THE ARDEN SHAKESPEARE

THIRD SERIES

General Editors: Richard Proudfoot, Ann Thompson,
David Scott Kastan and H.R. Woudhuysen

MUCH ADO
ABOUT NOTHING

REVISED EDITION

D0064045

THE ARDEN SHAKESPEARE

ALL'S WELL THAT ENDS WELL	edited by G.K. Hunter*
ANTONY AND CLEOPATRA	edited by John Wilders
AS YOU LIKE IT	edited by Juliet Dusinberre
THE COMEDY OF ERRORS	edited by R.A. Foakes*
CORIOLANUS	edited by Peter Holland
CYMBELINE	edited by J.M. Nosworthy*
DOUBLE FALSEHOOD	edited by Brean Hammond
HAMLET	edited by Ann Thompson and Neil Taylor
JULIUS CAESAR	edited by David Daniell
KING HENRY IV PART 1	edited by David Scott Kastan
KING HENRY IV PART 2	edited by A.R. Humphreys*
KING HENRY V	edited by T.W. Craik
KING HENRY VI PART 1	edited by Edward Burns
KING HENRY VI PART 2	edited by Ronald Knowles
KING HENRY VI PART 3	edited by John D. Cox and Eric Rasmussen
KING HENRY VIII	edited by Gordon McMullan
KING JOHN	edited by E.A.J. Honigmann*
KING LEAR	edited by R.A. Foakes
KING RICHARD II	edited by Charles Forker
KING RICHARD III	edited by James R. Siemon
LOVE'S LABOUR'S LOST	edited by H.R. Woudhuysen
MACBETH	edited by Sandra Clark and Pamela Mason
MEASURE FOR MEASURE	edited by J.W. Lever*
THE MERCHANT OF VENICE	edited by John Drakakis
THE MERRY WIVES OF WINDSOR	edited by Giorgio Melchiori
A MIDSUMMER NIGHT'S DREAM	edited by Harold F. Brooks*
MUCH ADO ABOUT NOTHING	edited by Claire McEachern
OTHELLO	edited by E.A.J. Honigmann
PERICLES	edited by Suzanne Gossett
SHAKESPEARE'S POEMS	edited by Katherine Duncan-Jones and H.R. Woudhuysen
ROMEO AND JULIET	edited by René Weis
SHAKESPEARE'S SONNETS	edited by Katherine Duncan-Jones
THE TAMING OF THE SHREW	edited by Barbara Hodgdon
THE TEMPEST, Revised	edited by Virginia Mason Vaughan and Alden T. Vaughan
TIMON OF ATHENS	edited by Anthony B. Dawson and Gretchen E. Minton
TITUS ANDRONICUS	edited by Jonathan Bate
TROILUS AND CRESSIDA, Revised	edited by David Bevington
TWELFTH NIGHT	edited by Keir Elam
THE TWO GENTLEMEN OF VERONA	edited by William C. Carroll
THE TWO NOBLE KINSMEN, Revised	edited by Lois Potter
THE WINTER'S TALE	edited by John Pitcher

* Second series

MUCH ADO ABOUT NOTHING

Edited by
CLAIRE McEACHERN

THE ARDEN SHAKESPEARE
LONDON • NEW YORK • OXFORD • NEW DELHI • SYDNEY

THE ARDEN SHAKESPEARE
Bloomsbury Publishing Plc
50 Bedford Square, London, WC1B 3DP, UK
1385 Broadway, New York, NY 10018, USA

BLOOMSBURY, THE ARDEN SHAKESPEARE and the Arden Shakespeare logo
are trademarks of Bloomsbury Publishing Plc

This edition of *Much Ado About Nothing*, edited by Claire McEachern, 2006
Revised Edition published 2015 by Bloomsbury Arden Shakespeare
Reprinted 2016, 2017 (twice), 2018, 2019 (twice), 2020

The general editors of the Arden Shakespeare have been
W. J. Craig and R. H. Case (first series 1899–1944)
Una Ellis-Fermor, Harold F. Brooks, Harold Jenkins and
Brian Morris (second series 1946–82)
Present general editors (third series)
Richard Proudfoot, Ann Thompson, David Scott Kastan
and H. R. Woudhuysen

Cover design: Sutchinda Rangsi Thompson.
Cover images: Venetian mask © Bruno Passigatti, and
First movement of 2nd symphony, by Jan Sibellius © The Art Archive / Alamy

A catalogue record for this book is available from the British Library.

A catalog record for this book is available from the Library of Congress.

ISBN: HB: 978-1-4725-2030-2
PB: 978-1-4725-2029-6
ePDF: 978-1-4742-1610-4
eBook: 978-1-4742-1609-8

Series: The Arden Shakespeare Third Series

Typeset by RefineCatch Limited, Bungay, Suffolk
Printed and bound in India

To find out more about our authors and books visit
www.bloomsbury.com and sign up for our newsletters.

The Editor

Claire McEachern is Professor of English at the University of California, Los Angeles, where she teaches sixteenth and seventeenth-century English literature. She is editor of the *Cambridge Companion to Shakespearean Tragedy* (2nd edition, 2014), a contributor to the *Cambridge Companion to Shakespeare* (2010), ed. Margreta de Grazia and Stanley Wells, and *The Spenser Handbook*, ed. Richard McCabe (2014). Her other editions of Shakespeare's plays include five volumes of the Pelican Shakespeare (*1* and *2 Henry IV, Henry V, King John* and *All's Well that Ends Well*), *King Lear* (Pearson, 2004), and *Twelfth Night* (Barnes and Noble, 2007); her other previous publications include *The Poetics of English Nationhood* (1996) and (with Debora Shuger) *Religion and Culture in the English Renaissance* (1997).

For Warner Mandeville (4.1.267–8)

CONTENTS

Contents

LIST OF
ILLUSTRATIONS

GENERAL EDITORS' PREFACE

The earliest volume in the first Arden series, Edward Dowden's *Hamlet*, was published in 1899. Since then the Arden Shakespeare has been widely acknowledged as the pre-eminent Shakespeare edition, valued by scholars, students, actors and 'the great variety of readers' alike for its clearly presented and reliable texts, its full annotation and its richly informative introductions.

In the third Arden series we seek to maintain these well-established qualities and general characteristics, preserving our predecessors' commitment to presenting the play as it has been shaped in history. Each volume necessarily has its own particular emphasis which reflects the unique possibilities and problems posed by the work in question, and the series as a whole seeks to maintain the highest standards of scholarship, combined with attractive and accessible presentation.

Newly edited from the original documents, texts are presented in fully modernized form, with a textual apparatus that records all substantial divergences from those early printings. The notes and introductions focus on the conditions and possibilities of meaning that editors, critics and performers (on stage and screen) have discovered in the play. While building upon the rich history of scholarly activity that has long shaped our understanding of Shakespeare's works, this third series of the Arden Shakespeare is enlivened by a new generation's encounter with Shakespeare.

THE TEXT

On each page of the play itself, readers will find a passage of text supported by commentary and textual notes. Act and scene divisions (seldom present in the early editions and often the product of eighteenth-century or later scholarship) have been retained for ease of reference, but have been given less prominence than in previous series. Editorial indications of location of the action have been removed to the textual notes or commentary.

In the text itself, elided forms in the early texts are spelt out in full in verse lines wherever they indicate a usual late twentieth-century pronunciation that requires no special indication and wherever they occur in prose (except where they indicate non-standard pronunciation). In verse speeches, marks of elision are retained where they are necessary guides to the scansion and pronunciation of the line. Final -ed in past tense and participial forms of verbs is always printed as -ed, without accent, never as -'d, but wherever the required pronunciation diverges from modern usage a note in the commentary draws attention to the fact. Where the final -ed should be given syllabic value contrary to modern usage, e.g.

> Doth Silvia know that I am banished?
>
> > *(TGV* 3.1.214)

the note will take the form

> 214 **banished** banishèd

Conventional lineation of divided verse lines shared by two or more speakers has been reconsidered and sometimes rearranged. Except for the familiar *Exit* and *Exeunt*, Latin forms in stage directions and speech prefixes have been translated into English and the original Latin forms recorded in the textual notes.

COMMENTARY AND TEXTUAL NOTES

Notes in the commentary, for which a major source will be the *Oxford English Dictionary*, offer glossarial and other explication of verbal difficulties; they may also include discussion of points of interpretation and, in relevant cases, substantial extracts from Shakespeare's source material. Editors will not usually offer glossarial notes for words adequately defined in the latest edition of *The Concise Oxford Dictionary* or *Merriam-Webster's Collegiate Dictionary*, but in cases of doubt they will include notes. Attention, however, will be drawn to places where more than one likely interpretation can be proposed and to significant verbal and syntactic complexity. Notes preceded by *discuss editorial emendations or variant readings.

Headnotes to acts or scenes discuss, where appropriate, questions of scene location, the play's treatment of source materials, and major difficulties of staging. The list of roles (so headed to emphasize the play's status as a text for performance) is also considered in the commentary notes. These may include comment on plausible patterns of casting with the resources of an Elizabethan or Jacobean acting company and also on any variation in the description of roles in their speech prefixes in the early editions.

The textual notes are designed to let readers know when the edited text diverges from the early edition(s) or manuscript sources on which it is based. Wherever this happens the note will record the rejected reading of the early edition(s) or manuscript, in original spelling, and the source of the reading adopted in this edition. Other forms from the early edition(s) or manuscript recorded in these notes will include some spellings of particular interest or significance and original forms of translated stage directions. Where two or more early editions are involved, for instance with *Othello*, the notes also record all important differences between them. The textual notes take a form that has been in use since the nineteenth century. This comprises, first: line reference, reading adopted in the text and closing square bracket; then: abbreviated reference, in italic, to the earliest edition to adopt the accepted reading, italic semicolon and noteworthy alternative reading(s), each with abbreviated italic reference to its source.

Conventions used in these textual notes include the following. The solidus / is used, in notes quoting verse or discussing verse lining, to indicate line endings. Distinctive spellings of the base text follow the square bracket without indication of source and are enclosed in italic brackets. Names enclosed in italic brackets indicate originators of conjectural emendations when these did not originate in an edition of the text, or when the named edition records a conjecture not accepted into its text. Stage directions (SDs) are referred to by the number of the line within or immediately after which they are placed. Line numbers with a decimal point relate to centred entry SDs not falling within a verse line and to SDs more than one line long, with the number after the point indicating the line within the SD: e.g. 78.4 refers to the fourth line of the SD following line 78. Lines of SDs at the start of a scene are numbered 0.1, 0.2, etc. Where only a line number precedes a square bracket, e.g. 128], the note relates to the whole line; where SD is added to the number, it relates to the whole of a SD within or immediately following the line. Speech prefixes (SPs) follow similar conventions, 203 SP] referring to the speaker's name for line 203. Where a SP reference takes the form, e.g. 38+ SP, it relates to all subsequent speeches assigned to that speaker in the scene in question.

Where, as with *King Henry V*, one of the early editions is a so-called 'bad quarto' (that is, a text either heavily adapted, or reconstructed from memory, or both), the divergences from the present edition are too great to be recorded in full in the notes. In these cases, with the exception of *Hamlet*, which prints an edited text of the Quarto of 1603, the editions will include a reduced photographic facsimile of the 'bad quarto' in an appendix.

INTRODUCTION

Both the introduction and the commentary are designed to present the plays as texts for performance, and make appropriate reference to stage, film and television versions, as well as introducing the reader to the range of critical approaches to the plays. They discuss the history of the reception of the texts within the theatre and scholarship and beyond, investigating the interdependency of the literary text and the surrounding 'cultural text' both at the time of the original production of Shakespeare's works and during their long and rich afterlife.

PREFACE

Much Ado About Nothing is a play in part about the informing
pressures of community, pressures both constraining and
enabling. While I knew that upon undertaking this work I would
be engaging with several centuries' worth of editors and
editions, and was prepared to be duly humbled, I was less aware
of how much I would rely on colleagues yet breathing, and thus
how genuinely, and generously, collaborative a process this
kind of work can be. My greatest debt is to the Arden general
editor Richard Proudfoot, whose careful eye, astonishing
breadth and depth of knowledge, and unfailing tact had me
convinced that *Much Ado* must be his favourite play as well
(except that I suspect all other Arden editors feel the same about
his relationship to theirs). Never has so much information been
dispensed with such forbearance. I am also indebted to the two
other members of the general editorial trinity. David Scott
Kastan has been, as ever, the person to whom I can safely
address all the really stupid questions; for this, for the invitation
to edit, and for his unflagging friendship over the past twenty
years I salute him. Ann Thompson offered me detailed guidance
at the early stages of the project, and I hope she is pleased with
the result. I was also fortunate to have my UCLA colleague
Reg Foakes as my associate general editor; this edition was
strengthened by his trademark scepticism and my work buoyed
by his shared affection for the play. These people have read this
work as if it were their own, and saved me from many an error,
though probably not, alas, all.

My colleagues in the UCLA English Department have been
indispensable sources of obscure references and tidbits for the
commentary, as well as tolerant of my urge to explain to them
all of their own work as it relates to *Much Ado*. Lowell Gallagher,
Debora Shuger and Rob Watson have been most patient. The
sage A.R. Braunmuller saved me many a trek to the library;

Jayne Lewis read the Introduction in its entirety, and got the jokes. My chair Tom Wortham was incredibly accommodating in matters of scheduling. I am grateful to the university for research funding, which made it possible to hire two terrific research assistants in Claire Banchich and Christina Fitzgerald.

It was characteristic of the genial fates that oversaw the production of this book that Shakespeare Santa Cruz, at the University of California at Santa Cruz, chose to stage *Much Ado* in the summer of 1998. Artistic Director Paul Whitworth gamely invited me to serve as dramaturg despite my never having before seen the inside of a rehearsal room, and I can't wait to go back someday for another play. Professors Audrey Stanley and Michael Warren taught me much about the relationships between text and performance. Director Rick Seer of the University of San Diego more than graciously suffered my presence. I learned a great deal from him and all of his actors, Ursula Meyer and Jamie Newcomb in particular.

Another California institution that made the work of this edition pleasurable as well as possible is the Huntington Library. The staffs of the Reading Room, Reader and Reprographic Services were unfailingly helpful and generous with their time and expertise. I am especially indebted to Director of Research Robert C. Ritchie, who over the years that this work has been in progress has offered material support, workspace and lecture opportunities that furthered its progress immeasurably. On the other coast, the Folger Library was equally helpful when it came to a study of their promptbooks, and Barbara Mowat and Paul Werstine, twin engines of the Folger editions, helped launch this edition with a digitized copy of the Quarto, and shared works in progress with me. In Britain, the collections and staffs of the Shakespeare Centre Library, the Shakespeare Institute Library, the library of Cambridge University and the British Library were indispensable resources.

The expertise of the team at Thomson puts all other publishing houses to shame. Jessica Hodge was a constant and patient source of encouragement in all the years when this work was under gestation. Margaret Bartley has overseen its completion admirably, and Jane Armstrong has coordinated its production with good humour and good advice. Giulia Vincenzi and Philippa Gallagher were terrific when it came to hunting photographs and their photographers. The practical support of Fiona Freel was indispensable. My greatest debt is to my copy-editor, Hannah Hyam, without whose painstaking attention, care and good sense this book simply would not exist. As the final stages of this book's production coincided with a complicated pregnancy followed by a lively infant, all these women are to be especially commended for their flexibility and patience in working with a sleep-challenged editor.

Other people helped me by sharing unpublished work, discussing individual points, accompanying me to productions of the play, sharing notes on productions they had witnessed, and by offering support and encouragement. David Bevington, Juliet Fleming, Penny Gay, Phyllis Gorfain, Victoria Hayne, Jonathan Hope, Gordon McMullan, Pamela Mason, Barbara Ramsey and Jim Shapiro are among them, as are my parents and siblings.

Between the beginning and the completion of this work I acquired a family; I am grateful to my daughters Helena and Marielle for napping when the edition needed it most, and to my stepson Justice, who tells his teachers that his stepmother cleans the house for a living. This book is dedicated to my husband Chip Mandeville, who would challenge any number of Claudios if I needed him to.

I am indebted, in this second edition of the third series of *Much Ado*, to the eagle-eyed review of the previous 2006 issue of this edition by Eric Rasmussen in *Shakespeare Survey*, 59 (2006) as well as to the thoughtful correspondence of Michael Warren.

Claire McEachern
Los Angeles, California

INTRODUCTION

Much Ado About Nothing is best known for the 'merry war' between one of its two couples, and an oxymoron could also describe this comedy's identity as a whole. Shakespeare offers a play of light and dark, of romantic union wrested from fear and malice, and of social harmony soothing the savagery of psychic violence. *Much Ado* claims one of Shakespeare's most delightful heroines, his most dancing word-play, and the endearing spectacle of intellectual and social self-importances bested by the desire to love and be loved in return. It is undoubtedly the most socially and psychologically realistic of his comedies, in its portrait of the foibles and generosities of communal life. Shakespeare represents a world governed, even poisoned, by male rivalry, in which conventions of gender and status shape emotional attachments, in which men and women fear each other, and in which only the most accidental of providences can save an innocent woman from the effects of slander, and a man from death by combat. The battle of the sexes it portrays, for all its lighthearted wit, risks real consequences and casualties.

This dual identity appears in *Much Ado*'s double life in the theatre and in scholarship. The play has two pairs of lovers, with two different, though perhaps equally rocky, paths to the altar. One pair have been the darlings of the theatre, the other, a target of scholarly scrutiny. *Much Ado* has thrived on the stage ever since its inception. This popularity has chiefly been credited to the combatants in the 'merry war', Benedick and Beatrice, whose sparring and eventual capitulation to each other has kept people laughing and weeping for centuries. Scholarship, on the other hand, has tended to concentrate on the darker elements, and hence on the Hero and Claudio plot. Thus, on the page the play has largely come in for a censorious treatment, either (in the past) for its violation of the decorums of comedy and

1

character alike, or (more recently) for its portrait of patriarchy, the success of whose artistic realization is overshadowed by critical distaste for the object portrayed. Advocates of the play's power to delight hear in Shakespeare's title a throwaway catch phrase, his lighthearted, shrugging comment on the ultimate triviality of human resistances to going the marital way of the world; the more sceptical ear registers, as the Elizabethan pun would have (*nothing* was slang for the female genitalia, and was pronounced the same as 'noting', which could mean 'noticing' or 'knowing'), the adverse power of communal opinion over individual identity, and the lethal seriousness of the matter of female chastity to the male imagination.

An edition needs to do justice to both the theatrical and the scholarly strands of the play. Yet editing is, by the nature of the medium, more pitched to the latter. It is difficult to reproduce the experience of the stage in print, though attempts are made throughout this Introduction and the commentary to provide instances of staging choices. But the stage is best experienced from a centre seat in the orchestra section, especially if it's a comedy, since nothing ruins a joke more than trying to explain it, particularly with footnotes. Effervescence does not improve with explication. Copious guidance on historical materials, or the intellectual traditions behind Shakespeare's choices, can often estrange, as can attention to conventions of genre, word-play and semantic resonances perhaps ringing in Shakespeare's ears but not necessarily available to the modern or even early modern theatre-goer. This edition treats the play as a literary text, not a script; actors and directors must make choices, but editors get to multiply them, albeit within parameters set by history and cultural moment. The risk of such an assignment (especially in this edition, attentive, as is the play, to the struggles between the sexes) is being charged, like many feminists, with having no sense of humour, let alone a sense of theatre. On the other hand, actors and directors (if not always theatre-goers) must also begin by reading the text.

Ultimately, the position of this edition (for editions, too, have positions, even though the pretence of the convention is neutrality) is that the two sides of this play – its light and its dark, sometimes understood as the theatrical and the scholarly – require each other. If Benedick and Beatrice please, it is not in spite of the universe in which they find themselves, but because the triumph of their union is wrought through and against near-tragedy. We treasure them in part because of what they hold at bay. If the ultimate pairing of Claudio and Hero challenges our expectations of comic deserts, it is because Shakespeare offers another vision of the human power to change and to choose. The play's distinctive mixture of delight and pathos depends upon this symbiosis.

Another premise of this edition, and one that governs the organization of this Introduction, has to do with the matter of temporal location (for editions, too, are of their moment, which is why editors are always producing yet more of them). This premise is that *Much Ado About Nothing* is also produced in and of time, built in and of its original culture, and a contributor to the subsequent ones in which it has been experienced. I thus begin with an extended discussion of what are traditionally considered Shakespeare's sources, but also other literary contexts not so usually considered sources – from cuckold jokes to conduct books – which inform the ideas and identities of this play. Some of these, as is conventional in source study, precede the 1598 date of this play; some of them follow it. Some contexts are cited by the play; some indicate the larger discursive universe to which the play, in turn, contributes. This, the longest section of the Introduction, is followed by a discussion of the play's structure and style, its relation to comic convention and its place in Shakespeare's corpus. Then come two reviews of the play's reception history in two different arenas: one, of staging possibilities over the course of the play's theatrical life to date, and the other, a brief critical résumé of the ways in which the play has been read and understood. The penultimate section focuses on the original texts and the choices made in generating the text of this edition.

BUILDING A PLAY: SOURCES AND CONTEXTS

The usual definition of a Shakespearean source is the work to which a play's plot is indebted. In *Much Ado About Nothing* Shakespeare portrays the unions of two couples. Only one of these pairs, however – Hero and Claudio – has what is conventionally considered a literary source, in the sense of a storyline already available elsewhere at the time of the play's composition. Traditional thinking about this play's debt to source material has thus tended to identify the Beatrice and Benedick material, as well as the Watch, as Shakespeare's original inventions, grafted on as comic relief to the oft-told backbone story of the slandered woman and her deceived betrothed. This vision of the play's relation to its sources locates the divergent natures of the two different love plots in their respective origins: Hero and Claudio's pairing, based on pre-existing narratives, represents 'conventional' romance, whereas the unprecedented Beatrice and Benedick plot represents something more unusual in both style and substance, a product of Shakespeare's genius, his comment on convention itself. This discrimination usually comes with the reminder that the Hero–Claudio plot is the 'main' plot, and the other, despite its tendency to upstage it, the mere subplot. On the other hand, revisions of this account of origins and originalities point out that, despite the apparent autonomy of the Beatrice and Benedick plot from the story of the slandered woman, both plots, in fact, turn on staged scenes and on fabricated accounts of love (of Don Pedro for Hero, Hero for Borachio, or Benedick for Beatrice, and she for him). Thus in this light the Benedick and Beatrice plot also derives from the calumny material. This remains nonetheless a plot-derived account of literary indebtedness, with Shakespeare doubling the offerings of his source (much as *The Comedy of Errors* multiplies Plautus' one set of twins) in order to multiply comic possibilities.

The usual suspects: Ariosto and Bandello

The plot-centred notion of a source gets us far with this play. The tale of the unjustly slandered woman was indeed a popular one in Renaissance literature (see Bullough). It appeared in many genres – tragedy, farce, romance and homily – and served as a vehicle for various meditations: on evidence, on love, on the powers of the senses, the rashness of the passions and the madcap complications of marital intrigue. Sexual slander was also a real concern of sixteenth-century courts (see Sharpe; Kaplan, *Culture*). The story's most ancient analogue was the fifth-century Greek romance of Chariton, Chaereas and Kallirrhoe, although more recent renditions lay behind Shakespeare's. Of these there were at least seventeen versions (both narrative and dramatic) extant at the time of the composition of *Much Ado*. The fifth Canto of Ludovico Ariosto's *Orlando Furioso* was perhaps the most prominent instance, itself probably based on the fifteenth-century Spanish *Tirant lo Blanco* by Juan Martorell.

Ariosto sets the story in question, an episode in his larger romance, in Scotland, and recounts it from the perspective of the lady's maid Dalinda (analogous to the figure of Shakespeare's Margaret), who relates her own misguided part in the proceedings. Dalinda is a lover of the knight Polynesso, Duke of Alban. He in turn wishes to marry her mistress Genevra, daughter of the Scottish king, 'Because of her great state and hie condition', although he promises to love Dalinda still: 'notwithstanding wife and all the rest, / I should be sure that he would love me best' (Book 5, 13.3, 14.7–8; Bullough, 85). He persuades Dalinda to make his suit to her mistress on his behalf, and when it is spurned – Genevra unwaveringly loves the Italian knight Ariodante – Polynesso wishes to revenge

5

himself upon her. Polynesso asks Dalinda to make love to him in her mistress's clothing and hair-style, under the pretext that it will serve as a therapeutic exorcism of his love for Genevra ('Thus I may passe my fancies foolish fit'), but really of course to deceive Ariodante (26.1; 88). Dalinda agrees, not knowing the true audience of her actions, and eager to resecure Polynesso's undivided attentions no matter how peculiar the means.

Ariodante, when confronted with Polynesso's claim to having enjoyed Genevra's 'yvorie corps' (38.2; 91), stoutly defends his lady. However, while fearful for his life from one he intuits is 'this false Duke' (43.4; 92), he nonetheless goes to the appointed viewing place accompanied by his brother, Lurcanio. Ariodante witnesses Polynesso ascend to Genevra's room, and 'straight beleev'd against his owne behoofe, / Seeing her cloth[e]s that he had seene her face' (50.3–4; 94). Lurcanio dissuades Ariodante from suicide, and the latter departs the Scottish court and is soon reputed drowned. The brother subsequently accuses Genevra of unchastity and culpability for Ariodante's death. Though Genevra's father, the King of Scotland, attempts to get to the bottom of the matter by interviewing her maids (an action which prompts Dalinda to warn Polynesso), he is nonetheless bound by Scottish law to sentence his daughter to death, unless a champion appears who can kill her accuser in a trial by combat, and thus prove her innocence. Polynesso packs off Dalinda to one of his castles (or so she thinks), with instructions to his men to murder her en route, a plight from which she is rescued by the knight Rinaldo, the principal hero of Ariosto's romance, now journeying through Scotland. She tells Rinaldo her tale, and he speeds to the court of Saint Andrews in time to prevent the combat between Lurcanio and an unknown knight, who, it turns out, is Ariodante in disguise. The lover had thought better of drowning himself, and decided to fight for his lady's honour even though he believed her guilty and the combat was against his own brother. All is revealed; Rinaldo slays Polynesso, the lovers are united, and Dalinda heads for a nunnery.

Ariosto's tale produced many spin-offs. It was first translated into English by Peter Beverly in 1566, and his *History of Ariodanto and Genevra* seizes upon the story as a frame on which to hang much poetry on the varieties and miseries of lovesickness. George Whetstone's *Rock of Regard* rendered it in 1576 (his hero is Rinaldo, his heroine Giletta, and the villain, also a rival lover, Frizaldo). A verse translation by Sir John Harington, *Orlando Furioso in English Heroical Verse* (1591), was more loyal to Ariosto. By this time the story had acquired an exemplary force, and Harington's moral is multiple: for example, the virtue in Genevra's preference of a humble knight to a duke, 'how wicked men often bewray their owne misdeeds . . . how God ever defends the innocent . . . how wickednesse ruines it selfe' (Bullough, 105). Edmund Spenser also found the story of homiletic utility, and in Book 2 canto 4 of *The Faerie Queene* (1590) he uses it to illustrate the dangers of intemperate action. Phedon, the lover figure, is tricked by his so-called friend Philemon into thinking his lady Claribell false to him 'with a groome of base degree' (24.3). Philemon's motives are vague: 'either enuying my toward good, / Or of himselfe to treason ill dispos'd' (22.2–3); nonetheless, he tells the maid Pryene that her beauty is worthier than her station, and persuades her to wear her mistress's 'most gorgeous geare' at an assignation (26.8). Phedon witnesses their embrace and, 'chawing vengeance all the way' (29.2), slays Claribell, only to rue his actions when Pyrene confesses the ruse (he then poisons Phedon and pursues Pyrene with a knife). When Guyon, knight of Temperance, finds him, he is being tortured by Furor and his mother Occasion, and serves up his tale as a warning against lack of moderation. Spenser's is the only version of the story in which the heroine dies.

The story also provided matter for drama, although the tenor of the plays is more farcical and less didactic than the poetic accounts (narrative accounts being better equipped than drama to provide opportunity for homily). The root here is the Italian *Il Fedele*, by Luigi Pasaqualigo (1576). Fedele loves Vittoria, who, although married to Cornelio, loves a man named Fortunio. Fedele discloses the latter information to the cuckolded Cornelio, and arranges for him to see a servant (in love with Vittoria's maid) enter the house to court an alleged Vittoria. The incensed Cornelio plans to poison his wife, but she by a trick escapes her fate. The play was translated into English by Anthony Munday, as *Fedele and Fortunio, the Two Italian Gentlemen* (1585), although this account is less racy than the Italian: 'Victoria is no promiscuous married woman but a maid uncertain in her choice between two suitors, and, after a number of equivocations, the story ends in no fewer than four happy marriages.'[1] Other dramatic versions included the Cambridge Latin production of *Victoria* (1580–3), by Abraham Fraunce, a court performance of *Ariodante and Genevra* in 1583 by the boys of Merchant Taylors probably based on Beverly, and a piece by Leicester's men in 1574/5 called *Panecia*.[2] The Pasaqualigo-derived versions, however, while providing ample evidence that the matter was apt for dramatic treatment, differ from *Much Ado* in that the latter's heroine is clearly chaste, Shakespeare's play deliberately courts tragedy, and his comedy lies elsewhere than in the spectacle of the duped husband (although the latter's spectre perhaps registers in the play's many cuckold jokes).

A nearer relative of Shakespeare's play is the prose novella 22 of Matteo Bandello's *La Prima Parte de le Novelle* (1554). This tale was translated into French, with the standard homiletic

---

1 Giorgio Melchiori (ed.), *The Merry Wives of Windsor*, Arden Shakespeare (2000), 17.
2 Bullough, 68. The name 'Panecia' betrays a link with the Bandello tale, as an imaginable error for Phanecia (= Fenicia). There was also a play by Jacob Ayrer, written between 1593 and 1605, titled *Die Schoene Phaenicia*.

and rhetorical flourishes, by François de Belleforest in his *Histoires Tragiques* in 1569. Bandello's story, like Shakespeare's, is set in Messina, where the knightly and very wealthy Sir Timbreo de Cardona is a courtier of King Piero of Aragon, the latter having taken possession of the island in the wake of a Sicilian rebellion against the occupying French (there is virtually no mention of King Piero, however). During the courtly victory celebrations, Sir Timbreo falls in love with one Fenicia, daughter of an impoverished but ancient family. Her father is Messer Lionato de' Lionati. While Sir Timbreo's intentions are not initially honourable, he is forced by Fenicia's chaste conduct to offer her marriage, despite the great difference in their social positions, 'for she never replied to any of the letters and messages he sent her except to affirm that she intended to keep her maidenhood inviolate for the man who would be given her as a husband' (Bullough, 113). The alliance is received happily by the entire town, chiefly on account of the universal regard in which Messer Lionato is held, 'since [he] was a gentleman rightly loved as one who sought to hurt nobody but to help all as much as he could' (114).

The only person disappointed by the match is one Sir Girondo Olerio Valenziano, who also loves Fenicia. Sir Girondo is also a proven soldier and ornament of the court, and comrade to Sir Timbreo (though curiously not in his confidence on the amorous score). Stricken by lovesickness and disappointment at the news of Fenicia's betrothal, Sir Girondo 'allowed himself to be carried away into doing an action blameworthy in anyone, let alone in a knight and gentleman such as he was' (114). He plots to destroy the match so as to gain Fenicia's hand for himself, and confides his desire to another courtier 'whom [he] had for confidant and helper in his crime . . . a fellow of little upbringing, more pleased with evil than with good' (115). This henchman goes to Sir Timbreo, relates the tale of Fenicia's duplicity, and makes an appointment to witness it. The hour arrived, Sir Girondo suborns one of his servingmen (having 'perfumed him with the sweetest of scents', 116) to enter, by ladder, a wing of Messer Lionato's house. The three pass by the hiding place of Sir Timbreo, where the fragrant servingman (to further increase plausibility) audibly cautions the others to take care of the ladder's placement, 'for the last time we were here my lady Fenicia told me that you had leaned it there with too much noise' (117). The man then climbs onto the balcony and purposefully enters the house 'as if he had a mistress within' (117). On the morrow the disappointed Sir Timbreo discreetly sends word by messenger to Messer Lionato that he will not, after all, have his daughter, and 'that you should find another son-in-law . . . because he has seen with his own eyes something in Fenicia that he would never have credited' (118). He instructs Fenicia to 'find yourself another husband, just as you have already found yourself another lover . . . Sir Timbreo does not intend to have anything more to do with you, since you will make anyone who marries you a Lord of Corneto' (118). Messer Lionato, however, doughtily tells the messenger he is not surprised:

> I always feared, from the first moment when you spoke to me of this marriage, that Sir Timbreo would not stand firm to his request, for I knew then as I do now that I am only a poor gentleman and not his equal. Yet surely if he repented of his promise to make her his wife it would have been sufficient for him to declare that he did not want her, and not to have laid against her this injurious accusation of whoredom. It is indeed true that all things are possible, but I know how my daughter has been reared and what her habits are.

> (118)

The story resolves itself in the best fashion of Italian novellas. The ever-virtuous Fenicia, from her sickbed, and surrounded by sympathetic friends and relatives, claims that Sir Timbreo's reversal was a providential means of preserving her from the arrogance which might have followed upon such a grand match. She then falls into a coma, is believed dead, is awakened as she is laid out for burial by her mother, and is dispatched by her ever-resourceful father to his brother's house in the country, 'so that after Fenicia had grown up and changed her appearance, as is usual with age, he might marry her off in two or three years under another name' (122). Her funeral proceeds as scheduled, provoking a universal sympathy, for 'all the citizens firmly believed that Don Timbreo had invented the lie about her' (122). The latter, meanwhile, surrounded by such adverse public opinion, 'began to feel great sorrow and a heartstirring such as he would never have thought possible' (122). Weighing the sum of the evidence (the remoteness of her bedroom from the entered balcony, her bedfellow sister, the location of her parents' bedchamber), it occurs to him that there might well have been other reasons for what he witnessed: 'maybe the man who had entered the house might have been doing so for another woman than Fenicia, or even to commit a theft' (123).

However, the greatest impact of Fenicia's funeral is upon Sir Girondo, who has become virtually suicidal not only for the loss of his beloved but for his dishonour in having been a cause of such harm. His contrition provides for the discovery of the deception. Consequently, a week after the funeral he confesses his sins to Sir Timbreo, and before her supposed tomb offers him both his poniard and his bared breast. Not to be outdone in chivalry, Sir Timbreo cites his own over-credulity as equally culpable, and the two men decide to clear Fenicia's name (Sir Timbreo only scolds Sir Girondo for not having disclosed his love to him, claiming that he would have 'preferred our friendship to my desire', 124). The repentant duo repair to Messer Lionato, who secures Sir Timbreo's promise to wed a woman of the latter's choosing. A year later Sir Timbreo willingly weds the much-improved Fenicia, who, like the phoenix after whom she is named, has been reborn through her trial. Sir Timbreo discovers her true identity before the marriage, but only after he recounts his love for the dead Fenicia. Sir Girondo weds her sister.[1]

Shakespeare's transformations of his sources: the creation of a social world

Ariosto and Bandello have been singled out as the most likely influences upon Shakespeare's play, the former for the particular means of the deception, and the latter for its obvious links of setting and names (Messer Lionato of Messina, King Piero of Aragon, etc.). The social universe of Bandello's novella is certainly the more akin to Shakespeare's Messina. Rather than court intrigue or the accidental landscapes of romance, he chooses to set his story in the gossipy confines of a leisured household in a small town, places best suited to creating the sense of social proximity in which rumours are born and transmitted, in which the notable are much noted, mostly by each other. This sense of a provincial (if aristocratic) identity extends to the incongruously home-grown quality of Dogberry and his men (who, with their ostentatiously English names, may lend a comforting and plebeian familiarity to Messinese society, Messina being as remote as the moon to the majority of Shakespeare's audience). This sense of social proximity also accounts for the Watch's knowledge of and attention to their neighbour's doings ('I pray you watch about Signor Leonato's door, for the wedding being there tomorrow, there is a great coil tonight', 3.3.89–91). Shakespeare's portrait of communal and quotidian life – also conveyed by such details as the passing mention of Claudio's uncle (1.1.17), Benedick's trip to the barber (3.2.41–3), Margaret's account of the Duchess of Milan's wedding gown 'that they praise so' (3.4.15) – builds upon Bandello's implicit sense of the busy and close-knit Messinese society that rallies around the family of Messer Lionato and pressures Sir Timbreo to

1 For a fuller treatment of the differences of play and source, see McEachern, 'Fathering'.

re-examine his convictions (though in Shakespeare's play the Friar's plan is a deliberate – if ineffective – implementation of this effect: '[Hero], dying, as it must be so maintained, / Upon the instant that she was accused, / Shall be lamented, pitied and excused / Of every hearer . . . When [Claudio] shall hear she died upon his words, / Th'idea of her life shall sweetly creep / Into his study of imagination', 4.1.214–16, 223–5). At the same time, the play's social universe, with its visiting dignitaries and fashionable speech, is not exclusively a provincial one. The leisured and literate universe of Baldassare Castiglione's *Il libro del cortegiano* (1528) provides another source of the play's social climate (as well as the typology of a courtly world in which beautiful people pass the time with elegant conversation and literary games).

Shakespeare's debt to Ariosto is a different one. If the exotic vistas, noble questants and providential accidents of romance are gone, to be replaced by the hothouse intimacies of small-town life (Rinaldo has become a householder with two gowns), Shakespeare retains Ariosto's chivalric register in the forms of Benedick's challenge to Claudio, as well as in Leonato's and Antonio's similar moves to defend Hero's honour.

Perhaps the strongest link of Shakespeare's play to the Ariostan version of the tale lies not so much in plot as in social custom, in his concern with the romance's attention to social distinctions. This is embedded in Shakespeare's response to the role of the maid Dalinda. She provides Shakespeare, in her tale of dressing in her mistress's clothes, with the sartorial means of the deception. Shakespeare then elaborates the social circumstances that condition Dalinda's own curiously abject role in Genevra's slander into an entire sociological climate in which rank and name are both subtle but crucial factors in determining the slander of Hero.

The maid

There is in Ariosto a clear sense of the social requirements of marital union. Dalinda's station is far below that of the Duke

Polynesso, even if we read her as a lady-in-waiting rather than a mere maid; in any case, she acknowledges the greater allure of her mistress's social position:

> Not all of love, but partly of ambition,
> He beares in hand his minde is onely bent,
> Because of her great state and hie condition,
> To have her for his wife is his intent:
> He nothing doubteth of the kings permission,
> Had he obtained *Genevras* free assent.
> Ne was it hard for him to take in hand,
> That was the second person in the land.

> (13.1–8; Bullough, 85)

The deception itself is heavily invested in the signs of clothing that mark Genevra's social identity: 'The gowne I ware' (recounts Dalinda) 'was white, and richly set / With aglets, pearle, and lace of golde wel garnished . . . Not thus content, the vaile aloft I set, / Which only Princes weare' (47.1–2, 5–6; 93). This impressive costume alone is sufficient to deceive Ariodante, who 'straight beleev'd against his owne behoofe, / Seeing her cloth[e]s that he had seene her face' (50.3–4; 94).

In Shakespeare's play, this emphasis on clothes and station provides the means and the rationale of Margaret's participation in the charade. Shakespeare sketches a character who like Dalinda is aware of her own relative lack of social status amongst the company: 'Why, shall I always keep below stairs?' she asks Benedick, flirting with him (5.2.9–10). She prides herself on her wit ('Doth not my wit become me rarely?', 3.4.63–4) in an environment where verbal prowess serves as a marker of social elegance, and her claim to having seen the dress of the Duchess of Milan adds to a similar social authority. The deception at the window, in which Margaret wears Hero's garments, and, in Borachio's words, 'leans me out at her mistress' chamber window, bids me a thousand times goodnight' (3.3.140–1), suggests that from Margaret's point of view the pair are engaged in an erotic game involving the impersonation of their social betters. Borachio has prepared his audience to see Hero making sport of her suit to Claudio by calling her lover Borachio by Claudio's name: 'hear me call Margaret "Hero", hear Margaret term me "Claudio"' (2.2.39–40). Margaret is innocent of her ultimate role in Hero's slander – Leonato says 'Margaret was in some fault for this, / Although against her will' (5.4.4–5), and Borachio claims she 'knew not what she did when she spoke to me' (5.1.291). But she is not innocent of social ambition, or at least a certain wistfulness about her inferior social station, enough so that we are asked to imagine that the game of mocking her betters is a plausible and pleasurable one for her to play.

'How many gentlemen?'

Margaret's charade in which she pretends to be Hero receiving a man into her bedchamber provides the particular mechanism of slander in this play, but Shakespeare locates her action in a larger social world shaped by concerns of status and place. The role of rank is present from the opening lines of the play: 'How many gentlemen have you lost in this action?' asks Leonato, and receives the reassuring reply: 'But few of any sort, and none of name' (1.1.5–7) – in other words, nobody of note. Much of this attention to status revolves around the presence of the Prince, the highest placed member of this society whose disarming gestures of *noblesse oblige* only accentuate his social superiority ('Please it your grace lead on?' 'Your hand, Leonato; we will go together', 1.1.152–3). It is a concern present in Leonato's enthusiasm for what he believes is a match of his daughter with the Prince; acknowledged in Beatrice's own refusal of Don Pedro's hand – 'No, my lord, unless I might have another for working days. Your grace is too costly to wear every day' (2.1.301–3); and in Don John's cruel request to Claudio to discourage the rumoured union of Hero and his brother – 'she is no equal for his birth' (2.1.150).

15

Don Pedro thus represents the apex of a social pyramid constructed out of relations of dependency and desire. (This is in striking contrast to Bandello's version, where the analogous figure receives only passing mention.) Some of these hierarchies are intellectual, but mostly they are matters of caste, so that the beautiful people can also lay claim to a beautiful language, and the less glamorous seek to better themselves through speaking elegantly. Shakespeare populates Messina with persons of social prominence and those who attend upon them. Don Pedro has his followers in Claudio and Benedick; Don John his, in Conrade and Borachio; Hero and Beatrice are attended by Ursula and Margaret. Antonio defers to Leonato, Verges to Dogberry, children to parents, soldiers to their leaders, the Watch to the constable. The lines of power are subtle, sometimes suspended, but ultimately firm. (Ursula and Margaret, for instance, are 'gentlewomen', take part in the dance in 2.1 and in Beatrice's gulling, but are also required to run errands. Some productions cast them as ladies-in-waiting; others, as ladies' maids.) The nub of the play's brush with tragedy is located in these social dynamics. While the Watch promptly discover the truth about Hero's slander in advance of the wedding, Dogberry's need first to impress upon Leonato his own importance, which he does by denigrating Verges, exhausts the harried Governor's short supply of patience and ultimately prevents the news from coming out in time to prevent suffering.

To say that Shakespeare gets all this from the fifth canto of *Orlando Furioso* is to over-privilege the latter and underestimate Shakespeare's accomplishment; what he does is to elaborate a suggestion of caste into an entire and nuanced social universe in which the distinctions between ranks are both insisted upon and overlooked (the social differences of Ariosto's chivalric and royal universe are, in fact, clearer and thus less treacherous). Hero, for instance, may not be Don Pedro's social equal but the fiction of his suit to Hero provokes no adverse comment and he proposes himself as a match for Beatrice.

In fact, the chief difference of *Much Ado* from its sources lies in Shakespeare's alteration of a fact of social status. It is crucial to Shakespeare's version that Hero's suitor, unlike Sir Timbreo, is not greatly above Leonato in rank, and perhaps not at all in fortune, if Claudio's enquiry about Hero's inheritance is to be credited (although such a question would have been routine and not necessarily over-mercenary). Unlike Ariodante, he is not significantly below her either. Claudio is also explicitly young – 'Lord Lack-beard' (5.1.187); 'young Florentine' (1.1.10); 'sir boy' (5.1.83) – and however distinguished in battle, clearly dependent upon Don Pedro's patronage and approval. Thus the explanation of the lover's snobbery which allows Messer Leonato de' Lionati to rebut Sir Timbreo's allegations with the confidence that he knows 'how [his daughter] hath been reared and what her habits are' is not available to Shakespeare's father character.

The difference results in a different figure of a father as well as a lover, and opens up an entirely new dimension of psychological depth and loss for this father: 'mine, and mine I loved, and mine I praised, / And mine that I was proud on – mine so much / That I myself was to myself not mine / Valuing of her' (4.1.136–9). Shakespeare's father character, in both the extremity of his loss and the bravado of his recovery, is quite different from the confident and expedient Messer Lionato. Shakespeare seems interested in authority figures generally, adding Antonio in addition to Dogberry, expanding the role of Don Pedro, and inventing the Friar, resourceful where Leonato is not. And if Shakespeare's alteration of Bandello's status relations between the lovers gives scope for parental pain, the chivalric posture, perhaps inspired by Ariosto, allows Leonato to recoup a kind of disinterested avuncular posture sorely lacking in him by the end of the church scene. In his challenge to Claudio, he thus differs not only from Messer Lionato, confident in his daughter's virtue, but from Ariosto's King of Scotland, constrained by his own law into a kind of impotence vis-à-vis his daughter's defence. Unlike the paternal blocking figure of comic convention, Leonato displays a great emotional range; measured by the extravagance and quantity of the poetry alone, he far more than Claudio might conceivably be seen as the protagonist of the play's semi-tragic plot.[1] Othello's Brabantio, dead of a broken heart at his daughter's defection, is his tragic counterpart. Eighteenth-century pictorial representations of 4.1 demonstrate this centrality (see Figs 8, 9 and 10).

The villain

The subtle pressures of social hierarchy and rivalry also account for the unique nature of Shakespeare's villain. Don John is the bastard brother of Don Pedro. He is referred to as a prince, but he is perhaps not as much a prince as his brother, and when the play opens he has been recently vanquished in a fraternal battle. His illegitimacy is not made explicit in the play until 4.1 (though it is present in the Quarto speech prefixes and stage directions). However, Don John's melancholy and enviousness, perhaps betokened in the original productions by black costume, may have emblematized the circumstances of his birth for a Renaissance audience, and served implicitly to explain his disgruntlement (so that the revelation in 4.1 of his illegitimate birth would have come as a confirmation of a suspicion already afoot). Like *King Lear*'s Edmund, Don John's ethical nature seems predetermined by the political and economic circumstances of his birth. That the villain of a play concerned with sexual fidelity is an actual bastard seemingly rationalizes its emphasis on the importance of social legitimacy by producing evidence of the unpleasant consequences of violating it. Cuckoldry leads to (and stems from) villainy, or so is the implicit moral of the anxiety. Shakespeare's wrong-side-of-the-blanket villain is not exactly base-born, in the etymological

---

1   Leonato speaks 24 per cent of the play's verse; Claudio, 16.

sense of *vilein*, but he is a kind of walking impersonation of the way in which illegitimate sexual activity can produce social malcontents.

Whether or not Don John's illegitimacy is literally worn on his sleeve, his role in the story of slander is a unique one. In all previous versions of the story excepting Spenser's, the slander stems from a jealous rival for the heroine's hand. The convention of friends divided by the love of an often changeable woman is a cliché of Renaissance literature, and generates much rhetoric on the fickleness of fortune, women and friendship. (John Lyly's *Euphues: The Anatomy of Wit* (1578) is another example, and many of the play's comments on female infidelity echo those of that text.) Given the conventions within which Shakespeare is working, then, the villain of the play would ordinarily be Claudio's 'new sworn brother' Benedick (1.1.68), or even Don Pedro (whom indeed Claudio suspects of appropriating Hero), not Don John – or at least Don John ought to be enamoured of Hero as well. (This theory is sometimes advanced by productions seeking to explain his actions by means of longing glances towards her.)

Don John's malignity, however, is motiveless or at least mixed – he is jealous of Claudio's position with his brother, perhaps disgruntled about his subjugation in the recent war (in which Claudio subdued him), or perhaps just a 'plain-dealing villain' (1.3.29–30), a machiavel whose desire to spoil the pleasures of others comes with the character type (George Bernard Shaw called him 'a true natural villain, that is to say, a malevolent person . . . having no motive in this world except sheer love of evil', 157). Yet Shakespeare softens his portrait of him as well as indicting him: for while in the sources the jealous rival (even the otherwise noble Sir Girondo) is wholly responsible for concocting his own plan, one in which subordinates of few scruples are mere agents, in *Much Ado* it is Borachio, identified as a drunkard by his name, who hatches the details to mobilize Don John's unformed desire to thwart

Claudio's suit. The diffusion of criminal responsibility between the two perhaps serves to dilute the sense of villainy so that it does not overwhelm the capacity of comedy to contain or forestall it. Evil in this play is muted by having been built by committee, and is thus a mirror image of the clumsy but ultimately providential collaborations of Dogberry and his men.

The lover

The place where Shakespeare most decisively departs from his predecessors is in the creation of his lover. Claudio is far more of a cad than his counterparts. Ariosto's Ariodante is positively saintly, defending his mistress against his brother's challenge despite thinking her guilty. Sir Timbreo, once 'his despite was now in great part cooled and reason began to open his eyes', begins to himself work out the possibility that he was mistaken (Bullough, 123). Unlike Sir Timbreo, who is close enough to the window to smell the alleged suitor, Claudio must form his judgement from 'afar off in the orchard', on a 'dark night' (3.3.144–5, 150), though, on the other hand, unlike Dalinda, Margaret is not veiled. For Sir Timbreo the seduction scene alone is sufficient to convince, while for Claudio the 'oaths' of Don John and Borachio's further testimony are crucial. And whereas Sir Timbreo's rejection of Fenicia is carried out by messenger, *after* he witnesses the window scene, Claudio responds to the mere allegation of Hero's infidelity with a ready plan of public vengeance: 'If I see anything tonight why I should not marry her, tomorrow in the congregation where I should wed, there will I shame her' (3.2.111–13).

The difference in these suitors' choices must partly have to do with the difference between a play and a prose account, and the dramatic opportunities of a scene of public rejection. But it is an unavoidable observation that Shakespeare deliberately provides us with a less than appealing suitor. Shakespeare may draw his heroine's name from the story of two loyal lovers, but the suitor in question resembles 'Leander the good swimmer' (5.2.30–1) – in Benedick's ironic term for the drowned swain – more in failure rather than steadfastness. Claudio's shortcomings in the trust department are also in keeping with his earlier lack of confidence in the loyalty of friends, when he suspects that Don Pedro has appropriated Hero for himself. His behaviour after the report of Hero's death is no less disappointing (the Friar's plan for instituting remorse seems not to have fully succeeded), which is consistent with the realism of this rendition. Shakespeare goes out of his way to give us a suitor who is morally faint of heart and faith, at a disadvantage in the lists of love and friendship.

This has rendered Claudio vulnerable to critical scorn, as 'a miserable specimen' (Ridley, 106), or 'the least amiable lover in Shakespeare' (Harbage, 192); another commentator claims that love never did have 'interest in his liver': 'The verb describing the young man's feeling is significantly "like" not "love" . . . What Claudio is really interested in is a good and suitable marriage' (Prouty, 42, 43). Defences of his behaviour, on the other hand, cite the conventional nature of his love: it is time for him to marry; Hero is an appropriate choice; Claudio has the support of his patron. J.R. Mulryne grants him a quasi-tragic status: 'Claudio lacks confidence in himself and is readily given to suspecting others . . . He is easy prey for Don John precisely because of a deeply ingrained mistrust of his own feelings; he cannot exclude the possibility of his being quite wrong about his most intimate beliefs' (Mulryne, 40). Other commentators point out that while the grounds of such a match may not be romantically thrilling, they are unobjectionable by the terms of the day. At the same time, as Sheldon Zitner aptly observes, 'the ensuing marriage of Claudio and Hero is not quite as everyone would like it. Nor can we condescend to Elizabethan audiences by assuming it was wholly as they liked it' (Oxf[1], 1). Benedick and Beatrice's courtship surely criticizes the younger pair's, and vice versa (much as in *The Taming of the Shrew*, where Shakespeare sketches a similar contrast between Petruchio and Kate and Luciento and Bianca).

These defences remind us, however, that while it would be inaccurate to interpret Claudio as contemptible, he is nevertheless somewhat of a disappointment. He is, above all, young: anxious for the approval of his elders and convention, unsure of himself, eager to do the right thing both in marrying and in extricating himself from a bad bargain.

The unpromising nature of Claudio as a hero deserving of comic happiness, as well as the enigma of his final union to a veiled woman, have suggested to Jonathan Bate another analogue for Shakespeare's play which might help to condition his status as a lover. This is Euripides' *Alcestis*, named after its heroine. She volunteers to die in place of her husband Admetus, whose hospitality to the gods has earned him in the event of his death the reprieve of a substitute (Alcestis is the only family member who volunteers for the mission). Hercules discovers her sacrifice, fetches her from the underworld and returns her to her husband in the veiled guise of a new wife. Admetus, however, has pledged not to remarry, and he protests at the gift. The occasion gives Admetus an opportunity to voice his own guilt at allowing his wife to die on his behalf: 'if Hero is an Alcestis, Claudio is an Admetus who repents of and learns from earlier unfair conduct . . . the mock death must make Claudio see Hero's virtues, must make him into a nobler lover' (Bate, 'Dying', 83). Unlike Sir Timbreo, but like Admetus, Claudio must accept his second bride without seeing her face, a stipulation that reverses the terms of his initial error (in which he identified a woman by outward signs rather than inner conviction), and forces him to have faith where once he lacked it. Hero's mock funeral, in turn, recalls and prefigures other of Shakespeare's mock deaths, such as Juliet's or Helena's or Hermione's, in which heroines undergo a trial passage to the underworld. Euripides' *Alcestis* is also structurally similar to *Much Ado* in its use of comic scenes (those of Hercules' drunken festivities during the heroine's funeral) to counterpoint the apparent tragedy and hint at the comic ending to come.

Claudio also bears comparison with other of Shakespeare's lacklustre suitors, in particular Bertram of *All's Well That Ends Well* and Proteus of *The Two Gentleman of Verona*, even Posthumus of *Cymbeline*, and his namesake Claudio of *Measure for Measure*. The type of the less than ideal protagonist who is nonetheless included in the redemptions of comedy may have been relatively unobjectionable to a Reformation audience not only familiar with the convention of the arranged marriage but unsurprised by the unregenerate quality of mankind in general.

Beyond the plot

The changes so far detailed concern for the most part matters of character, of Shakespeare's expansion of the psychological scope of his source materials chiefly by means of the manipulation of details of status. Don Pedro, for example, is transformed from a mere mention in Bandello to a type of *deus ex machina*, one of the 'only love-gods' (2.1.357), as well as a potentially melancholic figure isolated by his very privilege, 'too costly', in Beatrice's terms, to be worn in the workaday world of bourgeois marriage (2.1.302). He is in the party, but not of it, participating in disguise as a suitor, but not ultimately one of the final festive company: 'Prince, thou art sad – get thee a wife' (5.4.120). We still however are working within an understanding of source as referring to the origins of plot, and thus have yet to address the existence of Benedick, Beatrice or the Watch. If we are to account for these other elements, we need to move to a broader understanding of the cultural resources and generic exigencies that go into shaping an author's decisions. The intention is not to discount Shakespeare's originality, but better to illuminate the nature of his invention by comparison with shared cultural and dramatic assumptions that serve as foils to his own compositional choices.

Dénouement

Certainly the presence of the Watch can be in part attributed to the representational requirements of drama. Unlike a novella or a poem, a play (unless it is *The Winter's Tale*) usually cannot wait a year (or even Bandello's week) for the remorse of the villain to effect a denouement. In Shakespeare, indeed, it is not clear whether the villain does repent – although Borachio is contrite, Don John flees, and Claudio's own acknowledgement of culpability is potentially graceless and unlikely to provoke much in the way of reparation without further prompting. Furthermore, this play's peculiar emotional tenor, of a comedy whose rewards are hard won, depends upon the pleasurable frustrations of a villainy only slowly apprehended. Hence the utility of the Watch as the agent of revelation: their inadvertent discovery of the deception nearly as soon as it has occurred helps to build a sense of comic providence, while the subsequent failure of Dogberry to communicate this information in a timely fashion helps to make possible the broadening of the play's emotional register (to include pain) that distinguishes this particular comic resolution. A subplot of Pasaqualigo's *Il Fedele*, and Munday's *Fedele and Fortunio*, involves an interception by the police, and Lyly's *Endymion* (1591) includes a similarly simple-minded watch.

The inept quality of the police force in *Much Ado* may indeed owe more to the realities of Elizabethan policing than to any other source. For instance, the contradictions and difficulties of ordinary citizens policing their betters in a hierarchical society – 'If you meet the prince in the night you may stay him . . . marry, not without the prince be willing' (3.3.73–4, 77–8) – will be satirized in Thomas Dekker's *Gull's Hornbook* (1609) (see Fig.1). Dekker scorns the indolence and inefficacy of urban watches, easily smelled out by their excessive onion-eating ('to keep them in sleeping') and their preferential treatment of the gentry ('the watch will wink at you, only for the love they bear to arms and knighthood', 63). Dogberry's crew shares these assumptions

1 An early modern watchman, with his bill and lantern, from Thomas
  Dekker's *Gull's Hornbook* (1609)

about their responsibilities: 'We will rather sleep than talk; we
know what belongs to a watch' (3.3.37–8). The impulse to let a
sleeping watch lie may in fact have been a strategic choice of a
society with no standing army or police force, and suspicious, as
one historian puts it, of 'the over-efficiency of even good
enforcement systems' (Spinrad, 161). Thus while the semi-
competent watch may be a familiar dramatic device and social
reality, Shakespeare weaves it into the play's social texture, with
its concerns with rank and status. Although, as A.P. Rossiter

2 Title-page of Will Kemp's *Nine Days Wonder* (1600). Kemp was notorious for the athleticism of his jig, and jigs often followed the ending of a play.

comments, 'As a real official Dogberry would be a terror. Conceited ignorance and vast self-importance in local government officers is – and was, in the time of Elizabeth – as good a joke in fiction as a very bad joke in fact' (Rossiter, 53).

In addition, the improvisational and extemporal abilities of the actor Will Kemp, who may have originally played Dogberry (if we take the Quarto speech prefixes as evidence), may have suggested to Shakespeare a role that would accommodate and even satirize the desire to upstage his fellows. Dogberry's own desire for the spotlight (he is both eager and outraged to be 'writ down an ass', 4.2.88) stems from a desire for social importance and apes the clown's stage charisma and notoriety (see Fig. 2). Among Shakespeare's resources, then, if not 'sources' per se, we must also include the personnel of his company, their talents and reputations, and the need to make use of them.

Dialogue and debate forms

Another obvious requirement of drama is the need to transmit information through dialogue; hence the need for the play's many pairs: Leonato talks to Antonio, Beatrice to Hero, Claudio to Benedick, Don John to his followers Conrade and Borachio, Dogberry to Verges. Since information often unfolds through a process of debate, these pairs are often composed of foils: the demure miss and the sprightly spinster, the young cub and the cynical trencher-man, melancholy villain and deferential follower, despairing father and his consoling brother, all of which support the larger dialogic contrast of the two pairs of lovers. The use of such foils is arguably a device of any drama, indebted to the drama's roots in the scholastic convention of *in utramque partem* debate, in which contenders voiced opposing sides of an argument in order to demonstrate their rhetorical prowess (Altman). The prevalence of the dialogue convention in Renaissance prose fiction and rhetorical manuals – Castiglione's *Cortegiano*, Stefano Guazzo's *La civil conversazione* (1574), Lyly's *Anatomy of Wit* (1578) and *Euphues and His England* (1580) – bespeaks its availability for dramatic representation. Yet *Much Ado*, with its emphasis on wit, is particularly devoted to rhetorical contest, and these texts are especially pertinent. Many of Benedick's comments on the fair sex derive from Lyly, and Castiglione offers a model of intellectual contest and compatibility between the sexes, especially in his portrait of the exchanges between Lord Gaspare Pallavicino and Lady Emilia, the one a professed misogynist and the other a defender of her sex (Scott, 476). *Much Ado*'s stylistic register, from repartee to courtly exchange, is also indebted to debate forms. From Lyly's text comes the coinage for the very style in which the men of *Much Ado* often converse, 'euphuism' being the form of verbal exchange which consists in complicated syntactic parallelisms, chiasmus or inversions, and balanced structures, and above all in a competitive turning and returning of one's own terms and those of others (see 'Style', pp. 65–6 below).

However, euphuism is not a merely stylistic feature of this play, for its forms provide the currency by which the men create community. Male banter is a kind of verbal version of the secret handshake, cementing bonds and denoting hierarchy in much the same manner as the exchange of women. One of the reasons Beatrice is perceived to be 'an excellent wife for Benedick' (2.1.324) is that she talks so much like the men in the play (in the play's original staging, Beatrice's verbal masculinity would have been underscored by the fact of a boy actor playing the role). Euphuism is thus not just a source of the play's prose patterns but a medium of its gender roles, and dialogue is not merely a formal necessity of drama but a marker of social identity. The existence of dialogue manuals itself bespeaks a market of people who want to learn to exchange witticisms (Dogberry no doubt owns one, or would if he could read, whereas Beatrice is offended at the notion that her wit derives from a jest-book).

In Shakespeare's use of dialogue structures and styles we can see another instance of his use of forms in order to create a social world. Sexual slander requires a universe of rank and rivalry shaped by alliances between men, themselves shaped, among other ways, by the traffic both in words and in women (so that the semantic looseness emphasized by verbal badinage contributes to the imputed looseness of women). Thus in investigating Shakespeare's construction of gender identity we find other materials that might be considered as contributing to the intellectual conditions of possibility of this play. These materials include not only the formal patterns of dialogue and debate conventions, but contexts such as conduct books, theological and medical discourses, and the popular humour of cuckold jokes.

Sexual stereotypes

The debate model also helps, for instance, to contextualize Shakespeare's creation of Benedick and Beatrice, in that the types of the misogynist and the shrew that they can invoke belong to a prominent tradition of a rhetorical debate literature which specifically exercised itself on the question of woman's worth.[1] Thus while this pair are 'unconventional' in their shared suspicion of romantic love considered as a matter of 'soft and delicate desires' (1.1.284), their portraits nonetheless recall (although they are by no means reduced to) another set of conventions. As Linda Woodbridge has demonstrated, the debate on the question of woman's worth dates from the time of medieval universities, and received new momentum with the arrival of print culture: 'Humanism gave it its characteristic Renaissance form, most evident in its rhetoric, its humanist arguments, and its addition of classical materials to the characteristic set of *exempla*' (Woodbridge, 15). In woman's favour were cited models of chastity, thrift and heroism; against her lay charges of sexual promiscuity, and weakness of reason and body (among other faults). Authors weighed in on both sides of the question in order to demonstrate their rhetorical gifts, sometimes in different publications and sometimes in the very same work (e.g. Nicolas Breton, author of both *Cornucopiae* (1612) and *The Praise of Virtuous Ladies* (1606), or C. Pyrrye, *The Praise and Dispraise of Women* (1569)). No less a celebrant of profane love than John Donne was also responsible for a youthful exercise on the question of 'Why Hath the Common Opinion Afforded Women Souls?' (Donne, *Problems*, sigs G2ᵛ–3ʳ). Benedick's own sudden reversal from a man who swears 'till [love] have made an oyster of me he shall never make me such a fool' (2.3.24–5) to an advocate of

---

1   Woodbridge locates Benedick in the tradition of the 'stage misogynist', a company of soldiers that includes Troilus, Sextus in Thomas Heywood's *The Rape of Lucrece* (1608), Gondarino in Francis Beaumont and John Fletcher's *The Woman-Hater* (1607), Caratack in their *Bonduca* (1613), Acutus in *Every Woman in Her Humour* (anon., 1609), Posthumus in *Cymbeline*, Enobarbus in *Antony and Cleopatra*, Bosola in John Webster's *The Duchess of Malfi* (1612/13), Iago and Hamlet (Woodbridge, 279).

'No, the world must be peopled' (2.3.233) mimics the agility of authors whose goal was to show themselves equally dextrous in arguing both sides of a case. The scholastic range of Benedick's reference also perhaps reflects his hailing from Padua, 'nursery of arts' (*TS* 1.1.2).

As this edition's commentary documents, several of Benedick's tirades against women (e.g. in 2.3) resemble the conventions and details of the formal attack on women, particularly the invective of Demosthenes, which was reprised in *Of Marriage and Wiving: An excellent, pleasant, and philosophical controversy between the two Tassi* (1599) (where the Tasso brothers took up different sides of the question):

> *Demosthenes*, writing vnto the Tyrant *Corynthus* his friend, who had requested him to set downe his censure, what qualities one should seeke to finde in a woman that he ment to marry withal, returned him this answere: First, shee must be rich, that thou maist have wherewithall to live in shewe and carrie a port: next, she must be nobly borne, that thou maist be honoured through her bloud: then she must be yong, that she may content thee: then faire, that thou need not to hunt after other game; and lastly, honest and vertuous, that thou maiest not take the paines to provide a spie to watch her.[1]

This list demonstrates the conventional quality of Benedick's portrait of the ideal woman in 2.3. Shakespeare's account differs, of course, in the deft stylistic drollery with which it is presented: Benedick begins his meditation by disavowing love ('love . . . shall never make me such a fool', 2.3.25), but cannot resist contemplating what a possible mate might look like. He seemingly concludes his description with another protestation of disdain – 'till all graces be in one woman, one woman shall

1   Tasso, sig. B2[v]. Ercole Tasso was contra, Torquato pro.

not come in my grace' (27–8) – but then starts up again, as if he cannot resist the speculation. Shakespeare thus broaches the stereotype of the misogynist, but he animates it in the personality of one who seems to protest too much, a character who seems to need the convention as a defence against his own impulse to the contrary.

In describing a woman who is fair, wise, rich, virtuous, mild, noble and of good discourse, Benedick contemplates a kind of Renaissance fantasy girl, one who is all things to one man. She is not one who appears very often in the more practical-minded literatures of the day devoted to the process of mate selection (see pp. 39–43 – most caution against ambition in the choice of a wife). Even Benedick himself acknowledges the unlikelihood of his fantasy coming to fulfilment. More common was the notation of the failure to fulfil the ideal, and man's subservience to female domination brought on by the marriage yoke (see Figs 3 and 4). A chief obstacle to masculine happiness in marriage was a wife's failure to submit herself to being yoked, either verbally or sexually or both. Most of the Renaissance writings against women share the assumption about the link between verbal dexterity and sexual licence, and thus emphasize the threat of female loquaciousness to the security of patrilineal identity: 'A slow softe Tongue betokens Modestie, / But, quicke and loud signes of Inconstancy. / Words, more than swords, the inward Heart doe wound / And glib'd-tongu'd Women seldome chaste are found' (*Blazon*, sig. G1ᵛ). An ideal Renaissance woman was one seen but not heard, one who, in every sense, doesn't give anything away. We can sense in such statements the tenacity of medieval Christianity's idea of women as the heirs of Eve, that disobedient and fleshly creature who is punished for her disobedience with the arduous task of painfully peopling the world ('sure, my lord, my mother cried', 2.1.308). While the play ultimately repudiates many of these notions of female identity – Benedick readily decides to love his intellectual and verbal equal – they do inform both its jokes

Matrimonium :

3 A man bearing the servile yoke, punishing stocks and effeminizing skirt of matrimony. The fruit on his shoulder is the quince, symbol of fertility. From Henry Peacham's *Minerva Britannia* (1598)

about the male distrust of women and the psychological grounds of the slander plot. Indeed, while Benedick has no share in the slander of Hero, he is the voice of the play's most misogynist commentary: 'That a woman conceived me, I thank her; that she brought me up, I likewise give her most humble thanks; but that I will have a recheat winded in my forehead, or hang my bugle in an invisible baldrick, all women shall pardon me' (1.1.223–7).

The idea of woman as subordinate to man was a stereotype with biological as well as theological and political dimensions: even as women were thought inferior to men in reason and intellect, so they were considered a somewhat more primitive

Vis Amoris.

4 The emblem illustrating *Vis Amoris*, from Henry Peacham's *Minerva Britannia* (1598). Hercules, as the text reads, 'hath throwne his Clubbe away, / And weares a Mantle, for his Lions skinne / Thus better liking for to passe the day, / With Omphale, and with her maides to spinne . . . Loues affection, did disgrace and shame / His virtues partes' (1–10). *Much Ado's* many references to the emasculated Hercules recall this iconography.

life-form, whose blood, according to Galenic physiology, was colder, and whose metabolism more sluggish in nature than a man's.[1] In the humoral vocabulary which describes the Renaissance physique, the body is ruled by the four humours of

1 One anatomical theory of the period held that the ovaries and the uterus were an inverted penis and testicles that had not been conceived at a temperature high enough to expel them, right side out, of the foetus. See Thomas Lacqueur, *Making Sex: Body and Gender from the Greeks to Freud* (Cambridge, Mass., 1990).

blood, phlegm, choler and bile, and women were considered more phlegmatic than men. When Beatrice tells Benedick that she too loves none, and 'I thank God and my cold blood, I am of your humour for that' (1.1.123–4) (note that she vows not to love until a 'hot January', 1.1.89), she calls attention to her phlegmatic and thus essentially feminine nature.

Disdain

Beatrice, for her part, recalls in her alleged shrewishness the bane of much misogynistic writing, although the extent to which she fulfils descriptions of her as a 'harpy' (2.1.248), 'infernal Ate' (2.1.234) or 'my Lady Tongue' (2.1.252) has varied with the times and turns of productions (the eighteenth century tended to no-holds-barred shrew, whereas the nineteenth preferred the heart over the head). But this emphasis on Shakespeare's invocations of the Renaissance conventions of male suspicion of women should not obscure the fact that *Much Ado* portrays the resistance to marriage as characteristic of women as well as men. The characters of both Beatrice and Benedick draw on the convention of the 'disdainer of love' who comes to recant and even regret his or her former protestations of disinclination. Claudio swears off love at least twice. Spenser's *The Faerie Queene* includes both male and female versions: Prince Arthur, whose vow to eschew the distracting company of women is undermined by his erotic dream of a woman of no less persuasions than the Faerie Queene herself; and the arrogant Mirabella, 'borne free, not bound to any wight, / And so would euer liue, and loue her owne delight' (*FQ*, 6.7.30.8–9). Like Arthur, she is eventually humbled, though her comeuppance is significantly more abrading,[1] as she is brought

---

1   Much as Beatrice's is, compared with Benedick's: the latter is won by flattery and appeals to his chivalry; the former, by a scourging account of the harsh (rather than playful) nature of her wit.

before Cupid's court and sentenced to save as many loves as she had once scorned (twenty-two); her jailers on the journey are the tyrannous Disdain and the scourging Scorn, a pair which Hero describes as also riding 'sparkling' in the eyes of Beatrice (3.1.51) (though presumably directing their wrath towards her suitors rather than towards Beatrice herself). Beatrice is also stung in the masque scene by the allegation that she is 'disdainful' ('Well, this was Signor Benedick that said so', 2.1.118–19).

The 'scorner of love' who finds him or herself forced to recant was a familiar literary figure; the most prominent instance prior to Shakespeare lies in the first book of Chaucer's *Troilus and Criseyde*, where Troilus is punished as a heretic to love by falling for Criseyde. Among Shakespeare's works, *Love's Labour's Lost*, *Troilus and Cressida* and *The Two Gentlemen of Verona* provide male examples of the figure. Shakespeare's heroines almost to a woman display the ability to cast a cold eye upon the male of the species before themselves putting on the destined livery. Castiglione provides another precedent of disdain (or at least disinclination) being transformed by common opinion to the contrary: 'I have also seen a woman fall passionately in love with someone for whom to begin with she felt not the slightest affection, and this only from hearing that many persons believed the two were in love with each other.'[1] Beatrice, by contrast, believes 'better than reportingly' (3.1.116), and her reversal is prompted by her overhearing an account not only of Benedick's love but of her own allegedly uncharitable behaviour; however, the precedent

---

1 Castiglione, *The Courtier*, 269. The passage goes on to remark on the force of communal report: 'this, I think, was because she took what everyone thought as sufficient proof that the man concerned was worthy of her love, and it almost seemed that what was common opinion served to bring from her lover messages that were truer and more credible than his own letters or words, or any go-between, could have communicated'.

does point to the imaginative currency of the love-conversion experience.

Modifications of type

These kinds of indebtedness demonstrate not just how Beatrice and Benedick derive from Renaissance assumptions about gender identity, but how the play also challenges these assumptions. However much they may invoke such discourses, Benedick and Beatrice are not merely stereotypes; indeed, the fun of this play is the way in which they shake off these conventions of misogynist and shrew, and reveal them in the process as inadequate descriptions of human conduct. Benedick's reversal is as delightful as it is predictable, and Beatrice's bark lacks the bite of a more confirmed shrew such as Katerina. The charges of her shrewishness levied by her uncle and Antonio never really stick – as Leonato knows, 'There's little of the melancholy element in her' (2.1.316–17) – and part of what stings so about her gulling is the shock of Hero's exaggerated characterization of her as incapable of love: 'Stand I condemned for pride and scorn so much?' (3.1.108). Benedick's own allegations about her speech have more to do with the enviable speed and agility of her tongue rather than its mere logorrhoea. Bested as he often is by her wit, he is not a dispassionate judge.

As in the case of Benedick's acerbic bachelorhood, Beatrice's shrewishness is hardly a confirmed state, but rather a type which Shakespeare suggests only to bounce off, or back away from, in another demonstration of the play's concern with the frequent distance between who people imagine themselves to be and who they actually are. The sense throughout is that these two are using the conventions as a form of disguise or protective camouflage, or as a defence against the greater conventionality of being lovelorn; depending on the production, they throw them off either willingly or reluctantly, but throw them off they do. (Even if for yet another convention: Benedick, for instance, goes from being the most articulate source of the play's misogyny to a chivalric defender of woman's honour – a conversion from one norm of male behaviour to another. And Beatrice prompts this reversal by an acknowledgement of her own irretrievably female identity: 'O that I were a man . . . I cannot be a man with wishing, therefore I will die a woman with grieving', 4.1.315, 320–1.) Overall these gender stereotypes come across as rather archly staged roles; we can sense Shakespeare's nod to the conventional postures, but also his mockery of them.

The characterization of Beatrice in particular presents a striking departure from established Renaissance norms of gender identity. Despite the occasional dissenting voice (one nineteenth-century critic held her to be 'an odious woman' (Campbell, xlvi)), she is generally the most beloved of Shakespearean heroines, for her very vitality, generosity of spirit and wit, and the graceful but firm insistence with which she claims intellectual equality with men. Benedick's own characterizations of her as a 'harpy', 'infernal Ate' or 'my Lady Tongue' – all terms for a shrew – are comical in part because they are so far from the mark, as well as so obviously the slurs of one who has been bested by a woman who 'speaks poniards' (2.1.227). Her playful resistance to the thought of subjugation in marriage – 'Would it not grieve a woman to be overmastered with a piece of valiant dust? To make an account of her life to a clod of wayward marl?' (2.1.53–5) – smacks less of the shrew than of an intelligence truly indignant at the constraints social conventions impose upon selfhood (and a wit delighted with its own elaborative powers). The homicidal ferocity of her devotion to her cousin – 'Kill Claudio' (4.1.288) – is arresting but also cathartic, as is her thrilling cry against the unjustness of a world that so easily traduces a woman: 'What, bear her in hand until they come to take hands, and then with public accusation, uncovered slander, unmitigated rancour? . . . Talk with a man out at a window! A proper saying!' (4.1.302–4,

307–8). For all her intellectual pride, she is the first to admit that vanity is worth nothing when it is the cause of social divisiveness: 'Contempt, farewell; and maiden pride, adieu; / No glory lives behind the back of such' (3.1.109–10). Her wit works to produce pleasure and joy, with nothing truly grudging about it.

What is perhaps most surprising about Beatrice's relation to convention is that her flirtation with verbal prowess never seems to compromise her sexual reputation; it rather only argues for her intellectual parity with Benedick. This is significantly unlike the assumptions of much Renaissance misogynistic writing, where the link between verbal and sexual freedom is repeatedly underscored. Though Beatrice is called 'too curst' (2.1.18) by Antonio, and Leonato warns her 'thou wilt never get thee a husband, if thou be so shrewd of thy tongue' (2.1.16–17), and Benedick wishes 'my horse had the speed of [her] tongue, and so good a continuer' (1.1.135–6), her verbal powers never call her chastity into question, and they are more than anything a source of delight. (In fact, her speech is not characterized by excess or amplification – that would be Benedick – so much as by the darting, spare quip.) The point is explicitly made (perhaps in order to reassure?) that she is 'an excellent sweet lady, and, out of all suspicion, she is virtuous' (2.3.157–8).

Other characters in the play do imagine Beatrice in racy situations ('A maid and stuffed!', 3.4.59). When the men gull Benedick, they relate a racy joke about Beatrice writing in her nightgown, herself horrified at having found 'Benedick' and 'Beatrice' 'between the sheet' (2.3.137–8). The sheets here are paper, but the joke lies in the pun informed by the connection of women, words and sex that propels so much of the conventional writings against women. Further corroboration of Beatrice's unladylike affection for words comes in the play's closing revelation that she, like Benedick, has been writing sonnets, and in her quip in the first scene that if Benedick were in her books – i.e. her good graces – 'I would burn my study' (1.1.75). Hero says about Beatrice that 'I never yet saw man – / How wise, how noble, young, how rarely featured – / But she would spell him backward' (3.1.59–61); what she means is that Beatrice manages to convert any male virtue into a fault, but the phrase 'spell . . . backward' gives a sense of Beatrice's power to pervert meanings through her facility with words, and her Diana-like ability to metamorphose both meanings and men.

Yet despite these assumed links between loose words and loose women, so prevalent in the culture at large, the fact remains that the eloquent Beatrice's virtue is never in doubt. There is some acknowledgement in Lyly that women should be well spoken when occasion requires it, and heroines who are both articulate and nonetheless virtuous are common in Shakespeare. Thus when her uncle says that Beatrice apprehends 'passing shrewdly' in her estimate of marriage, we should hear it in the sense of perceptive, or sharp, rather than cross or lewd – as she replies, 'I have a good eye, uncle; I can see a church by daylight' (2.1.72–3). To see clearly is an important and rare feature in this play, and it is 'my Lady Tongue' (2.1.252) who persuades a man to believe in her cousin's honour. In a plot whose stumbling block is the fear of cuckoldry, it is the quiet ones, like Hero, that you have to watch out for.[1]

Chaste, silent and obedient

In seeking to explain this apparent paradox it may help to turn to other materials which, while they are not usually considered 'sources' of this play, do help to illuminate the cultural forces against and with which Shakespeare shaped his own characters and situations. Of particular interest is a class of writings

---

1   Bianca in *The Taming of the Shrew* is another superficially demure but troublesome figure (though more intentionally so than Hero).

concerned with the organization and regulation of the early modern family (see L. Wright). These 'conduct books' share many of the assumptions of the debate literature when it comes to the disputed nature of womankind, but unlike that tradition, do so without irony, in deadly earnest, and not primarily in the service of rhetorical performance.

The conduct-book tradition derived from the impetus of Protestant reformers eager to define marriage as an institution crucial to spiritual well-being (and hence necessary for priests); it was a genre also helped along by the increasing sense of the family as an economic unit, and the importance of a proper wife to its prosperity. Thus marriage in such texts begins to be defined not merely as a way to avoid the damnation attendant upon unregulated lust, or as a means of peopling the world, but as a source of companionship both intellectual and spiritual. Briefs for this new kind of marriage were written by and for men, but they introduced a woman different from her medieval sisters. Eve was rewritten as a solution to the problem of Adam's loneliness in paradise; according to the reformer Heinrich Bullinger, Eve was taken 'out of the syde of man and not from the erth, lest any man shulde think that he had gotten his wyfe out of the myre . . . the wyfe is the husbandes flesh and bone . . . even out of thy syde, as one that is set next unto man, to be his helpe & companyon' (Bullinger, sig. A4ᵛ). Citations of the Galatians verse 'there is neither Iew nor Grecian: there is neither bond nor free: there is neither male nor female' (3.28) helped to support this view of female spiritual fitness (if not parity). Bullinger is careful to stipulate that if woman was to be set alongside man, 'yet was she not made of the head' (sig. A4ᵛ); other writers pointed out that if a rib was not exactly dirt, it did derive from the flesh, and hence was in need of male control. St Paul underscored this hierarchy: 'the head of every man is Christ and the head of the woman is the man' (1 Corinthians, 11); 'Wives, submit yourselves to your husbands' (Ephesians, 5). Spousal companionship in this culture is officially thus perhaps less a marriage of true minds than a (re)absorption of female into male. But we can also see that Shakespeare's offering of a Benedick and Beatrice-type intellectual pairing ('if they were but a week married, they would talk themselves mad', 2.1.325–6) animates the notion of intellectual and spiritual compatibility. When Benedick asks Beatrice 'Think you in your soul the Count Claudio hath wronged Hero?' he is speaking to a Protestant woman: 'Yea, as sure as I have a thought or a soul' (4.1.325–7).

However, Beatrice is an uncommon figure, 'odd and from all fashions' (3.1.72). It is the dilemma of Hero as a victim of slander and impersonation that these texts illuminate most clearly. The centrality of companionship to marriage meant that the process of choosing a suitable wife – one meant to help you get ahead as well as into heaven – began to loom large in the male imagination. Women were by both nature and culture inscrutable, and hence a whole industry of what we would call self-help books, or, less kindly, consumer guides, began to appear. Texts with titles such as *How a Man May Choose a Good Wife from a Bad* (1602), *A Discourse of Marriage and Wiving* (1615), or *A Looking Glass for Married Folks* (1610) reminded prospective early modern bridegrooms how important the choice of a spouse was to one's domestic peace, prosperity and spiritual salvation – as well as how difficult it was.[1] The ideal wife was one designed to suit male needs for emotional, economic and reproductive profit: she should be devout, thrifty, even-tempered, hard working, and above all chaste.

The very existence of such guides suggests, however, that the ideal is easier described than found; their recommendations for proceeding suggest that the reason for the difficulty lies not only in the scarcity of good women but also in the limitations of the technologies available to discover them. How could a woman's nature and character be known? These guides are thus semiotic in nature, designed to enable the prospective suitor to

---

1 Heywood, *Man*; Niccholes; Snawsel.

41

discover a virtuous spouse by interpreting the marks of her speech, appearance and reputation. Yet the difficulty of finding a good woman lay not only in the ways in which bad women might impersonate the good; one author warned that 'thys undertaking is a matter of some difficulty, for good wiues are many times so like vnto bad that they are hardly discerned betwixt' (Niccholes, sig. B4ᵛ). More troubling still was that even though a bridegroom needed to look for signs of virtue, the very existence of legible signs ironically rendered a woman suspect. For a good woman was by definition inconspicuous, but hence at times potentially inscrutable.

For example, the standard advice in such manuals was to observe signs of behaviour, such as 'a sober and mild aspect, courteous behaviour, decent carriage, of a fixed eye, constant look, and unaffected gate, the contrary being oftentimes signs of ill portent and consequence' (Niccholes, sig. C1ʳ). Redheads were to be avoided, as well as women who were either too beautiful ('many times both to herself and to them that beholde her beautie is a prouocation to much euil') or too far above one in social station (liable to upset the gender hierarchy) (R.C., sig. K1ᵛ–2ʳ). But the difficulty in choosing a helpmeet on these grounds was that the viewer was always haunted by a sense that such signs might be dissembled, or be inadequate as denotative guides, especially as a meretricious sign is likely to be a warning one. A frequent dilemma is that a good woman can be known by her speech, but a truly good woman will be silent. Similarly, while 'the lookes' are an index of 'godliness in the face', the truly godly face will be veiled, 'to shewe how a modeste countenance and womanly shamefastnesse doe command a chaste wife; it is observed, that the word Nuptiae, doth declare the manner of her marriage. For it importeth a couering, because Virgins which should be married, when they come to their husbands for modestie and shamefastness did couer their faces' (R.C., sig. G4ʳ).

This paradox would bedevil John Milton, who nearly half a century after *Much Ado*'s composition writes in his divorce tracts that 'who knows not that the bashful muteness of a virgin may oftimes hide all the unliveliness and natural sloth which is really unfit for conversation?'[1] We can hear here the bewilderment of a man confronted by the contradiction between the cultural ideal of a woman who kept her signs to a minimum and his own definition of marriage as a 'happy conversation' (if not a couple talking themselves mad). Milton's plaintiveness here prefigures that of Henry Higgins in *My Fair Lady* ('Why can't a woman be more like a man?') but it also owes something to notions of companionate marriage and the incipient challenge it posed to and for traditional definitions of the ideal female identity as chaste, silent and obedient.

Hero

These difficulties in interpreting a woman's façade, the sense that she may be 'but the sign and semblance of her honour' (4.1.31), perhaps account for Hero's vulnerability, and the ease with which it is possible to slander her demure person. There is so little of her to go on. What there is is contradictory: she is silent in the presence of men, and pert in that of women – the discrepancy instances Shakespeare's psychological realism, surely, but also lends to her elusiveness. Both she and Claudio are very young, a 'forward March chick' (1.3.52) and a 'lamb' (1.1.15), and Hero is more often spoken about than a speaker herself. Ironically, however, and perhaps consequently, much of the play's thematic preoccupation with misinformation and misrepresentation – the 'noting' of its title – takes Hero as its object. She is rumoured to be Don Pedro's choice; she is rumoured to be unchaste; she is rumoured to be dead; she is masked, she is buried, she is veiled. The actual slander occurs by means of the manipulation of her clothing, in Spenser's version,

---

1   Milton, *The Doctrine and Discipline of Divorce* (1643), in Milton, *Poems and Prose*, 708. 'Conversation' at this time meant, in addition to verbal exchange, cohabitation or society (*OED* 2) as well as sexual intercourse or intimacy (*OED* 3).

the 'gorgeous geare' of Claribel (*FQ*, 2.4.26.8). (The play's leitmotif on the unreliable nature of fashion's significations is also voiced by Borachio in his disquisition on that 'deformed thief' (3.3.126ff.), and the Watchman's corroborative comments.) But the seeds of the slander are present in Claudio's initial choice of her, when he feels the need to ask both Benedick and Don Pedro for their warrants of her modesty, beauty and fortune – their own 'noting' of her. As his sense of Hero's attractiveness relies on the corroboration of his companions' second opinions of Hero's character, so it is vulnerable to the idea that others could desire her, and perhaps she them. (This dynamic of competitive desire is also invoked in the gulling of Benedick, where, to induce his interest, Don Pedro confesses to an attraction to Beatrice: 'I would she had bestowed this dotage on me. I would have doffed all other respects and made her half myself', 2.3.165–7). Claudio approaches Hero from the outside in, as it were, by judging the marks of her demeanour and reputation; given that in mixed company at least Hero is appropriately demure (unlike her forthright cousin), the task of deciphering her inner nature is one that requires the assistance of friends. But it remains a difficult one.

The enigmatic nature of Hero's appearance is made most clear at the moment of Claudio's rejection of her. He asserts that her blush, the conventional mark of female virtue, is a sign of shame, not embarrassment: 'guiltiness, not modesty' (4.1.40).[1] Her father agrees with this estimate: 'Could she here deny / The story that is printed in her blood?' (4.1.121–2). The Friar on the other hand has a different interpretation of Hero's visage: 'I have marked / A thousand blushing apparitions / To start into her face, a thousand innocent shames / In angel whiteness beat away those blushes' (4.1.158–61). Was a blush a sign of innocence, or experience?[2] Either reading demonstrates the

---

1   Compare with Isabella's enigmatic blush in *MM* 1.4.16–17.
2   See 4.1.32n., and McEachern, 'Blush'.

way in which knowledge of Hero's ethical identity relies on judgements about an appearance that is at once intrinsically ambiguous and imitable.[1] Hence while the docile Hero, the 'good daughter', is the enigmatic victim of others' manipulation of her representation, it is Beatrice, so clearly identified as the weaker sex by virtue of her unruly tongue, who paradoxically is transparently virtuous, 'out of all suspicion' (2.3.157).

Cuckolds

Much of this play's emotional process involves the need for discovery and disclosure – of Don John's villainy, of Benedick and Beatrice's mutual affections, of Hero's virtue and face, and so on. But if the revelation of a woman's true identity is necessary to marital security, the discovery of a man's is potentially horrifying (partly because the two are so interdependent). The dilemma of the conspicuous – what is visible and what is not – is also part of a popular tradition of cuckold humour that informs much of the play's comedy. While there are few actual cuckolds in Shakespeare's plays, Samuel Johnson wrote in some dismay, in a note on *Merry Wives* 3.5.140–1, that 'There is no image which our author appears so fond of as that of a cuckold's horns. Scarcely a light character is introduced that does not endeavour to produce merriment by some allusion to horned husbands' (*Johnson on Shakespeare*, 186). *Much Ado* is riddled with these jokes, as the characters make sport with the horn on their very way to the altar. Cuckoldry is not merely the matter of a running joke, but a theme that touches on the obstacle to love itself. Its prevalence warrants some explanation, especially given that what Johnson

---

1   The story of Susannah and the elders, in which the virtuous Susannah is slandered by two judges who attempt to blackmail her into sexual commerce by threatening her with a blot on her reputation, is another popular Renaissance instance of a woman being imprisoned by the very qualities she is trying to preserve; see Kaplan, 'Slander'; and e.g. Robert Greene, *Mirror of Modesty* (1584), 7ff.

found an excrescence is more often, to modern readers, obsolescence.

The idea that a deceived husband would grow horns which would reveal him to his community as a dupe of his wife and her lover is ancient and cross-cultural, although its ubiquity in Tudor–Stuart literature bespeaks a particular fascination for this moment. In addition to fuelling many a drama, the theme was the subject of many ballads and pamphlets, with titles such as *Cornucopiae* (Breton). There was even a place in London known as Cuckold's Haven, three miles east of St Paul's, and marked by a wooden pole sporting animal horns (see Bruster).

The word 'cuckold' comes from the word for cuckoo, the bird known to lay its eggs in another bird's nest in order that its chicks should be nurtured. The origins of the notion of horns are obscure, however; the *Oxford English Dictionary* points out that in German the word for cuckold comes from the word for capon, and is derived from the 'practice formerly prevalent of planting or engrafting the spurs of a castrated cock on the root of the excised comb, where they grew and became horns' (horn 7a). Another account explains that horns owe their origin to the practices of the Greek emperor Andronicus, who had horns placed on the houses of his conquests in order to signify the compensatory grant of hunting privileges to their husbands.[1] The most renowned source of the notion is Ovid's *Metamorphoses*, and its story of Diana and Actaeon (3.138–249). Actaeon, a notable hunter, is punished for his inadvertent glimpse of the chaste goddess of the hunt in her bath by being transformed by her into an antlered stag; he is then pursued and killed by his own hounds (see Fig. 5, and cf. *TN* 1.1.21–3).

---

1 *Brewer*. As Bruster records, this is similar to one account of the origins of Cuckold's Haven, which was attributed to the land grant of King John to the miller of Charlton, who caught the king kissing his wife; the miller was required to secure his title by walking once a year (on St Luke's day, patron saint of endurance) to the point marking his boundary with a pair of buck's horns affixed to his head.

5 Diana and Actaeon, from Henry Peacham's *Minerva Britannia* (1598).
Diana, goddess of the moon, sports the crescent horn which would become
the bovine property of the cuckold.

Ovid's version is helpful for explaining cuckolds in that it
associates horns with female power over men, although it is
also somewhat confusing in that Diana acts to protect her
chastity rather than to relieve herself of it. (Of course, from an
orthodox point of view any female sovereignty over sexuality
is an instance of unruly behaviour, and chastity is property to be
deployed in the service of male alliance, so even an aggressively
chaste Diana bears no small resemblance to an unfaithful wife,
in that she seeks to control her own sexual access.) There are
other differences as well: the plaintive vulnerability of Actaeon
is a far cry from the jolly comedy of the cuckold, who is usually
a figure less of pathos than of sport. Actaeon is punished for an

excess of vision, rather than a lack of it. And despite the use of the term 'Actaeon' to describe cuckolds, most Renaissance representations of cuckolds (with the exceptions of Falstaff, and the hunting chorus of *As You Like It*) involved not antlers but the bovine horn, as *Much Ado*'s jokes about 'the savage bull' (1.1.242–3, 5.4.43) and the 'curst cow' (2.1.20–1) underscore (cattle, like cuckolds, were servile beasts of burden and endurance). This horn bears a resemblance to the crescent moon sported by Diana herself, so that the cuckold, feminized by his wife's usurpation of sexual initiative, literally bears the emblem of female mutability.

The status of the cuckold's horn as both ludic and lucid is borne out by the uses of bovine horn in the period, as horn was known for its light-bearing and light-shedding properties; polished, it served as material for windows and lanterns (lant-horns) as well as hornbooks (alphabet primers in which the page bearing the letters was overlaid with a protective and transparent piece of horn). Crucially, this property of transparency only applies to bovine horn, not antler, which is opaque.[1] Horns are thus associated with visibility; they make the concupiscent conspicuous (see Fig. 6).

---

1   Rabelais supplements this material register by the mythic in Book 3 of *Gargantua and Pantagruel*, in which the quest of Panurge to find an answer to the question of whether, should he marry, he will be cuckolded, includes a dream vision (of his wife planting horns on his head), which he is advised to interpret according to whether the dream comes to him through the Gates of Ivory or the Gates of Horn. Whereas the former are misshapen and impenetrable, 'exactly the way you can't possibly see through ivory', the latter can be trusted, 'because [horn] is so diaphanous, so shining, and you can see them perfectly' (*Gargantua*, 2.68). The reference is to Book 19 of the *Odyssey* (probably the earliest site of the commonplace), where the chaste Penelope contemplates cuckolding Odysseus, and wonders aloud to a visiting stranger about a dream in which an eagle kills a flock of geese. When the (disguised) Odysseus assures her that it surely means that her husband will return and rout the suitors, she demurs that the authority of dreams depends on their gate: 'The dreams that pass through the gates of polished horn / are fraught with truth, for the dreamer who can see them' (19.637–8).

6 A seventeenth-century woodcut accompanying the ballad 'A Married Man's Miserie', which depicts the conspicuous plight of the cuckold. The figure on the right is winding a recheat (see 1.1.225). The cuckold wears the bovine horns (similar to those of his satyr-like rival) and seems to reside at the sign of the antler.

These features help to explain some of the function of the cuckold humour in this play, and reveal Shakespeare's preoccupation with the need for it not to be merely a matter of a recurrent locker-room gag. For while Shakespeare devotes many of the plot's twists and turns to questions of the enigmatic, also at work is the horror of the conspicuous, of having one's most intimate nature revealed in a society where social camouflage is of such supreme importance.

For Benedick the fear of such horns lies in their power to make a man visible; his fears of cuckoldry take the form of a fear of becoming a spectacle: 'pluck off the bull's horns and set them in my forehead; and let me be vilely painted, and in such great letters as they write "Here is good horse to hire", let them signify under my sign, "Here you may see Benedick, the married man"' (1.1.245–9); 'pick out mine eyes with a ballad-maker's pen and hang me up at the door of a brothel-house for the sign of blind Cupid' (1.1.234–6). This fear of becoming conspicuous is compounded by the status of the bovine horn as an instrument of sound as well as of sight, the vehicle of the 'recheat winded in my forehead' (1.1.225–6) (cf. Fig. 6). The dread of cuckoldry is a dread of becoming visible, the observed of all observers, of having your inmost domestic business revealed to the world. Thus a cuckold is emasculated, not merely by having his place taken by another, but in being rendered vulnerable to representation. The cuckold, who has failed to see his wife's behaviour, becomes a sign for others to see. What is funny about a cuckold is that not only can he not see his wife's faithlessness, he cannot see his own horns (hence Benedick's recourse to the figure of Cupid outside the brothel, emblematic not only of love's fated blindness, or that caused by venereal disease, but of that due to the failure of a husband's ability to see). Indeed a cuckold who is cognizant of his wife's behaviour is not technically termed a cuckold but a 'wittol', a word formed by splicing the word 'wit' onto the second syllable of cuckold.[1] He is in on the joke.

One of the comic attractions of the cuckold, and what differentiates him from the tragic Actaeon, is that it allows those around him to be in the know – to be, as it were, wits. He is funny because he provides a spectacle of ignorance that allows omniscience on the part of his audience. Cuckoldry thus

---

1   Middleton's Allwit, in *A Chaste Maid in Cheapside* (1613), is such an instance.

personifies the structure of dramatic irony, that phenomenon by which a certain group of people (including us) is privy to information not available to others (certain characters). In its most comfortable, silliest form, this is knowledge at the expense of a dupe, and productive of the pleasures of complicity (*Merry Wives*); in a less comfortable form, we get *Othello*, or *The Winter's Tale*, in which we are tortured by what we know but cannot share.

Much Ado veers between these two kinds of knowledge, the comic and the tragic. The spectacle of Beatrice and Benedick deluded is funny, that of Claudio and Leonato just the opposite. This is a play known for its wit; to have wit is to be in the know. It is the superior wit of both Benedick and Beatrice that marks them out as tempting victims for a kind of structural cuckolding, a desire to turn them into the butts of others' wits, and so rob them of their preening immunity to the bestial foolery of love, to dupe them into 'a mountain of affection th'one with th'other' (2.1.338–9) on false pretences, a transformation which will, or so it is hoped, rob them of their wit: 'The sport will be when they hold one an opinion of another's dotage, and no such matter . . . which will be merely a dumb-show' (2.3.208–11). The hope is that these two who pride themselves on their intellectual distance from human foibles will become, in love, a spectacle for others, unwitting of the deception practised upon them.

Thus the cuckold provides Shakespeare not merely with a species of joke, but with a design of comedy. The play is built around the question of who knows what, and when. It is formed by a series of movements of confusion and disclosure. The knowledges at stake include: the question of Hero's true suitor, mistaken by Leonato and Antonio, then Claudio and Benedick; the content and effects of the gulling plots; the discovery of the Watch, in which we are comforted by the knowledge of villainy apprehended (and frustrated, Othello-like, at its failure to be disseminated); Hero's mock 'death', and the forging of a bond between Beatrice and Benedick (by which they become, in effect, wittols, or complaisant in their own deception). In each situation some character or characters are at an epistemological disadvantage, and so provide the sport of others and ourselves. The conversion of characters into effective 'cuckolds' not only provides for the figural attention to the play's imagery of metamorphosis, but prepares for the greater emotional transformations of sceptics into lovers. Much of a production's closing tenor is determined by whether Beatrice and Benedick remain 'cuckolds' – that is, not fully cognizant of the origin or impetus of their mutual attraction – or become 'wittols': having some ownership of their own feelings. For one unusually cynical critic, for instance, they are merely victims of a 'social conspiracy': 'They are tricked into marriage against their hearts; without the pressure that moves them to professions of love, they would have remained unmarried . . . they constantly tantalize us with the possibility of an identity quite different from that of Claudio and Hero, an identity deliberately fashioned to resist the constant pressure of society. But that pressure finally prevails' (Greenblatt, 1386). An alternative vision might find the two in full possession of their own emotions, having united over and beyond the ways in which their community has prompted them. Either way, Shakespeare asks us to ponder the complicated relations of self- and social knowledges.

STRUCTURE AND STYLE

A distinguishing feature of *Much Ado About Nothing*'s architecture is the structure not merely of discrepant awareness, but of discrepant tones: it generates multiple emotional movements – towards sadness, towards happiness – sometimes contrapuntally, sometimes simultaneously.[1] This variety

---

1   See B. Evans for the notion of discrepant awareness.

sometimes occurs in the form of a disjunction that reassures, as in the awareness of comic providence at work even as tragic events unfold (granted, for instance, in the apprehension of the garrulous Borachio prior to the scene in which we know Claudio has vowed to denounce Hero). Or, as Barbara Everett has written of 5.3 (the monument scene), 'the fact that [Hero] isn't dead, and that we know she isn't, and that her family, too, know that she isn't, turns this grieving ceremony at the tomb into something like the masked dances which characterize this sophisticated comedy: an art, a game, a pretence' (Everett, 'Unsociable', 72). At other times the mixture can produce apprehension, such as when our trust in an ultimate comic direction must suffer impatience at the inability of providential action to prevent malign forces from having a certain sway. The Watch moves in inefficient if not mysterious ways.

This mixture of tones can also produce moments in which the comic and the tragic are so fused that one is not sure whether laughter or tears is the appropriate response, such as in Beatrice's command to Benedick to 'Kill Claudio' (4.1.288), or in the pathos of Leonato's own challenge to Claudio in 5.1, in which he seems to forget that Hero is not really dead (though of course, from a father's perspective, she might as well be). *Much Ado* is not classified as a tragicomedy (perhaps it is rather, à la Polonius, a comitragedy?) for it can and probably should wear its tragic potential lightly, but I would argue that it is unique among Shakespeare's comedies in its temporary proximity to the edge of the cliff (off which both Othello and Leontes will fall). Like Beatrice, who knows that at her birth 'sure . . . my mother cried; but then there was a star danced' (2.1.308–9), this play acknowledges the ways in which human joys and sorrows can often travel together.

'The course of true love'

Harmony clouded by discord is a defining aspect of comedy. While Aristotle cannot help us explicitly here, his model of the narrative sequence of tragedy – a fall from high to low – is echoed and reversed by definitions such as that of William Webbe, in *A Discourse of English Poetry* (1586). Webbe writes that comedy provides an inverse image of the tragic transit from felicity to misfortune: 'The Comedies, on the other side, were directed to a contrary ende, which, beginning doubtfully, drewe to some trouble or turmoyle, and by some lucky chaunce alwayes ended to the joy and appeasement of all parties' (Webbe, 39).[1] This is an essentially medieval, which is to say a Christian, apprehension of the function of comedy's providential conversions of trouble into joy (such that comic harmonies model and prefigure an eternal felicity). Classical models were also pertinent to Shakespeare's comic process; their plots presented the manoeuvrings of a young man towards a young woman, and the confrontation between the erotic ambitions of youth and social obstacles thereto (usually fathers, or discrepancies in social rank, or both – or, as Lysander puts it, 'differen[ce] in blood / . . . misgraffed in respect of years / . . . Or else it stood upon the choice of friends / . . . Or . . . / War, death, or sickness did lay siege to it', *MND* 1.1.135–42). But even this formula, as Frye pointed out, includes a relationship to tragedy:

> Even in New Comedy the dramatist tries to bring his action as close to a tragic overthrow of the hero as he can get it, and reverses this movement as suddenly as possible . . . Thus the resolution of New Comedy seems to be a realistic foreshortening of the death-and-

1 The majority of Renaissance definitions of comedy were satiric or homiletic, e.g. Philip Sidney: 'Comedie is an imitation of the common errors of our life, which [the poet] representeth in the most ridiculous and scornful sort that may be; so that it is impossible that any beholder can be content to be such a one' (although Sidney also considers comedy a source of delight) (Sidney, *Defence*, 44); George Puttenham: '[comedies] tended altogither to the good amendment of man by discipline and example' (Puttenham, 47); or Thomas Lodge: 'their matter was more plessant [than tragedies] for they were such as did reprehend' (Lodge, 37).

resurrection pattern, in which the struggle and rebirth of a divine hero has shrunk into a marriage, the freeing of a slave, and the triumph of a young man over an older one.

(Frye, 169)

Shakespeare's modifications of this model are many (for example, the questing hero of classical comedy is more often a hardworking heroine in boy's clothing, so that gender identity rather than social rank must be corrected). It has also been argued that Shakespearean comedy is equally indebted to native folkloric rituals of social regeneration, although *Much Ado* is in a minority among his comedies in its lack of even a metaphorical green world (a world that the 1993 Kenneth Branagh film did, however, provide). Messina is resolutely its sociable self – although the inversions of gulling, masquerade, slander and false death, and the hallucinatory social universe created by the resolutely social practices of eavesdropping and rumour could be argued to produce a climate akin to that of the forests of Arden and Athens.[1] However, Shakespeare's greatest elaboration upon his comic models lies in his transformations of the blocking mechanism, and *Much Ado* occupies a pivotal role in its evolution.

Shakespeare begins most of his comedies with a problem in need of a solution; they differ in regard to what kind of problem, how seriously we are meant to take it, and what collateral damage it does before it can be put right. In his early plays the obstacles are more akin to those of the classical models: uncooperative fathers (*Taming of the Shrew, Midsummer Night's Dream*), or social obstacles needing to be finessed by a discovery of hidden identity (*Comedy of Errors*).

---

1 Barber, who also notes an affinity between the verbal skirmishes of Benedick and Beatrice and the 'customs of Easter Smacks and Hocktide abuse between the sexes' (7).

The convention of comedy requires us to have confidence that these are puzzles that will be duly solved in due time. In the comedies of the later 1590s, however, we begin to meet more intractable obstacles, which have to do with the psychological rather than social barriers to desire's satisfaction. As in the comedies which cluster near *Much Ado* – *Merchant of Venice*, with its threat of death, or *Twelfth Night*, with its elegiac melancholy and wilfulness – the troubles of *Much Ado* come not from a meddling father or a problem of social rank but from within the self.

In fact, the play begins without a problem of the conventional sort; there is no social or paternal objection to the match of Hero and Claudio; if anything, all parties concerned are eager, even automatic, in their approval. Even in the case of a match for the unparented Beatrice it is clear that neither station nor parental permission is wanting to render her marriageable (and Benedick admits she is beautiful). So according to comic convention, the problem is rather that there is no problem; hence we are poised to anticipate one. When it comes, it comes from inside the lovers, not without; while the origins of Don John's villainy may be obscure (so to speak), his disruption of the course of true love works by playing upon overt elements of male psychology which appear in the play as commonplaces ('I think this is your daughter.' 'Her mother hath many times told me so', 1.1.98–100). In this respect the impediments to love in both pairs originate in the same source: male suspicion of female sexual inconstancy and its corollary, rival male predation. Don John's first attempt to 'cross' Claudio relies on nothing more than a lie about Don Pedro's own preference for Hero, so that by the end of Act 2 we have already experienced a miniature comedy, of error and its discovery, in which the obstacle derives from fears about male rivalry and female perfidy: 'Friendship is constant in all other things, / Save in the office and affairs of love . . . for Beauty is a witch / Against whose charms faith melteth into blood' (2.1.160–1, 164–5).

Benedick's reluctance to wed seems to stem from the same distrust of women that Claudio demonstrates (and the elder soldier's attitude perhaps serves as the model for the younger). While it is true that Beatrice's reluctance must be included in this catalogue of psychic obstacles, and while she does make the standard joke about marital infidelity ('to a cow too curst he sends none', 2.1.21), there is evidence that we are to construe her aversion to marriage, like Claudio's, as a response to Benedick's own ('Indeed . . . he lent it [his heart] me awhile, and I gave him use for it, a double heart for his single one. Marry, once before he won it of me with false dice; therefore your grace may well say I have lost it', 2.1.255–8). In Shakespeare's location of the barrier to sexual harmony within the human heart, *Much Ado* is, despite its gaiety, kin to the 'problem plays', with their dispiriting vision of the unequivocally fallen nature of human beings.

Another feature of *Much Ado*'s comic trouble is the way in which Shakespeare delays both its gestation and resolution. He mounts it in a staggered fashion, and once afoot, it is long brewing and difficult, perhaps impossible, to shrug off (the play may end with characters who have overcome their distrust of women enough to proceed to the altar, but they are still making jokes about cuckolds). No doubt this is partly because the mood is one of relief and celebration. After 2.1, with the resolution of the mini-comedy in Claudio and Hero's betrothal, Don John reapplies himself to his task, but we know as of 2.2 that an entire week must elapse before Borachio's incriminating masquerade will take place, as Leonato has fixed that term for the preparations of the wedding, and the plot is laid for the eve thereof. The interim is a halcyon time that does not, in Don Pedro's phrase, 'go dully by us' (2.1.336). Hence *Much Ado* can be played as the frothiest of Shakespeare's comedies. Its central acts are filled with the gullings in 2.3 and 3.1, and the contemplation of the 'limed birds' in 3.2 and 3.4. While Don John is presumably lurking (and a production may choose to underscore this in various ways), it is easy to forget this amidst the general gaiety of prenuptial high jinks. The conversions of Benedick and Beatrice give a sense that psychic obstacles to love are yielding, and provide another comedy in miniature, so that by the end of 3.1 we have them nearly aligned with each other even as Hero and Claudio were at the end of 2.1.

Don John reappears and approaches Claudio and Don Pedro with news of Hero's transgression at the end of 3.2, but, reinforcing the sense of quiescence, the Watch expeditiously apprehend Borachio in the very next scene. Like the gullings of Benedick and Beatrice, this apprehension is almost too easy (indeed, the loves of Benedick and Beatrice will be forged again at a higher heat). The ease signals that the trouble is not over yet. Hero's heart is unaccountably heavy in 3.4, and with 3.5 (Leonato brushing off the tedious Dogberry and Verges) arrives that familiar component of tragedy, haste, which rushes us into the church scene, where the plot of Don John nearly achieves its intended effects: 'to misuse the prince, to vex Claudio, to undo Hero and kill Leonato' (2.2.25–6).

The staggered arrival of trouble lies partly in Shakespeare's countervailing of its advances with the antidotes of a different momentum: Don John dupes Claudio in 2.1, and then Don Pedro corrects the error; Borachio recounts his dastardly deeds only to be immediately apprehended. But the difficulty of the villains in getting traction lies also in our own desire to forget their existence (while the comic obstacle here can be described as lurking and creeping – and Don John's malevolence is in some sense all the more threatening for being unexplained – it can also be imagined as effervescently transcended or held at bay by 'festival terms').

Shakespeare's use of time contributes to this effect. The play can be apprehended in three movements. The first (through 2.1) comprises some 760 lines (nearly one-third of the total), and represents the actions of one afternoon and evening. The second movement, just described, occupies another 870 lines, and represents a week; the remaining 1,000 lines depict the preparations for the wedding, its interrupted course, Beatrice and Benedick's troth-plight, Benedick's challenge to Claudio, the revelation of truth, the monument scene, and the re-betrothal scene, all of which occur in a twenty-four-hour period. In other words, the first and last thirds of the play each represent the events of a day, and the middle section a week, so that the latter operates like a kind of hammock of time, in which all seems well. However, the first and last movements are compacted and busy; the middle, indolent (this overall structure is replicated in the construction of scenes, so that long ensemble moments – the opening (1.1), the dance (2.1), the church scene (4.1) and the challenges (5.1) are interleaved with series of shorter, two- or three-person scenes[1]).

Thus, whereas many comedies spend their entire length embroiled in a crescendo of compounded confusion, *Much Ado* maintains a seeming innocence for two-thirds of its length. Or rather, while its participants are embroiled in the psychic obstacles which provide the comic oyster with its grit, they do not *know* they are embroiled until 4.1. While it is true that the finer details of this treatment of time may go unnoticed in performance, the general effect is of difficulty held at bay for a rather long period, followed by a protracted flurry of resolution, rather than, as with much comedy, a problem foregrounded from the beginning and compounded to a pitch of comic imbroglio, then solved in a single revelatory denouement.

Once the denunciation occurs, Shakespeare modulates the tone of the play significantly, and it becomes explicitly rather than implicitly tragic. In a masterly stroke, he moves in 4.1 from the formal verse drama of the church scene, in which emotions

---

1   This is somewhat of a false distinction, in that the longer scenes do not involve the entire ensemble at all times, but are composed of a series of smaller conversational groupings which while occupying continuous time and space do serve to keep the action dynamic and shifting. See Jenkins.

are wrought to a high pitch, to the relatively diffident – yet no less emotionally staggering – prose cadences of Beatrice and Benedick's professions of love. Benedick and Beatrice exchange confessions of love, but they do so, as Beatrice acknowledges, in sorrow and because of it: 'It were as possible for me to say I loved nothing so well as you. But believe me not – and yet I lie not. I confess nothing, nor I deny nothing. I am sorry for my cousin' (4.1.269–72). Leonato's grief at the perverse course of events exceeds comfort in 5.1, and Benedick's challenge quite spoils the (now uncouth) attempt of the Prince and Claudio to return to the teasing banter of 3.2. The audience of course views all of these sadnesses from the privileged knowledge that help is on the way, but in the meantime we also witness real suffering and the birth of real seriousness of feeling. Beatrice's desire to kill Claudio, and the Friar's plan for Hero – a mock death perhaps, followed by incarceration in a convent – both reveal a potential for irrevocable pain and danger. If the young pair are not exactly reborn in their ending, they both certainly escape forms of death, so even this third movement contains a third comedy, of joint resurrection, in miniature.

When the ending finally comes, all is well, but emotions are nonetheless raw (as in the sparring between Benedick and Claudio: 'some such strange bull leaped your father's cow / And got a calf in that same noble feat / Much like to you, for you have just his bleat', 5.4.49–51). Thus while *Much Ado*, like any comedy, performs a ritual of social renewal, this also includes the renewal of less than desirable aspects of the human creature. Hence, perhaps, the recurrence of the cuckold humour in virtually the final line – 'Prince, thou art sad – get thee a wife, get thee a wife! There is no staff more reverend than one tipped with horn' (5.4.120–2). The ending thus in a recursive fashion circles to reprise several earlier actions – the wedding, the masque, the merry war and the cuckold banter – and the reiteration gives a sense of the persistent quality of the play's problems.

Considered as a linear narrative, then, the structure of this play works by means of alternating scenes of hope and trouble. In one scale are male distrust of women, rivalry between men, and the sliding vices of social climbing; in the other, the fierce loyalty of Beatrice to her cousin, Benedick's willingness to take her word over his fellow soldiers', the Friar's hope and resourcefulness and the providential efficacy of the Watch and its captain. Also, perhaps, Claudio's willingness to trust in a veiled woman. One can consider the mixed emotional palette as producing a comedy whose harmonies are haunted by darker forces, or, more genially, as a supremely balanced, even temperate portrait of human experience comprising both positive potentials and flaws.

Two plots?

One thing which makes this play difficult to discuss in terms of structure is that one is not sure whether to treat its design diachronically or synchronically: that is, we could treat it either as a series of actions unfolding in time, designed to raise and condition our expectations sequentially – as we experience them when we first read or see the play – or as plots and situations that exist in parallel and antithetical relations (which are more usually recollected in scholarly tranquillity). The latter apprehension of *Much Ado* as an organic structure (rather than a narrative sequence) also yields the sense of its layered action, and Shakespeare's construction of psychic textures and truths that are melded of both hope and despair. Even as the plot reprises certain actions, so Shakespeare interweaves ostensibly separate but mutually illuminating strands of action, so that we are drawn into a sustained comparison of different characters as part of an ongoing enquiry into what constitutes a human being. It is an enquiry that extends from externals such as rank, role, speech, manners and dress, to more interior concerns such as self-knowledge, humanity towards others and openness to change. (It may be no coincidence that the word 'man' and its cognates occur more frequently, by a substantial margin, in *Much Ado* than in any other work of Shakespeare's.[1])

Traditional thinking about this play's structure has concentrated on the notions of main plot and subplot, one of a near-tragic tone, the other of a comic. This sense of the play as bifurcated is compounded by the realization that most of the first, or 'comic' half, leading up to the church scene of 4.1, is in prose, and the remainder of the play, dealing with more sombre matters, is in verse (the actress Maggie Steed, who played Beatrice, refers to this as a 'broken backed' structure (Steed, 42)). This unflattering sense of the play's discontinuity has been countered by other visions that emphasize the continuity and intersection of the two romances by means of various features of its design, including thematic parallels between the two plots. Some of these parallels are representations of behaviour. The most obvious is that signalled in its title, that of 'noting', the way in which social creatures perceive each other. This practice occurs in all of the 'discrete' plots and social groupings, and is staged in several scenes. Borachio overhears Don Pedro and Claudio in 1.1, as does Antonio's servant; Don John sours the betrothal by means of a masquerade staged for Claudio's benefit; Hero gulls her cousin by devising 'honest slanders' (3.1.84); Benedick and Beatrice are both prompted to love by overhearing themselves and their admirers described; the Watch overhear Borachio's relation of his perfidy. The play is full of instances in which characters perceive each other indirectly, and hence often erroneously. The effect is that Messina seems a world of many social proximities, where it is easy to come by information and misinformation about oneself and others. The prevalence of noting gives a sense of a community closely, claustrophobically knit together.

---

1 The runners up are *As You Like It*, then *Twelfth Night*; I owe the point and its statistics to RP.

A similar pattern of repetition and echoing occurs in episodes that call attention to social rank. Leonato's solicitude towards the Prince (1.1) is echoed in Dogberry's fawning upon Leonato (3.5). Margaret imitates her mistress in masquerade, and then flirts with Benedick about her social aspirations: 'Will you then write me a sonnet in praise of my beauty?' (5.2.4–5). Both Beatrice and Don John call attention to Don Pedro's high status, and the Watch are assured that 'If you meet the prince in the night you may stay him . . . marry, not without the prince be willing' (3.3.73–4, 77–8). The repeated noting of social place helps to create the texture of a social world homogenous in its assumptions. The repetition of similar motifs in different keys helps give the sense of a community bound at all levels by a consensual sense of its boundaries. This sense of the world is also created through Shakespeare's attention to incidental social details: the passing mentions of Claudio's uncle and Antonio's son, Margaret's chatty report on the Duchess of Milan's gown, Benedick's visit to the barber, the passing notations of time and place – all of these conjure a universe vivid, even solid, in its quotidian particulars. These details are not essential to the plot (to the extent that some of them have prompted debate about Shakespeare's compositional method), but they create a sense of a busy social world, of offstage lives and possibilities, and (in keeping with the play's themes) a sense of the audience's overhearing or witnessing a portion of a universe complete only in another dimension.

Another feature common to several of the play's strands is the amusing spectacle of a self-regard that fails to fully describe the self in question. The alacrity with which the confirmed bachelor Benedick resolves to be in love and the earnestness with which Lady Disdain vows to tame her maiden pride are two such instances, in which a character's self-professed reputation is no match for the more insistent desire to love and be loved. To these we must add the pomposity of Dogberry, whose exorbitant sense of self-importance quite outpaces the regard in which he is held by others. A more poignant version of these self-misconceptions is provided in Leonato, a father whose affectionate avuncularity gives way to a radical emotional investment in his daughter with infanticidal overtones.

Not just actions but situations are reiterated. One gulling scene follows another, and the challenge of Benedick to Claudio comes on the heels of Leonato's (and Antonio's). The love song of 2.3 ('Sigh no more, ladies') is echoed in the tomb ritual's song in 5.3 ('Pardon, goddess of the night'); the masquerade of 2.1 is reversed by the veiled women of 5.4; Hero receives the proposal of a disguised suitor in 2.1, and Claudio must accept a veiled bride in 5.4. The impersonation of Hero occurs at night; so does her mock burial. With each of these repetitions we sense the congruence of situations, as well as their individual particularity. The gulling of Benedick, for instance, works by flattering him, whereas Beatrice's gullers undertake a kind of scourging of her faults. Leonato's challenge is full of pathos; Benedick's of grim sincerity. The reiterations generate a series of foil effects, which give a sense of the commonality and the idiosyncrasy of persons – a nuanced portrait of a community. *Much Ado* bears comparison in this architectural respect with the *Henry IV* plays, which Shakespeare had recently completed, and in which he also works along these mirroring lines, so that rebellion in the tavern echoes rebellion in the state, the robbery of purses prefiguring the suppression of Percies. So too, parts of *Much Ado* echo and haunt each other, prefigure and invert their counterparts.

The construction of variation within symmetry, and symmetry within variation, is also the property of the 'dual' plot. The play opens with two pairs ostensibly belonging to antithetical romantic traditions: Hero and Claudio represent the marriage of partners suitable in age, wealth and station, and who conduct their courtship in the terms of stylized romance: 'Lady, as you are mine, I am yours. I give away myself for you,

and dote upon the exchange' (2.1.282–4). The more ornery
couple, 'too wise to woo peaceably' (5.2.67), seem compatible
only in their wit, their shared contempt for romance – 'I had
rather hear my dog bark at a crow, than a man swear he loves
me' (1.1.125–6) – and, of course, their obsession with each
other. But as the play moves on, both couples are tested, and
modify the extremity of their positions. Claudio acts most
unchivalrously, and Beatrice is forced to seek a champion. One
couple gains experience, and emotional texture; the other has
recourse to convention. Both unions take the form of an initial
approach followed by a severance, followed by a rapprochement,
so that marriage comes about as a result of experience and loss
as well as desire and momentum. The play begins with Benedick
and Beatrice estranged; the crisis between Claudio and Hero
helps to unite the former pair, even as it drives Claudio and
Hero apart. The figure of a dance comes to mind here, as
Shakespeare poses the two pairs as foils and then tempers their
differences. The overall effect, as in the emotional tenor, is of
balance, symmetry and temperance, shadows in light, and light
breaking through shadows.

Style

Relations of similarity and variety also characterize this play's
language. In *Much Ado* Shakespeare explores the powers and
the pleasures of speaking well. The dialogue is formal,
mannered and elegant, but also enlivened by the well-turned
phrase, the quick retort, and the punch-line, governed by the
tension between the decorous and the daring. The contrast
between these two forms is in part what pleases: the way in
which the energies of witty badinage can be sparked from the
elegant cadences of a more formal and mannered conversation,
and vice versa. Conversation is both a dance and a form of
combat. Words are swapped, tossed and stolen. Some speakers
are more nimble than others, but all aspire. The best in this kind
endow a mannered language with a sense of the impromptu and

the improvisational, while others study their forms in a hope of mastering their patterns. Above all we have the sense of being in the presence of a kind of everyday eloquence, all the more enviable because seemingly effortless. Additionally, in its very linguistic textures the play explores the larger thematic questions of the pleasures of artifice and the corresponding paranoia about semantic stability.

Prose and the prosaic

Shakespeare demonstrates in *Much Ado* a rare devotion to prose structures; nearly 70 per cent of the play's lines are prose, of which Benedick, with 399 of 2,485 lines, possesses the lion's share.[1] Only *Merry Wives*, at nearly 90 per cent, has a higher proportion (*Twelfth Night* and *As You Like It* following behind), and *Much Ado* makes prose the choice of principal characters as well as of the more usual suspects such as the Watch (and critics dedicated to the main plot / subplot distinction have cited these allocations in support of their position). This prose comes in several styles, and before examining its kinds we might consider a few critical assumptions about Elizabethan dramatic prose.

Even Shakespearean prose, for all its glories, tends to be treated somewhat as a poor relation in critical evaluations. One of the first things schoolchildren are taught about Shakespeare is that verse typically belongs to the aristocratic main characters, and prose to the motley speakers of the non-noble subplots, as if social station was a prerequisite for verbal ornament, and learning the prerogative of the line break. We are reminded that prose is most often the property of madmen and the lower orders: 'the normal mode of speech in the [Elizabethan] play was verse, and the introduction of prose signified the failure of

---

1   The figures belong to Vickers, 433, table 1, and T. King, 193.

a character to conform with the prevailing mode of his world' (M. Crane, 3). True in some degree as such statements are, they carry with them the implicit assumption of prose as a debased and undisciplined, or even unlearned and unadorned, medium, as if the absence of the governing regularity and pressure of a verse line opens the door to all manner of social ills. In its favour, on the other hand, prose can be considered (at least by modern students) more 'natural' and colloquial, and more true to how people really talk (although actors do cite the similarity of the iambic rhythm and a heartbeat): 'prose, the form of common speech, introduces an atmosphere of realism; and prose speakers in Shakespeare constantly recall the existence of a world which, although not the 'real world' of the audience, is nevertheless somehow physically nearer than the poetic world' (M. Crane, 100). In this light, prose exists merely to get the job done with a minimum of flourish.

Such assumptions have some utility in approaching the style of *Much Ado*. The prose in the play is indeed often easy and direct, even utilitarian: 'I learn in this letter that Don Pedro of Aragon comes this night to Messina' (1.1.1–2); 'Was not Count John here at supper?' (2.1.1); 'In my chamber window lies a book. Bring it hither to me in the orchard' (2.3.3–4). Socially subordinate characters can be very prosaic, on occasion: 'I like the new tire within excellently, if the hair were a thought browner. And your gown's a most rare fashion, i'faith. I saw the Duchess of Milan's gown that they praise so . . . By my troth, 's but a night-gown in respect of yours . . .' (3.4.12–18). Verse is reserved for moments of high formality (or moments which aspire thereto), such as Claudio's wooing and rejection of Hero, and Leonato's lethal disappointment in his daughter. In general the prose cadences of this play contribute to its portrait of a world replete in everyday detail.

However, such a distinction is also misleading. Some of Shakespeare's most virtuoso speakers often conduct themselves in prose: Falstaff and Hal ('the most comparative, rascalliest, sweet young prince', *1H4* 1.2.77–8), to cite two most immediately antecedent to *Much Ado*; Hamlet comes soon after. *Much Ado*'s prose is not exclusively plebeian, and, on the contrary, the efforts of social climbing and striving are conducted through attempts to master its distinctive, and decidedly elitist, patterns. While in the hands of the more eloquent these forms can seem unpremeditated and effortless, they are not unornamented or unlearned, or without artifice. Far from it.

Euphuism

Much Ado's prose style is influenced by and comments upon (although it rises above) the category of Renaissance literary style known as 'euphuism', after the writings of the dramatic and prose fiction writer John Lyly, in particular his prose works *Euphues: An Anatomy of Wit* (1578) and *Euphues and His England* (1580). These texts both feature a young man named Euphues ('Wellborn') who engages his friends in protracted discourses on the nature of friendship, love, women, and other subjects of philosophical merit. It is a style characterized by techniques of amplification such as parallelism and antithesis, chiasmus, strings of rhetorical questions, structural symmetries and turns of logic, and full of internal poetic effects generated by alliteration, syllabic echoing, the repetition of verbal roots, rhyme, puns, phrases patterned on sound and syntax, and myriad rhetorical figures identifiable only to the connoisseur. Crowning these aural effects were displays of humanist learning: epigrams, aphorisms, proverbs, classical allusions and examples, fables, and information from natural and un-natural history. In other words, this is a prose as complicated, and as figurally rich, as any verse.

While the term 'euphuism' credits Lyly with this style, he was less the originator than the popularizer of a mode that had been a hallmark of Renaissance humanism. This was a prose modelled after Ciceronian oratory in its copiousness and ornament; its balances and symmetries were meant to connote not merely rhetorical poise but ethical temperance.[1] At the same time, like all Renaissance rhetoric, euphuism is eloquence in the service of persuasion, or 'moving' (in Sidney's term), intended to shape the response of its recipient. As such it is indebted to the tradition of *in utramque partem* debate; authors employ its argumentative line in order to persuade or dissuade a presumed antithesis, and the syntactical register is itself replete with antithesis, balance and reversals. Its figures and methods were circulated in handbooks of rhetoric, such as *The Civil Conversation of M. Steven Guazzo* (1581), as well as promulgated by the mimetic methods of Renaissance schooling. This prose was written by 'wits', whose personae conveyed an ease, balance, temperance, agility and all-round suaveness (their number included John Donne, Thomas Nashe, Thomas Lodge and Ben Jonson); it achieved a vogue in the years 1590–1612.[2] The intellectual poise and apparent disinterestedness of Benedick and Beatrice model this pose as well.

It is not, at first glance, a prose style particularly suited to drama; in Lyly's prose the processes of amplification produce monologues that, however enlivened at the level of the clause, are daunting (and mind-numbing) in their stamina. An example apropos to the sexual mistrust that pervades *Much Ado* is provided by the disappointed Euphues, in his warning against love in the vein of Ovid's *Amores*:

> This is therefore to admonish all young Impes and nouices in loue, not to blow the coales of fancie wyth desire, but to quench them with disdayne. When love tickleth thee decline it lest it stiffle thee, rather fast than surfette, rather starue than striue to exceede. Though the

1 See W. Crane: '[wit] connoted . . . a flow of ideas and words ample for the development of any topic at length, along with quick comprehension of thought and readiness in answering' (9).

2 As well as a backlash, in the anti Ciceronian rhetoric of Justus Lipsius, Francis Bacon and others. See Croll.

beginning of loue bringeth delyght, the ende bringeth destruction. For as the first draught of wine doth comfort the stomacke, the second inflame the lyuer, the thirde fume into the heade, so the first sippe of loue is pleasaunt, the seconde perilous, the thirde pestilent. If thou perceiue thy selfe to be entised with their wanton glaunces, or allured with their wicked guyles, eyther enchaunted with their beautie or enamoured with their brauerie, enter with thy selfe into this meditation. What shall I gayne if I obtayne my purpose? nay rather what shall I loose in winning my pleasure? If my Lady yeelde to be my louer is it not lykely she will bee an others lemman?

(Lyly, *Anatomy*, 248)

This is a mere portion of a passage that has been underway, and continues, for hundreds of lines. Indeed, part of the point is the authorial staying power to sustain the subject while generating interest and texture with marks of ingenuity and invention. The writer must aspire to an encyclopaedic range of reference and reiteration, whilst managing to stay on topic, balancing digressive expansion against thematic pertinence. This is a style that Benedick might call 'so good a continuer' (1.1.136).

Some of *Much Ado*'s set pieces are akin to this not only in style but also in subject, such as Benedick's monologue against love in the beginning of 2.3 ('I do much wonder that one man, seeing how much another man is a fool when he dedicates his behaviours to love, will, after he hath laughed at such shallow follies in others, become the argument of his own scorn by falling in love . . .', 2.3.8ff.). This, the longest prose speech in *Much Ado* (27 lines), is rivalled only by the speech at the end of the same scene in which Benedick recants his position. In performance it is usually highly entertaining, chiefly because of the sense of argument that propels it; even as he scorns Claudio, Benedick is slowly persuading himself. This sense of suasion derives from Shakespeare's focus on the meditative and dialogue-like features of Lyly's prose, as he builds on and improves upon its patterns of call and response, internal echoes and retorts, rhetorical questions and answers, reversals and symmetries. (If Lyly's marathon style seems untheatrically static, it does contain within it the dialogic structures that make it surprisingly adaptable to drama, albeit in much smaller doses. Lyly himself exploited these.)

Yet the Shakespeare passage is infinitely more flexible than the Lyly, and more agile in sketching the drollery of a personality in debate with itself. It is true that Benedick unfurls parallel balanced structures: three sentences in succession list the contrasts between the 'before' and 'after' versions of Claudio, with respect to his musical tastes, clothing and speech ('I have known when . . . and now . . .'; 'I have known when . . . and now . . .'; 'He was wont . . . and now . . .', 2.3.12–19). But where Lyly's prose would be just beginning to warm up, Benedick stops and shifts the enquiry to himself, and the mesmeric repetitive queries give way to a blunter, more flat-footed idiom: 'I cannot tell; I think not' (22). Then, just when it seems that Benedick has resolved the matter with the seal of logic ('till he have made an oyster of me he shall never make me such a fool', 24–5), he starts up yet again with musing on the features of women: 'One woman is fair . . .' (25). He concludes again, with a chiastic flourish: 'But till all graces be in one woman, one woman shall not come in my grace' (27–8). But then he begins *again*, this time even more specifically: 'Rich she shall be . . .' (28–9). The 'continuer' features of the style are harnessed here to paint a mind irresistibly returning to a closed subject with a moth's attraction to a flame, so that the length of Benedick's argument simultaneously sustains and undermines his conviction. At the beginning of the speech Benedick is perplexed by the notion of a soldier in love, but by the end he is contemplating the colour of her hair, so that the audience begins to anticipate (if it hasn't already concluded) that Benedick himself might 'become the argument of his own scorn by falling in love' (11–12). Shakespeare's prose conjures a mind divided despite itself.

The agonistic aspect of euphuism's verbal one-upmanship is evident most clearly in dialogue rather than soliloquy, such as the first exchange between Beatrice and Benedick (also a disavowal of love):

BENEDICK   What, my dear Lady Disdain! Are you yet living?
BEATRICE   Is it possible Disdain should die, while she hath such meet food to feed it as Signor Benedick? 115 Courtesy itself must convert to Disdain if you come in her presence.
BENEDICK   Then is Courtesy a turncoat. But it is certain I am loved of all ladies, only you excepted; and I would I could find in my heart that I had not a hard heart, for 120 truly I love none.
BEATRICE   A dear happiness to women – they would else have been troubled with a pernicious suitor. I thank God and my cold blood, I am of your humour for that: I had rather hear my dog bark at a crow, than a man 125 swear he loves me.
BENEDICK   God keep your ladyship still in that mind, so some gentleman or other shall scape a predestinate scratched face.
BEATRICE   Scratching could not make it worse, an 'twere 130 such a face as yours were.
BENEDICK   Well, you are a rare parrot-teacher.
BEATRICE   A bird of my tongue is better than a beast of yours.
BENEDICK   I would my horse had the speed of your 135 tongue, and so good a continuer. But keep your way, o'God's name; I have done.

BEATRICE   You always end with a jade's trick; I know you
　　of old.

(1.1.112–39)

This exchange is always greeted with delight in the theatre; it
contains the first shots across the respective bows. As Brian
Vickers comments, 'repartee is more than a linguistic device
here: to Beatrice and Benedick it is a way of life, a mutual witty
antagonism which has evidently long continued and seems
destined to go on' (Vickers, 176). Here, instead of a speaker
punning upon his own terms, the contest of antagonists
personifies and animates the push-and-pull features of
euphuism's internal debate. Words of one speaker are taken and
turned by the other, returned inverted or askew, transported,
and otherwise perverted. Puns are crucial. Shakespeare moves
here beyond the polished, patterned verse of plays like *Love's
Labour's Lost* towards a more improvisational and realistic
repartee, which, while it may commence as elegant twists and
turns, degenerates into little more than name-calling, as both
speakers strain to sustain the rally.

It is no coincidence that the passages in *Much Ado* that
display the most virtuoso instances of euphuism are those
either where a debate is underway, or a character is engaged
in argument with himself, or where high feeling – either rage
or contempt – propels the language. Indignation and
invective, contempt and disdain are the motive forces of
this style. Don John's speech on his melancholy in 1.3 ('I
had rather be a canker in a hedge than a rose in his grace',
25ff.), and Beatrice's excoriation of Claudio in 4.1 ('Count
Comfit', 314), are two moments where Shakespeare fuels
the persuasive features of the style with the implosive pressures
of disdain.

Verbal handshakes

The combative aspect of euphuism – whether it appears as
persuasion or invective – derives in part from its roots in debate

forms, but also from the social function of the style as it is rendered in Lyly's works. Euphuism is the currency of social alliance and competition, the means by which Lyly's characters (and the real-life wits they inspired) signal their associations and their rivalries. It is as much sociolect as aesthetic, an identity which Shakespeare's practice in *Much Ado* makes clear. The language is the means by which members of this group signal their membership in the group, and their relations to each other, relations of both rank and gender (while euphuism is a primarily male discourse here, Beatrice's usage marks her out as both fashionable and an 'excellent wife for Benedick', 2.1.324). Speakers are distinguished by their relative proficiency in its patterns, a proficiency that is linked in part to social position. It is a dialect that signals the relations of a courtly class of persons, and is the means by which they display their membership in this class, and also the means by which others display their aspirations to the fashionable company.

The most slavish speakers of the idiom, for instance, include the Messenger and Balthasar, those subordinate male figures attending upon, and imitating, their betters. Don Pedro's nameless messenger, harbinger of the troop's arrival at Leonato's dwelling, signals the arrival of the courtly gentlemen in his description of Claudio: 'He hath borne himself beyond the promise of his age, doing in the figure of a lamb the feats of a lion; he hath indeed better bettered expectation than you must expect of me to tell you how' (1.1.13–16). This speech is met with Leonato's rather laconic comment on Claudio's uncle; the Messenger tries again in a description of his embassy: 'there appears much joy in him, even so much that joy could not show itself modest enough without a badge of bitterness' (20–2). Again, Leonato (bemused?) translates this ornate speech into the vernacular: 'Did he break out into tears?' (23), but then he too meets the challenge, matching the Messenger's *polyptoton* (repetition of the same word root

74

in different forms), and raising it with an *antimetabole* (the inversion of word or clause order within a sentence): 'A kind overflow of kindness; there are no faces truer than those that are so washed. How much better it is to weep at joy than to joy at weeping!' (25–7). By the time the troop arrives, Leonato himself is at full throttle: 'Never came trouble to my house in the likeness of your grace, for, trouble being gone, comfort should remain; but when you depart from me, sorrow abides, and happiness takes his leave' (94–7).

Don Pedro and Leonato as the two most important political figures in the play use this language as a form of mutual acknowledgement (hence perhaps Leonato's reluctance to match the Messenger's style). Their speech is courtly, decorous and balanced, trading and complementing each other's terms with the measured elegance of a formal dance. Don John, on the other hand, disdains this language in the first scene in order to signal his reluctant membership in this fellowship: 'I am not of many words' (150). (Later, however, with Conrade, he shows himself quite voluble in these very cadences, and 'the closeness of the patterning concentrates his ruthlessness still more' (Vickers, 178).)

The dilatory, even flowery, habits of euphuism render it vulnerable to cutting in modern productions; indeed, even this play's own characters can find an over-dedicated speaker tiresome. Dogberry is the prime exhibit here, but to his tediousness we can add Balthasar's – whose thematic punning on his 'notes' invites Don Pedro's impatience in 2.3: 'Why, these are very crotchets that he speaks' (2.3.54). Margaret's attempt to subject Beatrice to her own treatment in 3.4 receives a similar response. As with Balthasar, the efforts of the lower-status figure invite the contempt of the higher: 'O God help me, God help me, how long have you professed apprehension?' 'Ever since you left it. Doth not my wit become me rarely?' (3.4.61–4). Even as Margaret dresses herself in her mistress's clothes, she seeks to speak her betters' language, and even as Beatrice matches and betters Benedick by means of repartee, Margaret vies with her social superior by means of verbal one-upmanship.

It is chiefly the socially subordinate characters who have become over-literal (or would that be over-figural?) in their upwardly mobile emulation of the fashionable stylistic patterns. For more prized than a slavish imitation are the improvisational renditions of euphuism's best speakers. Beatrice and Benedick reign supreme here. What distinguishes them from the more formal or tedious speakers of the idiom – much as Shakespeare himself transcends Lyly – is their ability to animate its forms, chiefly by means of aggressive appropriations and inversions of the meanings of the speech of others.[1] If Don Pedro and Leonato exchange decorously calibrated compliments, Beatrice and Benedick take off the gloves. The two chief weapons in their arsenal are amplification and the turning of terms. Benedick excels at the former and Beatrice at the latter, which means that Benedick entertains chiefly by means of the longer speech (e.g. 2.1.219–39), whereas Beatrice tends to get the better of him in repartee (occasions which, in turn, give rise to Benedick's diatribes). Both characters convey a vibrant sense of verbal energy, whether in Benedick's talent for heaping image upon image or in Beatrice's dancing puns. This energy carries a sexual charge (not merely because of its production of *double entendres*, reproved by nineteenth-century critics as unbecoming to them both); it is the energy of

---

1 Indeed, there are places where Benedick cites Lylyean formulations almost scornfully, as if they were clichés, such as his phrasing of his disdain for Claudio's choice of Hero as herself undistinguished: 'too low for a high praise, too brown for a fair praise' (1.1.163–4); cf. 'I know not how I should commend your beauty, because it is somewhat too brown, nor your stature, being somewhat too low' (Lyly, *Euphues*, 261).

flirtation, the dance of attraction and elusiveness that constitutes the mating ritual of these two wits. The semantic fluidity they both exploit in making words dance for them, the ability to 'fright' a word 'out of his right sense' (5.2.52–3), dramatizes at a linguistic level the larger thematic questions in the play, the way in which signs are unstable, unpredictable and subject to manipulation, whether in play or in perversion.[1] This aspect of language also provides for one of the play's funniest moments, when the newly amorous Benedick, confronted with the as yet unconverted Beatrice, tries to parse her harsh words in his favour: 'Ha! "Against my will I am sent to bid you come in to dinner" – there's a double meaning in that' (2.3.248–9).

While euphuism is a distinctive feature of this play's prose style, it is not an exclusive one, and it would be a mistake to describe the style as steeped in euphuism, nor is word-play as a hallmark exclusive to that idiom. Like his use of gender stereotypes, Shakespeare's stylistic debts are more a matter of allusive citation, of the deft mining of a resource, or the pointed and strategic deployment of a pattern. Above all, one senses the way in which his writing animates its resources.

'The even road of a blank verse'

Prose is the dominant form of this play's language, but verse also plays a part in marking character and situation. Much of it (16 per cent) belongs to Claudio: his announcement to Don Pedro of his affection for Hero, his first speech of disappointment when misled about Don Pedro's intentions

---

1 Lynne Magnusson argues that not only does the play recognize language 'as productive of mistakes and misapprehensions' but also its characters 'deploy a complex range of prevention and repair mechanisms to compensate' for this aspect (Magnusson, 158).

towards her, and his rejection of her in the church scene all occur in a rather serviceable, primarily end-stopped line. Hero too, though not of many words herself, speaks most of them in verse, in the gulling of Beatrice (13 per cent of the total). The other prime verse speakers are Leonato (24 per cent), in the wake of Claudio's rejection, and the Friar, with his long practical and philosophical speech in 4.1 (9 per cent). Most of the verse arrives with the wedding scene and its aftermath, although a notable exception is the moment when Beatrice comes forward after the gulling scene to acknowledge her conversion into a lover, in the form of a truncated sonnet.

As this moment suggests, verse serves as a marker of the conventional romance (so much so that Benedick, new-styled as a lover, finds himself struggling to write poetry, and we find in the final scene that both members of the couple have authored sonnets). It is also the marker of high formality: the masked dance, the tomb scene, or the final encounter of Claudio with a veiled bride. Other abstractions of the self are also registered in verse: the Friar's meditation on the retrospective effects of loss, and Leonato's complaints of his injuries in 4.1 and 5.1. Indeed, Shakespeare gives to Leonato the verse most adventurous in construction, and most psychologically expressive, in that it displays a syntactic responsiveness and dynamism, as well as a richness of imagery. Tellingly, this is the language of pain, belonging to the play's most tragic moments, moments whose protagonist, at least as is measured by poetic intensity, is Leonato. Compared with the figural business of the prose, the verse is rather unathletic in its imagery, but given that verse here appears at moments of emotional intensity its function seems to be to provide a measured dignity of expression rather than a sense of inventive elaboration. Its figures seem to arise as a consequence of emotional pressure rather than calculation.

Introduction

Image patterns

The dominant 'donor-field'[1] of *Much Ado*'s metaphors belongs
to the beasts: Claudio is a 'figure of a lamb' doing the 'feats of
a lion' (1.1.14–15), a 'poor hurt fowl' (2.1.185), a calf (5.4.50);
Hero is a 'forward March chick' (1.3.52) and accused of having
the lust of 'pampered animals' (4.1.59); Don John is 'trusted
with a muzzle' (1.3.30) and decrees not to 'sing in my cage'
(1.3.31–2); Margaret has a 'greyhound's mouth' (5.2.11) and
her tongue keeps pace at 'Not a false gallop' (3.4.86). The 'two
bears' (3.2.70) Beatrice and Benedick are the most often
transfigured: he is a 'jade' (1.1.138), a 'savage bull' (1.1.242–3,
5.4.43), an 'oyster' (2.3.24), a 'kid-fox' (2.3.40) and a fish
(2.3.110). Beatrice is a 'harpy' (2.1.248), a 'lapwing' (3.1.24),
a 'haggard' (3.1.36), also a fish (3.1.29), and speaks of taming
her own 'wild heart' to Benedick's hand as if it were a bird
(3.1.112). Dogberry, of course, is an ass (4.2.75). The effect of
this menagerie is to underscore the carnal nature of humans in
love, to depict them as the prey of Cupid's hunting and trapping,
as well as to give a sense of the Ovidian stature of the
metamorphosis performed by love. This range of reference is
underscored by the play's second greatest figural resource, the
classical: 'infernal Ate' (2.1.234); 'Hercules' (2.1.231–2, 337;
3.3.131–2; 4.1.319); 'My visor is Philemon's roof' (2.1.85);
'You seem to me as Dian in her orb, / . . . But you are more
intemperate . . . / Than Venus' (4.1.56–9); 'the wheels of
Phoebus' (5.3.26). This latter register both complements and
offsets the bestial litany, providing a veneer of learned civility
over the sex: 'lusty Jove / When he would play the noble beast
in love' (5.4.46–7).

Another prominent strain of imagery is that belonging to
that 'deformed thief' fashion.[2] Shakespeare frames Borachio's

1 The term belongs to Thompson & Thompson.
2 A preoccupation of *Hamlet* and *All's Well* as well. See Ormerod.

extended discourse on fashion in 3.3 (that on the unreliable indices of fashion's representations, the discrepancy, for instance, between the size of a codpiece and that of its contents) with a series of similar images: Don Pedro hopes to 'fashion' (2.1.340) a match between Beatrice and Benedick; Benedick 'wears his faith but as the fashion of his hat: it ever changes with the next block' (1.1.70–2); Beatrice is an 'infernal Ate in good apparel' (2.1.234), who thinks a beardless husband fit only to be 'Dress[ed] . . . in my apparel and [made] . . . my waiting-gentlewoman' (2.1.29–30). Don John says that the word 'disloyal' is 'too good to paint out [Hero's] wickedness' (3.2.98–9); Benedick's transformation into a lover is signalled by the 'fancy that he hath to strange disguises' (3.2.30); and Hero's wedding is prefaced by a scene which details the complicated artifice of an Elizabethan bridal regalia, with its false hair, layered gowns and perfumed millinery. Shakespeare emphasizes with such incidents fashion's fickleness and power to obscure the truth of identity.

Songs

Another subset of the play's stylistic modes is that of its explicitly musical measures. *Much Ado* is a play replete with the melodious conventions of aristocratic courtship: masked balls, serenades before chamber windows, lute warbling and sonnet writing. The intrigue begins with a stately dance in 2.1, and is resolved with one in 5.4, the latter intended to 'lighten' not only 'our wives' heels' (117) but also the foregoing gloom. In between occur a number of musical interludes: Balthasar's song 'Sigh no more' (2.3.60ff.); Margaret's injunction to 'Clap's into "Light o'love"' (3.4.40); Benedick's attempt at 'God of love' (5.2.26–9); and the song of contrition at Hero's alleged tomb, begging 'Pardon, goddess of the night' (5.3.12ff.). Early performances (at Blackfriars theatre) may have punctuated intervals in the action with yet more music, and most plays were followed by a jig, perhaps once upon a time performed by the fleet-of-foot Will Kemp, who played Dogberry. Beatrice may skip a few steps of Scotch jig, measure or the cinque-pace to accompany her discourse on marriage in 2.1 (64–70). The play is punctuated and structured by song, perhaps not surprisingly, given its many meditations on the harmonies and dissonances of human connection.

Much of this music is more disconcerting than decorative in the content of its lyrics. A song whose refrain is 'Men were deceivers ever' (2.3.61) in a play replete with cuckold jokes provides a rare acknowledgement of the way in which men too can violate love's faith; as W.H. Auden wrote, 'the serenade convention is turned upside down in Balthasar's song, and its effect is to suggest that we shouldn't take sad lovers too seriously . . . If one imagines the sentiments of the song being an expression of character, the only character they suit is Beatrice' (Auden, 115).[1] Margaret's invocation of 'Light o' love' is another such grace note recommending a carefree attitude to love's trials. Indeed, the one relatively 'sincere' attempt at a romantic song comes from Benedick, in his attempted warbling of the plaintive and popular (even hackneyed) Elizabethan song 'God of love', but he is the first to admit that the tune sits ill in a throat more used to other registers. In this company, the 'song of woe' sung by the mourners at Hero's tomb strikes a rare sombre note, but the gravity of that, too, is undercut by our knowledge that the virgin knight in question is not really dead. In this light, the references to yawning graves, the heavy rhyme of 'moan' and 'groan', risk sounding overdone. The music throughout the play thus stands a degree askance to its action, in a way that provides an ironic commentary, respite from, or alternative perspective on that action. The individual settings of a given performance will, of course, shape the degree of distance invoked here. Of the three songs sung in the play, a

---

1   Kenneth Branagh's film took Auden's hint and had Emma Thompson as Beatrice read it at the start of the film.

probable original setting exists only for 'God of Love', sung to the dance tune of 'Turkeylony' (after the Italian 'Tordiglione'), which was initially printed in 1562 by the actor William Elderton, and much imitated.

STAGING *MUCH ADO*

Much Ado About Nothing is rife with representations of theatre, not merely, as in some of Shakespeare's works, as a metaphor for human experience, but as an actual practice of the play's characters. Some of this registers as the habit of certain characters of imagining themselves, or being imagined by others, as playing established roles: for instance Benedick's tendency to 'speak after [his] custom, as being a professed tyrant to their sex' (1.1.160–1); Don John's sense of himself as a confirmed melancholic; or Beatrice's reflexive perversity in describing men: 'How wise, how noble, young, how rarely featured – / . . . she would spell him backward' (3.1.60–1). But in addition to this sense of theatrical identity, as that of a reputation to be upheld, the play instances explicit performances, involving costumes, scripts, and even blocking, intended to persuade their audiences of a given understanding about themselves or another. While critics have noted the importance of eavesdropping to the play – an instance of an auditor, such as Borachio, or Antonio's servant, inadvertently overhearing an exchange – many scenes are also deliberately staged by characters for the consumption of an unwitting onstage audience, the difference from conventional theatre being that the audience in question – Benedick, Beatrice – is under the impression that he or she is eavesdropping, rather than attending an explicitly fictional performance; as Benedick avouches, 'I should think this a gull, but that the white-bearded fellow speaks it' (2.3.119–20). These scenes most obviously include the two intended to capture Benedick and Beatrice's affections, but also the dance masquerade by which Don Pedro secures

Hero for Claudio, the performance of Borachio and Margaret at Hero's window, and the plotted humiliation of Hero at the wedding by a Claudio who casts himself in advance of the event in the part of a scorned bridegroom: 'If I see anything tonight why I should not marry her, tomorrow in the congregation where I should wed, there will I shame her' (3.2.111–13). The ritual at the tomb, the masked dance and the final tableau of four veiled women present other species of theatre.

This is, then, a play for which Shakespeare writes characters who repeatedly stage actions in order to shape the response of an audience, and a play that thematizes the role of theatre in shaping human identity.[1] *Much Ado* thus dramatizes the practice of using theatre to create a deliberate effect – namely, to induce or to dissuade love.[2]

The effect of a given production of *Much Ado* itself is of course harder to specify, although we could say, safely (if blandly), that amusement, and hence a certain pleasure, are the desired goals (if only to secure an audience's continued custom). In its reliable ability to deliver such amusement, *Much Ado* has been a mainstay of the Anglo-American Shakespearean repertory. The title-page of the Quarto indicates that it has 'been sundrie times publikely acted', although the first documented evidence is of a court production in 1613. It was the seventh most popular of Shakespeare's plays staged by the late eighteenth century, and between 1879 and 1964 it was staged thirty-five times at Stratford-upon-Avon (roughly every three years) (Hogan, vol. 2, 717). It is a staple of American summer Shakespeare festivals, particularly in the wake of the 1993 Branagh film, and at the beginning of the twenty-first century the sixth most popular performance among Shakespeare's plays

---

1   Nova Myhill indicates this aspect of the play (Myhill).
2   As Jean Howard discusses, early modern anti-theatrical voices cited the production of illicit erotic identity as an undesirable function of the public theatre (Howard).

at the two leading Shakespeare venues of Britain and North America.[1] What constitutes its appeal has changed, however, with the moment, place and culture of production. But as in the playlets performed by its characters, its general effect comprises many local choices.

In many respects *Much Ado*'s production history follows the general contours of Shakespearean stage history: it was rewritten in the Restoration, revived in the eighteenth century, popularized by David Garrick, bowdlerized in the nineteenth century, and made spectacular by Victorian production values. Berlioz wrote an opera loosely based upon it, and Wagner's *Das Liebesverbot* treats William Davenant's *The Law Against Lovers* (1662), itself in part a reworking of the play. The early twentieth century saw a return to minimalist Elizabethan staging practices, but also film treatments that expanded the possibilities of realistic stagings (for instance location shootings in real villas). John Cox has amply narrated these changes, and points out that the two recurrent features of this play's staging include the fortunes of its portrayal of a strong heroine, and the temptations of the courtly milieu for designers (Cox, *Shakespeare*). This account will not rehearse the chronological stage history of the play per se, but will rather take up questions of staging, certain answers provided in the history of productions and their implications for the play's effect.

Tonal choices

In the case of *Much Ado*'s production history, the presiding question has usually been one of how 'light' or 'dark' a production is: to what degree is the war between the sexes (comedy's usual topic) a 'merry' one, or a conflict with real casualties to minds and hearts? How corrosive a portrait does

---

1 The Royal Shakespeare Theatre and the Stratford Shakespeare Festival in Ontario, Canada. See Taylor, 'Proximities'.

a production paint of male suspicion of and anxiety about women, and the social universe in which it is permitted to prosper? Is the event of Hero's slander easily repaired, shrugged off like one of the play's many witticisms, or does the play depict a more sombre picture of damaged and damaging relations between the sexes? To what degree, in other words, can the play be rendered a 'happy' comedy, a portrait of regenerative energies triumphing over obstacles to sexual and social union – or are its harmonious conclusions in dance and reunion precarious and provisionally engineered? Another way of putting this question has been to ask to what extent the play belongs to Benedick and Beatrice – an instance of a man able to break ranks with his own sex in order to cast his faith with a woman's word ('Think you in your soul the Count Claudio hath wronged Hero?', 4.1.325–6). Or is the joyfulness of their coupling clouded by its location in a universe in which a known villain's word trumps a woman's honour? (These questions rephrase that of the subplot / mainplot debate in a different guise, although the association of 'darker' elements with the Hero and Claudio plots fails to acknowledge the degree to which Benedick is the most eloquent speaker of the play's slanders against the fair sex.) Perhaps the simplest formulation of this choice, in post-modern terms, is how ruthlessly 'patriarchal' a world emerges in production, in which patriarchy is principally understood as a system of male alliance and rivalry conducted through the exchange of and competition for women.

Terminologies aside, the degree and inflection of patriarchy is not merely a concern that arises with modern political sensibilities. For instance, nineteenth-century productions tended to cut much of the play's bawdy and cuckold humour, a habit that displays in itself a patriarchal gesture. The goal was presumably to purify the play of material offensive to the tender sensibilities of a middle-class audience, or unbecoming to actresses in search of a new gentility and respectability for their profession. Bell's Shakespeare edition, for instance, notes that

Beatrice's comment to Don Pedro about Benedick – 'So I
would not he should [put me down], my lord, lest I should
prove the mother of fools' (2.1.261–2) – 'rather trespasses on
virgin diffidence; archness and real modesty are no ways
incompatible; therefore it is a pity the author should have
suffered this pleasant lady to even peep over the line of decency
. . . In this and in her next speech, she is again too knowing'
(Bell, 2.236). The cuts also had the effect of rendering the male
characters of the play more idealized than they appear in the
Quarto text – again, all to the good, at least for George Steevens,
editing *Much Ado* in the late eighteenth century: 'It is to be
lamented, indeed, that [Benedick's wit] is disgraced by
unnecessary profaneness; for the goodness of his heart is hardly
sufficient to atone for the license of his tongue' (Steevens,
2.163). The practice of editing such language out of production
had the side-effect of rendering much of this humour unfamiliar,
with the consequence that it continues to be cut from more
recent productions in a period less squeamish about sexual
material.

For similarly sentimentalizing and sanitizing reasons, most
nineteenth-century productions changed Benedick's farewell to
Beatrice in the concluding lines of 4.1 from a relatively brisk
envoi to a more protracted, and potentially cloying, dialogue
originally inserted by J.P. Kemble in 1788. The Quarto text
reads:

> *Bened.* Enough, I am engagde, I will challenge
> him, I will kisse your hand, and so I leaue you: by this
> hand, Claudio shal render me a deere account: as you
> heare of me, so think of me: goe comforte your coosin,
> I must say she is dead, and so fare-well.

The rewritten lines read:

> *Ben.* Enough I am engag'd, I will challenge him.
> *Beat.* Will you?

86

> *Ben.* Upon my soul I will. I'll kiss your hand, and so
> leave you. By this hand, Claudio shall render me a
> dear account.
> *Beat.* You'll be sure to challenge him.
> *Ben.* By those bright eyes, I will.
> *Beat.* My dear friend, kiss my hand again.
> *Ben.* As you hear of me so think of me. Go, comfort
> your cousin – I must say she is dead and so farewell.
> *Beat.* Benedick, kill him, kill him if you can.
> *Ben.* As sure as he is alive, I will.[1]

Despite her repeated insistence on Claudio's death, Beatrice becomes here, paradoxically, more querulous, less adamant, and hence more conventionally 'feminine'; Benedick, by contrast, emerges as more gallantly reassuring to his damsel in distress, rather than grim or troubled by the charge he has accepted. Cox notes:

> Kemble's ending built the scene to a climactic curtain
> line, significant in the eighteenth- and nineteenth-
> century theatre where each scene was a discrete unit
> marked by the fall of the curtain. However, Kemble's
> dialogue made the developing relationship between
> Beatrice and Benedick seem less provisional at this
> point than in the quarto text, and tended to sentimentalise
> the passage.
>
> (Cox, *Shakespeare*, 197)

Here, practical concerns of the theatre have an impact on the depictions of gender and romantic union. Ellen Terry, the great actress of Beatrice in the late nineteenth century, objected to what she termed 'the buffoonery' of this business in Henry Irving's 1884–5 production: 'I had been compelled to give way

---

1   J.P. Kemble, Partbook for Beatrice, marked in Kemble's hand (Shattuck, S5)

87

about a traditional "gag" in the church scene . . . I protested, and implored Henry not to do it. He said that it was necessary: otherwise the "curtain" would be received in dead silence' (Terry, 127). The preference here was for applause rather than sobering reflection, a choice not necessarily pressing for a Renaissance staging in which neither the structure of acts nor the technology of curtains applied.

As this example shows, a given production's inflections of the play can involve quite broad measures, and for reasons of stagecraft as well as thematic considerations. However, a production need not go so far as rewriting the dialogue, as the factors influencing its tones are many and minute, and can be as subtle as a gesture, such as the abstention of Judi Dench's Beatrice from the final dance of John Barton's 1976 production of the play (she was left awkwardly holding Benedick's sword, while he joined in the dance, a choice which complicated the symmetries and sexual harmonies that a dance might reinforce) (Cox, *Shakespeare*, 235). Like a musical score, a script is only fully realized through the instruments of voice and gesture. Such details of nuance are not always recoverable from reviews or prompt copies. Yet it is important to underscore, especially for the reader of a play, that every production aggressively rewrites as well as inflects the text, whether through cutting, sequencing, the timing of entrances and exits, or the addition of business and dumb-shows not scripted in the original (see Fig. 7). For instance, cuts and amplifications change with historical moment, political context and cultural taste. If nineteenth-century productions cut the bawdy (and much else, in order to accommodate changes of elaborate scenery), more recent productions keen to delineate a swift-moving plot have jettisoned the play's euphuistic language, and, with it, the verbal medium of male bonding. The eighteenth century was not fond of puns; the nineteenth, of sexual banter; the twentieth, of complicated rhetorical exhibitions (comic productions tend to favour plot over poetry, whereas tragedy's poetry is more often

9

Leonato
If you swear, my lord, you shall not be forsworn.
(To Don John, who drops L of C. Don Pedro has
his hand on Don John's R shoulder)
Let me bid you welcome, my lord; being reconciled to the
prince your brother, I owe you all duty.
(Don John accepts Leonato's hand)

Don'John
(L of Don Pedro)
I thank you; I am not of many words, but I thank you.
(Antonio at steps. Don John steps back)

Leonato
Please it your grace lead on?

Don Pedro
Your hand, Leonato; we will go together.
(Prince, turning, gives Leonato his L hand - Antonio
at steps indicating the way - bowing and smiles)
(No. 3 till Beatrice is off)
(7th Lady and 2nd Gentleman cross to upper side of
porch)

1 Don Pedro and Leonato.
2 7th Lady and 2nd Gentleman follow Don Pedro and Leonato
  into house.
3 4th Lady and 3rd Gentleman exeunt into house.
4 6th lady and 1st Gentleman and 3rd Lady exeunt into house.
5 6 soldiers exeunt L.U.E.
6 Messenger, Conrade and Margaret cross up R and
  Messenger shows them upper door L.3.E
  They exeunt.
7 Borachio and Ursula follow them - Messenger follows them
  off.
8 Benedick's Pages followed by Don Pedro's Pages exeunt
  L.U.E.)

(Beatrice crosses to stool by table R.)
(Benedick up to Antonio. Claudio X's to Hero to take her
hand, and lead her off, is intercepted by John - who suddenly seeing movement, drops to Hero - (who is disappointed)
Don John and Hero start up steps. Claudio looking after
Hero. At steps Hero gives flower to Claudio. He springs
forward and takes it and kisses it. Claudio crosses, below
porch, looking after Hero. Benedick crosses to Beatrice
and off. She looks at him, laughs, and crosses toward
Antonio, who crosses and takes her hand. As she passes
Benedick she tosses rose over her shoulder. He picks it
up, laughs. She turns, he offers rose. She sweeps it
out of his hand and exeunts with Antonio into house. He
kicks flower down stage)

7 1.1 (146–53), from a promptbook of a 1904–5 touring American production
   by E.H. Southern and Julia Marlowe which spells out details of stage
   actions. Note the business between Don John, Claudio and Hero, meant to
   motivate Don John's plot against the two lovers.

indulged). Each period, each production – each performance – offers an individual moment in the play's history.

Social representations

Much of a production's tonal range depends on its depiction of the world of male privilege. Choices must be made about big effects – the appearance of the soldiers as brilliant or battle-worn – as well as the more local details of character. Such tones often pivot on the presentation of Claudio. Despite historicist caveats about the unremarkable or conventional nature of his conduct, he has often been the recipient of treatments that seek to excuse that conduct (for example, being cast as very young). For instance, how is his rehabilitation as a non-cad accomplished (if at all) by the play's end? Is the ritual at the monument (5.3), assigned to him and Don Pedro by Leonato as a kind of reparation, played as in the Quarto text (in which Claudio doesn't speak except to direct others to speak on his behalf), or is Claudio allowed to take on the burden of most of the penitential language? Modern productions eager to bolster this character's sympathetic aspect, and associating penance with a personal voice (Elizabethans may have found a corporate grief equally, if not more, contrite), choose the latter, and, as in the Branagh film, include a semi-concealed Hero as witness to Claudio's grief, along with music and lighting effects that solemnize and elevate the moment. (In the same sensitizing spirit, they have also cut the banter of Don Pedro and Claudio with Benedick in 5.1.) Yet most eighteenth- and nineteenth-century productions, interestingly, cut the epitaph scene entirely, despite their general tendency to render the male characters as more gallant in their behaviour than in the Quarto text (perhaps the scenic requirements of a verisimilar attempt at a family monument were daunting, and impeding, in productions given to lavish staging and yet eager to move towards a happy ending in under four hours; or perhaps they preferred not to dwell any further on Claudio's error). Motives for such choices are not always as recoverable as their effects – and even those are elusive after the fact.

In addition to mitigating Claudio's 'mistaking' in the final fifth of the play, a production can soften or intensify his culpability in the acts leading up to it, for instance by means of casting and acting choices. Claudio can be played as particularly young, impressionable and vulnerable, torn between Hero and hero-worship (of Benedick and his contempt for marriage). His unsavoury decision to 'shame' Hero 'in the congregation where I should wed' (3.2.112–13) can be delivered as either reluctant or ready. Declan Donnellan's 1998 Cheek by Jowl production presented Claudio as 'sexually awkward . . . however much Bohdan Poraj's . . . Claudio professes to love Hero, he loves his cohorts more: in one of Donnellan's several comic coups, when Hero accepts his offer of marriage, Claudio runs not into her arms, but Don Pedro's instead' (Logan).

Perhaps most influential on the portrayal of Claudio has been the decision whether or not to stage the balcony scene described by Borachio: 'she leans me out at her mistress' chamber window, bids me a thousand times goodnight . . . Claudio and my master, planted and placed and possessed by my master Don John, saw afar off in the orchard this amiable encounter' (3.3.140–5). This scene is not staged in Shakespeare's text. However, some productions do choose to represent it, a decision that, if it results in a convincing action, can help make Claudio's reaction plausible, or (more usually) if too transparent, can undermine sympathy for him.[1] Fidelity to the Quarto text

---

1 Gary Taylor recounts another such intervention in the 1998 production at the Stratford Festival, Ontario, directed by Richard Monette, who 'moved "Fear no more the heat of the sun" from *Cymbeline* 4.2, into 2.1, giving Jennifer Gould's Hero a chance to sing and therefore a prolonged moment of center stage attention . . . the song then reappeared just before the intermission, in an interpolated scene outside Hero's bedroom window: Don Pedro and Claudio never saw Hero, but the sound of Margaret's voice singing a song we all associated with Hero made their mistake immediately understandable. This addition not only clarified the plot; it also unfortunately exculpated the men' (Taylor, 'Proximities', 340).

leaves the audience reliant only on what is suggested to our imaginations by Borachio's drunken account. A similar instance of directorial supplementation often occurs in the placement of Hero as a visible witness to the epitaph scene – such as 'a sudden shocking glimpse of the wanly immured Hero' – a blocking decision that seeks to address the problem of *her* feelings about Claudio's penance.[1]

Another intervention has occurred in the fate of 1.2, the scene where Antonio relates to Leonato his servant's inaccurate report of Don Pedro's plan to woo Hero; Garrick's 1777 production rewrote the scene to correct the error: 'It was agreed upon, that the prince / should in a dance, woo Hero, as for himself; and / having obtained her, give her to Count Claudio' (Cox, *Shakespeare*, 104). Many other eighteenth- and nineteenth-century productions adopted this 'correction', thus removing one instance of mistaken information; others relocated the scene to the beginning of 2.1 (the dance scene), so that Don John's malevolent plan follows immediately upon the exchange between Don Pedro and Claudio. The change renders villainy less casual, in a world where information is more mediated.

The treatment of the character of Claudio is just one example of how a production shapes its general portrait of its world through local choices. Other means of doing so include how the other male characters, and the bonds between them, are rendered. For example, how does Leonato react to Claudio's repudiation of Hero in the church scene (4.1)? Eighteenth-century depictions of Hero's swoon in this scene demonstrate an increasing focus upon Leonato's experience: in the frontispiece to Nicholas Rowe's edition (Fig. 8), he is indistinguishable; in the William Hamilton painting (Fig. 9), he is foregrounded in the lower left corner, and more prominent than Claudio; in the etching by Edward Francis Burney (Fig. 10), he is central and virtually

---

1   Michael Billington, review of Gregory Doran's 2002 RSC production, *Guardian*, 5 May 2002.

8 Hero swoons after Claudio's repudiation in the church scene (4.1), the frontispiece to Nicholas Rowe's edition of 1709, with an undifferentiated Leonato

9 Hero swoons after Claudio's repudiation in the church scene (4.1), engraving by Jean Pierre Simon of the painting by William Hamilton (1790), with Leonato foregrounded at the left

10 Hero swoons after Claudio's repudiation in the church scene (4.1), engraving by Edward Francis Burncy (1791), with a distraught Leonato in central place

Lear-like in his distraught domination over the fallen form of his daughter. Is his subsequent rejection of Hero vicious or pained – i.e. is his long speech of betrayal and rejection (120–43) cut, or perhaps accompanied by physical violence towards the actress playing Hero? Cox relates that nineteenth-century Leonatos were dignified and idealized by abridgement of their words, whereas 'Tony Church (RST 1971), on the other hand, reacted with "Victorian paternal outrage"' (Cox, *Shakespeare*, 182) – ironically, the Victorian actors habitually rendered fatherhood more benevolently.

Similarly, is Leonato's challenge to Claudio in 5.1 played as a comedy, of two old geezers rushing for their rusted swords à la Capulet (perhaps with an Antonio literally deaf to Leonato's cries of 'Brother'), or with dignity and pathos? (In the 2002 Gregory Doran RST production, set in Mussolini's 1936 Sicily, 'Hero's aged uncle suddenly draws a nasty little knife to threaten Claudio' (Hemming).) Are Benedick's cuckold jokes, or diatribes against 'my Lady Tongue', delivered teasingly or tinged with malice – for instance, does Beatrice enter during his speech in 2.1 in which he compares her to 'infernal Ate', and thus herself hear his excoriation of her (and if so, is Benedick aware of her presence)? Is the exchange between Don Pedro and Benedick in 5.1 (with Don Pedro's return to bawdy jokes about Beatrice) kept or cut (frequently the latter)? A notable strength of Franco Zeffirelli's 1967 BBC television production is that the socially superior sneering of Don Pedro and Claudio at this point was not cut, in keeping with a general impression of how far both fall short of any kind of courtly ideal.

How much is made of the military context of the play? Is it presented as a pretext for dashing uniforms or does it provide a continuing framework of male alliance based on aggression towards each other and towards women, 'a bastion of laddishness', in one reviewer's words, describing Donnellan's 1998 Cheek by Jowl production? Or, as another reviewer described it, 'This *Much Ado* is about men behaving badly', in which Don Pedro is 'clearly the sort of chap for whom towel-flicking in the locker-room is not just hearty fun'.[1] For instance, do the men appear in uniform, and when do they change into civilian costume, if at all? Do all of them do so? John Gielgud writes of his attempt to distinguish Benedick by means of costume from the elegant atmosphere urged by the staging:

> I kept trying to make Benedick into more of a soldier. At first [the designer] encouraged me to be a dandy, wearing comic hats [which] used to get laughs the moment I came on in them . . . I gradually discarded them, and wore leather doublets and thigh boots and became less of a courtier. I tried to inject a good deal more bluffness and strength into the part. Benedick ought to be an uncouth soldier, a tough misanthrope, who wears a beard and probably smells to high heaven.
>
> (Gielgud, 135–6)

Michael Billington noted in a *Guardian* review of the 1976 Barton production that in his colonial setting 'what Barton makes more clear than I ever remember is that, in this world of privileged impishness, Don John's pointless destructiveness is simply an extension of the prevailing officers' mess ethical code'.[2]

Also significant is the play's portrayal of the role of social caste in the relations between men, given the ways in which this play binds sexual rivalry to social rivalry. Is Leonato a grand governor of Messina, secure in his position with respect to Don Pedro (and thus one who can plausibly entertain the

---

1   John Peter, *Sunday Times*, 14 June 1998; Benedict Nightingale, *The Times*, 8 June 1998. This production attempted to counter the weight of male privilege by turning uncle Antonio into aunt Ursula.
2   *Guardian*, 10 April 1976.

initial, erroneous, idea of his daughter's alliance with the Prince)? Or is he a more provincial sort, a genial gentleman farmer (as in Branagh's 1993 film) eager to ally himself with the Prince despite the truth of Don John's claim that Hero is 'no equal for his birth' (2.1.150)? Does Dogberry provide a hyperbolic or an eccentric instance of this concern with rank? For example, is his officious attempt in 3.5 to impress Leonato with his own importance at the expense of Verges presented as an idiosyncratic foible or an extreme symptom of the same social system that has Leonato so eager to forge an alliance with the Prince or his protégé? Many nineteenth-century productions cut this scene altogether. Barton's production, set in British India, cast Dogberry and the Watch as turbaned Sikhs, and the other characters as British military, thus adding a racial and colonialist dimension to Dogberry's pomposity and malapropisms (see Fig. 11).

Other productions have set the play in Italy but depicted the Watch as English provincials (in keeping with the hints of region suggested by their names, Oatcake and Seacoal). This latter choice can render the Watch as stalwart John Bulls doggedly in pursuit of justice amidst their decadent Latin betters. As one commentator put it,

> the very figure of Dogberry is reassuring – evil cannot be rampant in a city which he and his 'most quiet watchmen' sufficiently protect . . . It is part of the irony, grave but not yet bitter, which underlies the play, that in this community of brilliantly accomplished men and women, it is not by dint of wit but through the blind channels of accident and unreason that the discovery makes its way.

(Gollancz, 142)

The tradition of depicting Dogberry as corpulent also has ramifications for our sense of his pomposity and efficacy (see Fig. 12); the nineteenth-century critic Henry Giles opined that

Dogberry is, I am persuaded, of an ample size – no small man speaks with his sedate gravity. There is a steadiness of bearing in him which you never observe in men of deficient length, breadth, or rotundity. No man of the lean and dwarfish species can assume the tranquil self-consequence of a Dogberry.

(cited in Furness, 353)

The Elizabethan Dogberry, on the other hand, was originally played (if we go by the Quarto's speech prefixes) by the athletic clown Will Kemp, whose notoriety – 'one . . . that hath spent his life in mad jigs and merry jests' (Wiles, 24) – may have contributed to his presence and popularity (and mostly likely would have seen him leading the jig which traditionally followed the close of a play) (see Fig. 2).[1] Kemp, if the actor of Falstaff, was no stranger to padding.

Not just the heroes but the villain are shaped by directorial choice. Is Don John himself portrayed as motiveless in his malignity, or is he given some pretext, such as an unrequited attraction to Hero (indicated by means of longing glances or some other non-verbal business), or a clear designation as the sore loser in the recent war with Don Pedro, a view reinforced by 1.3.30–1? (Recall that he is not identified as a bastard until 4.1, and while his envy and melancholy would have been legible to a Renaissance audience as signs of his bastardy, they do not function so for a modern audience, even if bastardy itself served for us as a sufficient cause of his discontents.) In the 1999 East Los Angeles Classic Theatre production, directed by Tony Plane, 'a betrothal between the Mexican Hero and Anglo Claudio strikes a chord of racial hatred within the cruel Don John – designating a specific reason for his treachery that one

---

1   Wiles argues that Kemp's public persona was that of a plain common man eschewing pretension, in which case Dogberry would have been in some tension with Kemp's other identity.

11 Dogberry and the Watch (4.2), in the 1976 RSC production, directed by John Barton. Left to right: Conrade (Brian Coburn), Borachio (Bob Peck), Watchmen (Paul Whitworth, Greg Hicks, David Howey, Leonard Preston), Dogberry (John Woodvine) and Sexton (Keith Taylor)

12 Dogberry addresses the Watch in 3.3, engraving by Henry Meadows (1845)

rarely finds in the play' (Provenzano). A 1995 production at the Old Globe in San Diego was directed by Jack O'Brien as a comedy 'through and through. Even the baddest villain, Don John, gets inventive bits of visual gags that pay off at terrific rates . . . tall, scowling, harbors an unnatural fear for a flower pot that no matter what he does he cannot avoid knocking over'.[1] Conversely, Helena Kaut-Howson's Royal Exchange production in Manchester in 1997 had Don John 'addressing the unfortunate Conrade as he shaves . . . holding his minion's head under water for a frighteningly long time and . . . pressing the open blade of a cut-throat razor against Conrade's tongue' (Lindop). In the 1996 Royal Shakespeare Company production directed by Michael Boyd, an inebriated Borachio actually urinated on the (raked!) stage, a choice that sought to underscore the villainous with the uncouth, and at the risk of total alienation of the audience. The tendency of many modern productions is to emphasize the brutality of the world of male privilege at the expense of the play's delight in union, a tendency which can unbalance the play; as Peter Holland has written of Bill Alexander's 1990 RSC production,

> the exploration of [Susan Fleetwood's] Beatrice, so firmly structured into the play, was endlessly compromised by the production's self-congratulatory and comforting return to a fascination with the difficulties of masculinity. Such treatment of gender looks ostensibly modern, in being prepared to critique the male world at all, but it is a regression and an evasion of the challenge to masculinity that could be achieved by a sustained re-examination of the spaces left by patriarchy.

> (Holland, 36)

Choice of place and time

Some of the decisions that inflect a production are quite specific matters of gesture or tone of delivery. Others are made

---

1 *Los Angeles Times*, 21 January 1995.

through more general choices of setting and design. Productions have rendered Messina as a courtly and idealized world, full of a beautiful and brilliant leisured class of people, with corresponding time on their hands for intrigue and games (much like their literary precursors, the inhabitants of Castiglione's urbane universe). This staging works well both in Renaissance guise and for later periods suggestive of leisure (Regency, Edwardian), although high-Renaissance Italianate settings have been a favourite choice for the play's portrait of an elegant and indolent social world.

Other productions have delivered it as a more gritty and grubby provincial outpost, full of provincials eager to entertain the troops; another choice is the rural idyll, unsophisticated and innocent by contrast with the intruding military universe. A 1987 production at the Shakespeare Santa Cruz Festival set Messina in the California Rancho era; their 1998 staging, directed by Richard Seer, chose a post-First World War provincial Sicily, all hanging laundry in sun-baked streets (also a choice of Doran's 2002 RSC production). Robert Smallwood compares the opening tableaux of two different 1988 productions, one of 'bored wealth . . . a society rich, decadent, and selfish' (Di Trevis's modern-dress production at Stratford, in which Don Pedro's party descended from a noisy hovering helicopter for the 1.1 entry); one of 'co-operation and mutuality . . . contented interdependence' (Judi Dench's direction of the Renaissance Theatre Company): 'one director wished the disintegrating events of the play to be unsurprising, almost what such a society deserved; the other made them seem a shocking intrusion into harmony, eliciting from us a response of pain and pity' (Smallwood, 192). Such effects depend of course on the audience's reaction to wealth as something either to spurn or to identify with.

Both of these productions were instances of what is called 'Directors' Shakespeare', late twentieth-century mountings of the play influenced by academic understandings, which sought to present a strong interpretative angle, almost an argument, about it, often making thematic points by decisions about staging and scenery. So the striking mirrored floor of Terry Hands's 1982–5 RSC production conveyed both brilliance and the sense of a world of confusingly inverted images; in the 1996 main-stage version of Michael Boyd's Stratford production, the large onstage picture frame made the point about how our knowledge of each other is conditioned by its framing representations.

Such decisions often also reflect changing theatre fashions as well as the immediate constraints of theatre architecture, budget and personnel. Shakespeare's theatre used little scenery, and eighteenth-century stagings used stock scenery, whereas Victorian productions were notoriously sumptuous exercises in pictorial realism, entailing substantial cuts to the text in order to allow for scene-shifting; running time could still approach four hours (Charles Kean 1858; Irving's Lyceum 1884–5; Beerbohm Tree 1905). On the other hand, our own age achieves a comparable running time by playing so slowly that even heavily cut texts can seem interminable. Shaw described Herbert Beerbohm Tree's lavish 1905 production as having 'all the lovely things Shakespeare dispensed with . . . in bounteous plenty. Fair ladies, Sicilian seascapes, Italian gardens, summer nights and dawns (compressed into five minutes), Renascential splendours, dancing, singing, masquerading, architecture'.[1] Such extravagances produced a backlash of sorts, and early twentieth-century productions moved towards a simpler, more gestural style, influenced by the stagings of William Poel, Harley Granville-Barker and Edward Gordon Craig, who sought to 'recover' Elizabethan stage practices. The full-blown cathedral scenery of the Irving

---

1   *Saturday Review*, 11 February 1905.

production, complete with rood screen, pillars, altar, etc., became in the 1903–4 Craig production a matter of a simple curtain and sophisticated lighting effects:

> The only illumination in this dimly lit 'church' came from an imaginary stained-glass window above the proscenium arch that cast a great pool of light on the floor below . . . The characters were only lit when they entered the acting area which was the pool of coloured light; outside it, they became silhouettes like the columns.
>
> (Cox, *Shakespeare*, 50)

The change was indebted to new technological possibilities as well as to shifts in taste (see Fig. 13).

Such choices are also historically, politically and above all practically determined: casting Benedick and Beatrice as middle aged, and potentially more world weary than their younger counterparts, may have been an option unavailable to the all-male Elizabethan theatre company, where Beatrice's pertness was also that of the boy actor. William Davenant's 1662 rewriting of the play, *The Law Against Lovers* (in which the Benedick and Beatrice plot is grafted onto a retooled *Measure for Measure*), increases the quotient of salacious banter between Beatrice and Benedick (now a Restoration libertine). The adaptation may have been fuelled by a desire to compound the racy novelty of women playing the female roles, of which the revised play had four prominent ones plus two bit parts. Davenant was granted a theatrical monopoly (the other went to Thomas Killigrew) in the Restoration, and *Much Ado* was one of nine Shakespeare plays to which he had the rights (Killigrew claimed the rest). As Victoria Hayne writes, the decision to reduce his repertoire by conflating *Much Ado* and *Measure for Measure* seems odd, except when we consider Davenant's need to generate roles for his new company of

13 Edward Gordon Craig's preliminary sketch for the church scene (4.1) in his production of 1903–4

female actors; one of the roles, that of Beatrice's sister Viola, seems gratuitous:

> her primary function is to dance, equipped with castanets, and to sing two songs, including a quartet with Beatrice, Benedick, and Lucio entitled 'Our Ruler Has Got the Vertigo of State' . . . [yet] Pepys regarded her performance as the highlight of the evening.
>
> (Hayne)

Cultural moment

The changing force of theatrical taste is demonstrated most clearly through the interpretation of Beatrice throughout the centuries. Much as productions are judged to range between light and dark, portrayals of Beatrice range between the shrewish and the more pliably tender-hearted. Her command to 'Kill Claudio' (4.1.288), for instance, has been received as either the unladylike vengeance of a virago, or the fierce loyalty of a woman moved by sisterly feeling for her cousin (Cox, 'Stage'). Whether this moment gets a laugh (and whether that laugh is a nervous one) can indicate the degree to which a production attempts to move into a serious vein – or is allowed to do so by its audience. The prefatory remarks to the Kemble text noted that 'her generous indignation at the slander cast upon Hero tends very happily to heighten our admiration of her character, which has previously appeared somewhat open to suspicion of insensibility and shrewishness' (Kemble). In the 2004 Globe production, on the other hand, directed by Tamara Harvey and played by an all-female cast, the line was 'said snappily to guffaws . . . in a production . . . gently feminist in mood ("as you are a man" is said with an equal measure of disdain and pity)' (Mahoney).

That the play presents us with an outspoken yet upright female argues that such a figure was conceivable in 1599 (even if played by a boy and dressing like an Ate in good apparel).

However, stage tradition throughout the centuries has qualified the anomaly of her initial appearance, often in the direction of muting any unladylike tendencies. Restoration performances found the verbal agility of Beatrice attractive; James Miller's 1737 *Universal Passion*, another rewriting of the play (splicing it with Molière's *La Princesse d'Elide*), recast Hero and Claudio as another pair of witty lovers, thus 'doubling the possibilities for witty raillery' (Cox, *Shakespeare*, 10). (The clergyman Miller's play was, however, largely sanitized of salacious dialogue.) Shakespeare's original text returned to the stage in 1721 and 1737 (at Lincoln's Inn Fields and Covent Garden, respectively), on the latter occasion as part of the response to lobbying by the Shakespeare Ladies' Club, described by Michael Dobson as 'an informal pressure group which lobbied theatre managements to revive more Shakespeare, insisting that his patriotic and uplifting drama should drive both the libertine excesses of Restoration comedy and the invading irrationality of Italian opera from the corrupted contemporary stage' (Dobson, 63). Dobson notes that 'As Shakespeare's status as a British hero rose, so the practice of rewriting his plays came to be seen as positively treasonous' (64). With Garrick's 1748 rendition, Beatrice (played by Hannah Pritchard) continued to be valued for her verbal sportiveness: 'Every scene between them was a continual struggle for superiority; nor could the audience determine which was the victor' (Davies, 146). As Cox writes, the main interest in this period was focused on 'the social status which the actress's manners gave to Beatrice'; her verbal elegance thus largely functioning to denote her social position rather than indicate unladylike outspokenness (Cox, *Shakespeare*, 14).

During the nineteenth century, however, the emphasis shifted from Beatrice's mind to her heart. Helena Faucit played the role for forty-three years, from 1836 (when she was 19, to the 61-year-old Charles Kemble's Benedick) to 1879 (the latter at the opening of the Shakespeare Memorial Theatre in Stratford-upon-Avon). The tenor of her performances can perhaps be judged from her reflections upon the role. Beatrice posed somewhat of a challenge to her understanding of 'the part women have played, and are meant to play, in bringing sweetness and comfort, and help and moral strength, into man's troubled and perplexing life'; 'I cannot write [of Beatrice] with the same full heart, or with the same glow of sympathy, with which I wrote of Rosalind.' Nonetheless, she allows that 'a young, beautiful, graceful woman, flashing out brilliant sayings, charged with no real malice, but with just enough of a sting in them to pique the self-esteem of those at whom they are aimed, must always, I fancy, have a peculiar fascination for men of spirit' (Faucit, 300). A review of her performance corroborates her modulated pitch:

> When Beatrice was left in the Chapel with Benedick, Miss Faucit rose to the greatest height of her acting; her alternations of grief for Hero, of indignation at the treatment which her cousin had received, her eagerness to have Claudio killed, and her wish that she were a man . . . were rendered with great force, but did not exceed the display of a true womanly spirit.

Or, as another estimate put it, 'high spirits run away with the tongue but not with the manners, this is the key-note struck by Miss Faucit'.[1]

While some nineteenth-century actresses continued to emphasize Beatrice's asperity, the general tendency was in the direction of 'true womanly spirit', a tradition epitomized at the century's end by the actress Ellen Terry (see Fig. 14), who managed to temper the termagant by means of performances most frequently described by the terms 'sunny', 'boisterous'

---

1 *Manchester Guardian*, 11 April 1866, cited in Furness, 388; *Manchester Examiner and Times*, 11 February 1866, in Furness, 389 (reviews of Charles Dillon production, Broadway Theatre, Manchester, 1866).

14 Ellen Terry as a kinder, gentler Beatrice in Henry Irving's Lyceum
production, 1884–5

and 'merry' (as opposed to 'caustic', 'contemptuous' or 'tart') (Cox, *Shakespeare*, 35–43 *passim*). Here, ebullience provided a context for Beatrice's verbal combativeness that took the sting out of the zingers:

> enchanting in her tenderness, full of an admirable vivacity, never once playing the shrew, and though her words were sharp as steel, they seemed always sheathed in velvet and to convey the idea that she loved Benedick; she softened the wordy blow that she struck him and turned it to nought by the tender light of her eyes, or by a manner deviously arch and winsome, which in itself was ever half-caressing.[1]

With the twentieth century, and the advent of a popular political feminism, one would have thought that the spikier aspects of Beatrice's character would have become more plausible, but the sentimentalizing nineteenth-century tradition held on strong until mid-century. Then, after the Second World War, actresses of the part such as Katharine Hepburn, Peggy Ashcroft, Maggie Smith and Janet Suzman began to inject a bit more spirit into their renditions; Emma Thompson's Beatrice, in the 1993 Branagh film, 'seemed representative of twentieth-century feminism in its mature phase: not edgily assertive . . . but assured of her powers as a woman, and confident from the beginning of her ascendancy in the "merry war"' (Cox, *Shakespeare*, 83). Nonetheless, the production cut 180 lines of banter between Beatrice and Benedick, so whatever assurance Thompson conveyed had to be managed without them.

If Beatrices range between women of feeling and women of wit, Benedicks too have parameters: these are most often the gruff and the urbane, or the soldier and the courtier, or Garrick's vivacious humorist, or Charles Kemble's elegant courtier (see Fig. 15). Recent productions have cast him as somewhat

---

1   L. Clarke Davis, *Philadelphia Inquirer*, 19 March 1884.

15 Charles Kemble as Benedick, drawing by J.H. Lynch, published by Engelmann, London (1828)

dissolute. Nicholas Le Provost, in the Doran RSC 2002 version, 'is a lank-haired, unshaven old louche for whom even the plink and fizz of soluble aspirin proves too vexatious the morning after the night before' (Marmion).[1] The nature of the union between the two characters is another measure of a production's pitch: does the prospect of love occur as a surprise to them, or is it afoot from the beginning? How do the actors choose to deal with the text's suggestions that there has been some romantic history between them? 'You always end with a jade's trick' Beatrice tells Benedick, 'I know you of old' (1.1.138–9). How do they deliver their final exchange in 5.4 ('BENEDICK They swore that you were almost sick for me. / BEATRICE They swore that you were well-nigh dead for me', 80–1)? Is this a dead-earnest reprise of an earlier pique, or is it delivered with a knowing eye to their audience, and a recognition of their own collaboration in their gullings? Finally, how egalitarian a match is their union finally rendered? Most editions and productions since Lewis Theobald's edition have assigned the line at 5.4.97, 'Peace! I will stop your mouth', to Benedick, rather than to Leonato (as in the Quarto, and this edition), and accompany his command with a direction to kiss her; what happens if this line is delivered by a Leonato intervening in the renewed combat, and handing Beatrice to Benedick, who then kisses her (or, if one is going to emend in the absence of bibliographical evidence for likely error, why not change 'mouth' to 'mouths'?). It may remain a gesture of male authority, but there is a difference whether it comes from an incipient husband or an uncle and guardian (especially an uncle whose own paternal authority has been qualified by his behaviour in 4.1).

---

1   In the 1998 Cheek by Jowl production, it was Saskia Reeves's Beatrice who over-indulged: 'a spiky, sparky young spinster who bums drags from her uncle's cigar and gets drunk at her cousin Hero's engagement party' (Charles Spencer, *Daily Telegraph*, 8 June 1998).

Afterlives

My emphasis here on Beatrice and Benedick is also that of the tradition of stage reviews, and the tendency of productions in the direction of lighthearted comic warfare rather than a distressing indictment of male privilege (the reasonable assumption being that audiences expecting the latter do not go to comedies). The play's identification with its nominal subplot is on record from its earliest stage history, as Benedick and Beatrice became a trope both for the play and for the portrait of sexual attraction – of kindred yet combative minds – that they depict. The title-page of the Quarto notes that it was 'sundrie times publikely / acted by the right honourable, the Lord / Chamberlaine his seruants', but by the second recorded mention the couple have moved downstage. The Lord Chamberlain's accounts of 20 May 1613 record payment to John Heminge for 'presenting [at Whitehall] before the Princess highnes the Lady Elizabeth and the Prince Pallatyne Elector fowerteene severall playes', including 'Benedicte and Betteris' (Chambers, 2.343). This staging occasion presumably found the play suitably festive for a wedding celebration. So too Charles I's copy of the Second Folio notes 'Benedik and Betrice' next to the title. For Robert Burton, in his *Anatomy of Melancholy* (1628), the pair had become a shorthand or type for those lovers 'which at the first sight cannot fancy or affect each other, but are harsh and ready to disagree, offended with each other's carriage, like Benedick and Beatrice in the comedy, and in whom they find many faults' (for Burton, it was an antipathy most readily resolved by proximity: 'by this living together in a house, conference, kissing, colling, and such like allurements, begin at last to dote insensibly one upon another') (Burton, 3.107). Leonard Digges's dedicatory poem to the 1640 edition of poems groups the pair with the Eastcheap gang as guaranteed crowd-pleasers: 'Let but *Falstaffe* come, / *Hal*, *Poines*, the rest you scarce shall have a roome / All is so pester'd: let but

Beatrice / And *Benedick* be seene, loe in a trice, the Cockpit Galleries, Boxes, all are full.'[1]

And like Falstaff, whose presence warranted him a play of his own in *Merry Wives*, the popularity of these inevitably allied antagonists is confirmed by their own 'excerptability', not only in Restoration adaptations such as Davenant's and Miller's, but in the sparkling literary imitations of Restoration wit comedy, of Jane Austen's sparring Elizabeth Bennett and Mr Darcy, or the cinema's tart Katharine Hepburn and suave Spencer Tracy. Berlioz's opera of 1861, titled *Béatrice et Bénédict*, converted the figures of Claudio and Hero into merely the instigators of the former match,

> and the vocabulary that admirers of [Beatrice and Benedick] exhaust in describing them – sprightly, vivid, animated, vital, vivacious, and so on – is perfectly appropriate to describe the effects Berlioz achieves with the jazzy syncopations, veering melodic lines, trills and arpeggios, dotted and cross-rhythms, and lilting triplet figures.
>
> (Schmidgall, 275–6)

If the repulsion and eventual attraction of kindred spirits wasn't a convention before Shakespeare's play (and *The Taming of the Shrew*), it certainly became so in its wake. Other stage conventions bequeathed, or at least popularized, by this play, include the distracted father of the bride, and the witty or bookish woman (Beatrice's sisters include not just Elizabeth Bennett, but Jane Eyre and *Little Women*'s Jo March). The contrasting use of two romantic plots as foils to each other is

---

1 Preface to the 1640 edition of Shakespeare's poems, printed in Chambers, 2.233. Other indices of the play's cultural currency were its citation in Thomas Heywood's *Fair Maid of the Exchange* (1607): 'I could not indure the carrier of her wit' (4.3.50, cf. 2.1.251–2); 'I am horribly in love with her' (4.3.57, cf. 2.3.226–7); ''tis most tolerable and not to be endured' (4.3.157–8, cf. 3.3.35–6).

another lasting legacy. As recently as 2001, for instance, Mira Nair's film *Monsoon Wedding* pits the arranged bourgeois marriage against the more untoward union of two servants.

Origins

While modern audiences are used to imagining the play's staging in verisimilar terms (and a high-Renaissance Italianate setting has always proved tempting to designers with big budgets), the Elizabethan stage on which the play originally appeared (perhaps the Curtain, north of the city of London, but the Globe is also a possibility) required a different kind of imagination. While specific details are inevitably speculative, this stage probably would have been a thrust stage, about forty feet across, surrounded by a standing-room pit and tiered galleries. At the rear of the stage would have been the 'tiring-house', a space with two or three curtained openings, and perhaps a gallery above; above the stage (though not covering it entirely) may have been an overhanging roof, supported by downstage pillars. The outdoor Renaissance theatre space was not dedicated to realistic staging; there was no representational scenery per se (although there may have been properties, such as an arbour, or a monument, both of which are in Henslowe's list of properties for the Rose playhouse). Shakespeare wrote his play for this kind of stage. It would have been a fast-paced production. The rapid Elizabethan delivery would have fuelled the bantering quality of the language, and the unlocalized nature of its settings works well with the shifting continuity of Shakespeare's scenes.

For instance, the editorial controversy over whether Don Pedro and Claudio's conversation, an exchange which seems to take place wherever the play opens – somewhere in the vicinity of Leonato's house – but is overheard by a man of Antonio's in 'a thick-pleached alley in mine orchard' (1.2.8–9), and then also by Borachio while being 'entertained for a perfumer, as I was smoking a musty room' (1.3.54–5), has posed problems for productions dedicated to realistic scenery (unless we imagine it as a conversation continued out of our earshot in successive locations). The Elizabethan stage, however, does not require that the scenery change with the language – rather, the language creates the scenery. Borachio's 'arras' (1.3.57) could be one of the tiring-house curtains or its gallery; the 'penthouse' of 3.3 (100) the tiring-house roof. But such concrete locations are not essential; the governing distinction of this play's settings in the early acts is that of indoors and outdoors, and an architecture of the social proximity conducive to overheard conversations. In Acts 4 and 5 a church, a jail and a monument are indicated by the language, as are the distinctions of night and day.

Such flexibility is particularly useful in the gulling scenes; both Benedick and Beatrice are said to conceal themselves in a honey-suckle arbour (see Fig. 16). The chief criteria of the humour of these scenes, particularly that involving Benedick, depend on their listeners being visible to the audience, but thinking themselves invisible to their gullers. However, the scene can be often far funnier, and more dynamic, the less it is particularized by actual props (see Figs 17 and 18). Also, since the gulling scenes follow each other, the actress playing Beatrice is often hard put not to repeat the same gags as Benedick, a risk compounded by actual furniture (and perhaps contrary to the rather different emotional tenor of the later gulling scene). Many productions hence cut 3.1 heavily, and 'load it with comic business' (usually involving water, e.g. garden hoses, duck ponds, and wet laundry, in order to account for Beatrice's head cold in 3.4) (Cox, *Shakespeare*, 145), despite the fact that there is something inherently more sobering about Beatrice's gulling, with its charges of cruelty and perversity, and her epiphany (with her first launch into verse) is less droll than Benedick's. In general, the less verisimilar the staging, the more imaginative flexibility exists for both an actor and an audience. Barton's 1976 production kept Judi Dench's Beatrice immobile and shrouded behind a screen

The Spanish Tragedy:

Or,

HIERONIMO is mad againe.

Containing the lamentable end of *Don Horatio,*
and *Belimperia*; With the pittifull Death
of HIERONIMO.

Newly Corrected, Amended, and Enlarged with new
Additions, as it hath of late been diuers
times Acted.

LONDON,
Printed by *Auguftine Mathewes*, and are to bee fold by
Iohn Grifmand, at his Shop in Pauls Alley, at the Signe
of the Gunne, 1 6 2 3.

16 Title-page of Thomas Kyd's *The Spanish Tragedy* (1623), showing a
stage-property arbour

118

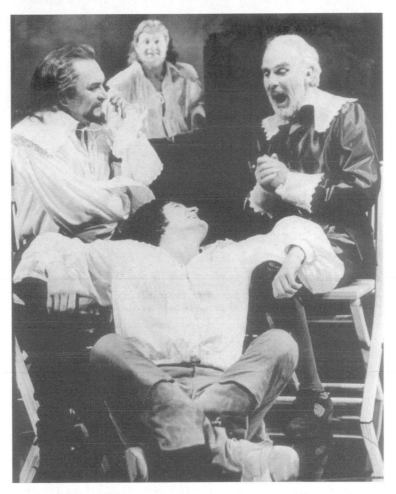

17 A relatively minimalist staging of Benedick's gulling scene (2.3) in Terry
   Hands's 1983 RSC production, with Derek Jacobi as Benedick (standing),
   and left to right Don Pedro (Derek Godfrey), Claudio (Robert O'Mahoney)
   and Leonato (Edward Jewesbury)

18 A more realistic staging of Benedick's gulling scene (2.3), with a property arbour akin to that pictured in Fig. 16. John Gielgud as Benedick, in his production at the Shakespeare Memorial Theatre, 1950, with left to right Leonato (Andrew Cruickshank), Don Pedro (Leon Quartermaine) and Claudio (Eric Lander)

(see Fig. 19); in 1998, Shakespeare Santa Cruz's Ursula Meyer made what she could of the cover provided by a redwood tree and the parasols of her fellows. The 1990 Bill Alexander RSC staging 'exercised a sexually discriminatory policy that gave Benedick a cypress tree to climb up and fall out of in 2.3 but left Beatrice in 3.1 propped up against the proscenium arch looking unsure whether she was effectively invisible or not' (Holland, 35). Incidentally, this latter scene was the most illustrated of the play during the nineteenth century (Altick; and see Fig. 20).

19 3.1 in John Barton's 1976 production, with Ursula (Marilyn Taylerson, left) and Hero (Cherie Lunghi); Judi Dench's Beatrice is behind the curtain, with a collection of servants watching from above

20 3.1 in the engraving by James Heath of W. Peters's painting for Boydell's
    Shakespeare Gallery (1791); in the nineteenth century, the most frequently
    illustrated scene of the play

In casting the play a director can range from a minimum casting, with as much doubling as the play permits (see Appendix), to a plethora of extra non-speaking attendants suggestive of luxury and high society. The original staging would have required at least twelve adult actors for fifteen male speaking parts (not including the Watch). All female parts were played by boy actors, of which four are required. These sixteen actors speak 97 per cent of the lines.[1] The actors playing Hero and Margaret can be cast as physically similar, for example in height (or not – either way conditions our understanding of Claudio's susceptibility to 'mistaking'). We know from the text that Hero is, in Benedick's phrases, 'Leonato's short daughter' (1.1.200–1), 'too low for a high praise, too brown for a fair praise and too little for a great praise' (1.1.163–5), in other words, that she was short and maybe portrayed as a brunette (although 'brown' could refer to complexion as well as to hair colour), probably played by a boy actor younger and less accomplished than the actor required for Beatrice (at 262 lines, the fifth largest part, after the four principal men, Benedick, Leonato, Don Pedro and Claudio). The other casting information provided by the Quarto text is that the parts of Dogberry and Verges were perhaps written for and played by the comic actors Will Kemp and Richard Cowley.

The innovation of modern technologies and tastes notwithstanding, productions based on such original choices remain remarkably viable. Perhaps the only constant requirement among these choices is the necessity that the play be given a period and a setting in which male honour is dependent on female identity, and sexual chastity is a matter of life and death. This has tended to dictate settings in moments prior to the sexual revolution of the late twentieth-century West, although a reliance on stereotypes of Latin machismo has

---

1   The statistic is T.J. King's (T. King, 86). See also Weil.

pushed it as far as the decades immediately before the First World War, and Mira Nair's 2001 film *Monsoon Wedding* gracefully transposes many of the play's themes and structures to modern bourgeois India. For Elizabethans, too, Latin countries represented passionate tendencies; as Benedetto Varchi put it in 1615,

> people in hot climates are more jealouse, eyther because they are much giuen and enclined to Loue naturally, or else that they hold it a great disparagement and scandal, to have their Wiues or their Mistresses taynted with the foul blot of unchastitie; which thing those that are of contrarie regions, and such as liue under the North Pole, take not so deepe at the heart.

> (*Blazon*, sig. E3$^\mathrm{v}$)

At the same time, it must be a culture in which the relative independence of Beatrice is possible, anomalous but not unintelligible. She has, for instance, been played as a wartime nurse, a Wallis Simpsonesque socialite, and an aspiring painter. Hence the preference for setting the play in moments of transition in sexual politics (which, opportunely, most moments seem to be).

CRITICISM

The unusual emotional palette of *Much Ado* was a main topic of commentary from very early on in the play's critical history. In 1709 Charles Gildon in his 'Remarks' included with Rowe's edition observed that 'this play we must call a comedy, tho'' some of the incidents and discourses are more in a tragic strain; and that of the accusation of Hero is too shocking for either Tragedy or Comedy' (Gildon, cited in Furness, 347). This estimate was still current in 1873: 'Here is no stuff for a comedy. A girl slandered and ill-treated to an unutterable extent is not an object to awaken merriment. And it is degrading that she should finally, without hesitation, marry her slanderer.'[1] Such estimates of the play's violation of comic decorum continue, although they seem to have had little effect on the play's popularity on the stage, no doubt due to the theatrical dominance of the Beatrice and Benedick material, which has carried the rest of the play in its wake.

Of chief interest to Gildon and many who followed him is what was understood to be Shakespeare's realistic representation of character, such that aesthetic stumbling blocks (the problematic nature of this comedy) were often apprehended as ethical ones (the dubiousness of certain moral portraits): 'he always draws men and women so perfectly, that when we read, we can scarce persuade ourselves but that the discourse is real and no fiction' (Gildon, cited in Furness, 348). With the nineteenth century (and the habit of novel reading) comes a strong attention to the construction of character, judged according to its psychological verisimilitude and historical plausibility. For William Hazlitt in 1817, for instance,

> Dogberry and Verges in this play are inimitable specimens of quaint blundering and misprisions of meaning; and are a standing record of that formal gravity of pretension and total want of common understanding, which Shakespeare no doubt copied from real life, and which in the course of two hundred years appear to have ascended from the lowest to the highest offices in the state.

(Hazlitt, 303)

Hazlitt's attention to Dogberry and Verges is unusual (although see also Aubrey; H. Evans; Allen), in that most commentators in his century focused their gaze upon Benedick and Beatrice: their comportment, their language, and the

---

1   Roderich Benedix, *Die Shakespearomanie* (1873), cited in Furness, 377.

probability and suitability of their tempers as measured by both current and Elizabethan mores. In spite of their power on the stage, they were often found lacking in the decorum department: 'If Benedick and Beatrice had possessed perfect good manners, or just notions of honour and delicacy, so as to have refused to become eavesdroppers, the action of the play must have stood still.'[1] Even as the play's version of comedy was sometimes considered ungainly, so, often, were its jokes and its portrayal of personality. More than one response attributes what was seen as the indelicacy of the play's humour to another form of realism, deriving from Shakespeare's submission to his own age's crude sensibility:

> Beatrice's wit, let it be frankly avowed, is uncommonly Elizabethan. It would have been called 'chaff' if our rude forefathers had known the word in that sense . . . This kind of merry combat would be thought blunt by a groom and a scullion . . . The wit combat must be judged historically.[2]

George Bernard Shaw located what he felt was the play's uncouth sense of humour (redeemed only by the music of the language) in Shakespeare's own artistic immaturity:

> The main pretension in *Much Ado* is that Benedick and Beatrice are exquisitely witty and amusing persons. They are, of course, nothing of the sort. Benedick's pleasantries might pass at a sing-song in a public house parlor, but a gentleman rash enough to venture on them in even the very mildest £52 a year suburban imitation of polite society today would assuredly never be invited again . . . It took the Bard a long time to grow out of the provincial conceit that made him so

---

1   Mrs Inchbald, *British Theatre* (1822), cited in Furness, 348.
2   Andrew Lang, *Harper's Magazine*, September 1891, cited in Furness, 362.

fond of exhibiting his accomplishments as a master of gallant badinage.

(Shaw, 141)

To the sense of Shakespeare's violation of comic protocol, then, was added the sense of his violation of polite manners. Shaw's deliberate and typically antibardolatrous overstatement no doubt misses the point that Benedick and Beatrice are amateurs, whose wit deliberately varies in achievement, but his caricature nonetheless relies on the equation of formal and ethical decorums.

At the same time, many of these nineteenth-century estimates were influenced by the current stagings of the play, dominated by their successful Benedicks and Beatrices. Responses rapidly came to concentrate on the figure of Beatrice as a trope for the play's mixed palette. For instance, Mrs Jameson, in her *Characteristics of Women* (1833), writes:

> Shakespeare has exhibited in Beatrice a spirited and faithful portrait of the fine lady of his own time . . . In Beatrice, high intellect and high animal spirits meet, and excite each other like fire and air. In her wit, (which is brilliant without being imaginative,) there is a touch of insolence, not unfrequent in women when the wit predominates over reflection and imagination. In her temper, too, there is slight infusion of the termagant; and her satirical humour plays with such an unrespective levity over all subjects alike, that it required a profound knowledge of women to bring such a character within the pale of our sympathy. But Beatrice, though wilful, is not wayward; she is volatile, not unfeeling . . . we are yet more completely won by her generous enthusiastic attachment to her cousin.

(Jameson, 1.128)

Here, again, is the sense of Shakespeare's psychological realism, filtered through contemporary mores about appropriate female behaviour. Beatrice's wit is only fully redeemed and balanced by her loyalty to Hero. Not surprisingly, Benedick and his wit tend to come off in such accounts as far more palatable, 'because the independence and gay indifference of temper, the laughing defiance of love and marriage, the satirical freedom of expression . . . are more becoming to the masculine than the feminine character' (Jameson, 1.128). Beatrice appears rather as a more risky (if ultimately temperate) blend of traits.

In general, as went Beatrice, so went the play. Not everyone was convinced of Shakespeare's power to err on the side of good taste. In 1838 Thomas Campbell called Beatrice 'an odious woman', a sentiment not without its supporters over the centuries:

> Mrs. Jameson concludes with hoping that Beatrice will live happy with Benedick, but I have no such hope . . . I once knew such a pair: the lady was a perfect Beatrice; she railed hypocritically at wedlock before marriage, and with bitter sincerity after it. She and her Benedick now live apart, but with entire reciprocity of sentiments, each devoutly wishing that the other may soon pass into a better world.

> (Campbell, xlvi)

Not surprisingly, the relatively silent Hero comes off much better in this kind of response. Nineteenth-century codes of gender propriety were not one-sided, however, and Claudio comes in for his fair share of censure, as giving gentlemen a bad name: 'arrogant, faint-hearted, liable to hasty change of mood, and in anger capable of heartless cruelty, he repeatedly brings into question his qualification to be the hero of the Play, the fortunate lover'; 'aesthetically impossible'; 'the most hateful young cub'.[1] It was not until the twentieth century, with the critical pressure to move towards investigating historical

---

1   F. Kreyssug, *Vorlesungen ueber Shakespeare* (1862), cited in Furness, 374; Heinrich Bulthaupt, *Dramaturgie der Classiker* (1884), in Furness, 378; Andrew Lang, *Harper's Magazine*, September 1891, in Furness, 361; Faucit, in Furness, 361.

contexts, that such opinions began to be countered by insistence on the conventionality and historical aptness of Claudio's actions (Neill; Page).

Opinions of *Much Ado*'s characters – their probability, likeability and propriety – dominate much of the first two centuries of response. Concerns with other elements did appear, in the rare formalist diagnosis ('one of Shakespeare's few essays at what may be called genteel comedy' (Coleridge, 2.135)), or attempts to locate the play within Shakespeare's corpus, 'its reach backward and forward' (Furnivall, lv). But if Shakespeare's characters were considered psychologically probable, his plot was deemed less so, although, interestingly, the failings of genre were often linked to the failings of moral character: what was unpleasant about Claudio, for instance, is tied to what is ungainly about the play's status as comedy (Claudio's inclusion in a comic ending). Conversely, defenders of the overall artistry of the play tended to defend the ethical nature of its characters as well:

> For power of composition, for faultless balance and blameless rectitude of design, there is unquestionably no creation of his hand that will bear comparison with *Much Ado About Nothing* . . . As for Beatrice, she is as perfect a lady, though of a far different age and breeding, as Celimène or Millamant, and decidedly more perfect woman than could properly or permissibly have trod the stage of Congreve or Molière . . . But Alceste would have taken her to his own.
>
> (Swinburne, 152)

This 1880 account by A.C. Swinburne no doubt bears the influence of the actress Ellen Terry's gracious and graceful Beatrice, and in his reading the play, far from being a botched version of comic and drawing room decorums alike, approaches a classical ideal of both dramatic proportion and female self-sacrifice.

Some of Shakespeare's works turn on enigmas that repeatedly fuel critical approaches (Why does Hamlet delay? Is Henry V nasty or nice?), so that different critical generations return time and again to the same question, trying to answer it with the tools and vocabulary of the particular moment. If *Much Ado*'s critical history offers such a touchstone, it is in fact this question of the play's tonal and generic mixture. In the formalist era, for instance, this sometimes showed up in criticism as the question of *Much Ado*'s stylistic 'unity' (usually answered in the negative), or of its formal coherence (one plot or two?), or of its relationship to its multiple sources.[1] Historically *Much Ado* has been judged a rather motley effort, though agreeable in parts; it is the rare reader who perceives Shakespeare's mixture as, in fact, the point. To wit: 'Shakespeare . . . generate[s] a novelistic sense of the real, of a world where people live together to a degree that is socially and psychologically convincing, and new in the poet's work . . . by *embracing* contradictions everywhere' (Everett, 'Unsociable', 73; see also Craik).

In more recent times, questions of aesthetic unity have become less fashionable, as have questions of character and morals, but attempts to find coherence in the play's construction have persisted, only moving from the formal to the thematic register. Shakespeare comes across in such accounts as concerned throughout the play with some governing preoccupation that works to unify otherwise discordant elements: for instance, with knowledge,[2] or fashion,[3] or slander,[4] or social status,[5] or self-regard,[6] or the power of language,[7] or the role of wit.[8] The standard dialectical move of such analyses is to note the play's

---

1   See, for instance, D. Cook; Mueller; Osbourne; Prouty; Traugott.
2   Berry; Fergusson; Henze; Lewalski, 'Love'; Myhill; Rossiter.
3   J. Evans; Friedman, 'Man'; Ormerod.
4   Cerasano; Sexton.
5   Kreiger; M. Taylor.
6   Rose.
7   Dawson; Dobranski; Drakakis; Hunt; Jorgensen; Magnusson; Straznicky.
8   W. King; McCollum.

formal and ethical disparities, but then to overcome them by pointing to the overriding currency of the theme in question.

This play, like most of Shakespeare's works, has run the twentieth-century critical gauntlet that stretches from formalism[1] through psychoanalytic,[2] feminist, and materialist and new historicist criticisms.[3] Not surprisingly, feminist criticism has struck the richest vein, as the play's portrait of patriarchy outrages and encourages in equal measure. Thus the nineteenth-century study of the morality of character became the study of the morality of a political system. Interestingly, as a result of these recent attentions to power structures, the Hero and Claudio plot, for so long upstaged (quite literally) by Beatrice and Benedick, has begun to achieve a new prominence. Beatrice and Benedick, by contrast, have begun to return to their ornamental status, perhaps because they are harder to assimilate to a grim view of power's deforming effects upon personhood, and the figure of Beatrice challenges rigid notions of patriarchy's comprehensive or coercive force. No doubt the pendulum will keep on swinging.

TEXT

First impressions

Much Ado About Nothing exists in one authoritative early text, the Quarto of 1600 ('quarto' refers to the format of a book made of sheets folded twice, to provide four leaves, or eight pages). The first official mention of this text occurs on 4 August 1600, in an entry in the Stationers' Register (the record of the Stationers' Company, in which a member paid a fee to enter the name of a book to which he wished to establish a claim). The entry reads as follows:

---

1   There are, surprisingly, given the role of language in the play, few analyses of the style per se. See Barish; Vickers, 171–249.

2   C. Cook; Girard.

3   Berger; Howard; McEachern, 'Fathering'; Neely, 24–57; Williams, R.

as yo^w like yt: / a booke Henry the ffift: / a booke Euery
man in his humo^r. / a booke The com[m]edie of muche
A doo about nothinge. / a booke to be staied

(Greg, 1.15)

This list follows a series of entries of plays registered in 1600
as belonging to the Lord Chamberlain's Men, Shakespeare's
company, the leading one in London at the time. The meaning
of the phrase 'to be staied' is unclear; it was perhaps an attempt
to protect these texts from unauthorized publication.[1] It was
somewhat unusual for an acting company to publish its texts, for
it was more lucrative to disseminate them in performances to
which admission was paid, rather than in exchange for the one-
time fee – about forty shillings – that a publisher would give for
the rights; eighteen of Shakespeare's plays, for instance, did not
appear in print until the publication of the First Folio in 1623 (a
folio is a book made from sheets folded once to produce two leaves
and four pages). But in 1599–1600 a batch of play manuscripts
belonging to the Lord Chamberlain's Men (plays were typically
the property of the company, not the author, who sold them to the
players along with his rights) was sold and published in authorized
editions, including *Romeo and Juliet* (Q2), *A Midsummer Night's
Dream*, *The Merchant of Venice*, *2 Henry IV*, *A Warning for Fair
Women* (anon.), and Ben Jonson's *Every Man Out of His Humour*.
It has been conjectured that the sale of these plays was occasioned
by the move into the Globe theatre in 1599–1600, which would
have required capital and publicity, or that the Privy Council's
limitation, on 22 June 1600, of the number of London theatres
to two, and restriction of their performances to twice a week,
imposed a similar fundraising exigency.[2]

---

1 *As You Like It* did not see print until the 1623 Folio, Jonson's *Every Man in His
   Humour* appeared in 1601, and *Henry V* was published in an inferior text in 1600.
2 Taylor, 'Introduction', 86; *Acts*, 395–8; Blayney, 386; Erne, 115–28, offers another view.

The next record of *Much Ado*'s existence occurs nineteen days later, on 23 August, when the Register records:

Andrewe Wyse Willm Aspley Entred for their copies vnder the / hand[e]s of the wardens. Twoo book[e]s. the one called: Muche a Doo / about nothinge. Thother the second p[ar]te of the history of kinge henry / the iiij[th] w[th] the humo[r]s of S[r] Iohn ffallstaff': Wrytten by m[r] Shakespere / xij[d]

(Greg, vol. 1, 216)

Later that year both quartos duly appeared, printed for the publishers Wise and Aspley by Valentine Simmes, who also printed several other Shakespeare quartos around this time (the title-page for *Much Ado* reuses type set for the quarto of *2 Henry IV*). The title-page reads:

[Ornament] Much adoe about / Nothing. / *As it hath been sundrie times publikely* / acted by the right honourable, the Lord / Chamberlaine his seruants. / *Written by William Shakespeare*. / [Ornament] / LONDON / Printed by V. S. for Andrew Wise, and / William Aspley. / 1600.

Here, then, is our first and, as it turns out, most authoritative text: identified as a record of a play whose calling card was its performance on more than one occasion by the most prominent playing company in London. (The name of the author was likely, as listed, to be a selling point of only secondary or recent importance, and indeed the entry of 23 August is the first time Shakespeare's name appears in the Register, though plays had been printed with his name since 1598 (Arber, 2.170).)

We can conclude from other sources that the play was a relatively fresh item, in addition to being presented as a popular and prestigious one. *Much Ado* is not mentioned in the survey of notable works of English writers, entitled *Palladis Tamia*, compiled by Francis Meres and registered in 1598, which means either that Meres overlooked it or that it postdates the composition of his (otherwise quite up-to-date) list.[1] As for a terminal date of composition, we know from the Quarto speech prefixes referring to the clown Will Kemp (designated to play Dogberry) that the play must have been performed (or been intended to be performed) prior to early 1599, when Kemp left the Chamberlain's company to embark on his marathon jig to Norwich. Perhaps a more intuitively conclusive if less objective measure is provided by stylistic patterns, which locate *Much Ado* in a prosy phase, on the heels of *1* and *2 Henry IV* (1596–8) and in the vicinity of *Merry Wives* (1597–1600).[2] And while the sequencing of Shakespeare's works is a notoriously tendentious exercise, it could be argued that *Much Ado*'s sophistication of comic structure (in which circumstantial blocking mechanisms have become psychological ones) indicates that its theme and character anticipate the problem comedies of the early 1600s. The earliest conjectured date of composition is thus the middle to latter part of 1598, with a closing limit of the early months of 1599.

Making a book

The representations of the title-page notwithstanding, truth in advertising has been in dispute as long as salesmanship has existed. The text of the Quarto does not in fact derive from a performance 'sundrie times publikely acted'. It was instead printed from Shakespeare's 'foul papers' – or early complete draft of a play – which had not as yet 'undergone such polishing as might have been necessary before it could be held to represent a satisfactory performance' (Wells, 'Foul-paper', 1). We know this because

---

1   Meres rated the up-and-coming Shakespeare's plays as 'the most excellent in both kinds [i.e. comedy and tragedy] for the stage . . . his *Gentlemen of Verona*, his *Errors*, his *Love Labours lost*, his *Love labours wonne*, his *Midsummers night dream*, and his *Merchant of Venice*' (Chambers, 2.194); scholars once surmised that *Love labours wonne* was an alternative title for *Much Ado*, but this was disproved by evidence that in 1603, by which time the *Much Ado* Quarto was identified as such on the title-page, a bookseller named Christopher Hunt listed the former play as being in stock. See Baldwin, 31.
2   The dates are taken from Bevington.

of certain marks of composition (e.g. a characteristic lightness of punctuation), a certain sketchiness of stage directions, as well as certain inconsistencies of dialogue and speech prefixes (e.g. characters designated variously both by function and by given name). For instance, characters are named in entry directions who not only never speak in the scene in question but never appear in the play at all. This kind of evidence stands as witness to Shakespeare's compositional process, a kind of picture of his mind in action, making it up as he goes along, changing his mind as the story line emerged, and not necessarily backtracking to render his document internally consistent.

Had the Quarto been a record of a 'satisfactory performance' akin to others that we possess, it probably would have travelled the following route: Shakespeare's draft would have been recopied for a promptbook, which would then have been licensed by the Master of the Revels for theatre performance. (The licence would have rendered this text a valuable piece of company property, and hence unlikely to be passed along to a printer.) This 'prompt copy' would then have been annotated for performance by a bookkeeper (the person who cued entrances and prompted forgotten lines), who presumably would have regularized the text with respect to stage directions (although this is to assume that the company's practice was to record details which may have been tacitly understood, or nailed down only verbally, by actors). In some instances such bookkeepers noted the names of individual actors, especially in minor roles, a practice that at one point was the basis for the theory that the Quarto SPs of '*Kemp*' and '*Cowley*' for Dogberry and Verges meant that the Quarto was indeed derived from the promptbook. (This notion has since been dismissed as implausible, and the names attributed to Shakespeare's own use of the names of the actors he had in mind for the parts.[1]) The 1623 Folio version of the play is a reprint of Q based on a copy of Q

---

1 See Wilson, 67–8. The Quarto displays the variety of the ways in which Shakespeare thought of his characters as he scribbled his way through: by function (*Const., Dog., Ke.*); type (*Bastard, Don John, Old, Antonio*); and title (*Don Pedro, Prince*).

(no longer extant) lightly annotated by reference to the company's promptbook. The name of '*Iacke Wilson*' in the entry SD at 2.3 is that of a singer cast in the role of Balthasar and must be presumed to be derived from a theatrical document.[1] The ample evidence for direct reprinting of F from Q rules out the alternative possibility of the promptbook having itself served as printer's copy for F. Differences of the Folio are noted in the textual collation.

In addition, the text of the Quarto lacks such bookkeeperly detail as has sometimes been held characteristic of promptbooks, revealing instead various features consistent with the alternative of its having been printed from an informal and incompletely revised authorial draft of the play. Bibliographers imagine the genesis of Q in these terms: Shakespeare's draft, once having been copied for a promptbook, became available, and was considered serviceable, for a printer's use (as copying was costly and laborious, this would have been an economical use of this superseded but good-enough document). At the printer's workshop, it would have been set into type by hand. In the case of *Much Ado*, it was (somewhat unusually) set by a single typesetter, Simmes's 'Compositor A'. Identification of this workman involves his participation in setting other playtexts, from which it appears that, among his various working habits, leaving the unabbreviated forms of SPs unpunctuated is distinctive. Compositor A would have set his text into type choosing one of two methods of page formatting. If he did so by 'formes' (a forme was a block of type printing one side of an entire printed sheet), he would have set at one time the four pages contained on a single side of the sheet to be printed, that is, pages 8, 1, 4 and 5 on one side, and 2, 7, 6 and 3 on the other. Setting by formes required the advance estimation

---

1 Other differences of the Folio from the Quarto include its division into five acts (though scenes are not indicated after '*Actus primus, Scena prima*'); SD changes seeming to reflect playhouse practice; commonsense SD changes not necessarily involving playhouse origin; erroneous SD changes; omission, or addition, of dozens of words, and omission of five short passages (at 1.1.290–1; 3.2.31–4; 4.1.18; 4.2.19–22; and 5.4.33 (see textual notes)); many minor textual variations.

(or 'casting off') of copy to instruct the compositor exactly what section of the text to set for each page, a process that could sometimes result in crowded pages (or the contrary) if miscalculations occurred. The crowded final sig. L1ʳ of *Much Ado* in the forme-set Folio, for instance, betrays such an error; as casting off is more difficult to do with prose than verse, verse might then be strategically set as prose in order to make up the required space, and *Much Ado* is a prose-heavy play. (Other space-saving stratagems could include the abbreviation of names in SPs, the omission of lines, or the condensation of SDs.) Despite the calculations required, however, setting by formes is a relatively efficient method of typesetting, as one entire side of a sheet can then go to press and be printed while the compositor sets the remaining four pages. It would have been unusual to set a play quarto (presumably not a large or exceptionally lucrative print run) according to the other, less time-saving method, namely, 'seriatim', in consecutive order, so that a forme will be complete and ready to print only when seven of the eight pages (in quarto) or three of the four (in folio) are set in type. The scholar John Hazel Smith argued further on the basis of typographical evidence (the apparent pattern of roman and italic type usage for the letter 'B', required by this B-heavy play) that Q was indeed set by formes.[1] The crowded Q page G1ʳ, with thirty-nine instead of thirty-seven lines of text, seems to be an instance of compensating for casting-off errors (another explanation could be that the proofreader discovered that the compositor, by eye-skip or other mishap, had left two or three lines out in his initial setting – this is less likely, of course, with cast-off copy, where the number of lines per page is the basis of the calculation and such an error would presumably come to light at the end of the page).

Charlton Hinman, whose detective work is discussed in his introduction to the Q facsimile, argues however that despite such

1 Smith, 'Quarto'. Smith argued that the heavy demand for italic B 'was met by regularly removing the italic Bs from the newly wrought-off type pages for use in the composition of the immediately following sheet' (Hinman, xiii).

persuasive analysis, the pattern of type usage in *Much Ado* (as well as the preponderance of prose) in fact points 'for the most part' to a seriatim setting (e.g. distinctive type recurs in alternate sheets in a pattern indicative of consecutive composition). Hence he argues that the peculiarities of Q's text must be the result of something other than casting-off errors – obscurities in the copy itself, perhaps (Hinman, xv). Correction of hand-printed books took place immediately after a forme of type went to press, when a proof sheet was run off. However, the printing of the uncorrected forme continued while the proof was read and marked up, with the consequence that the corrections, made at press during a pause in printing, do not appear in every copy of the pages in question. In general, stop-press correction was carried out early in the printing of the forme, so that many more corrected than uncorrected copies of a given forme were printed. Corrected and uncorrected states of several formes have been identified among the seventeen surviving copies of Q, distributed at random among those copies. The corrections made to *Much Ado* in this manner are of minor errors of typesetting and unfortunately have no bearing on the play's few verbal cruces.[1]

So, while the odds are that the Quarto text of *Much Ado* may depart in minor ways from its 'foul papers' copy, this is in all likelihood mainly at the level of insignificant detail. Hinman concludes that Compositor A's work is 'not obviously corrupt, even when it does not follow its original' (Hinman, xvii).[2] And, it is important to re-emphasize, these foul papers were themselves merely an initial-to-intermediate step on the way to a hypothetical promptbook (which in turn may not have been as

1   See the full record of variants given by Hinman in his introduction to the Shakespeare Quarto Facsimile of *Much Ado* (a record later emended at F2v.4, where '*Leonati*' is a misprint for '*Leonato*').

2   For an alternative estimate of Simmes' reliability, see Alan E. Craven, 'Simmes' Compositor A and Five Shakespeare Quartos', *Studies in Bibliography*, 26 (1973), 37–60 and 'The Reliability of Simmes' Compositor A', *Studies in Bibliography*, 32 (1979), 186–97.

ideally tidy and consistent as scholars have liked to imagine, and which, in any case, is not the same as a text, such as that of this edition – or Q or the First Folio – prepared for the imaginative experience of reading rather than the embodied practices of the theatre).

This edition, like any previous edition, has thus sought to modify and modernize the original text so as to make the play legible to the mind's eye. The pages reproduced here (Fig. 21) give some sense of the work that takes place in producing today's text. Speech prefixes have been regularized, and entrance and exit directions made consistent with the required personnel. Some more substantive changes apply to the language (though not many, as the Quarto is generally quite free of such confusion). Some concern matters of punctuation. The Quarto text is lightly punctuated – potential full stops, for instance, are at a minimum, and colons occur instead. This allows for some flexibility in determining meanings, and such instances have been indicated in the textual notes.

The majority of alterations concern logistical matters of personnel and action. For instance, Quarto SDs have been clarified when necessary, with additions enclosed in square brackets. What is presented here is not the text of the original performance. It is not the text of any performance, and indeed it is intended to be open ended rather than restrictive (not to be confused with indecisive) in suggesting possibilities for stage action, despite the editorial temptation to block the play – a temptation made inevitable if not irresistible by the fact that this reader, like any other, builds in the course of her experience of the play expectations about how its characters might or might not behave. An edition truly scrupulous about these matters would perhaps provide multiple-choice SDs; however, there are enough notes on these pages as it is, the number of choices is unwieldy if not infinite, and my assumption is that other readers will have their own opinions about how characters might or might not behave, and will undoubtedly exercise them.

Much adoe

eate his heart in the market place.

Bened. Heare me Beatrice.

Beat. Talke with a man out at a window, a proper saying.

Bened. Nay but Beatrice.

Beat. Sweete Hero, she is wrongd, she is slaundred, shee is vndone.

Bened. Beat?

Beat. Princes and Counties! surely a princely testimonie, a goodly Counte, Counte Comfect, a sweete Gallant surely. O that I were a man for his sake! or that I had any friend woulde be a man for my sake! But manhoode is melted into cursies, valour into complement, and men are only turnd into tongue, and trim ones too : he is now as valiant as Hercules, that only tels a lie, and sweares it : I cannot be a man with wishing, therfore I will die a woman with grieuing.

Bened. Tarry good Beatrice, by this hand I loue thee.

Beatrice Vse it for my loue some other way than swearing by it.

Bened. Thinke you in your soule the Count Claudio hath wrongd Hero?

Beatrice Yea, as sure as I haue a thought, or a soule.

Bened. Enough, I am engagde, I will challenge him, I will kisse your hand, and so I leaue you : by this hand, Claudio shal render me a deere account: as you heare of me, so think of me: goe comforte your coosin, I must say she is dead, and so farewell.

Enter the Constables, Borachio, and the Towne clearke in gownes.

Keeper Is our whole dissembly appeard?

Cowley O a stoole and a cushion for the Sexton.

Sexton Which be the malefactors?

Andrew Mary that am I, and my partner.

Cowley Nay thats certaine, we haue the exhibition to examine.

Sexton But which are the offenders? that are to be examined let them come before maister constable.

Kemp Yea mary, let them come before mee, what is your
name,

21 *Much Ado About Nothing*, 1600 Quarto, sigs G3ᵛ–4ʳ (4.1.305–4.2.54). Note the variety of speech prefixes for Dogberry (*Keeper, Andrew, Kemp, Ke.*); the use of actors' names (*Cowley, Kemp*); the use of colons where a

about $\mathcal{N}othing$.

name, friend?

Bor. Borachio.

Ke. Pray write downe Borachio. Yours sirra.

Con. I am a gentleman sir, and my name is Conrade.

Ke. Write downe maister gentleman Conrade : maisters, do you serue God?

Both Yea sir we hope.

Kem. Write downe, that they hope they serue God : and write God first, for God defend but God shoulde goe before such villaines: maisters, it is prooued alreadie that you are little better than false knaues, and it will go neere to be thought so shortly, how answer you for your selues?

Con. Mary sir we say, we are none.

Kemp A maruellous witty fellowe I assure you, but I will go about with him: come you hither sirra, a word in your eare sir, I say to you, it is thought you are false knaues.

Bor. Sir, I say to you, we are none.

Kemp VVel, stand aside, fore God they are both in a tale: haue you writ downe, that they are none?

Sexton Master constable, you go not the way to examine, you must call foorth the watch that are their accusers.

Kemp Yea mary, thats the eftest way, let the watch come forth : maisters, I charge you in the Princes name accuse these men.

Watch 1 This man said sir, that don Iohn the Princes brother was a villaine.

Kemp Write downe, prince Iohn a villaine : why this is flat periurie, to call a Princes brother villaine.

Borachio Maister Constable.

Kemp Pray thee fellowe peace, I doe not like thy looke I promise thee.

Sexton VVhat heard you him say else?

Watch 2 Mary that he had receiued a thousand duckats of don Iohn, for accusing the Ladie Hero wrongfully.

Kemp Flat burglarie as euer was committed.

Const. Yea by masse that it is.

Sexton VVhat else fellow?

Watch

modern edition might use full stops; and the lightness of the punctuation generally.

Who's in, who's out

In practice, this means that most clarifications of the Quarto's irregularities are fairly obvious ones: who is on stage in a particular scene, when they arrive, when they need to leave. The dialogue itself will give the reader clear answers to many such questions (which is probably why the writer didn't overload his script with stage directions): for instance, 'exit' for a character who says goodbye, or otherwise needs to be got offstage (e.g. 1.2.21, 2.3.7). Sometimes, however, characters are given an entry when they shouldn't have been (2.1.195); sometimes, an exit when they need to remain on stage (2.1.145). A slightly more complicated category involves those instances when a character says goodbye, but doesn't leave promptly, or makes a false exit (e.g. 3.3.85, not atypically involving Dogberry, who displays a frequent reluctance to quit the stage when prompted).[1] But none of these adjustments should be open to serious objection.

Other unremarkable editorial supplements relate to addressees or stage action, and are also evident from the dialogue: for example '[*Hero falls.*]' (4.1.109); '[*Hands Seacoal the lantern.*]' (3.3.24); '*Enter* Beatrice[, *who hides*].' (3.1.23). The one SD of this type in this edition most likely to raise eyebrows is that provided at 5.4.97, describing the stage action which accompanies the line: 'Peace! [*to Beatrice*] I will stop your mouth. [*Hands her to Benedick.*]'. This speech is given in Q (and F) to Leonato, but since Theobald's 1733 edition has been assigned to Benedick, with the accompanying supplemental direction '[*He kisses her.*]'. This edition returns the line to Leonato, and in restoring the line to its Quarto speaker my

---

1 The Folger edition makes the not unattractive suggestion that Dogberry does indeed return yet again at the end of 3.3, in response to a watchman's 'Call up the right master Constable' (159) and by reading the uncorrected Quarto's SP '*Conr.*' as an error for *Con.*, or constable (Qc = *Con.*). My sense however is that unless we imagine Dogberry's offstage location to be extremely close to hand, the disruption to the general hubbub of the scene's closure required by the time necessary to summon Dogberry is not theatrically plausible in terms of pacing or character: 'Shakespeare has left remarkably little time for the proposed action to take place' (Wells, 'Crux', 85–6).

assumption is that Leonato, a directing presence throughout this scene, intervenes to impose himself upon the bickering couple ('Peace!') and then addresses himself to Beatrice, who has just spoken ('I will stop your mouth.'), signalling his intent to silence her merely by giving her to a husband. As a directive delivered by a third party to a couple, it has the precedent of Beatrice's own command to Hero at 2.1.285–6 ('Speak, cousin, or, if you cannot, stop his mouth with a kiss and let not him speak neither.'). I confess I also feel that if Leonato speaks the line it provides for a more egalitarian accommodation between the lovers, one that seems in keeping with the tenor of their relationship throughout. This edition's SD here is thus more prescriptive than most in the same category (though, I'd argue, less so than Theobald's), and according to a principle of editorial abstemiousness that restricts itself to spelling out only actions indicated by the dialogue, I probably ought to refrain. But I thought the direction necessary to counterbalance the weight of editorial precedent being shifted aside here. (In defence of said abstemiousness, I have left it to the reader's imagination whether or not Benedick does kiss Beatrice, although I confess in mine he does, or perhaps she him.) Obviously, other actions may accompany the line; the important point here is its speaker.

A somewhat stickier category of entry SD involves uncertainty about when certain actors need to arrive on stage. For instance, Margaret and Ursula are members of the dance in 2.1, where they also speak, but they are never given an entrance in the scene. Rowe introduced them in the initial entry, but since they do not speak until the dance, it is also possible to have them enter, as they do here, with the revellers at 75. Arguments against the latter choice are that this somewhat violates the convention by which masked revellers entered a family party from without (as in *Romeo and Juliet*); arguments for it are that since the two women are given no lines until the dance, it might be awkward to have them enter with the immediate family (and social betters) at the beginning – although, as discussed below, Shakespeare seems to have no problem with occasionally bringing on extra actors just to give the impression of social bustle. The decision may depend on whether a production imagines the two women as ladies-in-waiting, or more like household servants – the former might well be part of the intimate family group, the latter might still be cleaning up after the supper, and thus enter with the general throng. Alternatives of this kind are discussed in the commentary throughout.

A similar case involves the entry of Leonato and Hero in the same scene, after the confusion over whom Hero is to marry has been cleared up. The Quarto locates their entry with Don Pedro at 2.1.192 (although it also erroneously includes Don John, Conrade and Borachio); the Folio (again, perhaps cued by the promptbook) has them enter with Beatrice and Claudio at 239. This choice is attractive since neither of them speaks until then, and it has been thought awkward to have them present during Benedick's discussion of the confusion over Hero's suitor, and Benedick's subsequent diatribe against Beatrice. As Zitner points out, 'this' in his phrase 'your grace had got the good will of this young lady' (198) is not necessarily demonstrative (Oxf[1]).[1] However, their entry with Beatrice somewhat dilutes the force of her entry with the sullen Claudio, and in my imagination Benedick is playing to a crowd, despite (or perhaps because of) the indelicacy involved in abusing Beatrice in earshot of her kin, or even that of discussing the disposition of Hero's hand in her earshot (tact is not his strong suit). In other words, either decision can be rationalized. I have adopted the Quarto direction; like the entry of Margaret and Ursula, the choice in a production will have certain atmospheric consequences, but in neither instance is much at stake.

So much for the relatively neutral choices. There are, however, a few places in the Quarto that require a somewhat more radical decision. For instance, in the entry directions to 1.1, Q lists '*Innogen his wife*', repeating '*his wife*' at the start of 2.1; she,

---

1 Zitner, following a conjecture by Harold Jenkins, boldly has Leonato and Hero enter with Beatrice and Claudio at 2.1.275 but at separate doors.

along with '*a kinsman*' (also at 2.1.0), is known as a 'ghost' character, that is, one who enters but is not otherwise invoked or given anything to do or say. The 'kinsman' is perhaps the same man Leonato mentions in 1.2: 'where is my cousin your son? Hath he provided this music?' (1–2); by 5.1.280, however, Antonio is childless, and Beatrice in 4.1 without a supportive kinsman to champion Hero. This figure's lack of substance is an instance of Shakespeare's working method of conjuring up a raft of personnel, and then streamlining as he goes along, finding (or not finding) things for them to do, sorting out the action and necessary bodies as the plot thickens and occasion requires. The Florentine Claudio's Messinese uncle, mentioned in passing in the dialogue of 1.1 (at 17) but never again, seems to materialize from a similar desire to create and populate a social universe. There are also instances of characters mentioned in entry directions who have nothing to say in the scene in question – for example Balthasar at 1.1.90.1, or the Sexton at 5.1.248.1. These are not as ghostly, in that they do speak elsewhere, and, as they seem not out of place in these scenes (Balthasar is a member of Don Pedro's company, the Sexton has just apprised Leonato of Borachio's trick), they have been left in their mute peace. Again, in this play about social foibles Shakespeare seems to generate a sense of society through a critical mass of actual bodies on stage and references to others elsewhere, a choice that can be followed or not according to the resources of a particular production (e.g. doubling constraints; see the Appendix).

Unlike the kinsman, however, mother Innogen is not explicitly written out of the play; such a figure is present in the Bandello tale, and recent arguments (in a thematic and political rather than theatrical vein) have been made for her silent presence (Friedman, 'Hush'd'; Baker), especially as she does not vanish after 1.1 but persists in the entry direction to 2.1.[1] She is referred to indirectly

---

1   Grounds for supposing either that Shakespeare might have written 2.1 first, or that he thought she might still be useful.

in 1.1: 'DON PEDRO . . . I think this is your daughter. / LEONATO Her mother hath many times told me so. / BENEDICK Were you in doubt, sir, that you asked her? / LEONATO Signor Benedick, no, for then were you a child' (98–102). This jocular little exchange might conceivably have been imagined by Shakespeare to be carried out in the presence of the woman in question (although it would be unseemly, given the relative formality of the occasion).[1] But there is no other mention of her in the play (even when we might expect one, as when Leonato disowns Hero in 4.1). Shakespeare moves quickly to the father–motherless daughter dyad, one dramatically and psychologically profitable elsewhere in his work (e.g. Lear, Prospero, Shylock). By 4.1, Leonato and Dame Nature alone are her parents (128–9), which adds to the sense of Hero's vulnerability and isolation in her lone parent's abandonment of her. It has traditionally been difficult for editors to imagine Innogen as a Hermione-like bystander to her daughter's trials; and it seems equally important that Beatrice give full and sole cry to a female and familial defence of Hero. (The mother in Bandello is also silent, but she does succour her daughter in her moment of trial. But nurturing mothers are scarce in Shakespeare's plays, to put it mildly, and a figure with the maternal instincts of Lady Capulet or Volumnia might have strained comic credibility too far.) Editors since Theobald have concurred that despite her persistence in the entry SDs Shakespeare ultimately found her more powerful in her absence than her presence, and so she has been retired from the fray.

Who gets to say what?

The choice to delete Innogen is clearly not one of a merely tidying-up nature, or at least it is one that also involves notions of character and context. Similar questions are also involved in

---

1 The exchange moved Shaw to comment: 'From his first joke, "were you in doubt, sir, that you asked her?" to his last, "There is no staff more reverend than one tipped with horn," he is not a wit, but a blackguard . . . [*MM*'s] Lucio is much more of a gentleman than Benedick, because he keeps his coarse sallies for coarse people' (Shaw, 141).

addressing the Quarto's speech prefixes. For instance, in the dance in 2.1, Q initially partners Margaret with Benedick (*Bene.*) for three exchanges, and then switches the male partner to Balthasar (*Balth.*) for the last two. The '*Bene.*' SPs spread from sig. B4^r (2) to B4^v (1), while both '*Balth.*' SPs are on B4^v. Edward Capell supported the change of partners with a SD '[*turning off in Quest of another*]', and there are grounds for some bantering relationship (reprised in 5.2) between Benedick and Margaret (although of course the male dancers are masked here).[1] From Theobald on, however, all five of the male partner's speeches have usually been given to Balthasar (the exception being J. Dover Wilson's Cambridge edition, which thought Borachio apropos, and argued that in the Quarto SD '*Balthaser, or dumb Iohn*', '*or*' was a misreading of '*B or*', for Borachio). Wells, however, thinks it 'more likely that "*or*" is a misreading of ampersand, or even of "and"', or even that the compositor misread all the SPs (all those Bs again) and that what we have, as elsewhere, is another instance of the 'foul-paper' traces of Shakespeare's rethinking of the action as he worked through his plot: first he conceived of a Benedick–Margaret exchange, then realized in the course of writing that a more powerful climax to the scene lay in partnering Benedick and Beatrice (Wells, 'Foul-paper', 12). This edition rests with this conclusion, though I'd argue that a Beatrice and Benedick pairing was always the intended destination – the only real problem is finding a partner for Margaret.

The speaking members of the Watch in 3.3. and 4.2 present another instance of the Quarto in need of some clarification in ways that entail notions of character. In 3.3, at their first appearance, Q begins by distinguishing between the first speaker ('*Watch* 1') and the man identified by him as George Seacoal ('*Watch* 2'). But after line 27 ('*Watch* 2 How if 'a will

---

1   See Mason; other partner-switchers include Malone, Collier, Stevenson, and most recently the Folger edition.

not stand?') the various voices of the band are all prefaced from sigs E3^v to E4^v with a mere '*Watch*', until the very end of the scene, at 157, from whence '*Watch* 1' and '*Watch* 2' alternate the last four Watch speeches (on sig. F1^r). There are, I would argue, at least three watchmen on stage: Watch 1, Hugh Oatcake and George Seacoal ('they can write and read', 12); there may be at least one other, from whom Watch 1 distinguishes them (unless he is merely eager to distinguish them from himself). As Wells argues of the undifferentiated lines, 'Each speech could be spoken by the same man, and he could be any one of the three who are certainly present. Equally, each speech could be spoken by a different actor, none of whom need have spoken before' (Wells, 'Foul-paper', 11). The lack of specificity among their SPs may have a typographical or compositorial origin, or be due to casualness on Shakespeare's part. A different explanation would be that Shakespeare left the speeches undifferentiated so as to provide for the flexibility required by a given performance (perhaps he had no idea how many bodies would be available once the play came to be staged). This edition follows as much as possible Q's omission to individuate these speeches, on the assumption that this allows for a certain choral flexibility of voices and in the confidence that a reader will not be unduly confused.

Two final SP issues need a word here, as they represent instances of this volume's departure from the usual editorial consensus. The first concerns 5.3, the scene at Leonato's family monument, where he has formerly instructed Claudio to 'Hang her an epitaph upon her tomb / And sing it to her bones' (5.1.274–5). In the Quarto, which I have followed, the text of the epitaph follows the SP of an anonymous and unprecedented figure of 'A Lord', who also speaks the couplet which follows the song: 'Now unto thy bones good night; / Yearly will I do this rite' (5.3.22–3). Claudio, according to Q, speaks twice during the actual ceremony, first to ask 'Is this the monument of Leonato?' (5.3.1), and then to direct: 'Now music sound, and sing your solemn hymn' (5.3.11). But all editions since Rowe have also assigned the epitaph and the couplet to Claudio, in view of Leonato's instructions. The voice of the Lord may be felt to dilute the force of Claudio's penance, and, according to Capell, the copy or the compositor may simply have failed to provide a speech prefix for Claudio in these places. While I cannot be accused of a wish to go lightly on my imagined Claudio, I would argue that the sheer anomaly of the unprecedented Lord suggests that he is meant to be there, doing what he does; and also, given the highly formal, public and ritual nature of this ceremony, it need not appear callous for a delegate to speak on Claudio's behalf and the collective behalf of the male community which slandered Hero (quite the opposite). It is also clear that contrary to Leonato's directive Claudio instructs others to sing and that the singer who was (and perhaps still is) Balthasar, unless he is doubling as the Lord, may be the likeliest singer here too. In Claudio's defence, following Q's SPs means that here (and only here) for the first time does Claudio initiate and control the action, becoming in effect director or stage manager of the scene; rather than discrediting his sincerity, these assignments lend him a new and needed authority and weight. It is for these reasons that I have remained with the Quarto.

Finally, I have also returned two speeches of 5.4 to their Quarto speaker, Leonato. The second, at line 97, is discussed above; the first appears at line 54, and accompanies the delivery of Hero to Claudio: 'This same is she, and I do give you her.' This line has since Theobald been assigned to Antonio, as Leonato has said earlier to him 'You must be father to your brother's daughter / And give her to young Claudio' (15–16). Theobald's assumption is that Shakespeare forgot he had written the earlier instruction; my sense is rather that Leonato is the one who forgets, steps in to take over from his brother, and begins again to direct the action, as he does at 56, 66, 118, and, as I've argued above, at 97 (we don't assume 56 is a mistake, so why 97?). Admittedly, these decisions are governed by a mental picture of a character, but that is always the case, and not, I think, something for which to apologize. All these original SPs represent workable, stageable choices, consistent with character and context, even if they are not as sentimentally attractive as other possible alternatives.

I risk labouring these choices as instances of this edition's general tendency (always difficult to describe, since editing is mostly a series of very local and often inconsistent choices) to have as much confidence in Q as possible. This is to discount neither its origin in a pre-theatrical text, nor the evidence it offers of Shakespeare's exercise of the authorial right to change his mind in the course of composition, nor, certainly, that productions and readers will reassign these matters as desired. Nor is it an attempt to abdicate editorial responsibility; the choice to follow Q is a choice like any other, and it has the virtue of not obscuring the identity of the original text. It is rather an attempt to give weight to Shakespeare's instincts (if we are right in supposing that Q gives evidence of them), in the understanding that a conscientious reader will take all such decisions with a grain of salt and an eye to the textual notes. *Much Ado* is a play deliberately designed by its author to stage the processes of misinformation, misapprehension and misdirection: for instance, there are at least two different accounts of who will propose to Hero and five different accounts of the event at her bedchamber window; and Don John is named as a bastard in the Quarto SPs and SDs, but, in a manner emblematic of the play's concern with confusion and disclosure, he is not so defined in the dialogue until the fourth act. This kind of architecture of misinformation compounds the editorial challenge of a base text which is clearly a work in progress, as one is forced to ponder whether inconsistencies are evidence of a playtext not yet fully realized, or, rather, of a playtext very fully realized. Given the degree to which Shakespeare is actively concerned in *Much Ado* with the vagaries of human communication, I believe one is well advised not to compound matters with an idea of an author more absent-minded than is strictly necessary. The assessment of what constitute theatrically unviable loose ends in an Elizabethan playscript is always going to require a large measure of caution, and of care not to impose standards of our own imagining onto it.

ADDITIONS AND RECONSIDERATIONS

'Hasn't that been done already?' Whether this question be posed by a concerned friend or a sceptical colleague, I doubt I am the first editor of a Shakespeare play who has been found herself required to supply an answer to it. In the case of an edition revised in advance of the standard two-score years of a scholarly generation, the answer might well be, more than is usually the case, 'well, yes'. Yet, as is also always the case, it is also 'yes and no'. For like certain other kinds of work, textual editing, especially of Shakespeare's writing, rarely *stays* done. However, unlike, say, housework, the cause here is not entropy but vitality. The combination of the ever-receding movement backwards in time of the plays' compositional moment with the ever-lengthening list of performances, critical interpretations and scholarly excavations in the present means that his plays are very much a moving target. This is especially true of a play as perennially popular as *Much Ado About Nothing*. An edition that pretends to just documentation and appraisal of its ongoing cultural currency must hustle to keep pace.

* * *

What a relief to encounter a production of a Shakespearean comedy where not once does a character thrust his or her groin to highlight a dated double-entendre.

(J. Kelly Nestruck, review of Stratford Ontario's *Much Ado About Nothing, Toronto Globe and Mail*, May 20, 2012)

Performance first. Several recent productions testify to the continuing imaginative appeal of this play, whether in the theatre or on screens big and small. Another feature-length film from a major Hollywood director, a play written in response to Shakespeare's, and a television 'retelling' of the play have joined several high-profile stage versions since 2006. (The majority of the productions discussed below have been chosen for their availability on digital recordings.) While generalizations about performance trends can be challenged not just by a given production, but by any given performance of that production, the most recent fashion is a turn to the darker elements of the play, particularly the sinister sides of militarism and male bonding; the fear of romantic commitment; and as ever the imaginative provocations of an independent woman who, for all her defiance of male dominion, eventually bumps her head against the glass ceiling of gender conventions.[1] In attending to the darker aspects of the play's gender politics, several productions reflected the trend of much scholarship of the past few decades.

It is not every play of Shakespeare's that can lay claim to two commercially and critically successful Hollywood treatments within the space of twenty years. The comedies in particular have been a tough sell for the silver screen. As Michael Hattaway has written, the histories have found a congenial medium in the spectacular potentials of film, and the tragedies profited from the camera's converse power to represent interiority through close-ups and the generation of 'salient visual images . . . [that] conjure portentous themes appropriate to the genre'. But Shakespeare's comedies have not proved as appealing to filmmakers, and such films of the comedies as do exist have generally been constrained by commercial imperatives to 'make the medium as transparent as possible'; in films of the comedies, auteurs need not apply.[2] This expectation contrasts with what is anticipated of theatre audiences, who may be more likely to come to a performance

---

1 For a helpful overview of performance possibilities, see Findlay.
2 Michael Hattaway, 'The comedies on film' in Russell Jackson (ed.), *The Cambridge Companion to Shakespeare on Film*, 2nd edn, (Cambridge, 2007), 86–7, 92.

154

with a set of expectations about a director's interpretive and argumentative responsibilities. So the fact that there are two relatively proximate (as these things go) major film versions of *Much Ado About Nothing* is a truly unique circumstance among not merely the films of Shakespearean comedy, but all of the plays.

Famously now, Kenneth Branagh's 1993 film of *Much Ado* made a persuasive case for the commercial power of Shakespeare's plays in the multiplex. Like Baz Luhrmann's *Romeo + Juliet* (1996), the production's goal was to grasp the brass ring of the teenage demographic of moviegoers. Like his full-throated, rousing rendition of *Henry V*, Branagh's star-studded vision of *Much Ado* is a bumptious one, full of Mediterranean sunshine, tanned and physically striking celebrity actors in freshly starched linen exuding the dewy glow of youth and cavorting on the grounds of a gorgeously framed Italian villa whose own beauty did much to highlight the lighter side of the play. As in his subsequent Shakespearean filmography, Branagh here makes a case for translating Shakespeare's works into the specific language and history of film. His *Much Ado* coyly cites both *The Magnificent Seven* and *Singin' in the Rain*, while his use of the panoramic power of the crane shot conjures a sweeping perspective and lays claim to an idiom of cinematic grandeur. As is often the case with off-stage couples, in the casting of Beatrice and Benedick the (then) real-life couple Kenneth Branagh and Emma Thompson supercharged the sense of romantic history present in the play. The sole note of menace resided in Michael Keaton's inscrutable Dogberry, whose gurgled elocution of Shakespeare's words further insulted malapropism's prior injuries to intelligibility.[1]

Fast-forward twenty years and cue the cellos. Probably the most eye-catching production in any venue of recent times is the

---

1 For a discussion, see Samuel Crowl, 'Flamboyant realist: Kenneth Branagh' in *The Cambridge Companion to Shakespeare on Film* (Cambridge, 2007), 226–44.

2012 film directed by Joss Whedon, a screenwriter and director known for his work in popular film and television, much of which features strong female protagonists, e.g. 'Buffy the Vampire Slayer'; 'The Agents of Shield' (his *Avengers*, which also debuted in 2012, is the third-highest grossing film of all time). Like Branagh's cast, Whedon's included actors known to the director's youthful fan base from other contexts. (It should be noted that despite occasional critical scorn for the draws of celebrity casting, the 'small world' upshot of the digital universe in which many of us consume performance enables familiarity with the work of film and television actors in a range of roles, affording an experience of allusion and memory akin to that provided by repertory theatre companies.) Both films luxuriate in their settings. In the Branagh film the glamour of the villa conjures fantasy vacations in Tuscany; in Whedon's the lifestyles of the rich and famous relocate to the tony, sybaritic environs of Santa Monica CA, an upscale neighborhood of Los Angeles' Westside, where celebrity homes (or at least their security gates) are hunted by tourists. Cinematographer Jay Hunter shot the film in Whedon's own Spanish-style home over a period of twelve days, in an elegant black and white – an aesthetic as sleek as that of the smartphone that reports the capture of Don John.

This film also asks the viewer to think about the history and possibility of the medium, but where Branagh cites Sturges and Sinatra and the wide-open spaces of cinematic pastoral, Whedon asks us to think about Hitchcock and Welles – to attend to the covert possibilities of indoor eavesdropping and conspiratorial conversations. Whedon also makes use of flashbacks to fill in suggestions in the text about backstory or offstage events. Where the Branagh film is, literally, light-filled, the 2014 rendition is sombre – reflecting the director's understanding of the play as 'dark and manipulative and strange and cynical'.[1]

---

1 http://www.theskinny.co.uk/film/features/304769-joss_whedon_much_ado_
   about_nothing

Surveillance technology plays its part in creating the film's atmosphere: Don Pedro and his men arrive in a convoy of town cars with tinted windows, and seemingly hail from the world of modern-day military surveillance (á la Blackwater, Halliburton or the NSA), where terse security personnel pack concealed heat and lurk with headsets discreetly tucked behind ears. Dogberry and his crew oversee their charges from video screens in the home's security command center, and the outsized lens of the wedding photographer mimics the intrusions of other eyes. Many conversations are staged *sotto voce*, in groupings of two or three filmed in close-up in confined spaces. The camera makes fine conspiratorial use of the Chandleresque sightlines of the home's architecture and the eavesdropping potentials of its acoustics, with many scenes shot through windows, with the use of mirrors or other ostentatious framing devices – although a decision to open the French doors in the gulling of Alex Denisoff's Benedick would have soothed the viewer distracted by the question of him actually hearing the exchanges. The staging of Amy Acker's Beatrice's comparable scene, 3.1, where she tucks herself out of sight under the envious expanse of a granite kitchen island, is more successful. Many productions seek to alleviate the repetition factor and the formal tenor of the verse in Beatrice's gulling scene with assaults on an actress' physical dignity. This version, however, is less gag-ridden than 2.3 is for Benedick, despite being prefaced by a tumble down a flight of stairs from which it seems unlikely even the most avid eavesdropper would recover without a stint in hospital.

In interviews Whedon claimed that in his stylistic choices he sought to cultivate an air of 'Kennedyesque' glamour: 'We referred to Leonato's estate as the Kennedy compound, the idea that everybody looks fabulous, is fabulous, is having a martini at noon'.[1] But it could also be argued that the noir palette, the

---

1   http://www.vulture.com/2013/06/joss-whedon-much-ado-about-nothing-interview.html

Hitchcockian use of aspects of the house, Denisoff's passing resemblance from some angles to Jimmy Stewart, and the cut of the dresses of the female characters echo the tropes of 1930s and 40s 'screwball comedy' films. In this choice the film brings to the fore a potential often noted in *Much Ado's* genetic influence upon subsequent romantic comedy.

Literary and film historians have long remarked upon the resemblances between the Beatrice and Benedick pairing and the sparring couples in the comedic films starring actors such as Katharine Hepburn and Spencer Tracy, often depicted wrangling their way back into love amidst what Stanley Cavell describes as settings of 'unmistakable wealth; the people in them have the leisure to talk about human happiness, hence the time to deprive themselves of it unnecessarily'.[1] Cavell has dubbed such films the comedies of remarriage: 'the drive of this plot is not to get the central pair together, but to get them back together, again . . . the genre of remarriage [undertakes] to show how the miracle of change may be brought about and hence life together between a pair seeking divorce become a marriage.' He argues that leisured settings – which possessed a special charisma in the years of the Depression – and energetic conversation between a central pair are essential to the utopian function of such films: 'we can expect the characters in them to take the time, and take the pains, to converse intelligently and playfully about themselves and about one another'.[2] Also crucial to the genre's composition is a strong female character, which Cavell sources to the unacknowledged feminist history of post-depression years.[3] Conspiring circumstantially to the genre's emergence were the technological innovation of sound and the fortuitous provision of a crop of actresses such as Hepburn,

1 Cavell, 5.
2 Ibid.
3 Ibid, 17–18.

Claudette Colbert, Irene Dunne, Rosalind Russell, and Barbara Stanwyck: 'all around thirty years old as the genre is forming itself, neither young nor old, experienced but still hopeful'.[1]

Cavell famously traces the debt of these films to Shakespearean comedy and romance. Yet he does not cite *Much Ado* as an influence, despite the fact that it arguably possesses in Beatrice and Benedick an almost textbook case of mutual acknowledgement through discourse. Given the hints of a previous and soured romantic history between Beatrice and Benedick, it also hews most closely among Shakespeare's plays (with the exception perhaps of *The Winter's Tale*) to a portrait of remarriage – and, of course, Hero and Claudio head to the altar not once but twice. Descriptions of Beatrice in the company of mercurial goddesses ('an infernal Ate in good apparel' (2.1.234)) prefigure heroines such as *The Philadelphia Story*'s heiress Tracy Lord (Hepburn), who is chastised by Cary Grant's C.K. Dexter Haven for her Diana-like moral austerity. Of course, for all her claims to independence, Shakespeare's heroine is relatively constrained in her freedom, e.g. ultimately required to rely upon Benedick's assistance as a vehicle of her violent desires. What Cavell's citations reveal about our play is that *Much Ado* is not as lighthearted in tenor as the earlier comedies or as utopian as Shakespeare's romances, nor does its solution depend on a remove to an alternate location (even mercantilist Venice has a Belmont). It hence lacks a crucial element of Cavell's typology: 'A place in which perspective and renewal are to be achieved . . . a perspective that presents itself as a place, one removed from the city of confusion and divorce'. For Cavell, at least, 'this locale is called Connecticut'.[2]

---

1 Ibid, 18.
2 Ibid, 19, 49.

Seventy years on from the films he discusses, the site of new beginnings has, in typical American fashion, migrated westward. In what might be called an attempt to 'Connecticut-ize' his setting Whedon's film makes terrific use not only of his home's many creature comforts but its Southern California terraced garden, where nature both well-cultivated and lush serves as a backdrop to the moneyed Angeleno lifestyle. In the opening credits the camera travels up the virtually animate voluptuous folds of a coral tree in a manner that suggests we may be in a world of near-magical transformation. The ball scene of 2.1 transpires around an infinity pool and a firepit, with fairy lights twinkling in the treetops; the wedding is set on a hillside overlooking what could well be the greensward of either the Brentwood or the Palisades Riviera golf course, framed at one remove further by a verdant canyon vista (or so at least the black-and-white palette allows us to imagine what in fact, in colour, would have been revealed as drought-parched chaparral). In a sly local reference to workout-cum-mating habits of Santa Monica singles, the newly converted Benedick attempts to get fit by 'running the stairs' of the home's many-tiered grounds.

Ostentatiously modernizing productions always confront the task of how to translate the play's emotional concerns into the present day despite the differences between the sexual mores of an imaginary early modern Messina – where honour killing of one's daughter is, at the very least, not unspeakable – and our own allegedly less extreme moment. Of Claudio's rejection, Whedon said:

> 'he called off the wedding because he thought he saw her sleeping with another guy the night before the wedding. That's different than, "Are you a virgin?" That's, "Do you love me? Are you lying? Are you cheating on me? Is this a joke to you?" That's hurt and betrayal and jealousy, and I think that's very modern. I

don't think he's thinking about her hymen. It's the human, not the hymen.'[1]

In one of several tweaks to the script that work to soften the edges of Claudio's potentially unpleasant aspects, the 2.3 speech in which he states his intention to publicly humiliate Hero at the very altar is cut, and he responds to Don John's charges with physical assault. The latter's appearances are relatively fleeting, and the burden of the villainy shifts to the baby-faced Borachio, who acquires a motive beyond either service or lucre (Whedon again: 'the only way Borachio makes sense to me is if he's in love with Hero'.)[2]

In keeping with the effort to modernize the themes of sexual betrayal and disappointment, the film opens with an interpolated morning-after-the-hookup dumb show where Alex Denisoff's Benedick attempts to tiptoe out undetected from the bed of a Beatrice who only feigns sleep. The scene casts over the exchanges that follow the long shadows of our modern versions of confirmed bachelor and shrew: the commitment-phobic male and the woman whose mimicry of the vaunted sexual nonchalance of men masks the wounded heart of a woman scorned. During Beatrice's 2.1 speech to Don Pedro about her having once lent her heart to Benedick there is a flashback to the passionate, even tender lovemaking of this pre-play night. Continuing the theme of explicit eroticism, the casting of Conrade as a smoldering and sulky blonde converts the exchange about Don John's discontent into a form of foreplay ('if I had my mouth I would bite'), and adds a tone of menacing sexuality to the aura of material decadence.

This gender-switching casting choice somewhat dilutes the homosocial presence of the play's men's club, and the sexual

---

1   http://www.vulture.com/2013/06/joss-whedon-much-ado-about-nothing-interview.html.
2   Ibid.

freedom on display certainly obfuscates the self-explanatory power of bastardy as a motive for villainy, but for Whedon, 'I did like the idea that the only actual stable relationship in the movie is between the villains.'[1] The party scene of 2.1 is highly eroticized as well; the camera dwells on the embraces of a pair of female acrobats, and Beatrice fends off the paws of an anonymous drunken admirer while she taunts Benedick. The dawn after the party, even the otherwise unimpeacheable Ursula and Balthasar fondle each other in the kitchen, careless of nearby observers. The copious detritus of bottles and glasses throughout the home and grounds suggests that at some point during the night the ample host of maidservants abandoned their catering duties for pleasures more attractive. In some respects, the debauchery on display jars with the many references to the elegant social world and arch innuendo of the 1930s and '40s comedies; Hepburn and Grant these folks are not. This is perhaps 'Kennedy compound' as Chappaquiddick, rather than Hyannisport.

As has become standard performance practice, a 'window scene' is invented. This is also a sex scene, and also appears in flashback during Borachio's voice-over narration of it to Conrade in 3.4, intercut with shots of Claudio's dismayed reaction. The camera moves from the interior of the bedroom, where Margaret vamps under Borachio's direction in a series of Hero's dresses, to Claudio's vantage point, with its vision of Margaret-as-Hero and Borachio copulating in standing silhouette, Margaret with Hero's dress rucked up around her hips. There is a final cut back to the interior of the room and Margaret's face over Borachio's thrusting shoulder, a lost expression on her face. As well as serving to render Claudio's response sympathetic, this staging provides for a nice moment of scruple for Margaret's character in the following morning's wedding preparation scene. When the

1 Ibid.

latter prepares to don the dress in question, Margaret's insistence that 'your other dress [sic] were better' comes across as another morning-after repentant desire to direct Hero away from what is at the very least a figuratively soiled wedding gown.

Somewhat more difficult to situate in this sexually permissive climate is Leonato's wish in 4.1 that he and / or his daughter were dead – the sense that Hero's shame is his as much his own as hers (if not more so). His speech in the church scene is severely cut, and the scene ends with him tenderly embracing his daughter. To a lesser extent, the transformation of an honour culture into a world of hurt feelings also strains the intelligibility of Beatrice's lethal commission for Benedick. Absent a universe where a duel-by-combat is a plausible means either of avenging a lady's honour or establishing the truth, 'Kill Claudio' veers close to spite and vengeance. Much like Margaret's face in the window scene, Beatrice is shown speaking 'Kill Claudio' over Benedick's shoulder during an embrace, her mind far afield from his; the possibility of his comical double-take response to the request is wholly foreclosed.

More uneasily rendered in this climate of equal-opportunity sexual opportunism is Beatrice's frustration at the alleged limits her gender enforces upon her actions – although the delicate, almost ethereal frame of the actress does help emphasize a sense of her frailty, particularly dwarfed as she is by the much taller and broad-shouldered Benedick; in this performance, it is Leonato's niece who is short, Hero being a willowy head taller than her cousin. However, given the setting in a world where female agency seems relatively less fettered than we imagine it to have been four hundred years ago, and where it is hard to credit that an accusation of female disloyalty would amount to a sentence of social death, it is not entirely clear why Beatrice *requires* a champion.

In addition to the sidling by the question of female subordination, the contemporary American context seems nonplussed by the element of rank and consequent jockeying for position that permeates the social world of Shakespeare's text, or rather these are reshaped as youthful envy of the one-percenters on the part of the wannabes of their entourage. The actors playing Margaret, a prettily androgynous Borachio, and Conrade are younger even than Hero and Claudio. Margaret's black-and-white maid's costume sets her off from the company as an employee rather than lady's attendant (and excepting the rather unlikely Anglo casting of an LA maid, her social indeterminacy vis à vis the family nicely echoes the complicated relations of domestics and their employers in another Westside film, James L. Brooks' *Spanglish*). Antonio's role is eliminated, and with it the initial mis-noting of the proposal relayed by Antonio in 1.2, i.e. that Don Pedro intends to woo Hero for himself. This means that the advice of Beatrice to Hero in 2.1, that she say 'Father, as it please me', comes across as a generalized maxim in favour of personal choice rather than a suggestion that Hero resist her father's instructions for alliance with the highest-ranking visitor; this daddy is clearly on board with Claudio as a suitor from the outset.

Prominently substituting for what, in another setting, could be phrased as a function of social caste or homosocial rivalry are copious amounts of alcohol. Almost the very first shot of the film frames two empties amidst Beatrice's fallen lingerie; Don John's initial attempt to undermine Claudio's confidence occurs in the pool in the dawn hours following the party, where he and his companions swim up behind the besnorkled Claudio like two sharks and a malicious mermaid as he quaffs what must be his umpteenth martini; his wounded response is clearly formulated under this influence. Characters pour themselves a glass of wine or down a shot of tequila at nearly every turn. In one of the many publicity interviews he gave about the film, Whedon admitted his reliance on the explanatory function of alcohol:

> The reason there's so much drinking in *Much Ado* was
> that I read the text and I said, "These people are making

> incredibly silly decisions, they're at a party for the
> entire time" . . . there were also a couple of decisions,
> like, "This only makes sense if the people are drunk
> enough to decide this is a good idea."[1]

Nevertheless, much about this film is sexy and stylish; while there may be less effervescence in the exchanges of Benedick and Beatrice than there is in the champagne, their final union feels both tender and strong, a comedy of remarriage indeed.

Alcohol also served as the implied explanation of now-opaque human motives in other recent productions. The much-publicized West-End stage production at the Wyndham directed by Josie Rourke in the summer of 2011, with David Tennant and Catherine Tate (of *Dr. Who* fame) as the bickering couple, was set in a harshly-lit British navy outpost of Gibraltar styled with a 1980s Costa del Sol vibe; the soldiers arrive in crisp white dress uniforms, and members of the watch are retirees in combat fatigues. There was a coarse quality to the over-tanned and patently *nouveau-riche* members of Leonato's household. Tate's Beatrice had a hardened air (beer bottles and cigarettes); Hero was a bit of a sexpot. Margaret's impersonation of her mistress takes place (via bridal veil and flashing disco lights) during an extremely drunken bachelorette party, with Claudio, enjoying his own version of shore leave, hovering nearby. However, as the *Times* critic pointed out, 'It is hard to believe that a girl who had a hen night as raucous as Hero's would swoon at the altar when accused of wantonness.'[2] Claudio, for his part, mimes an attempted suicide in response to the deception, with alcohol also implied as a factor. The excesses of the wedding scene were consequently fueled by hangovers all round.

---

1   Ibid.
2   http://www.theguardian.com/culture/2011/jun/02/much-ado-david-tennant-catherine-tate

This production was notable for taking the cue of the Quarto stage directions and casting an Innogen figure in the place of uncle Antonio (is she aunt or distant stepmother?); however, there were few signs of contact between her and Hero, and her silent and immobile presence became downright distracting in the church scene. This choice was first rolled out in Rourke's Sheffield production in 2007, which also cast the members of the watch (with the exception of Hugh Oatcake) as female, a choice that made Leonato's failure to listen to Dogberry in 3.5 a function of sexism rather than tediousness.[1] Both gulling scenes were staged amidst painter's scaffolding for the new McMansion; Beatrice, typically, fared far worse than Benedick. While he merely ended up bedaubed with paint, she awkwardly managed to get herself tangled in the painter's rigging, and her responses to the dialogue of Hero and Ursula were obscured by the fact that she was for the majority of the scene hanging virtually upside down, limbs a-flailing. Tennant distinguished himself among the play's speakers of Shakespeare's language, with the drollery of his trademark Scottish intonation adding a further dissenting note to Benedick's scepticism about going the way of the world.

The award for most inebriated rendition of *Much Ado* in this period, however, needs to go to the play *Days of Significance,* commissioned by the RSC from playwright Roy Williams as part of a series of new plays set the task of responding to Shakespeare's works. Premiering at the Swan Theatre, Stratford-upon-Avon, in the winter of 2007, Williams' play transports vestigial versions of Shakespeare's characters to the setting of a provincial market town, where tensions about the Iraq war aggravate conventional standoffs between young men and women, and the college-bound and the dole-bound. There

1   Michael Dobson, 'Shakespeare performances in England and Wales', *Shakespeare Survey*, 59 (2007), 309.

is very little of Shakespeare's world left: Hannah's (Hero) betrayal of Jamie (Claudio) takes the form of her confiding his apprehensions about shipping out to Iraq to a girlfriend in the Ladies. The first scene takes place on the eve of some local soldiers' deployment to Iraq; the second in Iraq, during a shoot-out with the enemy; and the last at a boozy wedding back in England, where Jamie is facing a court-martial for having followed orders to 'prolong the shock of capture'.[1] 'Ben' is dead, and the foulmouthed and bereft 'Trish' seeks soused consolation in the arms of another. While inspiration would probably be the wrong word for the function of Shakespeare's model with respect to Williams' – not a shred of glamour remains, and the characters are virtually inarticulate rather than witty – Williams' play dwells powerfully on the homosocial military underbelly implicit in its predecessor, and the demands of that culture upon both manhood and morals. And certainly part of the harrowing effect of Williams' work is how it makes us feel the brutalizing loss of Shakespearean pleasures.

The translation of Shakespeare's plays to historical periods closer to our own is undoubtedly a genre-specific exercise. The histories, the roman plays, and the tragedies may have an easier time of it, given the perennial congruence of certain state and military formations. In such cases, part of the thrill of using Shakespeare's plays to probe the character of subsequent historical moments (why so seldom earlier?) relies on the continuities rather than differences between moments. Sexual politics can prove a bit trickier to 'update', however, for while fear of romantic commitment or the battle between the sexes may be just as persistent cultural formations, sexual equality is something we generally feel (or hope) separates us from the past, occasional evidence to the contrary notwithstanding. *Much Ado*'s simultaneous representation of institutionalized

---

1   *Days of Significance* (London, 2007), 70

misogyny and a vociferous feminist protest against it offers a challenging blend of elements that, while hardly unique, nevertheless can be deceptively difficult to update. Efforts to emphasize the brutality of the sexual politics often jeopardize the play's vision of romantic promise.

Instructive in this company of contemporizing productions was a performance directed by Jeremy Herrin at the reconstructed Globe during the same summer of 2011 as the Tennant / Tate vehicle at the Wyndham. The Globe's calling card lies in its attempts to reimagine allegedly authentic early modern performance conditions. The tenor of this production, set in Morocco, was broad and bawdy (as opposed to sexy); the open-air stage meant that most lines were delivered at a nearly bellowed pitch, which meant that the stagy and operatic qualities of the church scene shone through. In wearing its patriarchal mores less self-consciously than some modernized productions, there was less insistence on the towel-snapping aspects of militarism, which meant in some respects that the strain of feminist resistance came through more clearly. Ony Uhiara's Hero was in many moments as feisty as her cousin.[1] In an interesting twist on the epitaph scene which neatly answered many a production's desire to have a semi-concealed Hero witness her suitor's contrition, Claudio sung his song – supported by a chorus of his fellows – to the bier (allegedly) bearing Hero's body. Eve Best's Beatrice was a sometimes barefoot, gangly, rumpled-haired eccentric, in contrast to Charles Edward's rather debonair Benedick; in the words of Carol Chillington Rutter, 'feisty and spiky, pained and rueful, outrageous and maddening, gawky, frequently graceful, very, very funny, and ultimately

---

1   For a discussion that highlights Hero's agency in the play, see Diana Henderson, 'Mind the gaps: the ear, the eye, and the senses of a woman in *Much Ado About Nothing*' in Lowell Gallagher and Shankar Raman (eds), *Knowing Shakespeare: Senses, Embodiment and Cognition* (Basingstoke and New York, 2010).

wonderful'.[1] As this description suggests, reviewers were generally kinder to this production than the Wyndham's, citing its warmth and buoyancy in comparison with the brittle surfaces of the 'celebrity' vehicle.

A far more cheerful version of this play than any of these was that directed by Brian Percival for the 2005 BBC series *Shakespeare Retold*. The setting is a provincial Wessex newsroom, with no military in sight – albeit much laddishness. Beatrice and Benedick (Sarah Parish and Damien Lewis) are mutually hostile co-anchors reunited on camera three years after Benedick stood her up; 'Claud' (Tom Ellis) is a puppyish sportscaster; and Hero (Billie Piper) the toothsome weather girl and daughter of the show's producer Leonard (Martin Jarvis). The eavesdropping deftly takes place via television monitor and (once again) a bathroom stall in the Ladies; an overzealous, portly, yet curiously dignified security guard provides a modern Dogberry ('I'm only 5'4 – just this much more [height] and I'd have been out there on a stakeout.'). The villain is 'Don' (Derek Riddle), a former beau of Hero (as is the case in Shakespeare's sources), who in the beginning of the story is demoted from his position as executive producer due to drinking on the job. His stalker-like conduct erupts when he overhears at a party that she only slept with him during their brief fling out of pity; he perpetrates his deception via stolen photos and forged text messages.

Like Whedon's film, this one begins with an opening credit sequence that shows where Beatrice and Benedick went wrong prior to the events of the play. The camera cuts back and forth between them as they appear to be preparing for a date with each other: Benedick sprays aftershave down his pants; Beatrice strews rose petals on her bed and then, grimacing, hoovers

---

1 Carol Chillington Rutter, 'Shakespeare performance in England and Wales' *Shakespeare Survey*, 65 (2013), 455.

them up with a handvac. It turns out, however, that Benedick is headed to the airport, texting his regrets to Beatrice awaiting him in an expensive restaurant ('no hard feelings!'). At the show's conclusion, they meet again at the same table, where Beatrice tartly replies to Benedick's query about whether he is late with: 'only about three years'.

Ron Kerrigan's script does a deliciously clever job of mixing elements of Shakespeare's text with rephrasings in a modern idiom (such as Benedick's soliloquy: 'love is just one of those things a man grows into, like jazz, or olives . . .'; Beatrice to Benedick, *sotto voce*, as the cameras begin to roll: 'You really do put the "w" in anchorman'; Leonard to Beatrice, trying to convince her that Benedick will be good for ratings: 'All the housewives love him.' 'They're called women, Leonard.' 'Well, the women all love him.' 'Not all the women, Leonard – not all.'). Lewis plays Benedick as a bit of a dandy, hoping that a hipster goatee and dreams of the BBC will propel him far from his ignominious beginnings as a late-night antiques show and children's television host. Beatrice is hands-down the intellect of the pair, and repeatedly typed by other characters as that notorious pant-suited career woman in her mid-thirties whose odds of being hit by a bus are higher than her chance of romantic happiness (Margaret, in Beatrice's gulling scene: 'That Katharine Hepburn ice-queen act won't be so pretty in five years' time.'). When reluctantly enlisted as best man and matron of honour to the younger couple, they luminously come together as Beatrice helps Benedick to interpret Sonnet 116, which he thinks, bless him, will prove a novel choice of nuptial reading. The pretext for the gulling is not that the two smartest people in the room are the only possible match for each other, but that if something isn't done to rein in their hostility the show will not go on.

This rendition is undoubtedly the most successful of recent efforts when it comes to modernizing the darker themes of sexual betrayal without jeopardizing Shakespeare's light touch.

'Kill Claudio' is uttered by a Beatrice miserable for her friend and scandalized that none of the men present in the church came to her defence; when she walks out of the frame Benedick responds not by promising to challenge Claudio to a duel but to make all right again. The character of Hero is the most thoroughly transformed in the translation. After recovering from a coma suffered as a result of her flying into an attack upon Don – a coma that permits him a version of the epitaph scene at her hospital bedside – she tells a repentant Claudio that she cannot, in fact, forgive him, making the very apt point that had he really loved her he would never have treated her as he did. Nevertheless, the story concludes with the wedding of a giggling Benedick and Beatrice, with the latter transformed by her wedding gown into the spitting image of that more ladylike Hepburn, Audrey. Meanwhile best man Claud and maid of honour Hero cast sweet looks at each other across the aisle. Some endings are hard to resist.

* * *

MORE ADO ABOUT CUCKOLDS

In concentrating on the more sombre elements of the play, these recent productions find themselves in accord with the work of much latter-day scholarship, which has tended to focus on excavating the historical prompts for Shakespeare's ideas in early modern social and political history.[1] The bent of recent

---

1   See, for instance, Philip Collington, 'A "pennyworth" of marital advice: bachelors and ballad culture in *Much Ado About Nothing*,' in Karen Bamford (ed.), *Shakespeare's Comedies of Love: Essays in Honor of Alexander Leggatt*, (Toronto, 2008), 30–54, and ' "Stuffed with all honourable virtues": *Much Ado About Nothing* and the Book of the Courtier,' *Studies in Philology*, 103, no. 3 (2006), 281–312; Clegg; Wright, N., 'The legal interpretation of defamation in Shakespeare's *Much Ado About Nothing*', *Ben Jonson Journal*, 13 (2006), 281–312; Bronfen; Fleck.

generations of Shakespearean scholars towards cultural history, the search in such history for the *gravitas* of political struggle, the consequent critical attraction to plays that explicitly treat social contest, and the lack in *Much Ado* of what is generally agreed upon to be the politically redeeming feature of an otherwise quiescent genre – the politically subversive 'green world' – have combined to direct critical attention towards the sobering slander material rather than the romantic delights of minds and hearts well-matched. Combined with the prevalent taste for 'edgy' rather than idealizing productions, and the tendency to associate modernization with disenchantment, such trends mean that the tonal qualities of the Hero and Claudio story have come to absorb and overshadow the possibility of making love rather than war promised by the prospect of wits well matched. In previous decades (even centuries), the Beatrice and Benedick plot largely eclipsed the rest of the play's offerings, and this continues to be the case in the less intellectually glamorous summer festival circuit; now, at least in these high-profile performances, the reverse is true. The upshot of this trend is that in watching this play in recent years it can sometimes be difficult to believe in love at all.

The convention of editorial neutrality behooves circumspection about such trends, and the citation of 'original historical meanings' in order to scold interpretations is what gives editors and scholars a bad name. But editors, despite having more reasons than most to know there is no such thing as the Platonic ideal form of their play, may also have more reasons than most to treasure a mind's-eye version of it (for me in this case, it is best expressed by the 1984 RSC Terry Hands production, starring Derek Jacobi and Sinéad Cusack as Benedick and Beatrice, although this enchantment may well have something to do with the fact that it was also the first Shakespeare performance my nineteen-year-old self had ever seen.) That said, in the cause of advocating for the play's joyful elements,

I believe it worth calling attention to some previously unacknowledged historical information that may serve to bring back into focus the play's lighter side. It also further clarifies the grounds for Shakespeare's fondness for the cuckoldry *topos*, that plot designed around the self-suspecting male who discovers himself, for good or for ill – which is to usually say in time or too late – to be mistaken in his conjectures about sexual loyalty.[1]

Much recent scholarship on Shakespeare's plays has been concerned with the consequences of the seismic effects of the Reformation in English society. I would suggest that a number of pressing cultural questions of a religious nature could be said to resonate with *Much Ado About Nothing*. For instance, the preoccupation of the play's characters with possessing advantageous knowledge at others' expense recalls similar concerns provoked by predestination, that theological doctrine which decreed that an individual's salvation was known to God, humans meanwhile labouring under an epistemological disadvantage with respect to this very intimate information. In many respects, the fear of cuckoldry bears many of the same epistemological markers as the quest to know salvation; both 'am I loved?' and 'am I saved?' concern a domain proper to the self and in which a person's self-recognition depends mightily upon another's estimate. Similarly, the play's focus on the difficulty of fixing and interpreting meanings – manifest in the verbal sparring of Benedick and Beatrice; in Dogberry's inadvertent mangling of terms; in Borachio's power to misrepresent Hero's actions; and in the contested readings of her blush in the church scene – recalls the ambivalent burden of soteriological thought, which urged the sinner to examine his life for the evidence of salvation in one breath even as it

---

1   For a fuller discussion of these materials, see McEachern.

cautioned him to beware of the 'carnal' interpretations of the human mind in the next.

Such points of contact still concern what might be thought of as the 'darker' aspects of *Much Ado*, as well as of Reformation religion, i.e. their shared anxieties about the difficulties of knowing and being known about, or loving and being loved. Scholarship has, in fact, considered cuckold humour as a comical release of, or displacement for, some ulterior social anxiety. For instance, the horn has been glossed as 'a metaphor of labor and economic relationships defined by gender' or as 'a complex analogy to theatrical performance and response that tends to conceive of theatrical experience in erotic terms'.[1] If we wished to add Reformation religious concerns to such a list, we could consider Actaeon's story a resonant instance for a culture concerned with knowing and noting in the following ways: as a mortal condemned by a deity for reasons beyond his ken, trapped in the mute form of a beast unable to make himself known to his hounds, Actaeon expresses a terror of mistaken identity, one that reprobation may bespeak as well. In this light, the Ovidian source of the cuckold mythos presents a rich site for humanist syncretism.

However, not only is the tragic story tonally at odds with much cuckold humour, but Actaeon's form is anatomically discrepant from that of most cuckolds. He sports not a ox's horns but a stag's antlers, and it is only possible, in Benedick's phrase, to 'wear [one's] cap with suspicion' (1.1.187) if the horns in question will fit under a cap. Actaeon is a man first mystified by having become the prey of his hounds, who then discovers that he *does* have horns; that is, he is relieved of one mystery (why he can run so swiftly) only to be

---

1 Bruster, 195–215, 198; Maus, 561–83, 563.

confounded by a greater (why has the goddess done this to him). By contrast, many of Shakespeare's plays dramatize the plight of a man who erroneously suspects he has horns, but then discovers he does *not*. Depending on what events have transpired during the period of benighted belief, dénoument comes to the deluded either as a relief (Claudio) or a horror (Othello).

These discrepancies cry out for a cultural provocation for horns somewhat more homegrown than Ovid, one that might explain both the bovine anatomy of the Elizabethan cuckold as well as what early modern authors and audiences may have found so genuinely funny about him – a figure not just to laugh *at*, but to laugh *with*. As it so happens, there was in the Reformation another instance of a horned human whose horns result from an encounter with a deity, an individual whose plight may help to explain the cultural roots and comic power of the figure of the self-suspecting-but-ultimately-mistaken cuckold.

Throughout much of what we now term medieval Christianity, Moses travels as a horned man. This is due to Jerome's notorious Vulgate translation of the Hebrew 'qeren' (Exodus 34:29), or 'rayed' as 'cornuta' (as in the translation of the Douai-Rheims bible: 'And when Moses came down from the mount Sinai, he held the two tables of the testimony, and he knew not that his face was horned from the conversation of the Lord.')[1] Michaelangelo's sculpture is the most famous commemoration of this metamorphosis, and visual representations are common in medieval manuscripts and other iconographic sites. Ruth Mellinkoff's 1970 study of the visual tradition argues that the visual literalization of the horn as an organic outgrowth of Moses' own head initially appears in fact in an English context,

1   Martin (Sig. Hhr).

in the eleventh-century *Aelfric Paraphrase*.[1] The choice of horns to visually represent Jerome's metaphor is, she suggests, likely to have been influenced by the iconographic conventions of helmet-horned chieftains in the Scandanavian legacy of pre-conquest Britain, in which the horn functions as a sign of power. Jerome's translation is thus not a mistranslation of the Hebrew, but a reasoned choice of the metaphor that best figures the way in which Moses was rayed with light (recall the discussion above p. 48 about the ancient uses of horn as a light-conducting material). This figure is then literalized by the tradition of visual representation pitched towards a lay audience – a picture-perfect instance, as it were, of what Protestantism would later come to criticize about the over-literalizing iconic visualizations of Roman Catholic practice.

Moses' horns are, in their original incarnation, a sign of strength and power. His metamorphosis comes in the wake of his second visit to Sinai, when, troubled by the backsliding idolatrous tendencies of the Israelites, he asks God for a token that will convince them to forsake their golden calf and return to the one true God: 'I beseech thee that thou will go with us (for it is a stiff-necked people) and take away our iniquities and sins, and possess us.' God promises him that 'I will do signs that were never seen upon the earth, nor in any nations: that this people may see, in the midst of whom thou are, the terrible work of the Lord which I will do.'[2] The sign is Moses himself; the transformation of his appearance is designed to awe, terrify and convince.

Yet Moses' horns also carry a disturbing cachet. When he returns to the Israelites, Moses is unwitting of his transfiguration: 'he knew not that his face was horned by the conversation of the talk of our Lord. And Aaron and the children of Israel seeing

---

1 Mellinkoff.
2 *The Geneva Bible* (London, 1599), (Sig. E2r).

the face of Moses horned, they were afraid to come near.' Like Bottom greeted by his fellow mechanicals ('Bless thee, Bottom, thou art translated!'), or Actaeon cued by his hounds' bloodlust to the fact that he has become unrecognizable, Moses' self-knowledge is reflected back to him in the faces of his fellows. That his horns disturb others and perhaps even Moses himself is revealed by the fact that henceforth, quite unlike the nonchalant Bottom, he veils himself except when speaking to God. We might say he henceforth wears his cap with suspicion.

As Mellinkoff details, as Christianity sought over the course of the medieval period to distance itself from its parent religion, the negative connotations of the horn began to take precedence over the positive. In time Moses' veiled horns come to represent not only the inability of the children of Israel to accurately perceive the law, but the limitations of the Old Testament and the Law itself: 'At least in the thinking of some, Moses seems to have been guilty by association or transferred identity.'[1] Originally a token of privileged immediacy to the divine, a souvenir of the time when God went about giving face-to-face meetings, Moses' horns become the mark of shame, a sign of eclipsed belief – that which is outdated and superseded (just as many a cuckold was December to his wife's May?). By the end of the sixteenth century, horns are fully stigmatized, changing from a mark of their (fore-?)bearer's spiritual superiority to his inadequacy. To be horned is not so much to be cuckolded as it is to believe the wrong thing.

As we approach closer in time to Shakespeare's moment, the Reformation's process of confessional differentiation delivers yet another turn in the story of the horn's power to denote errant belief. The shift in the horn's associations begins with the Wycliffe bible, where the figurative usage implicit in Jerome's term is restored: 'he wist not that his faced was *horned of*

---

1   Mellinkoff, pp.125–8.

the fellowship of God's word'.[1] With Tyndale this becomes 'he wist not that his face *shone with beams of his commening* with the Lord', and by Coverdale, 'Moses wyst not that the skin of his face *shone in manner of an horn*, while he talked with him'. With the Geneva Bible the horn disappears completely: 'now Moses wist not that the skinne of his face shone bright, after that God had talked with him'.[2] The Douai Rheims Bible of the later sixteenth century retains 'horned' without a modifying claim (as Catholic bibles do to this day), but by 1609 its own marginal note also refiguralizes the horn: 'So his face appeared to the beholders, by reason of the glistering beams of his countenance shining gloriously, after his conversation with God forty days.'[3] By 1550, then, Moses has been relieved of his horns by Protestant philologians seeking to strip away the veil of the Vulgate in order to rebuke the carnal superstition of their own rival and parent religion. Or, as Shakespeare might have put it, 'Bless thee, Moses, thou art *re*-translated!' Unlike Actaeon's tragic horns, then, Moses' horns are only a temporary aberration, something not only to be laughed at, but, ultimately, off.

My point here is not that original audiences of *Much Ado* would have thought about Moses's horns whenever they heard a cuckold joke. But I would argue that the story of mistaken belief corrected – exemplified by an embarrassed patriarch relieved after a period of benighted belief of his suspected and secret shame – was a particularly charged one for Reformation audiences, in which case the original bearers of the cuckold's horns included not just Actaeon or Diana, but Moses. In fact, for the unlettered among Shakespeare's audience, their reputation was more likely to be indebted to the iconographic

---

1   Forshall and Madden, p.277.
2   Tyndale, Sig. Siiiiv; Coverdale Sig. Siiir; *The Bible* (1599), Sig. E2v.
3   Martin, Sig. Hhr.

traditions available in bible plates and – to cite Borachio – 'old church window[s]'. Like a cuckold, Moses is the last to know he is horned; he finds out from his neighbours and seeks to conceal his horns from public view; so too in the middle ages, Judaism, like an old husband, finds its place usurped by a more youthful contender (note Borachio's emphasis on the outmoded idolatry of the *old* church window and the *reechy* – i.e. smoke-begrimed – painting). Most of all, however, like a man relieved of his erroneous belief, Moses is eventually and presumably joyfully restored to his original form.

The story of misbegotten belief set to rights is of course an ancient one for drama, but this material suggests that the spectacle of a man misled, as Claudio is, by the combination of his own fears and undue confidence in the powers of sense perception is a plot point with both perennial and local as well as *joyful* power for the Elizabethan moment.

More specifically still, the analogue may help to shed light upon a passage that has puzzled modern editors, namely, Borachio's drunken citation of the idolatrous priests of the dragon god Bel in support of his point about fickle fashion's deforming transformations of the body's visual appearance ('sometimes fashioning [young men] like Pharoah's soldiers in the reechy painting, sometimes like god Bel's priests in the old church window' (3.3.129–31)). Editorial tradition has struggled to make sense of what seems at best an inebriated form of free-association. However, like *Much Ado*, the story of Daniel and Bel's priests is a story of nocturnal gullers caught out by shrewd forensic methods: seeking to prove to King Cyrus that his sumptuously attired priests are deceitful and their god a mere idol, Daniel sprinkles ashes around the offerings to the idol, and the following morning is able to point to the captured footprints as evidence that the greedy priests themselves consumed the offerings in order to perpetrate the hoax of the god's power. Dogberry is certainly no Daniel; his malapropisms render words virtually unrecognizable. But not unlike reformist philologians returning words to their original meanings, he and his watch nonetheless manage (with a little help from the Sexton), to unmask the makers of false reputations, in which case Borachio here unwittingly provides a foreshadowing of his own undoing.

In other words, the plot of mistaken belief overturned may help us to recover a more joyful link between the experience of the play's two couples and their cultural context: instead of viewing them as linked in tragic terms – in a concern with slander, or the ways in which societal pressures enforce conformity upon romantic choice, or epistemological anxieties – we might consider how both pairs of lovers undergo conversion experiences in which former prejudices are cast off, false beliefs are exchanged for true ones, as the parties concerned feel themselves recognized for who they truly are ('May I be so converted and see with these eyes?'(2.3.21–2)). In short, in addition to anticipating modern critiques of authority, both plots turn on the miracles of repair and forgiveness, both of which *require* disappointment in order to woo wisely rather than too well; *only* love tested is love true. While the idea of conversion may have less religious currency in our own moment than it did in Shakespeare's, the power of love to transform a heart retains its appeal.

This native history of the horn also helps to explain an important and, to our ears, often perplexing feature of cuckold humour, namely, the inclusiveness of the condition (recall Benedick's closing words to Don Pedro: 'Prince, thou art sad – get thee a wife, get thee a wife! There is no staff more reverend than one tipped with horn.' (5.4.120–22)). Certainly, one way to hear the assumption that, by definition, to be married is to be cuckolded is as a species of gallows humour. But the universal haplessness of the human condition – our vulnerability not only to the deceits of others but our own self-deceit – is a tenet of all Christian confessions. Particularly in Protestantism, acknowledgement of one's own insufficiencies is the first and necessary step on the path to salvation. Cuckold jokes fly fast and thick in the closing moments of *Much Ado* in a manner that, especially to modern ears, resounds rather sourly with the thinly-veiled and bitter one-upmanship, mutual suspicion and rivalry among men that provokes the trouble in Messina to begin with. Hero's acceptance of a grudgingly contrite Claudio ('nor sinned I not but in mistaking' (5.1.264–65)) has proven difficult for audiences to bless. But we can also hear something reassuring, maybe even redemptive, in these invocations of the alleged universality of the temporary cuckold experience, not only in the hopeful spectacle of otherwise inscrutable vices made visible, but in the reminder of the common condition of human vulnerability before God. As Moses' example exhibits, mistaken belief can happen to the best of us. In its celebration of cuckoldry's erosion of boundaries between people – cuckolds and cuckolds-in-waiting, your wife and your neighbour – *Much Ado*'s horn humour may even signal an effort to elide the differences between pre- and post-Reformation religions.

MUCH ADO
ABOUT NOTHING

LIST OF ROLES

THE SOLDIERS

DON PEDRO	*Prince of Aragon*	
DON JOHN	*illegitimate brother to Don Pedro*	
Signor BENEDICK	*a lord of Padua*	
Signor CLAUDIO	*a lord of Florence*	
BALTHASAR	*an attendant to Don Pedro*	5
CONRADE		
BORACHIO	*companions to Don John*	
LORD		

THE HOUSEHOLD OF THE GOVERNOR OF MESSINA

LEONATO	*Governor of Messina*	
ANTONIO	*brother to Leonato*	10
HERO	*daughter to Leonato*	
BEATRICE	*niece to Leonato*	
MARGARET		
URSULA	*waiting women to Hero*	
BOY		15

TOWNSPEOPLE OF MESSINA

FRIAR Francis		
DOGBERRY	*master constable*	
VERGES	*a headborough*	
Members of the WATCH		
George SEACOAL		
Hugh Oatcake	*members of the Watch*	20
Francis Seacoal, *a* SEXTON		

OTHERS

MESSENGERS

Attendants, Musicians

LIST OF ROLES   Rowe's was the first edition (1709) to list the characters, classifying them according to both rank and gender.

1   DON PEDRO   The *Prince of Aragon* hails from a region in north-west Spain, unlike his followers, who are Italian. Messina, a port city of north-east Sicily, was under Spanish rule in Shakespeare's time. The Quarto entry SDs often list him merely as '*Prince*', or '*Prince Pedro*'; these have been emended to Don Pedro throughout.

2   DON JOHN   Don John's bastard status is not voiced in the play until 4.1.188, though he is designated in Q's SPs as such, and bears telling character traits typical of literary bastards (see 1.1.90.2n.) Unlike the villains of his sources, Shakespeare's villain is not a rival lover of Hero.

3   **Signor** BENEDICK   Benedick's name derives from *benedictus* or *benedict*, he who is blessed, or a blessing; etymologically, it also refers to a good saying or one of 'good speech' (*bene dicte*), perhaps an apt name for one known for verbal dexterity. Padua was a commune of north-east Italy to the west of Venice, renowned for its university – 'nursery of arts', according to *TS* (1.1.2).

4   **Signor** CLAUDIO   Claudio's youth is mentioned several times in the text, and he shares his name with other of Shakespeare's young lovers, notably *MM*'s unfortunate swain; the name was derived from the Roman Claudii, a family of despotic fame; in Shakespeare's Bandello source, 'Sir Timbreo de Cardona'. Florence was known in Elizabethan England for its trade and cultured and ostentatious power.

5   BALTHASAR   Shakespeare also uses the name in *CE*, *MV* and *RJ*. The Folio substitutes the name of '*Iacke Wilson*' in the entry direction at 2.3.34.1–2; though this was a common name, at least two men have been identified as possible candidates for the performances which may have provided the copy-text for F (neither would have been old enough for the original performances, though some other Jack Wilson may have served). The first is John

Wilson (1595–1674), who graduated as Doctor of Music at Oxford in 1644 and became Professor of Music in 1656 (see Rimbault). Cam[1] identifies him with 'Mr. Wilson the singer', who was a guest at Edward Alleyn's 28th wedding anniversary, 22 October 1620.

6   CONRADE   by his own account (4.2.15), a gentleman

7   BORACHIO   The name derives from the Spanish word for 'drunkard' (*borracho*, from the term for a leather wine bottle); cf. '*Bourrachon:* A tipler, quaffer, tossepot, whip-canne; also little Bourrachoe' (Cotgrave). See Thomas Middleton, *The Spanish Gypsy* (1625), 1.1.2–8: '*Diego:* Art mad? / *Roderigo:* Yes, not so much with wine . . . I am no Borachio . . . mine eye mads me, not my cups' (Middleton, 6.118).

8   LORD   This person is identified in Q only in the SPs in 5.3; it is unclear whether he is associated with Leonato's household or the soldierly contingent.

9   LEONATO   The governor of the Sicilian city of Messina would have been a medium fish in a small pond. In Shakespeare's Bandello source, 'Messer Lionato de' Lionati' is of significantly lesser rank than his daughter's suitor. Benedick describes him at 2.3.120 as the 'white-bearded fellow'.

10   ANTONIO   is referred to in Q's SDs / SPs as '*old man*' / '*Old*', and (by 5.1) '*Brother*' or '*Bro.*' He appears to live either with or adjacent to his brother Leonato (he refers to the garden where much of the play's action takes place as *mine orchard,* 1.2.8–9). While he is described as having a son in 1.2, no such person appears in the play.

11   HERO   The name was notorious from Christopher Marlowe's poem *Hero and Leander* (1598), where it belongs to a priestess of Venus who forsakes her vestal duties for her lover. In George Chapman's continuation of Marlowe's unfinished poem, when Leander drowns on Hero's behalf, she returns the compliment; thus she is a figure

of a complicated sexual loyalty, and an overriding devotion. Her counterpart in Bandello is Fenicia (from 'phoenix', a bird noted for its capacities of resurrection). See also 4.1.79n.

12 BEATRICE from the Latin Beatrix, for 'one who blesses'; in Elizabethan pronunciation probably *Bettris* or *Betteris* (as metre requires)

13 MARGARET based on the gentlewoman Dalinda of Ludovico Ariosto's *Orlando Furioso* (1532), waiting lady to the princess Genevra, and lover of Polynesso; the latter, ambitious of Genevra's hand in marriage and desirous of separating her from her own beloved Ariodante, persuades Dalinda to dress in her mistress's clothes (on the pretence that he can then imagine himself Genevra's lover and exorcise his love for her), and arranges to have Ariodante view their assignation.

14 URSULA spelled Ursley (e.g. 3.1.4) and so pronounced

15 BOY appears only in 2.3

17 DOGBERRY from the decidedly English rustic botanical name for the fruit of the wild cornel or dogwood, a common shrub. Perhaps played in the Lord Chamberlain's Men by the hearty and nimble actor of clown roles Will Kemp, prior to his departure from

the company in 1599. See 3.3.0.1n. on *constable*, and p. 134.

18 VERGES (1) from the dialect form of verjuice, the sour juice of unripe grapes of the agresto vine (one upon which the ripe fruit and flowers appeared simultaneously), and perhaps a reference to the lean physiognomy of the actor Richard Cowley, who first played the role; (2) an oblique reference to the Court of the Verge (responsible for policing trespasses within 12 miles of the royal person); (3) a reference to the verge, the staff associated with the office of constable, upon which the latter would presumably lean. A headborough is a parish officer one rank below constable.

19 Members of the WATCH This neighbourhood citizen patrol is composed of at least four officers (see 3.3.0.2n.), two of whom are named in the play (see 20, 21n.).

20,21 George SEACOAL and Hugh Oatcake northern provincial British names

22 SEXTON Francis Seacoal, also called 'town clerk' (4.2.0.2). A sexton was a minor church official.

23 MESSENGERS There are three SPs for a messenger in the play, in 1.1, 3.5 and 5.4. They need not be the same person; the one who appears in 1.1 seems to be of the military party.

MUCH ADO ABOUT NOTHING

[1.1] *Enter* LEONATO, Governor of Messina,
HERO *his daughter and* BEATRICE *his niece,*
with a Messenger.

LEONATO I learn in this letter that Don Pedro of Aragon
comes this night to Messina.

MESSENGER He is very near by this. He was not three
leagues off when I left him.

LEONATO How many gentlemen have you lost in this   5
action?

1.1 Act divisions originate with F (from the Blackfriars' practice of breaking continuous action into parts punctuated by musical intervals); scene divisions (apart from F's '*Actus Primus, Scena prima*') were enumerated by eighteenth-century editors. The early texts do not designate locations; Pope was the first to do so. A courtyard, garden or entryway before Leonato's dwelling is a typical production choice, and Don Pedro's greeting – 'are you come to meet your trouble?' (91–2) – implies that Leonato encounters his guests near the threshold of his home. Antonio's reference to *mine orchard* (1.2.8–9) as the site of the conversation between Don Pedro and Claudio which concludes this scene further suggests that it is a verdant space, and that its architecture may contain a structure conducive to eavesdropping (but see 1.3.54–9 for confusions on this score). Productions often use this opening scene to

set the tone; choices have included aristocratic splendour, military milieu and rural idyll. See pp. 102–5.

0.1 *LEONATO . . . Messina** Q also lists '*Innogen his wife*' after Leonato, in this SD and at the entrance to 2.1, although she is given no lines. Beginning with Theobald in his 1733 edition, editorial tradition omits her. Theobald surmised that Shakespeare 'in his first plan designed such a character, which, on a survey of it, he found would be superfluous'. Some recent scholars however have suggested she be a silent presence in the play. See pp. 144–6.

1, 9 *Pedro** Q has *Peter* instead of the Spanish Pedro, or Bandello's Italian Piero.

1–2 Aragon . . . Messina See List of Roles, 1n.

3–4 three leagues a distance between 7 and 13 miles. The Messenger has ridden ahead of the troop to announce their arrival.

6   action battle

1.1] *Actus primus. Scena prima. F*   0.1–2 Messina, HERO] *Theobald (Leonato, Hero); Messina, Innogen his wife, Hero Q*   1, 9 Pedro] *Rowe; Peter Q*

187

MESSENGER   But few of any sort, and none of name.

LEONATO   A victory is twice itself when the achiever brings home full numbers. I find here that Don Pedro hath bestowed much honour on a young Florentine   10
called Claudio.

MESSENGER   Much deserved on his part, and equally remembered by Don Pedro. He hath borne himself beyond the promise of his age, doing in the figure of a lamb the feats of a lion; he hath indeed better bettered   15
expectation than you must expect of me to tell you how.

LEONATO   He hath an uncle here in Messina will be very much glad of it.

MESSENGER   I have already delivered him letters, and there appears much joy in him, even so much that joy   20
could not show itself modest enough without a badge of bitterness.

7   **sort** rank, reputation (see *MM* 4.4.18) or possibly kind, since *name* designates noble family. Cf. *H5* 4.8.74, where the king asks 'What prisoners of good sort are taken, uncle?' and later a recital of English casualties by rank concludes with 'None else of name, and of all other men / But five-and-twenty' (4.8.104–5). This is a verse line, although perhaps an involuntary or accidental one; or the Messenger could be attempting to initiate a more formal register, which Leonato declines to match.

8   **twice itself** double
    achiever victor

9   **full numbers** i.e. all the soldiers who set out to the battle

10–11 **young . . . Claudio** Leonato's comment could suggest that he is teasing his daughter with news of an admirer. Claudio's youth is emphasized here, and in the Messenger's reply.

12–13   **equally remembered** properly acknowledged, duly rewarded

14–15 **in . . . lion** The Messenger speaks, and Leonato replies, in the mannered

cadences of the 'euphuistic' style (noted for inversions and balanced syntactic structures; see pp. 68–73); such forms of verbal exchange serve as a way for the men in this play to create and recognize alliance. These lines and others like them are often cut in productions committed to a less mannered stylization of characters, or to moving the plot along more expeditiously.

15–16 **better bettered expectation** more than merely fulfilled his promise

17   **an uncle** No further reference to or appearance of this person occurs, though his mention can give a sense of a 'wider and more intimate background to the characters, and to create in us the illusion of lives and homes apart from the action of the stage' (Ard¹).

20–2 **that . . . bitterness** His happiness demanded some mark of sadness so that it would not seem excessive; a badge is 'a mark of service worn by the retainers of a nobleman' (Wright) (hence, a sign of subordination). For adverbial use of *much* see Abbott, 51.

LEONATO   Did he break out into tears?

MESSENGER   In great measure.

LEONATO   A kind overflow of kindness; there are no faces   25
truer than those that are so washed. How much better
is it to weep at joy than to joy at weeping!

BEATRICE   I pray you, is Signor Mountanto returned
from the wars or no?

MESSENGER   I know none of that name, lady; there was   30
none such in the army of any sort.

LEONATO   What is he that you ask for, niece?

HERO   My cousin means Signor Benedick of Padua.

MESSENGER   O, he's returned, and as pleasant as ever he
was.   35

BEATRICE   He set up his bills here in Messina and

---

24   i.e. copiously, although the term *measure*
also connotes a sense of (manly)
temperance

25   **kind ... kindness** natural show of family
feeling; cf. *Ham* 1.2.65: 'A little more than
kin, and less than kind.'

25–6   **no faces truer** 'that is, none honester,
none more sincere' (Johnson)

27   **weep ... weeping** an inversion typical of
the euphuistic style. Cf. *Mac* 1.4.33–5: 'My
plenteous joys, / Wanton in fulness, seek to
hide themselves / In drops of sorrow.'

28   **Signor Mountanto** i.e. Signor Upthrust,
from *montanto* or *montant*, a fencing
term for an upward thrust, as Capell first
recognized, citing Ben Jonson, *Every Man
in His Humour* (1598), 4.7.76–9: 'I would
teach [them] the special rules, as your
punto, your reverso, your stoccata, your
imbrocatto, your passada, your mountanto'
(Jonson, 3.262). The term implies a type of
overweening fashionable fencing-room
combat (akin to witty banter), rather than
doughty soldiership, and perhaps also a
sense of the braggart soldier, as well as a
sexual innuendo (e.g. both the thrust of a
penis and the 'mounting' of a partner). Cf.
2.1.338–9, and Don Pedro's aim to bring
Benedick and Beatrice into a 'mountain of
affection, th'one with th'other.'

34   **pleasant** agreeable

36   **bills** handbills, or posters, to announce
what is in this case an archery contest; cf.
Thomas Nashe, *Have with You to Saffron
Walden* (1596): 'setting up bills, like a
Bearward or Fencer, what fights we shall
have, and what weapons she will meet
me at' (Nashe, 3.121). Beatrice jokingly
describes Benedick as having challenged
Cupid, the blindfolded and winged god of
love (and child of Venus) notorious for his
wayward archery, which suggests that
Benedick had either sought to enter the
contest of love (i.e. become a lover), or, on
the contrary, sought to fight against (or
perhaps shoot at?) the bird-like Love (since
he later professes himself an apostate to
that religion).

28+   Signor] *(Signior)*   Mountanto] Montanto *Pope*

challenged Cupid at the flight; and my uncle's fool,
reading the challenge, subscribed for Cupid and
challenged him at the bird-bolt. I pray you, how many
hath he killed and eaten in these wars? But how many   40
hath he killed? For indeed I promised to eat all of his
killing.

LEONATO   Faith, niece, you tax Signor Benedick too
much, but he'll be meet with you, I doubt it not.

MESSENGER   He hath done good service, lady, in these   45
wars.

BEATRICE   You had musty victual, and he hath holp to

---

37 **flight** either a type of arrow, light and
well feathered, suited for long-distance
shooting, or, more likely, a long-distance
shooting contest, of the most challenging
kind, using such arrows. There may be also
a pun on 'flyte'; a 'flyting' was a kind of
Scottish insult contest (such as that which
Beatrice and Benedick engage in at their
first meeting).
my uncle's fool A fool was a type of house
jester or entertainer, but Beatrice may be
elliptically referring to herself, given her
role in her uncle's household – much as she
later terms Benedick the 'prince's jester,
a very dull fool' (2.1.125). No such
character appears in Leonato's household
in the course of the play. Barbara Everett
observes: 'certain speeches of Beatrice . . .
do cohere into an attitude that utilises a
"fool's" uncommitted wit and detached
play of mind, together with a clown's grasp
of earthy reality, yet committed in such
a new way that they are given the effect
of female veracity against a masculine
romanticism or formality' (Everett, 'Much
Ado', 326).
38 **subscribed for** signed up on Cupid's
team, as his representative; took the part
of; vouched or answered for

39 **bird-bolt** a short blunt arrow (as opposed
to the *flight*), the child Cupid's weapon
of choice ('Proceed, sweet Cupid, though
hast thumped him with thy birdbolt under
the left pap', *LLL* 4.3.22–43), or that of
other less than proficient archers, as in John
Marston's *What You Will* (1607): 'Some
boundlesse ignorance should on sudden
shoote / His grosse knobbed burbolt'
(Induction, 39–40). Beatrice's (enigmatic)
sense is either that the fool insisted on using
the blunter and less swift weapon in order
to mock Benedick's pretensions to be a
ladies' man; or that the fool (as Beatrice?)
clumsily transformed the nature of the
contest from swift shooting to more
fumbling childish attempts.
41–2 **promised . . . killing** a proverbial
phrase (Dent, A192.2) deriding someone's
swaggering ferocity, suggesting that he
didn't kill any at all. Cf. *H5* 3.7.94: 'I think
he will eat all he kills.'
43 **Faith** in faith; truly
   tax accuse, censure
44 **be . . . you** pay you back; get even with you
(perhaps with a pun on 'meat', as well as
'mate' or 'checkmate', all of which were
pronounced similarly)
47 **holp** helped

39 bird-bolt] *Pope² (Theobald);* Burbolt *Q*   47 victual] *F (*victuall*);* vittaile *Q*

eat it. He is a very valiant trencher-man: he hath an
excellent stomach.

MESSENGER　And a good soldier too, lady.　　50

BEATRICE　And a good soldier to a lady; but what is he to
a lord?

MESSENGER　A lord to a lord, a man to a man, stuffed
with all honourable virtues.　　*⇒Fake*

BEATRICE　It is so indeed, he is no less than a stuffed man;　55
but for the stuffing – well, we are all mortal.*⇒that bey human*

LEONATO　You must not, sir, mistake my niece; there is a
kind of merry war betwixt Signor Benedick and her.
They never meet but there's a skirmish of wit between
them.　　60

BEATRICE　Alas, he gets nothing by that. In our last
conflict, four of his five wits went halting off, and now

48　**trencher-man** hearty eater, glutton;
'trencher' from the French *trenchoir* =
wooden platter; although in the later
Middle Ages trenchers were made of day-
old bread, so perhaps a trencherman ate
even his very plate.

49　**stomach** (1) digestive organ; (2) appetite:
see 2.3.246–7, 'You have no stomach,
signor?'; (3) courage

51　**soldier . . . lady** (1) i.e. compared to a lady;
(2) an aggressive (with sexual suggestion)
suitor; or, alternatively, (3) a man who treats
women like a soldier rather than a suitor
(cf. *H5* 5.2.148–9: 'I speak to thee plain
soldier'); (4) braggart soldier (i.e. only a
soldier among ladies). Beatrice's turn on the
Messenger's terms signals her entry into the
verbal one-upmanship which characterizes
the exchanges of men in this play, whereby
terms and meanings are appropriated and
returned, transformed, to their speaker.

53　**A . . . to a man** i.e. he behaves with an
awareness of both social rank and common
decency

stuffed well provided or fortified with (in a
military sense); cf. *RJ* 3.5.181, 'Stuff'd, as
they say, with honourable parts', and *WT*
2.1.184–5, 'whom you know / Of stuff'd
sufficiency'.

55　**stuffed man** rich person; scarecrow
dummy; fat man (especially if he is
one of 'excellent stomach'), replenished.
See also 3.4.59, 'A maid and stuffed!',
where *stuffed* = pregnant and / or sexually
penetrated. Dent, S945.1, citing T. Becon's
Principles of Christian Religion (1552),
sig. A3ᵛ, lists this phrase as both proverbial
and flattering: 'Your father is learned
and hath a brest stuffed with al godlye
virtues.'

59　**skirmish** battle; the metaphor indicates the
rivalrous nature of the euphuistic mode.

62　**five wits** sometimes synonymous with
the five senses – cf. Chaucer, *The
Parson's Tale*, 272 – but also, as here,
the mental capacities of wit, imagination,
fantasy, judgement and memory. Cf.
Son 141.9–10: 'But my five wits,

---

48 eat] ease *F*　He is] he's *F*　trencher-man] *(trencher man)*, *F*　56 stuffing – well] *Theobald;*
stuffing wel, *Q*　61 that. In] *F;* that, in *Q*

is the whole man governed with one, so that if he have
wit enough to keep himself warm, let him bear it for a
difference between himself and his horse, for it is all the   65
wealth that he hath left to be known a reasonable
creature. Who is his companion now? He hath every
month a new sworn brother.

MESSENGER   Is't possible?

BEATRICE   Very easily possible. He wears his faith but as   70
the fashion of his hat: it ever changes with the next
block.

MESSENGER   I see, lady, the gentleman is not in your
books.

BEATRICE   No; an he were, I would burn my study. But I   75

---

nor my five senses, can / Dissuade one
foolish heart from serving thee.'
halting limping (ignominiously); Beatrice
extends the military metaphor.
64 **wit . . . warm** proverbial: having sense
enough to come in out of inclement
weather (Dent, K10); cf. *TS* 2.1.260:
'PETRUCHIO Am I not wise? / KATHERINA
Yes, keep you warm.'
64–5 **bear . . . horse** keep it as a sign to
distinguish himself from his horse
65 **difference** a coat of arms designed to
differentiate branches of the same family;
cf. *Ham* 4.5.180–1: 'You must wear your
rue with a difference.'
66–7 **to . . . creature** in order to know himself
to be a rational human and not a beast,
reason being the quality that distinguishes
the two
68 **new sworn brother** newly pledged comrade
(in arms); 'sworn brother' was a chivalric
phrase (*fratres iurati*); cf. *H5* 2.1.11–12:
'we'll be all three sworn brothers to France'.
70 **faith** friendship (with his *sworn brother*)
71 **fashion** style. A charged word in the
play, with various meanings: as a verb, to
shape, to continue, to frame, transform,
counterfeit, pervert; as a noun, the action of
making, visible characteristics, appearance,

mode of behaviour, prevailing custom,
convention, a mode of dress (*OED* fashion
v. 1, 2a, 4, 4b; *sb.* 1, 2a, 6a, 8a, 9a, 10). See
1.1.92–3: 'The fashion of the world is to
avoid cost, and you encounter it'; 3.3.114–
37, *passim*.
72 **block** i.e. style; a block was a wooden
mould for shaping felt hats, changing with
the fashion of hat. Cf. Thomas Dekker,
Seven Deadly Sins of London (1606): 'the
blocke for his heade alters faster then the
Feltmaker can fitte him' (Dekker, *Sins*,
2.60); perhaps also contemptuously implies
that Benedick's friends are blockheads
(*OED* block *sb.* 15a).
74 **books** favour; proverbial (Dent, B534).
The phrase is of uncertain origin, possibly
from (1) record books of employers, in
which servants' names were listed; (2)
guest books; (3) books of a college listing
members; (4) heraldic registers, cf. *TS*
2.1.223: 'A herald, Kate? O, put me in thy
books'; (5) account books of a tradesman
in which creditable customers were listed.
As is typical in such shifting word-play,
Beatrice transposes the context to a
collection of books.
75 **an** if (common throughout, e.g. 130, 180,
189, etc.)

66 left to] *Collier;* left, to *Q*   67 creature.] *F;* creature, *Q*   75 an] *(and);* if *Pope*   study.] *F;* study, *Q*

pray you, who is his companion? Is there no young
squarer now that will make a voyage with him to the
devil?

MESSENGER   He is most in the company of the right noble
Claudio.   80

BEATRICE   O Lord, he will hang upon him like a disease!
He is sooner caught than the pestilence, and the taker
runs presently mad. God help the noble Claudio! If he
have caught the Benedick, it will cost him a thousand
pound ere 'a be cured.   85

MESSENGER   I will hold friends with you, lady.

BEATRICE   Do, good friend.

LEONATO   You will never run mad, niece.

BEATRICE   No, not till a hot January.

MESSENGER   Don Pedro is approached.   90

Enter DON PEDRO, CLAUDIO, BENEDICK, BALTHASAR
and [DON] JOHN *the bastard.*

76 **pray you** pray of you, beg of you
77 **squarer** swaggerer; trouble-maker (as one
    who 'squares' for a fist-fight)
82 **pestilence** plague **taker** victim
83 **presently** shortly, immediately
84 ***the Benedick** in Q, Benedict, its only
    instance of that spelling. Benedicts, or
    benets, were Catholic priests qualified
    to perform exorcisms, and madness was
    often thought to be caused by demonic
    possession, hence *caught the Benedict*. See
    also List of Roles 3n.
84–5 **cost . . . pound** i.e. friendship with
    Benedick is expensive (perhaps because of
    his appetite for fashion?)
85 **ere** before **'a** he
88 i.e. *you* are immune to catching the
    Benedick. The allegedly colder female
    humoral temperament was thought to

be less susceptible to love's passions;
see 119n.
90 **is approached** has arrived
90.1–2 Don Pedro's company has often entered
    with great ceremony in the theatre, and
    may on the Renaissance stage have been
    announced with a musical flourish.
90.2 *the bastard* Don John's illegitimate birth
    is not mentioned by another character
    until 4.1.188, although it could be reflected
    in his melancholy temperament and his
    estrangement, now *reconciled* (1.1.148),
    from his brother Don Pedro. Bastards were
    thought by nature, and nurture, to be
    covetous due to their lack of social legitimacy
    (and property); Francis Bacon writes in his
    essay *Of Envy* (1597) that 'Deformed
    persons, and eunuchs, and old men, and
    bastards, are envious. For he that cannot

84 Benedick] *F2;* Benedict *Q*   85 'a] he *F:* it *F2*   88 You will never] You'l ne're *F*   90.2 DON JOHN]
Rowe; Iohn *Q*

DON PEDRO   Good Signor Leonato, are you come to meet
your trouble? The fashion of the world is to avoid cost,
and you encounter it.

LEONATO   Never came trouble to my house in the likeness
of your grace, for, trouble being gone, comfort should   95
remain; but when you depart from me, sorrow abides,
and happiness takes his leave.

DON PEDRO   You embrace your charge too willingly. I
think this is your daughter.

LEONATO   Her mother hath many times told me so.   100

BENEDICK   Were you in doubt, sir, that you asked her?

LEONATO   Signor Benedick, no, for then were you a child.

DON PEDRO   You have it full, Benedick; we may guess by
this what you are, being a man. Truly, the lady fathers
herself. Be happy, lady, for you are like an honourable   105
father. [*Don Pedro and Leonato walk apart.*]

possibly mend his own case, will do what he can to impair another's' (Bacon, 25). Cf. the behaviour of Edmund in *KL*. It is apt that the villain of a play so preoccupied with male anxiety over cuckoldry and its social and emotional consequences be a bastard. Shakespeare departs from his sources in not making his villain a rival lover.

92 **trouble** i.e. the effort and expense of entertaining a guest **fashion** way, custom **cost** expense of guests

93 **encounter** come to meet

94 **likeness** appearance, person

98 **charge** expense; responsibility

100 the first of the play's many references to the dubious sexual fidelity of women. Cf. *KL* 2.2.320–4: 'REGAN I am glad to see your highness. / LEAR . . . If thou shouldst not be glad, / I would divorce me from

thy mother's tomb, / Sepulchring an adultress.' Leonato's reference to his wife's frequent verbal warrant ('many times told me') contrasts with the visual proof of Hero's physical resemblance to her father (Leonato's double proof differentiates him from Prospero, who can only affirm 'Thy mother was a piece of virtue, and / She said thou wast my daughter', *Tem* 1.2.56–7).

102 **a child** i.e. incapable of fathering a child upon my wife, implying not only that Benedick is a womanizer, but that he is the only one in the community

103 **full** fully answered, i.e. he's got you there

104–5 **fathers herself** physically resembles her father, and thus needs no other warrant of her paternity

105–6 **Be . . . father** i.e. it is Hero's good fortune to resemble her father, whose

91+ SP DON PEDRO] *Capell (D. Pe.); Pedro Q;* PRINCE *Folg²* are you] you are *F*   92 trouble?] *Collier;* trouble: *Q*   101 sir] *om. F*   106 SD] *Ard² (Don . . . Leonato talk aside); Oxf¹ (speaks privately with Leonato)*

BENEDICK   If Signor Leonato be her father, she would
not have his head on her shoulders for all Messina, as
like him as she is.

BEATRICE   I wonder that you will still be talking, Signor   110
Benedick; nobody marks you.

BENEDICK   What, my dear Lady Disdain! Are you yet
living?   *Dicth*

BEATRICE   Is it possible Disdain should die, while she
hath such meet food to feed it as Signor Benedick?   115
Courtesy itself must convert to Disdain if you come in
her presence.

BENEDICK   Then is Courtesy a turncoat. But it is certain
I am loved of all ladies, only you excepted; and I would
I could find in my heart that I had not a hard heart, for   120
truly I love none.   *entitled*

BEATRICE   A dear happiness to women – they would else
have been troubled with a pernicious suitor. I thank
God and my cold blood, I am of your humour for that:

honour consists not only in his own
attributes but in his possession of a chaste
wife and legitimate offspring (and also, as
Benedick's subsequent comment implies, a
venerably aged appearance)

107–8 **she . . . shoulders** i.e. she wouldn't want
to resemble his white-bearded appearance
exactly

111 **marks** notices, is paying attention to
(except, of course, Beatrice)

112 **Lady Disdain** Benedick refers to Beatrice
as if she were a personification in a morality
play or an allegorical debate, as she does
herself with *Courtesy* (116). The figure of
the disdainful woman was a conventional
one (Prouty, 54); Spenser's Mirabella in
The Faerie Queene (1596) was condemned
to wander the world, guarded by Disdain
and Scorn, in order to save 'so many loues,

as she did lose' (*FQ*, 6.7.37.9), and the
indifference of the Petrarchan mistress
fuelled many a sonnet-writer's powers of
pleading invention. Cf. 3.1.51–2, 'Disdain
and Scorn ride sparkling in her eyes, /
Misprising what they look on.'

115 **meet** appropriate, fit (with a pun on 'meat'
and 'mate', as at 44)

116 **convert** to change into

119 **only you excepted** all except for you

122 **dear happiness** stroke of good luck

124 **of your humour** i.e. of your mind
(medieval physiology designated four
humours – blood, phlegm, choler
and melancholy – thought to determine
health and temperament). If Beatrice
has *cold blood* she is phlegmatic, thus
apathetic or indifferent. Renaissance
medical thought considered women

I had rather hear my dog bark at a crow, than a man   125
swear he loves me. →progressive thoughts

BENEDICK   God keep your ladyship still in that mind,
so some gentleman or other shall scape a predestinate
scratched face.

BEATRICE   Scratching could not make it worse, an 'twere   130
such a face as yours were.

BENEDICK   Well, you are a rare parrot-teacher.

BEATRICE   A bird of my tongue is better than a beast of
yours. → All warm love is words

BENEDICK   I would my horse had the speed of your   135
tongue, and so good a continuer. But keep your way,
o'God's name; I have done.

BEATRICE   You always end with a jade's trick; I know you
of old. → Always ninth works never stays and
Follows through (horse

to be cooler of humour, and temperature,
than men, and the phlegmatic temperament
the more impervious to love: 'Now, as
women are much more moyste than men,
so in like manner we may discerne in them,
that frenzies and furiousness is not so
familiar with them as men, in regard they
will neuer runne mad for loue, or any other
worldly desire . . . whereas men from time
to time, make themselues as in a publique
theatre, the subject of very tragicall follies'
(Gibson, sig. B3ᵛ).

125 **dog . . . crow** presumably a frenzied and
aggravating noise, and one which drives
the crow away

128 **scape** escape
    predestinate for predestinated (i.e.
inescapable, fore-ordained); some verbs
with stems ending in *-d* or *-t* may form
participles which may drop the final *d* (see
Abbott, 342). Cf. 3.2.2, *consummate*.

132 **rare parrot-teacher** one who repeats
endlessly so that a parrot will learn a
phrase

133–4 i.e. better a talking bird than a mute
beast

136 **so . . . continuer** a horse of great stamina;
Beatrice (according to Benedick) talks at
great length (a stereotypically unappealing
trait in women in this period).
    keep your way i.e. carry on

137 **'o** in
    I have done i.e. I am done sparring with
you

138 **jade's trick** A jade is a wayward horse,
canny to devious ways of unseating a rider;
the term was rarely applied to men.
Beatrice, pursuing the equine metaphor,
accuses Benedick of ducking out of
the game of wits prematurely and
underhandedly (i.e. by denying her the
opportunity to reply).

138–9 **I . . . old** There is a suggestion here
of a history between them of such
premature abdications on Benedick's
part; cf. 2.1.255–8: 'Indeed, my lord,
he lent it me awhile, and I gave him use
for it, a double heart for his single one.

130 an] *(and)*   132 parrot-teacher] *(parrat teacher)*, *F2*   137 o'] *(a)*

DON PEDRO   That is the sum of all, Leonato. [*Addresses the*   140
   company.] Signor Claudio and Signor Benedick, my
   dear friend Leonato hath invited you all. I tell him we
   shall stay here at the least a month, and he heartily
   prays some occasion may detain us longer. I dare swear
   he is no hypocrite, but prays from his heart.   145

LEONATO   If you swear, my lord, you shall not be forsworn.
   [*to Don John*] Let me bid you welcome, my lord, being
   reconciled to the prince your brother. I owe you all
   duty.

DON JOHN   I thank you. I am not of many words, but I   150
   thank you.

LEONATO [*to Don Pedro*]   Please it your grace lead on?

DON PEDRO   Your hand, Leonato; we will go together.
                    Exeunt all but Benedick and Claudio.

CLAUDIO   Benedick, didst thou note the daughter of
   Signor Leonato?   155

Marry, once before he won it of me with
false dice; therefore your grace may well
say I have lost it.'

140 **sum of all** i.e. the full account (presumably
of the battle)

143 **a month** See pp. 58–9 for a discussion of
the play's time scheme.

146–7 **you shall . . . forsworn** i.e. I won't do
anything to falsify your vow

147 **being** now that you are

150 **not . . . words** Reticence was a hallmark
of the melancholic, a humoral personality
type also noted for being 'lean, dry, lank,
the face beneath pale, yellowish, swarthy
. . . enuious and jealous, apt to take
occasions in the worse part, and out of
measure passionate. From these dispositions
of the heart and braine arise solitarinesse,
weeping, and . . . melancholie laughter . . .
of pace slow, silent, negligent, refusing the
light and frequency of men, delighted more
in solitariness and obscurity' (Bright, sig.
H6ᵛ). On the Renaissance stage Don John
may have been dressed in black, the colour
symbolic of melancholy.

152–3 **lead on . . . go together** As the
person of highest rank, Don Pedro should
precede the company into the house;
he courteously refuses to enter before his
host.

154 **note** (1) take special notice of (hence
Benedick's reply); (2) remark, the first of
many instances of this usage in the play.
See also 2.3.55n.

140 That] This *F*   all, Leonato.] *Collier²*; all: Leonato, *Q*   140–1 SD] *Ard²* (*Turning to the company*);
Oxf¹ (*ending his talk with Leonato*)   142 tell him] tell you *F3*   147 SD] *Hanmer subst.*   147–8 lord, . . .
brother.] Lord; . . . brother, *Hanmer*   152 SD] *Oxf*   153 SD *all but*] *Rowe*; *Manent Q, Manet F*

BENEDICK   I noted her not, but I looked on her.
CLAUDIO   Is she not a modest young lady?
BENEDICK   Do you question me as an honest man should
do, for my simple true judgement? Or would you have
me speak after my custom, as being a professed tyrant 160
to their sex?
CLAUDIO   No, I pray thee, speak in sober judgement.
BENEDICK   Why, i'faith methinks she's too low for a high
praise, too brown for a fair praise and too little for a
great praise. Only this commendation I can afford her: 165
that were she other than she is, she were unhandsome;
and being no other but as she is, I do not like her.
CLAUDIO   Thou thinkest I am in sport. I pray thee tell me
truly how thou lik'st her.
BENEDICK   Would you buy her that you inquire after her? 170
CLAUDIO   Can the world buy such a jewel?

160 **custom** habit
   professed well-known
160–1 **tyrant to** slanderer of
163–5 **Why . . . praise** The implication is that
   the actor or actress playing Hero is to be
   short (low), slight and dark – perhaps as
   opposed to Beatrice, of whom the actress
   Helena Faucit said: 'if what Wordsworth
   says was ever true of anyone, assuredly it
   was true of her, that "Vital feelings of
   delight / Had reared her to a stately
   height" ' (Faucit, 297). 'Brown' was often
   contrasted with a more conventional
   beauty, as in *TC* 1.2.90ff., or *H8* 3.2.294–
   6: 'I'll startle you / Worse than the sacring-
   bell when the brown wench / Lay kissing in
   your arms, Lord Cardinal'; or the first line
   of John Donne's poem 'The Indifferent': 'I
   can love both fair and brown'. Benedick's
   formulation recalls the comments of John
   Lyly's Fidus to Euphues, in *Euphues and
   His England* (1580), concerning the virtues
   of witty women: 'And this is the greatest

thing, to conceive readily and answer
aptly . . . A nobleman in Siena, disposed
to jest with a gentlewoman of mean birth
yet excellent qualities, between game and
earnest gan thus to salute her: "I know
not how I should commend your beauty,
because it is somewhat too brown, nor your
stature, being somewhat too low, and of
your wit I cannot judge." "No," quoth she,
"I believe you. For none can judge of wit
but they that have it" . . . He perceiving all
outward faults to be recompensed with
inward favour, chose this virgin for his
wife' (Lyly, *Euphues*, 60).
165 **afford** provide
169 **how . . . her** Claudio's need for
   corroboration   of   Hero's   universal
   desirability will turn out to be closely
   coupled with fear of her faithlessness,
   and replicates a concern of Lyly's hero
   Euphues: 'If my lady yeeld to be my lover
   is it not likely she will be another's leman?'
   (Lyly, *Anatomy*, 95). Cf. 287n.

198

BENEDICK   Yea, and a case to put it into. But speak you
this with a sad brow? Or do you play the flouting jack,
to tell us Cupid is a good hare-finder and Vulcan a rare
carpenter? Come, in what key shall a man take you to   175
go in the song?

CLAUDIO   In mine eye, she is the sweetest lady that ever
I looked on.

BENEDICK   I can see yet without spectacles, and I see no
such matter. There's her cousin, an she were not   180
possessed with a fury, exceeds her as much in beauty as
the first of May doth the last of December. But I hope
you have no intent to turn husband – have you?

CLAUDIO   I would scarce trust myself, though I had sworn
the contrary, if Hero would be my wife.   185

BENEDICK   Is't come to this? In faith, hath not the world
one man but he will wear his cap with suspicion? Shall

---

172 **case** jewel case; clothing; Elizabethan
slang for vagina ('because it sheathes a
sword', Partridge)

173 **sad brow** i.e. in all seriousness
flouting jack irreverent rascal; 'jack' was a
term of contempt. To flout was to scorn,
and George Puttenham in his *Art of English
Poesy* (1589) describes the 'broad floute or
Antiphrasis' as 'when we deride by plaine
and flat contradiction' (Puttenham, 201).

174–5 **Cupid . . . carpenter** To describe the
blind archer Cupid as proficient in spotting
hares for a hunt, or the blacksmith Vulcan
(god of fire) as a carpenter (hence more
likely to burn wood than to build with it), is
akin to, or so Benedick implies, mocking
Hero by ascribing to her qualities she
does not possess. (Vulcan was, incidentally,
a notorious cuckold, whose wife Venus
consorted with Mars, god of war.)

176 **go** i.e. to join in, follow along

178 **I** This could also be heard as 'eye', a sense
which Benedick's reply perhaps punningly
seizes upon. Love was thought to enter
through the portal of the eyes: 'which
are the faithful spies and intelligencers
of the soul, steals gently through those
sences, and so passing insensibly through
the veines to the Liuer, it there presently
imprinteth an ardent desire of the object,
which is either really louely, or appears to
be so' (Ferrand, sig. E2ʳ).

179 **I . . . spectacles** Benedick's accurate vision
compares to Beatrice's 'good eye', which
can 'see a church by daylight' (2.1.72–3).

180 **cousin** Beatrice, niece of Leonato

181 **fury** passionate rage; avenging Greek
goddess with snakes in her hair sent to
torment or punish wrong

187 **wear . . . suspicion** the first of many
jokes about the cuckold's horns,
which presumably would be difficult

180 an] (and)

I never see a bachelor of threescore again? Go to,
i'faith. An thou wilt needs thrust thy neck into a yoke,
wear the print of it and sigh away Sundays. Look, Don   190
Pedro is returned to seek you.

Enter DON PEDRO.

DON PEDRO   What secret hath held you here that you
followed not to Leonato's?
BENEDICK   I would your grace would constrain me to tell.
DON PEDRO   I charge thee on thy allegiance.   195

to conceal inconspicuously under a cap,
and of course the wearing of which might
well draw attention. Cf. William Painter's
The Palace of Pleasure (1569): 'All they
that weare hornes, be pardoned to weare
their caps vpon their heads' (Painter, 2.37).
The conspicuousness of horn was seconded
by its use as an instrument of sound (cf.
225–6, 'have a recheat winded in my
forehead'); the horn's identity as a material
of notoriety was seconded by its function
as the translucent material used in lanterns,
as in *MND* 5.1.238: '*This lantern doth the
horned moon present*'). See pp. 45–52.

188 **threescore** sixty
    Go to go on, get away
189–90 **thrust . . . Sundays** The yoke, the
    wooden bar used to join pairs of oxen, was
    a symbol of marriage, and Sunday, the
    day of restrictions on public pastimes, was
    presumably less amusing when spent
    as a husband and father rather than as
    a bachelor; one would then also have, as
    Wright observes, 'most leisure to reflect
    on your captive condition' (Furness). The
    image of the yoke as a sign of marital

confinement was a common one. Cf.
Torquato and Ercole Tasso, *Of Marriage
and Wiving* (1599): 'He that will not
believe [that wives deprive us of our own
sweete naturall freedom] is as bad as a
pettie Hereticke . . . if he but call to minde
the picture of matrimonie itself as the most
wise Egyptians drewe the same, one while
painting it as man that had both his hands
and his feete manacled together, an other
while representing it with such a plain-
fashioned yoke as you tie horned Oxen in
thrall, which doubtlesse is a most manifest
imprese or signe of bondage, slaverie, and
continualle servile drudging' (Tassi, sig.
F4ʳ). (Oxen were cattle gelded only after
reaching maturity.)

190 **wear . . . it** be branded or stamped (by the
    impression left by the yoke upon the flesh);
    be made into a sign
191.1 *Q's stage direction (see t.n.) is faulty,
    since Don John first hears of the intended
    marriage from Borachio in 1.3.
194 **constrain** compel, order; the remark
    suggests that Claudio makes silencing
    gestures.

189 i'faith.] *Capell (*i'faith;*); yfaith, *Q* An] *(and)* 191.1] *Hanmer; Enter don Pedro, Iohn the
bastard. Q* 196 Claudio?] *Oxf¹;* Claudio, *Q* 203 'it] *Dyce;* it *Q* 204 so'] *this edn;* so *Q* so!] so!'
Dyce* 213 spoke] speake *F*

BENEDICK   You hear, Count Claudio? I can be secret as a
    dumb man; I would have you think so. But on my
    allegiance – mark you this, on my allegiance – he is in
    love. With who? Now, that is your grace's part. Mark
    how short his answer is: with Hero, Leonato's short   200
    daughter.

CLAUDIO   If this were so, so were it uttered.

BENEDICK   Like the old tale, my lord: 'it is not so, nor
    'twas not so'; but indeed, God forbid it should be so!

CLAUDIO   If my passion change not shortly, God forbid it   205
    should be otherwise.

DON PEDRO   Amen, if you love her, for the lady is very
    well worthy.

CLAUDIO   You speak this to fetch me in, my lord.

DON PEDRO   By my troth, I speak my thought.   210

CLAUDIO   And in faith, my lord, I spoke mine.

BENEDICK   And by my two faiths and troths, my lord, I
    spoke mine.

CLAUDIO   That I love her, I feel.

DON PEDRO   That she is worthy, I know.   215

BENEDICK   That I neither feel how she should be loved

---

197 **dumb man** mute
198 **allegiance** sworn loyalty to a prince or
    lord
203 **old tale** Benedick refers to the punch-line
    of a story (of the robber-bridegroom genre)
    in which a woman discovers her suitor
    to be involved in some criminal activity
    and convicts him before her family; he
    continually denies the charge but finally
    incontrovertible evidence is produced, to
    which the man in question replies with this
    formula.
205 **shortly** perhaps with a pun on *short* (i.e.
    with a reference to Hero's stature)
205–6 **God . . . otherwise** i.e. God forbid

I should not love her
207 **Amen** a response to Claudio's prayer
208 **well worthy** worthy of love; honourable;
    wealthy
209 **fetch me in** lead me on (and presumably
    invite ridicule for such an admission), trick
    me into confessing
210 **By my troth** i.e. on my word; *troth* = truth,
    and is similar to *faith*, as in the following
    line.
212 **by . . . troths** i.e. to both Claudio and
    Don Pedro, which could, as Benedick
    comically implies, refute each other (if one
    cannot swear allegiance to two persons
    simultaneously)

nor know how she should be worthy is the opinion that
fire cannot melt out of me; I will die in it at the stake.
DON PEDRO   Thou wast ever an obstinate heretic in the
despite of beauty.   220
CLAUDIO   And never could maintain his part but in the
force of his will.
BENEDICK   That a woman conceived me, I thank her; that
she brought me up, I likewise give her most humble
thanks; but that I will have a recheat winded in my   225
forehead, or hang my bugle in an invisible baldrick, all

218 **at the stake** Religious dissenters (cf. *heretic*, 219) were burnt at the stake in England in great numbers under Mary Tudor, 40 years prior to this play's Elizabethan staging, although the penalty was applied to a few under Elizabeth as well. Benedick's professed inability to confess to Hero's lovability despite his multiple troths and faiths parodies the obduracy of Protestant martyrs who refused to acknowledge the miraculous transubstantiation of blood and bread, the supremacy of the Pope, and other articles of the Roman Catholic faith.

220 **despite of** contempt or scorn of (the true faith of beauty)

221–2 **never . . . will** could not persist in his belief were it not for his obstinacy (wilfulness was thought to be a motivation of heresy); cf. Milton, *Of True Religion* (1673): 'Heresie is in the will and choice profestly against Scripture' (Milton, *Religion*, 109). There may also be a sexual innuendo (*part* = penis; *will* = sexual desire).

225–6 **recheat . . . forehead** a hunting call to summon hounds, blown on the (cuckold's) horn which will grow on Benedick's forehead if he marries. The *recheat* calls attention to the horn hidden by the *invisible baldrick* (see 226n.); horns and bugles

were fashioned of cattle horns or boar tusks. Jane Anger, in *Her Protection for Women* (1589), imagines horns to be the property of the cuckolder rather than the cuckold, and audible as well as visible: 'their sex are so like to Bulls that it is no marvel though the Gods do metamorphose some of them to give warning to the rest . . . for some of them will follow the smock as Tom Bull will run after the Town Cow. But lest they should running slip and break their pates, the Gods, provident of their welfare, set a pair of tooters on their foreheads to keep it from the ground' (Anger, 176). The Ovidian transformation of Benedick into a bull joins a pattern of similar imagery of metamorphoses in this play: Dogberry's desire to be 'writ down an ass' (4.2.88); Claudio's mutation from a *lamb* to a *lion* and a *hurt fowl* (1.1.15, 2.1.185); Hero into a *chick* (1.3.52); Beatrice into a *lapwing*, a *haggard* (hawk) and a *curst cow* (3.1.24, 36; 2.1.20–1); and Benedick and Beatrice alike as besieged animals (*kid-fox, two bears*, 2.3.40, 3.2.70).

226 **hang . . . baldrick** i.e. entrust my manhood to the unverifiable quantity of female chastity; a bugle is a horn but also a penis (the dual meaning suggests the vulnerability of phallic power, the ease with which a penis can become a

225   recheat] *Rowe²* *(recheate)*; rechate *Q*

women shall pardon me. Because I will not do them the
wrong to mistrust any, I will do myself the right to trust
none. And the fine is – for the which I may go the finer
– I will live a bachelor.   230
DON PEDRO   I shall see thee, ere I die, look pale with love.
BENEDICK   With anger, with sickness, or with hunger, my
lord, not with love. Prove that ever I lose more blood
with love than I will get again with drinking, pick out
mine eyes with a ballad-maker's pen and hang me up at   235
the door of a brothel-house for the sign of blind Cupid.
DON PEDRO   Well, if ever thou dost fall from this faith,
thou wilt prove a notable argument.

[handwritten margin note: won't do it to my thing to do with true love]

horn by the displacement of a husband
by another man). A baldrick is a belt
or girdle slung across the body to hold
a horn or sword; *invisible* suggests either
its immateriality (i.e. the difficulty of
securing, or proving, female fidelity), or its
obscurity (in which case Benedick wishes
not to need to hide his member – or his
shameful cuckold's horn – in a secret
place), or the ignorance in which a cuckold
sometimes sports his horns (Kittredge).
Invisibility can also denote insubstantiality;
the word 'nothing' was slang for the 'hole'
of the vagina (as in *Much Ado About . . .*) as
opposed to the 'something' of the penis,
and hence Benedick could also mean 'I
don't want to have to hide my shameful
cuckold's horn', or, more likely, 'You
won't catch me putting my penis / horn in
an untrustworthy hole.' See 2.3.55n.
229 **fine** conclusion
    finer more richly dressed (because freed of
    the expense of a wife). Some productions
    costume Benedick as a dandy; others, as a
    soldier.
231 **pale with love** The pallor of love-
    melancholy was thought to be caused by

the combination of 'yellow choler and
the waterish parts of the blood' (Ferrand,
sig. G5ᵛ).
233–4 **lose . . . love** The sighs of love were
    thought to draw blood dangerously away
    from the heart and towards the extremities;
    cf. *MND* 3.2.97: 'With sighs of love, that
    costs the fresh blood dear'.
234 **get . . . drinking** a reference to the
    restorative effects of wine, which reddens
    the complexion (hence rendering it more
    sanguine); proverbial: 'Good wine makes
    good blood' (Dent, W461)
235 **ballad-maker's pen** the writing implement
    dedicated to love songs and loved ones; cf.
    AYL 2.7.148–9: 'a woeful ballad / Made to
    his mistress' eyebrow'.
236 **sign . . . Cupid** Like taverns, houses
    of prostitution had signs denoting their
    trade and name. Benedick implies that
    the gruesome image of his blinded self
    (because Cupid is blind, and perhaps
    because venereal disease causes blindness)
    would be an appropriate advertisement for
    such an establishment.
238 **notable argument** notorious subject for
    discussion

236 brothel-house] *(*brothel house*)*, *F*

BENEDICK   If I do, hang me in a bottle like a cat and shoot
at me, and he that hits me, let him be clapped on the   240
shoulder and called Adam.

DON PEDRO   Well, as time shall try. 'In time the savage
bull doth bear the yoke.'

BENEDICK   The savage bull may, but if ever the sensible
Benedick bear it, pluck off the bull's horns and set   245
them in my forehead; and let me be vilely painted, and

239 **hang . . . cat** referring to the apparent
custom of suspending a cat (dead? alive?)
in a wicker basket (cf. *Oth* 2.3.141,
'twiggen bottle') as a target for a
shooting contest. Steevens–Reed[2] cites as
corroboration a pamphlet *Wars, or the
Peace is Broken*: 'arrowes flew faster than
they did at a catte in a basket, when Prince
Arthur, or the Duke of Shoreditch, strucke
up the drumme in the field'. Benedick's
image sustains the theme of gruesome
punishments visited upon heretics and
apostates, as well as the links between
archery and love.

240–1 **clapped . . . Adam** congratulated as the
best archer. As Theobald surmised, Adam
is probably a reference to the renowned
northern outlaw archer Adam Bell, who
together with Clym of the Clough and
William of Cloudesley comprised a
legendary trio of archers; see *English and
Scottish Ballads* (Child, 5.124).

242 **try** reveal, test; proverbial: 'Time tries all
things' (Dent, T336)

242–3 **In . . . yoke** proverbial (Dent, T303).
Shakespeare could have also heard or read
the phrase in Thomas Kyd's *The Spanish
Tragedy* (1592), 2.1.3: 'In time the sauage
Bull sustaines the yoke'; or in Thomas
Watson's *Ecatompathia* (1582), sonnet 47:
'In time the Bull is brought to weare the
yoake.' There are Italian and classical

antecedents for both, e.g. Ovid, *Tristia*,
4.6.1, and *Ars Amatoria*, 1.471. A bull
compelled to the yoke was more than likely
to be rendered an ox (i.e. castrated) in the
process (the ox, along with the camel and
the snail, was an emblem of endurance).

245 **horns** The association of horns with
cuckoldry is ancient and cross-cultural, but
of obscure origin; the *OED* (*sb.* I 7a)
suggests that it derives from the ancient
practice of 'engrafting the spurs of a
castrated cock on the root of the excised
comb, where they grew and became horns'.
Brewer (1142) cites the stag's battle for
herd dominance; when a stag is 'horned',
he loses his herd until he can return the
favour to another stag. The Ovidian myth
of Actaeon (*Met.*, 3.138–249), in which the
hunter views the chaste and divine huntress
Diana bathing, and is consequently turned
by her into a stag and slain by his own
hounds, also provides an association of
horn-wearing with female power over
men; however, Diana, goddess of the
moon, sported the emblem of crescent
horns (sign of the moon as well as of its
mutability), which most closely resemble
the bovine horns (rather than antlers)
conferred upon most cuckolds. See
pp. 45–52 and 174–78.

246 **vilely painted** i.e. have his portrait painted
in a crude or degrading style

246 forehead;] forehead, *Q*   vilely] *(vildly)*

204

in such great letters as they write 'Here is good horse
to hire', let them signify under my sign, 'Here you may
see Benedick, the married man.'

CLAUDIO   If this should ever happen, thou wouldst be   250
horn-mad.

DON PEDRO   Nay, if Cupid have not spent all his quiver in
Venice, thou wilt quake for this shortly.

BENEDICK   I look for an earthquake too, then.

DON PEDRO   Well, you will temporize with the hours.   255
In the meantime, good Signor Benedick, repair to
Leonato's, commend me to him and tell him I will
not fail him at supper, for indeed he hath made great
preparation.

BENEDICK   I have almost matter enough in me for such   260
an embassage. And so, I commit you –

251 **horn-mad** (1) stark raving mad; (2) mad
with jealousy; (3) angry as an enraged bull:
pun on the cuckold's horns intended. Cf.
MW 3.5.140–2: 'If I have horns to make
one mad, let the proverb go with me: I'll be
horn-mad'; *CE* 2.1.58–60: 'Why, mistress,
sure my master is horn-mad / . . . I mean
not cuckold-mad, / But sure he is stark
mad'; Dent, H628.
252 **quiver** i.e. of arrows (with sexual
suggestion of spending phallic power)
253 **Venice** renowned for its courtesans and
prostitutes. The traveller Thomas Coryat,
in his *Crudities* (1605), writes that 'The
name of a Courtezan of Venice is famoused
over all Christendom' (Coryat, 1.401).
   quake According to Ferrand, symptoms of
love-melancholy included 'loss of appetite,
weeping, sobbing and sighing, frequent
sighings, continuall complaints, languishing

countenance, feebleness of the knees'
(Ferrand, sig. E2ʳ).
254 **earthquake** a rare event, thought to herald
momentous changes. Benedick continues
Don Pedro's pun on *quiver*.
255 **temporize . . . hours** become more
temperate, or realistic in and with time
(Latin *tempus* = time, so the phrase could
mean 'delay the event'; *hours* could also
pun on whores, with whom Venice was
reputedly replete). Cf. *Cor* 4.6.16–17:
'All's well, and might have been much
better if / He could have temporiz'd.'
256 **repair** go
257 **commend me** send my regards
258 **fail him** fail to be present
260 **I . . . me** i.e. I believe I possess adequate
sense; cf. 2.1.303–4: 'I was born to speak
all mirth and no matter.'

251 horn-mad] *(*horn madde*)*, *Pope*   256 meantime] *(*meane time*)*   261 you –] *Theobald*; you. *Q*

CLAUDIO   'To the tuition of God. From my house' – if I
   had it –

DON PEDRO   'The sixth of July. Your loving friend,
   Benedick.'   265

BENEDICK   Nay, mock not, mock not. The body of your
   discourse is sometime guarded with fragments, and the
   guards are but slightly basted on neither. Ere you flout
   old ends any further, examine your conscience. And so
   I leave you.   *Exit.*

CLAUDIO

My liege, your highness now may do me good.   271

DON PEDRO

My love is thine to teach; teach it but how,
And thou shalt see how apt it is to learn
Any hard lesson that may do thee good.

CLAUDIO

Hath Leonato any son, my lord?   275

262–5 **To . . . Benedick** In these tags the
   men make epistolary closing formulae.
   The sixth of July was the quarter-day when
   rents were due, and hence a likely day for
   letter-writing.

262 **tuition** protection

266–8 **The . . . neither** i.e. the substance of
   your speech is often badly ornamented; the
   metaphor of Claudio's language as a body
   decorated (*guarded*) with ragtags of speech
   or clichés (*old ends*) which are loosely
   sewn (*slightly basted*) onto the garment
   uses the imagery of fashion itself to
   describe the fashionable discourse of puns
   and turns so prized by the men in this play.
   Benedick implies that Claudio's attempt at
   ornate speech is rather a motley effort.

268 **flout** quote or recite with sarcastic purpose
   (*OED v.* 1b)

269 **old ends** well-worn quotations, clichés

270 SD Borachio and / or Antonio's servant
   may perhaps enter unseen before the end of
   the scene, though they need not.

271 **liege** lord
   good a favour

271–2 **your . . . thine** Claudio uses the formal
   second person pronoun; the Prince the
   more intimate one.

272 **My . . . to teach** The love I bear you is at
   your service, to be instructed as to how to
   help you.

273 **apt** eager
   it i.e. his love for Claudio

275 This question need not appear as
   mercenary as it seems to a modern
   audience; any Renaissance count worth
   his salt would and should have been
   curious about the financial standing

---

262 'To . . . house'] *this edn;* to . . . house *Q*   262–3 – if . . . it –] *Capell subst.;* if I had it *Q*   263
it –] *Theobald;* it *Q*   264–5 'The . . . Benedick.'] *this edn;* the . . . Benedicke. *Q*   269 conscience.]
Steevens–Reed² (conscience:); conscience, *Q*

DON PEDRO

No child but Hero; she's his only heir.
Dost thou affect her, Claudio?

CLAUDIO   O my lord,

When you went onward on this ended action
I looked upon her with a soldier's eye,
That liked, but had a rougher task in hand   280
Than to drive liking to the name of love.
But now I am returned, and that war-thoughts
Have left their places vacant, in their rooms
Come thronging soft and delicate desires,
All prompting me how fair young Hero is,   285
Saying I liked her ere I went to wars.

DON PEDRO

Thou wilt be like a lover presently
And tire the hearer with a book of words.
If thou dost love fair Hero, cherish it,
And I will break with her and with her father,   290
And thou shalt have her. Was't not to this end

of his contemplated intended. 'Young'
Claudio can also be played as seeking to
establish the adult or business-like nature
of his interest. The question establishes
for the audience the fraternal isolation of
Hero, who has no male relative to avenge
her honour when need be; Antonio's *son*
(at 1.2.2) is, like Innogen of the SDs, a
character who vanishes once he becomes
an encumbrance to the plot (see 5.1.280).

277 **affect** love

278 **went onward on** set out on
     ended action completed military mission

280 **in hand** before me

281 **drive** convert

282 **that** now that

283 **left . . . vacant** deserted their posts
     rooms places

285 **young** The emphasis on Hero's youth
     accords with that on his own age at 1.1.10
     and 5.1.180.

287 **like a lover** Garrulousness was considered
     a trait of lovers, 'which proceeds from the
     fulness of their Heart, for loue, sayes
     Plutarch, is naturally a great Babler . . . For
     that louers haue a strong desire to enduce
     all others to the belief of that whereof
     themselues are already persuaded . . . they
     would willingly haue these opinions of
     their beloued confirmed also by all other
     men's judgements' (Ferrand, sig. G5ᵛ).
     presently instantly, in no time

290 **break** broach the question

291–2 **Was't . . . story** i.e. isn't this the reason
     you were setting out to weave so well-
     crafted a tale (*OED* twist *v.* 3b)

283 vacant,] *Capell;* vacant: *Q*   290–1 and . . . her] *om. F*

That thou began'st to twist so fine a story?

CLAUDIO

How sweetly you do minister to love,
That know love's grief by his complexion!
But lest my liking might too sudden seem,   295
I would have salved it with a longer treatise.

DON PEDRO

What need the bridge much broader than the flood?
The fairest grant is the necessity;
Look what will serve is fit. 'Tis once, thou lovest,
And I will fit thee with the remedy.   300
I know we shall have revelling tonight;
I will assume thy part in some disguise
And tell fair Hero I am Claudio;
And in her bosom I'll unclasp my heart
And take her hearing prisoner with the force   305
And strong encounter of my amorous tale.
Then after, to her father will I break,
And the conclusion is: she shall be thine. → No room for her choice
In practice let us put it presently.   *Exeunt.*

---

293 **minister to** assist
294 **complexion** appearance (love was thought to induce pallor); four syllables
296 **salved it** elaborated upon it (so as to soften the brunt of its sudden appearance); *salve* literally means to anoint or soothe (as in an ointment for an injury, such as that which causes love's grief).
297 i.e. why elaborate any more than necessary?
298 Don Pedro seems to mean that Claudio's need for his aid is his best motive for giving it.
299 **Look what** whatever
    once once and for all
304 **in her bosom** privately; in her heart

305–6 **take . . . tale** capture her with the forceful urgency of my love talk (Don Pedro employs a military idiom). Why Don Pedro feels that his masquerading as Claudio in order to woo Hero is an appropriate *remedy* (300) for Claudio's plight is not clear; the plan seems to speak to the Prince's penchant throughout to be one of 'the only love-gods' (2.1.357), as well as his tendency to imagine himself the lover of other men's women (2.3.165). The scheme represents the first instance of several in the play where a man takes (or is thought to take) Claudio's place with respect to Hero.

293 you do] doe you *F*

[1.2]   *Enter* LEONATO *and* [ANTONIO,] *an old man,*
brother to Leonato[, *meeting*].

LEONATO   How now, brother, where is my cousin your
son? Hath he provided this music?
ANTONIO   He is very busy about it. But brother, I can tell
you strange news that you yet dreamt not of.
LEONATO   Are they good?   5
ANTONIO   As the event stamps them, but they have a good
cover: they show well outward. The prince and Count
Claudio, walking in a thick-pleached alley in mine
orchard, were thus much overheard by a man of mine:
the prince discovered to Claudio that he loved my niece   10
your daughter, and meant to acknowledge it this night
in a dance; and if he found her accordant, he meant to
take the present time by the top and instantly break
with you of it.
LEONATO   Hath the fellow any wit that told you this?   15

1.2 The location is in or near Leonato's house.
This scene has often been cut or transposed
to the beginning of 2.1 (Cox, *Shakespeare*,
110).
1   **How now** hello there; Leonato's greeting
suggests he and Antonio enter separately.
1–2 **my . . . son** another relative who appears
only by report and disappears in the course
of the action (at 5.1.280 Antonio has no
son); 'cousin' (and 'coz') was used of all
close relations beyond immediate family.
5   **they** *News* is usually plural in Elizabethan
usage.
6   ***event stamps** outcome will reveal
6–7 **good cover** auspicious external appearance;
Antonio uses the imagery of books and

book-binding.
8   **thick-pleached alley** a path lined by
closely woven intertwined branches (and
hence an optimal site for potential
eavesdropping)
9   **man** i.e. servant; presumably this is
the same conversation overheard (more
accurately) by Borachio as well.
10 **discovered** disclosed
11 **your daughter** The designation is perhaps
to distinguish her from Beatrice.
12 **accordant** agreeable, willing
13 **by the top** by the topknot; proverbial:
'Take Time by the forelock, for she is bald
behind' (Dent, T311). Cf. *AW* 5.3.39.
13–14 **break . . . it** broach it with you

1.2] *Capell (*SCENE II*)   0.1 ANTONIO] *Rowe*   0.2 *meeting*] *Cam*   3+ SP] *Rowe (Ant.); Old Q*
4 strange] *om. F*   6 event] euent *F2;* euents *Q*   7 outward.] *Popo;* outward, *Q*   8 thick-pleached]
*(*thicke pleached*), Theobald*   mine] my *F*   9 much] *om. F*

209

ANTONIO   A good sharp fellow; I will send for him, and question him yourself.

LEONATO   No, no; we will hold it as a dream till it appear itself. But I will acquaint my daughter withal, that she may be the better prepared for an answer, if   20 peradventure this be true. Go you and tell her of it.

[Exit Antonio.]

[Enter Attendants, and cross the stage.]

Cousins, you know what you have to do. O, I cry you mercy, friend: go you with me and I will use your skill. Good cousin, have a care this busy time!   *Exeunt.*

[1.3]   *Enter* DON JOHN *the bastard and*
CONRADE *his companion.*

CONRADE   What the goodyear, my lord! Why are you thus out of measure sad?

DON JOHN   There is no measure in the occasion that breeds, therefore the sadness is without limit.

18 **hold it as** consider it but
18–19 **appear itself** materializes
19 **withal** with what you have told me
21 Depending on his speed, Antonio may exit only at the general dispersal at line 24, as he does in some productions and editions. As Oxf¹ notes, 'the text requires only bustle here'.
22–23 **cry you mercy** beg your pardon
24 **have a care** be careful (may suggest a stage action of clumsiness for the actor to whom it is addressed)
1.3 The location is in or near Leonato's house.

1   **What the goodyear** a benign expletive, similar to 'What the devil', possibly derived from the early modern Dutch exclamation 'wat goedtjarr': 'as I hope for a good year'
2   **out . . . sad** excessively melancholy, out of sorts
3   **measure in** moderation of; limit to
3–4 **occasion that breeds** source that causes his sadness. The term *breeds* may suggest that the irremediable cause of Don John's grief is his own bastardy; alternatively, it could refer to his melancholy or to the recent defeat at the hands of Claudio.

21 SD] *Boas*   21.1] *Capell (Enter several persons, bearing things for the banquet); Exit Antonio, Enter Antonio's son with a Musician / Boas; Exit Antonio. Enter Antonio's son, with a Musician and Others. / Kittredge; Several cross the Stage here / Theobald (after* to do *22); Enter Attendants Oxf*   22 Cousins] Cousin *Waters-Bennett*   **1.3**] *Capell (*SCENE III*)*   0.1 DON] *Rowe; sir Q*   1 goodyear] (goodyeere), *Malone*   lord!] *Hanmer;* lord, *Q*   3+ SP] *Iohn Q*   4 breeds] breeds it *Theobald*

CONRADE   You should hear reason.   5

DON JOHN   And when I have heard it, what blessing
brings it?

CONRADE   If not a present remedy, at least a patient
sufferance.

DON JOHN   I wonder that thou – being as thou sayst   10
thou art, born under Saturn – goest about to apply a
moral medicine to a mortifying mischief. I cannot hide
what I am. I must be sad when I have cause, and smile
at no man's jests; eat when I have stomach, and wait
for no man's leisure; sleep when I am drowsy, and   15
tend on no man's business; laugh when I am merry,
and claw no man in his humour.

CONRADE   Yea, but you must not make the full show of
this till you may do it without controlment. You have
of late stood out against your brother, and he hath ta'en   20
you newly into his grace, where it is impossible you

---

5   **reason** The term suggests the exorbitance
of Don John's sadness.

8   F's change of 'at least' to 'yet' is
perhaps to accommodate its erroneous
expansion of Q's 'brings' (6) to 'brin- /
geth'.

9   **sufferance** forbearance, endurance; cf.
5.1.38, pain, suffering.

11   **born under Saturn** saturnine, morose –
because born under that planet, described
by Stephen Bateman in *Upon Bartholomew*
(1582) as 'an euill willed Planet, colde
and drie, a night Planet and heauie . . .
and therefore a childe . . . that be conceiued
& come forth vnder his Lordship, [shall]
dye, or haue full euill qualyties' (Bateman,
fol.129ᵛ, cited by Furness). According
to Robert Burton in his *Anatomy of
Melancholy* (1621), those born under
Saturn were excessively melancholy
(Burton, 1.2001); Andrew Gurr suggests
that melancholics dressed emblematically

in black on the Renaissance stage
(Gurr, 182).

goest about attempt

12   **moral . . . mischief** philosophical remedy
to a mortal injury. Don John, like other
men in the play, is an accomplished
euphuistic speaker.

14   **stomach** appetite

14–15 **wait . . . leisure** do not wait until another
man is free to eat with me

16   **tend on** attend to

17   **claw . . . humour** soothe, flatter, stroke, no
man when he is moody (much as Conrade
seeks to do with Don John)

19   **till . . . controlment** until you are free to
act without risk of restraint

20   **stood out against** defied, fallen out with
(Don Pedro's recent military battle was
with Don John)

20–1 **ta'en . . . grace** recently forgiven you,
taken you into his favour; *ta'en* is
pronounced 'tane'.

---

7 brings] brin- / geth *F*   8 at least] yet *F*   12 moral] mortall *F2*   20 ta'en] *(tane)*

211

should take true root but by the fair weather that
you make yourself. It is needful that you frame the
season for your own harvest.

DON JOHN   I had rather be a canker in a hedge than a rose   25
in his grace, and it better fits my blood to be disdained
of all than to fashion a carriage to rob love from any. In
this, though I cannot be said to be a flattering honest
man, it must not be denied but I am a plain-dealing
villain. I am trusted with a muzzle and enfranchised   30
with a clog. Therefore I have decreed not to sing in
my cage. If I had my mouth I would bite; if I had my
liberty I would do my liking. In the meantime, let me
be that I am, and seek not to alter me.

CONRADE   Can you make no use of your discontent?   35

DON JOHN   I make all use of it, for I use it only. Who
comes here?

Enter BORACHIO.

22–3 **take . . . yourself** be firmly established
except by behaving well

23–4 **frame . . . harvest** behave so as to ensure
that you prosper; manipulate (by a pretence
of agreeableness) circumstances in order to
pursue your own goals

25 **canker** wild or dog-rose (hence, like
a weed, uncultivated but hardy; an
appropriate emblem for one whose social
position is of dubious legitimacy); cf. *1H4*
1.3.174–5: 'To put down Richard, that
sweet lovely rose, / And plant this thorn,
this canker, Bolingbroke?'

26 **grace** with pun on grass
fits my blood suits my humour and my
(illegitimate) birth

27 **fashion a carriage** adopt a demeanour

(as opposed to behaving without pretence)
rob love gain favour on false pretences

28 **flattering honest** The oxymoron conveys
his contempt of honesty.

29 **but** i.e. that

30–1 **trusted . . . clog** i.e. allowed into favour
only by virtue of harsh restrictions laid
upon my behaviour. A clog is a heavy block
of wood attached like a hobble to the leg or
neck of a man or animal in order to prevent
escape or straying. Don John imagines
himself as a dog, a horse and a bird in
succession.

32 **had my mouth** i.e. was unmuzzled

33 **my liking** what I please

35 **make . . . of** find no way to profit from

36 **I use it only** it is my entire occupation

22 true] *om. F*   29 plain-dealing] (plain dealing), *Rowe*   30 muzzle] *(mussell)*   33 meantime] *(mean time)*   36–8] *Pope; Q lines only, / Borachio? /*   36 I make] I will make *F*   37.1] *Capell; after 38 Q*

What news, Borachio?

BORACHIO I came yonder from a great supper. The
prince your brother is royally entertained by Leonato, 40
and I can give you intelligence of an intended marriage.

DON JOHN Will it serve for any model to build mischief
on? What is he for a fool that betroths himself to
unquietness?

BORACHIO Marry, it is your brother's right hand. 45

DON JOHN Who, the most exquisite Claudio?

BORACHIO Even he.

DON JOHN A proper squire! And who, and who? Which
way looks he?

BORACHIO Marry, on Hero, the daughter and heir of 50
Leonato.

DON JOHN A very forward March chick! How came you
to this?

BORACHIO Being entertained for a perfumer, as I was

---

39 **great** lavish
41 **intelligence** news
42 **model** blueprint, ground-plan
43 **What . . . fool** what manner of fool is he
44 **unquietness** discord; women were often
stigmatized as a source of unquietness.
45 **Marry** a common asseverative mild oath
(originally 'by the Virgin Mary')
46 **exquisite** dainty; perfect (cf. 4.1.314–15)
48 **proper** exemplary
squire youthful follower of a knight (and
knight-in-training), and also a stock figure
of an ideal lover, as in Chaucer's General
Prologue to *The Canterbury Tales*: 'A
lovere and a lusty bacheler / With lokkes
crulle as they were laid in presse' (Chaucer,
80–1)
And who i.e. and on whom does he look
50–1 Borachio's specification of Hero as
Leonato's heir could make explicit a

mercenary element in Claudio's motives,
although cf. 1.1.275n.
50 *on Q's 'one' is unlikely, as it suggests
that Hero is unknown to Don John and
Conrade as well as Borachio.
52 **forward March chick** upstart youth; the
phrase could equally apply to Claudio
(presumptuous *start-up*, 61), or Hero
(precocious, saucy, even immodest,
although there is no evidence of such a
character until the exchange with Don
Pedro in the dance in 2.1). A chick born in
March would be an early bird. Some
productions present a Don John with his
own interest in Hero; unlike Shakespeare's
sources, however, *MA*'s villain is not a
rival lover of Hero.
54 **entertained . . . perfumer** employed to
render a disused room sweet-smelling by
burning aromatic substances

---

45 brother's] *F;* bothers *Q* 48 squire!| squier, *Q* who? Which] *Rowe²;* who, which *Q* 50 on] *F;*
one *Q* 52 March chick] *(*March-chicke*)*

smoking a musty room comes me the prince and   55
Claudio, hand in hand in sad conference. I whipped me
behind the arras, and there heard it agreed upon that
the prince should woo Hero for himself, and having
obtained her, give her to Count Claudio. *give her → Object*

DON JOHN   Come, come, let us thither; this may prove   60
food to my displeasure. That young start-up hath all
the glory of my overthrow. If I can cross him any way,
I bless myself every way. You are both sure, and will
assist me?

CONRADE   To the death, my lord.   65

DON JOHN   Let us to the great supper; their cheer is the
greater that I am subdued. Would the cook were o'my
mind. Shall we go prove what's to be done?

BORACHIO   We'll wait upon your lordship.   *Exeunt.*

55   **comes me** come towards me
56   **hand in hand** The description could
provide a SD for the actors in 1.1.
   sad serious
   me myself; *me* here (and at 55) is an
obsolete form similar to the classical ethical
dative, where 'me' functions to draw
attention to the speaker, by making the
remark sound colloquial. See Abbott, 220.
57   **arras** tapestry wall-hanging (named after the
town in France where produced). Borachio's
comment suggests that the conversation he
overhears was not conducted in Antonio's
orchard after all (though it is continuous with
the opening setting of 1.1), or that it was
pursued indoors, or that the arras is outdoors
– or that Shakespeare is not overly concerned
with such specifics. Getting things slightly
wrong is a theme of the play.
58–9   **for . . . Claudio** Borachio either mishears
Don Pedro's plan, or renders it in its most
callous form by implying that Don Pedro
will 'obtain' Hero and then transfer her to
Claudio's ownership; either way, he does

communicate that the ultimate intention
is to acquire Hero for Claudio, but his
formulation points out to Don John a way to
harass Claudio at 2.1.148–53, by convincing
him that Don Pedro woos indeed *for himself.*
60   **thither** i.e. to the party
61   **food** i.e. fuel
   start-up upstart
61–2   **hath . . . overthrow** has reaped all the
benefits of my fall from (Don Pedro's) grace
(presumably by taking Don John prisoner)
62   **cross** vex, make trouble for; however,
taken in the sense of 'to make the sign of
the cross', the term also allows the play on
words with *bless.* Don John tends to turn
his own terms without the aid of an
interlocutor, perhaps a sign of his solipsism.
63   **bless** benefit
   sure firmly with me, loyal
67   **subdued** i.e. defeated
67–8   **o'my mind** i.e. possessed of poisonous
thoughts
68   **prove** investigate
69   **wait upon** attend upon (i.e. follow)

56 me] *om. F*   64 me?] *F; me. Q*   67 o'] *(a); of F*   69 SD] *F; exit. Q*

[2.1]   *Enter* LEONATO, *his brother* [ANTONIO],
             HERO *his daughter and* BEATRICE *his niece.*

LEONATO   Was not Count John here at supper?

ANTONIO   I saw him not.

BEATRICE   How tartly that gentleman looks! I never can
     see him but I am heart-burned an hour after.

HERO   He is of a very melancholy disposition.   5

BEATRICE   He were an excellent man that were made just
     in the midway between him and Benedick: the one is
     too like an image and says nothing, and the other too
     like my lady's eldest son, evermore tattling.

LEONATO   Then half Signor Benedick's tongue in Count   10
     John's mouth, and half Count John's melancholy in
     Signor Benedick's face –

BEATRICE   With a good leg and a good foot, uncle, and
     money enough in his purse, such a man would win any
     woman in the world – if 'a could get her good will.   15

2.1 The location is in or near Leonato's house, presumably in a space separate from the site of the *great supper* (1.3.66) and the rest of the company, who enter revelling at 75. Don Pedro's comment to Leonato at the end of the scene ('Go in with me', 357) suggests that the dance takes place either outdoors or in a relatively public space. The scene is usually set in night-time (post-supper), which in Renaissance staging would have been signified by torches.

0.1–2 Rowe provides an entry here for Margaret and Ursula, who need to be onstage by the dance (75), where this edition, after Capell, locates their entrance.

See 75.2–3n. and p. 143.

1 Leonato's question could suggest that as his party enters they cross paths with or glimpse the exit of Don John's.

3 **tartly** disagreeable, acid
  looks appears; regards one (perhaps a suggestion for Don John's stage action)

8 **image** statue; picture

9 **my . . . son** i.e. a spoiled heir apparent, licensed to chatter
  evermore tattling a charge that Beatrice has had laid against her as well; see 1.1.135–6.

13 **good leg** nice limbs, graceful bow

15 **good will** favour

2.1] *Actus Secundus F; scene i. / Rowe*   0.1 ANTONIO] *Rowe*   0.2 HERO] *Theobald; his wife, Hero Q; Innogen, Hero / Rowe   niece.] Oxf¹; neece, and a kinsman. Q; niece, Margaret and Ursula / Rowe*   2+ SP ANTONIO] *Rowe (Ant.); brother Q*   10+ Signor] *(signior)*   12 face –] *Rowe,* face. *Q;* face –. *F2*   15 world –] *F (world,);* world *Q*   'a] he *F*

LEONATO By my troth, niece, thou wilt never get thee a husband, if thou be so shrewd of thy tongue.

ANTONIO In faith, she's too curst.

BEATRICE Too curst is more than curst. I shall lessen God's sending that way; for it is said 'God sends a curst   20
cow short horns' – but to a cow too curst he sends none.

LEONATO So, by being too curst, God will send you no horns.

BEATRICE Just, if he send me no husband. For the which blessing I am at him upon my knees every morning and   25
evening. Lord, I could not endure a husband with a beard on his face! I had rather lie in the woollen.

17 **shrewd** shrewish, sharp, critical; observant or penetrating (and unladylike in its bawdy *double entendre*), as at 71

18 **curst** cantankerous, perverse; Antonio's estimate of Beatrice's excessive shrewishness would consign her to the choleric category of shrew occupied by *TS*'s Kate, although John Draper points out that according to Don Pedro 'she has "a merry heart," was "born in a merry hour," and truly by nature has "little of the melancholy element in her": in short, she seems, like Benedick, to be either sanguine by nature or mildly choleric under the influence of the sun: this marks her off from Kate the Shrew as less violent and more witty and amenable' (Draper, 265).

19 **Too** with pun on 'two'

20 **sending** something sent; gift, endowment **that way** in that respect

21 **short horns** i.e. providentially, the least harmful ones, in the case of an angry cow, but also, for a cuckold, the least conspicuous ones

24 **Just** exactly
send . . . husband Beatrice's reply to Leonato could imply either that she couldn't then cuckold her husband, or be

herself cuckolded (horns were an equal-opportunity side-effect of marital infidelity, in which case the wife would be called a cuckquean); see Painter's *Palace of Pleasure*: 'Behold Ladyes . . . this History which for example I have willinglye recited to thintente that when your husbands do make you hornes as big as a Goate, you may render unto him the monstrous heade of a Stagge' (Painter, 2.37). As with the cuts to the male banter of cuckoldry in 1.1, Beatrice's lines have often been censored in productions concerned to present her in a ladylike manner.

25 **I . . . him** I address myself to him

26 **Lord** This could be delivered as the invocation of a prayer.

27 **beard** Beards were a sign of virility and maturity (cf. Benedick's contempt for Claudio as 'Lord Lack-beard' at 5.1.187); Beatrice's preference contradicts contemporary opinions of what Renaissance women want. Ferrand (143) professes to the contrary that 'women cannot endure a man that hath but little beard; not so much for that they are commonly cold and impotent, as that, so

20–1 'God . . . horns'] *Capell subst.;* God . . . hornes *Q*

LEONATO   You may light on a husband that hath no beard.
BEATRICE   What should I do with him? Dress him in my
apparel and make him my waiting-gentlewoman? He   30
that hath a beard is more than a youth, and he that hath
no beard is less than a man; and he that is more than
a youth is not for me, and he that is less than a man, I
am not for him. Therefore I will even take sixpence in
earnest of the bearward and lead his apes into hell.   35
LEONATO   Well then, go you into hell?
BEATRICE   No, but to the gate, and there will the devil
meet me like an old cuckold with horns on his head,
and say, 'Get you to heaven, Beatrice, get you to heaven.
Here's no place for you maids!' So deliver I up my apes   40
and away to Saint Peter fore the heavens. He shows me

much resembling Eunuchs, they are for the most part inclined to baseness, cruelty, and deceitfulness'. In effect, Beatrice rejects both men with beards and men without. Benedick has a beard, which he shaves before 3.2.

in the woollen i.e. in rough blankets without sheets

28 **light on** find yourself with

29–30 **Dress . . . apparel** the fate of Hercules in the house of Omphale, who forced the captive Hercules to wear women's clothes and spin wool with her maids (Ovid, *Fasti*, 2.317ff.; *Heroides*, 9.55ff.); cf. Benedick's fear at 231–3: 'She would have made Hercules have turned spit, yea, and have cleft his club to make the fire too' (see 231–3n., 232n. on *turned spit*).

31 **more . . . youth** too old

32 **less . . . man** too young for marriage; insufficiently virile

34–5 **in earnest of** as an advance payment from

35 **bearward** someone who keeps bears (e.g. for bear-baiting) or trained apes. Q's 'Berrord' could be modernized as 'bearward' or 'bearherd', both of which were in use in the period (although 'bearward' was the more common word); both are homophones for the earlier *beard*. The aural link provides Beatrice with her shift to the notion of an animal herder and from there she moves to the proverbial idea (Dent, M37) that spinsters were doomed to lead apes in hell (presumably as punishment for having disdained human reproduction and concomitant childminding?). Cf. George Peele, *The Arraignment of Paris* (1584), 4.2.6: 'All that be Dian's maids are vowed to halter apes in hell.' Apes were considered mimics of men.

40 **no place** i.e. because maids are presumably pure of sexual taint

41 ***Saint . . . heavens** Q's punctuation (see t.n.) has invited dispute as to whether *fore the heavens* is either

28 on] vpon *F*   30 waiting-gentlewoman] *(*waiting gentlewoman*)*, *Rowe*   35 bearward] *Knight;* Berrord *Q;* bearherd *F3*   36 hell?] *Hanmer;* hell. *Q*   39–40 'Get . . . maids!'] *Capell subst.;* get . . . maids, *Q*   41 Peter fore . . . heavens.] *Oxf;* Peter, for . . . heavens. *Pope subst.;* Peter: for . . . heauens, *Q*

where the bachelors sit, and there live we as merry as
the day is long.

ANTONIO [*to Hero*]   Well, niece, I trust you will be ruled
by your father.   45

BEATRICE   Yes, faith, it is my cousin's duty to make
curtsy, and say, 'Father, as it please you.' But yet for
all that, cousin, let him be a handsome fellow, or else
make another curtsy, and say, 'Father, as it please me.'

LEONATO   Well, niece, I hope to see you one day fitted   50
with a husband.

BEATRICE   Not till God make men of some other metal
than earth. Would it not grieve a woman to be over-
mastered with a piece of valiant dust? To make an
account of her life to a clod of wayward marl? No,   55

a mild oath, or a reference to Saint Peter's location (before), or to the part of the heavens to which Saint Peter assigns Beatrice.

42 bachelors unmarried persons of either sex

42–3 merry ... long proverbial (Dent, D57)

46–7 make curtsy i.e. demonstrate respect (perhaps a suggestion for stage action)

49 Father . . . me Beatrice's advice to Hero anticipates the equally novel wish of Helena in *AW* (1.1.151–2), to 'lose' her virginity 'to her own liking'.

50–1 fitted with The metaphor is a sartorial one, but contains a sexual innuendo as well.

52 metal also play on 'mettle' (substance of character, as opposed to material component); cf. Barnaby Rich, *The Excellency of Good Women* (1613): 'But the better to make tryall of women's perfection in generall, let us examine their first creation, wherein it is to be noted the substance whereof they were formed,

which was of the purified mettall of man' (Rich, sig. A4ʳ).

53–4 over-mastered An early modern woman was supposed to acknowledge a husband as her master; the marriage service of the *Book of Common Prayer* (1559) reads: 'Ye women submit yourselves unto your own husbands as unto the Lord, for the husband is the wife's head even as Christ is the head of the Church' (*BCP*, 298). See also 259–60n.

54 valiant dust Cf. Genesis, 2.7: 'And the Lord God also made the man of the dust of the ground, and breathed in his face the breath of life, and the man was a liuing soule.' Beatrice's oxymoron recalls the warning of the Geneva Bible's marginal note: 'Hee sheweth wereof mans body was created, to the intent that man should not glorie in the excellencie of his own nature.'

55 wayward errant (because fallen)
marl soil of lime and clay, sometimes used for fertilizer

44 SD] *Rowe*   47, 49 curtsy] *(cursie)*   47 say, 'Father, as] *(say, father, as);* say, as *F*   47–9 'Father . . . me.'] *Theobald;* Father . . . me. *Q*   52 metal] *(mettal)*   54 an] *om. F*

uncle, I'll none. Adam's sons are my brethren, and
truly, I hold it a sin to match in my kindred.

LEONATO   Daughter, remember what I told you. If the
prince do solicit you in that kind, you know your
answer.   60

BEATRICE   The fault will be in the music, cousin, if you be
not wooed in good time. If the prince be too important,
tell him there is measure in everything, and so dance out
the answer. For hear me, Hero; wooing, wedding and
repenting is as a Scotch jig, a measure and a cinque-   65
pace. The first suit is hot and hasty, like a Scotch jig,
and full as fantastical; the wedding mannerly-modest as
a measure, full of state and ancientry; and then comes
Repentance, and with his bad legs falls into the cinque-

---

57   **kindred** relations too close for marriage;
Elizabethan devotional texts (such as
catechisms, or the *Book of Common
Prayer*) often list degrees of consanguinity
within which marriage is forbidden.

59   **in that kind** on that subject (of marriage);
Leonato believes that the Prince intends to
woo Hero for himself.

62   **in good time** at the appropriate moment;
rhythmically
important hasty (importunate, cf. *KL* 4.3.26
and *AW* 3.7.21); overbearing, too grand (as
in Beatrice's comment to the Prince at 302–3
that he is 'too costly to wear everyday')

63   **measure** moderation; a stately dance (see
68); temperate quality
measure in everything proverbial (Dent,
M806)

64   **the answer** a musical (and antiphonal)
response

65   **Scotch jig** an especially lively (even lewd)
dance in the round

65–6   **cinque-pace** a capering dance (galliard)
with a five-beat step followed by a leap
(hence difficult to perform); pronounced
'sink-a-pace', hence the pun, and the

incongruity, at 70). Thomas Middleton also
characterizes dances in this fashion in *Women
Beware Women* (1627), 3.2.215–18: 'Plain
men dance the measures, the sinquapace the
gay; / Cuckoldes dance the hornpipe, and
farmers dance the hay; / Your soldiers dance
the round, and maidens that grow big; / Your
drunkards, the canaries; your whore and
bawd the jig' (Middleton, 6.317).

66   **suit** courtship of a lover

67   **full as fantastical** every bit as extravagant,
passionate
mannerly-modest decorous

68   **state** pomp
ancientry tradition

69   **Repentance** Beatrice's personification
invokes the medieval morality play's plot
of human life, in which the protagonist
ideally finished by entering the grave
repenting of his worldly sins (and hence
accompanied by an actor representing
Repentance).
bad legs The literary device of
personification represented moral identities
in physiognomic terms, as in Spenser's
Faerie Queene, where Gluttony (for

---

62 important] importunate *Rowe³*   67 mannerly-modest] *(manerly modest)*, *Theobald*

pace faster and faster, till he sink into his grave.   70

LEONATO   Cousin, you apprehend passing shrewdly.

BEATRICE   I have a good eye, uncle; I can see a church by
daylight.

LEONATO [*to Antonio*]   The revellers are entering, brother.
Make good room. [*Antonio steps aside, and masks.*]   75

Enter DON PEDRO, CLAUDIO, BENEDICK,
BALTHASAR[, *masked, with a Drum,* MARGARET
and URSULA,] *and* DON JOHN[, BORACHIO *and others.*
Music and dancing begin].

instance) is a 'Deformed creature, on a
filthy swyne, / His belly was up-blowne
with luxury' (*FQ*, 1.4.21.2–3). The
penitent's weak legs would presumably
indicate the feebleness of old age (and by
extension his ward's reluctance to repent or
weakness of spirit), or, alternatively, his
propensity for kneeling.

71 **apprehend** perceive
passing shrewdly very satirically

72 **church** usually the most conspicuous
structure in a town; Beatrice's claim to
the ability to see what is patently obvious
contrasts with imagery elsewhere in the
play in which vision is considered as
a malleable and socially conditioned
quantity, e.g. 2.3.21–2, 'May I be so
converted and see with these eyes?';
3.4.84, 'methinks you look with your eyes
as other women do'; 3.2.107–8, 'If you
dare not trust that you see, confess not that
you know'; 2.1.163–5, 'Let every eye
negotiate for itself, / And trust no agent; for
Beauty is a witch / Against whose charms
faith melteth into blood.' The phrase could
also mean that she sees a wedding in the
near future (cf. *AYL* 2.7.52).

75 **Make good room** stand aside; clear the
space. Antonio is one of the masquers, so
this provides an opportunity for him to
either step aside and put on a visor (as the
SD indicates), or (as some editions choose)
to exit and re-enter masked.

75 SD It seems according to the SD and
Renaissance convention that only the men
mask (unless they are already masked; cf.
5.4), and perhaps only those (plus Claudio)
who participate in the dance, although
most productions mask both sexes.
Leonato, as host, may remain unmasked
(cf. *RJ* 1.5 or *H8* 1.4), as well as Don John
and his associates, Don John being
professedly hostile to social amusements.
The dance has often served in productions
as an occasion for great spectacle (Cox,
Shakespeare, 113).

75.2–3 Margaret and Ursula are given no entry
to this scene in Q. Rowe introduced them at
the opening, but since they have no
speaking parts until the dance they might
equally enter here (particularly to maintain
the pretence that Ursula is meant not to
know Antonio's identity); see Wells, 'Foul-
paper', 6.

74 SD] *Oxf¹*   75 SD] *this edn; Exit Antonio. Cam²; Leonato and his company mask. / Capell; He signals
the others to disperse and don masks Oxf¹*   75.1 DON] *Rowe; prince, Pedro Q*   75.2 *masked, with a Drum*]
F (*Maskers with a Drum*)   75.2–3 MARGARET *and* URSULA] *this edn* (Wells)   75.3 *and* DON JOHN] *Capell
(and Don* John); *or dumb Iohn Q*   BORACHIO] *Capell   and others*] *Rowe*   75.4 *Music . . . begin*] *Cam²
(The dance begins)*

DON PEDRO [*to Hero*]   Lady, will you walk a bout with
　your friend?

HERO   So you walk softly, and look sweetly, and say nothing,
　I am yours for the walk; and especially when I walk away.

DON PEDRO   With me in your company?   80

HERO   I may say so, when I please.

DON PEDRO   And when please you to say so?

HERO   When I like your favour – for God defend the lute
　should be like the case!

DON PEDRO   My visor is Philemon's roof: within the house   85
　is Jove.

HERO   Why then, your visor should be thatched.

---

76   ***a bout** a turn, a portion of the dance (but
the aural sense 'about' also applies); cf. *RJ*
1.5.17–18. 'Welcome, gentlemen, ladies
that have their toes / Unplagu'd with corns
will walk a bout with you.' Alan Brissenden
suggests that the dance here is the pavan,
'for in that elegant perambulation the
couples can be side by side with hands
linked at arm's length and the steps involve
turns back and forth, retreats and advances,
so that it is ideal for highlighting dramatic
conversation' (Brissenden, 49). It is also
possible that the dialogue between the
couples occurs as they pair off in
preparation for the dance.

77   **friend** partner, lover

78   **So** so long as

79   **walk away** probably a reference to the
movement required by the dance pattern;
see 76n.

83   **favour** face, looks
　　defend forbid (cf. the French *défendre*)

84   **like the case** This indicates that Don Pedro
wears a grotesque mask (it is doubtful that
Hero toys with the salacious meaning of
case here, though her playful speech in this

scene indicates some capacity for the
verbal dexterity of her peers).

85   **visor** mask
　　Philemon's roof Don Pedro compares his
ugly visor to the humble cottage roof
('thatched all with straw and fennish
reed') of Philemon and Baucis, an elderly
and impoverished couple in Ovid's
Metamorphoses, who nonetheless provided
unstinting hospitality to the gods Jove and
Mercury disguised as humble travellers
(8.616–735). Don Pedro's comparison of
himself to Jove hints at his (godlike, or at
least well-born) identity to Hero. The idea
of Jove, king of the gods, in a thatched
cottage was (like Christ in a manger) a
familiar trope of incongruity or paradox; see
AYL 3.3.9–10: 'O knowledge ill-inhabited,
worse than Jove in a thatched house!'

85–8   The couple trade lines here in a rhyme that
shares the 14-syllable verse line of Arthur
Golding's translation of the *Metamorphoses*
(Ovid / Golding, fol. 113ᵛ, sig. 07ᵛ).

87   **thatched** i.e. like a humble cottage;
whiskered; or Hero's reply could suggest
that he is balding.

76+   SP] *Capell (D. Pe); Pedro Q*   76 SD] *Cam¹   (Leading Hero forth)*   a bout] *Cam¹; about Q*
78   So you] *F;* So, you *Q*   80 company?] *Rowe³;* company *Q*   85–6] *Oxf¹ lines* roof. / Jove. / 86 Jove]
(Ioue); Loue *F*

DON PEDRO   Speak low if you speak love. [*They move
aside; Balthasar and Margaret come forward.*]
BALTHASAR   Well, I would you did like me.
MARGARET   So would not I, for your own sake, for I have   90
many ill qualities.
BALTHASAR   Which is one?
MARGARET   I say my prayers aloud.
BALTHASAR   I love you the better; the hearers may cry
amel!   95
MARGARET   God match me with a good dancer!
BALTHASAR   Amen!
MARGARET   And God keep him out of my sight when the
dance is done! Answer, clerk.

88 **Speak low** The instruction suggests a SD for
the tone of Hero's voice throughout; it also
provides for the invitation to private speech
necessary to Don Pedro's proposal, and
clears the way for the next pair of dancers.
89, 92, 94 SP *BALTHASAR This edition
follows Theobald in assigning these
speeches to Balthasar, in keeping with Q's
assignment at 97 and 100, and on the
grounds of symmetry ('so that every man
talks with his woman once round',
Furness). By the same logic, some
productions partner Margaret with her
friend Borachio (using Balthasar as a
musician), and yet other editors, and
productions, have posited, in keeping with
Q's assignments, that Margaret switches
partners (i.e. Balthasar cuts in on Benedick
at 97). Dyce asked 'is not the effect of the
scene considerably weakened if Benedick
enters into conversation with any other
woman except Beatrice?' (Dyce, *Notes*,
42); however, an exchange between

Margaret and Benedick here could prepare
for their flirtatious exchange in 5.2. Capell
hypothesized that the women are also
masked, and that 'Benedick, who is in
search of Beatrice, lights upon Margaret; a
sharp one, her voice, suiting her sharpness;
this voice (which she raises) betrays her to
Benedick, who quits her smartly and
hastily, a manner resented slightly by
Margaret, who expressed it in her prayer'
(Capell, *Notes*, 2.12). Pamela Mason
suggests that 'If Benedick is allowed to
speak these lines to Margaret it shows a
Benedick aware of his attraction to women
and following his superior's lead in not
respecting established alliances' (Mason,
247). Compositor error or typographical
necessity has also been adduced for the
change in SPs in the early texts.
93 **aloud** Religious enthusiasts were known
for their vocal declamation of prayers.
99 **Answer** i.e. say 'amen'
clerk respondent in a liturgy

88 SD *They move aside*] Capell *(Drawing her aside)   Balthasar . . . forward*] Folg² *(Benedick and
Margaret move forward)*   89, 92, 94 SP] Theobald; *Bene.* Q; *Borachio* Cam¹

BALTHASAR   No more words; the clerk is answered. [*They*   100
     move aside; Ursula and Antonio come forward.]

URSULA   I know you well enough; you are Signor
     Antonio.

ANTONIO   At a word, I am not.

URSULA   I know you by the waggling of your head.

ANTONIO   To tell you true, I counterfeit him.   105

URSULA   You could never do him so ill-well, unless you
     were the very man. Here's his dry hand up and down.
     You are he, you are he!

ANTONIO   At a word, I am not.

URSULA   Come, come, do you think I do not know you by   110
     your excellent wit? Can virtue hide itself? Go to, mum;
     you are he; graces will appear, and there's an end. [*They*
     move aside; Benedick and Beatrice come forward.]

BEATRICE   Will you not tell me who told you so?

BENEDICK   No, you shall pardon me.

BEATRICE   Nor will you not tell me who you are?   115

BENEDICK   Not now.

BEATRICE   That I was disdainful, and that I had my good
     wit out of *The Hundred Merry Tales*! Well, this was
     Signor Benedick that said so.

---

100 **the . . . answered** i.e. I get the message

103 **At** in (the word being *not*)

104 **waggling** tremor; like *dry hand* (107), a
'character of age'; *2H4* 1.2.180–2
specifies others: 'Have you not a moist
eye, a dry hand, a yellow cheek, a white
beard, a decreasing leg, an increasing
belly?'

105 **counterfeit** impersonate

106 **do . . . ill-well** imitate him so
effectively, by being so doddering,
'represent his imperfection so perfectly'
(Brooke)

107 **up and down** exactly, all over; cf. *Tit*
5.2.107: 'up and down she doth resemble
thee'.

111 **Go to, mum** go on, hush

112 **graces** good qualities
an end all there is to say

114 **shall** must

118 ***Hundred Merry Tales*** a collection of
comic stories and jokes of not very
sophisticated humour, printed by John
Rastell in 1526, apparently popular
(though only one copy is now extant, in
the Royal Library of Göttingen). Its

100 SD *Ursula . . . forward*] *Folg²; They move aside / Kittredge; parting different ways / Capell*
106 ill-well] *Theobald;* ill well *Q;* ill Will *Rowe;* ill, well *Pope*   112 SD *Benedick . . . forward*] *Folg²; They*
step aside / Kittredge; mixing with the company / Capell   118 *The . . . Tales*] *Hanmer;* the hundred mery
tales *Q*

BENEDICK What's he? 120

BEATRICE I am sure you know him well enough.

BENEDICK Not I, believe me.

BEATRICE Did he never make you laugh?

BENEDICK I pray you, what is he?

BEATRICE Why he is the prince's jester, a very dull fool; 125
only his gift is in devising impossible slanders. None but
libertines delight in him, and the commendation is not
in his wit but in his villainy, for he both pleases men and
angers them, and then they laugh at him and beat him.
I am sure he is in the fleet; I would he had boarded me. 130

BENEDICK When I know the gentleman, I'll tell him what
you say.

BEATRICE Do, do. He'll but break a comparison or two on

---

recitation was rumoured to be a solace of
Queen Elizabeth (Furness, citing a letter in
the Venetian correspondence of the State
Papers Office, 9 March 1603), though
Beatrice takes offence at the implication
that she owes her verbal prowess to such a
hackneyed text (or to any source at all,
other than her own imagination).

125 **jester** Beatrice returns the insult by
implying that Benedick is a court buffoon,
employed to keep royalty entertained
(though compare this with her own possible
equation with Leonato's fool at 1.1.37).

126 **only his gift** his only skill
impossible slanders incredible or
outrageous libels (such as Beatrice getting
her wit out of crude jest-books); the play's
plot turns on just such a slander.

127 **libertines** persons of loose morals or
lightweight intelligence
commendation recommendation,
approval

128 **in . . . in** of . . . of
villainy malice; acuity of his slander

128–9 **pleases . . . them** i.e. pleases by his
malice and angers by hitting the mark in

his slanders; or, pleases some men by
slandering others, and angers those whom
he slanders. Neither describes a portrait of
a very generous wit.

129 **beat him** a traditional punishment for
court fools

130 **in the fleet** i.e. among the dancers
boarded i.e. as one boards a ship, took on,
attempted, engaged with (as in a contest of
wit, but also with sexual innuendo); cf. *TN*
1.3.55–6, Sir Toby to Sir Andrew: 'You
mistake, knight. "Accost" is front her,
board her, woo her, assail her.'

133–4 **break . . . me** level (ineffectively) a few
slanderous comparisons at me; from the
metaphor for tilting, as a knight in a
tournament breaks a lance; cf. Lyly,
Campaspe (1584), 2.1.56–7: '*Psyllus:*
Why, you were at mortall iars [i.e. jars =
wars]. / *Manus:* In faith no, we brake a
bitter iest one vppon another' (*Works*,
2.328). A comparison was an insulting
simile; Beatrice implies that the unkind
figures of speech with which Benedick
will undoubtedly attempt to slander her
will fall short of their mark.

128 pleases] pleaseth *F*

224

me, which, peradventure not marked, or not laughed
at, strikes him into melancholy, and then there's a 135
partridge wing saved, for the fool will eat no supper
that night. We must follow the leaders.

BENEDICK In every good thing.

BEATRICE Nay, if they lead to any ill I will leave them at
the next turning. 140

Dance. Exeunt [all but Don John, Borachio and Claudio].

DON JOHN Sure my brother is amorous on Hero and hath
withdrawn her father to break with him about it. The
ladies follow her, and but one visor remains.

BORACHIO [*aside to Don John*] And that is Claudio; I
know him by his bearing. 145

DON JOHN Are not you Signor Benedick?

CLAUDIO You know me well. I am he.

DON JOHN Signor, you are very near my brother in his
love. He is enamoured on Hero. I pray you, dissuade

---

134 **peradventure** perhaps
  marked noticed, commended
136 **partridge wing saved** i.e. the *valiant
  trencher-man* (1.1.48) will be so
  melancholy that he will refrain from
  eating an entire partridge wing (a bone
  with very little meat). The diminutive
  partridge wing was considered a delicacy.
137 **We . . . leaders** i.e. we must keep pace
  with the dance; this could provide a SD for
  their falling out of step whilst bickering,
  and hence needing to regain their place in
  the dance pattern.
140 **turning** parting of roads; a change in
  dance figure
141–3 Whether or not Don John now believes
  that it is Don Pedro who is in fact *amorous
  on Hero*, or whether he is even at this point
  trying to goad Claudio (which he certainly

is by 149), depends on whether these lines
are spoken in Claudio's hearing or as an
aside (i.e. on how nefariously Don John
is played – or, alternatively, as how he too
is subject to misnoting the evidence of
his eyes). If the former, Borachio's
comment at 144–5 needs to be delivered,
and responded to, as a statement of what
is already obvious to Don John (i.e.
Borachio could be played as being
rather slow-witted – perhaps because
drunk?). In either case the speech is also a
signal of the masked Claudio's identity
to the audience. Garrick's 1777 text
clarified the issue by inserting 'now for a
trick of contrivance' at the beginning of
the speech.
148–9 **very . . . love** an intimate friend of his
149 **enamoured on** in love with

140 SD *Dance. Exeunt*] *Exeunt. / Musicke for the dance. F   all . . . Claudio.*] *Theobald subst.*   141 + SP]
Capell (D. Jo.); Iohn Q   Sure] *Aside to Borachio.* Sure *Oxf¹*   144 SD] *Oxf¹*   146 Are] *Approaching
Claudio.* Are *Oxf¹*

him from her; she is no equal for his birth. You may do   150
the part of an honest man in it.

CLAUDIO   How know you he loves her?

DON JOHN   I heard him swear his affection.

BORACHIO   So did I too, and he swore he would marry her
tonight.   155

DON JOHN   Come, let us to the banquet.

Exeunt all but Claudio.

CLAUDIO

Thus answer I in name of Benedick,
But hear these ill news with the ears of Claudio.
'Tis certain so; the prince woos for himself.
Friendship is constant in all other things,   160
Save in the office and affairs of love.
Therefore all hearts in love use their own tongues:
Let every eye negotiate for itself,
And trust no agent; for Beauty is a witch

---

150 **no ... birth** of too low a social station, for the *too important* Don Pedro (as Beatrice describes him at 62). (Not, apparently, something that occurs to Leonato, Antonio, Claudio or Benedick, all of whom at some time believe that the Prince woos on his own behalf.) René Girard's reading of the play emphasizes the intended slight here, to argue that 'If he, Claudio, is really allowed to marry Hero, it means that the Prince has no personal interest in her; immediately, she seems less interesting than when the opposite appeared to be true. Cut off from the model whose desire transfigured her, she looks less attractive ... [Claudio] wonders if some secret disgrace might not account for her willingness to bind her fate to such a lowly character as himself' (Girard, 86).

150–1 **do the part** perform the service

151 **honest** loyal; truthful

156 **banquet** a 'course of sweetmeats, fruit, and wine, served either as a separate entertainment, or as a continuation of the principal meal, but in the latter case usually in a different room' (*OED sb.*[1] 3). Cf. *TS* 5.2.9–10: 'My banquet is to close our stomachs up / After our great good cheer.'

158 **news** See 1.2.5n.

160–1 proverbial: 'When love puts in, friendship is gone' (Dent, L549). Male rivalry over women is a feature of the euphuistic plot.

161 **office** functions, business

162 **Therefore** i.e. therefore let

164 **Beauty . . . witch** Claudio attributes Don Pedro's behaviour to female sorcery rather than male perfidy; the conversion of faith into the more carnal blood (or passion) recalls Circe's transformation of Odysseus' men into

---

156 SD *all but*] *Rowe subst.; manet Q*

Against whose charms faith melteth into blood. 165
This is an accident of hourly proof
Which I mistrusted not. Farewell, therefore, Hero!

Enter BENEDICK.

BENEDICK Count Claudio.
CLAUDIO Yea, the same.
BENEDICK Come, will you go with me? 170
CLAUDIO Whither?
BENEDICK Even to the next willow, about your own business, county. What fashion will you wear the garland of? About your neck, like an usurer's chain? Or under your arm, like a lieutenant's scarf? You must 175 wear it one way, for the prince hath got your Hero.
CLAUDIO I wish him joy of her.
BENEDICK Why, that's spoken like an honest drover; so they sell bullocks. But did you think the prince would have served you thus? 180

swine in Homer's *Odyssey* (10.148–631), as well as Ovidian instances of persons and deities being converted into animal form.
165 **blood** passion, desire
166 **accident** event
  hourly i.e. frequent
167 **mistrusted not** never suspected; should have expected (more likely the latter, given the claim for frequency)
169 **the same** Perhaps Claudio has yet to unmask, though many productions have him do so before his soliloquy.
172 **willow** Willow garlands were the emblem of the forsaken (see *Oth* 4.3.50) or the merely lovelorn.
173 **county** count. This common form of 'count' is 'app[arently] an adoption of AF.

counte, or OF. and It. *conte*, with unusual retention of final vowel, confused in form with COUNTY (*OED* county²). 'Shakespeare uses both forms although one may be felt to add a little local colour' (*TxC*, 372).
174 **of** in
  usurer's chain a heavy gold chain worn by a money-lender, a reviled profession
175 **lieutenant's scarf** a sash worn diagonally across the body marking the rank of a lieutenant, that below captain; a lieutenant was empowered to stand in, or take the place (from the French *lieu tenir*) of his superior. Cam¹ glosses 174–5 as 'are you going to make capital out of this by claiming preferment from the Prince in return for your loss, or shall you challenge him to a duel?'
178 **drover** cattle-dealer

173 county] Count *F*   174 of] off *F*   178 drover] *(Drouier)*

CLAUDIO I pray you leave me.

BENEDICK Ho, now you strike like the blindman! 'Twas
the boy that stole your meat, and you'll beat the post.

CLAUDIO If it will not be, I'll leave you.   *Exit.*

BENEDICK Alas, poor hurt fowl, now will he creep into 185
sedges. But that my Lady Beatrice should know me,
and not know me! The prince's fool – hah! It may be I
go under that title because I am merry. Yea, but so I am
apt to do myself wrong. I am not so reputed; it is the
base, though bitter, disposition of Beatrice that puts the 190
world into her person and so gives me out. Well, I'll be
revenged as I may.

Enter DON PEDRO, HERO [*and*] LEONATO.

DON PEDRO Now, signor, where's the count? Did you see
him?

182–3 **strike . . . blindman . . . beat . . .
post** i.e. behave irrationally, as in blind
anger
183 **post** pillar; messenger
186 **sedges** reeds, a good hiding place for a
wounded bird. This image inaugurates a
chain of like references to the hunting and
trapping of wild animals.
188 **merry** high-spirited (rather than foolish)
190 **base** mean, low-minded
though bitter albeit stinging, cutting
190–1 **puts . . . person** claims to speak for
everyone else, represents her own opinion
as the world's
191 **gives me out** portrays me according to
that opinion
192.1 *Q includes Don John, Borachio and
Conrade in this entrance, though it is clear
from 2.2 that Don John has not been
present, and presumably nor have his

henchmen. F has the Prince enter alone
here, and Leonato and Hero with Claudio
and Beatrice at 239. As the latter choice
perhaps indicates, given that Hero and
Leonato have no lines until 277 (Hero is
mute until 346), their silent presence
during the exchange between Benedick
and Don Pedro about the latter's
purloining of Claudio's girl could be
theatrically awkward (though Benedick is
hardly a model of tact); alternatively, the
tone (and sting) of Benedick's subsequent
diatribe can be conditioned by his playing
to the additional audience of her uncle and
cousin, as well as by the timing of
Beatrice's own entry (some productions
have her enter when Benedick is in mid-
rant, which can produce humour or
embarrassment at the expense of either
party). Benedick's reference to *this young*

187 fool – hah!] *Capell (*fool? Ha!*)*; fool! – ha? *Johnson*; foole! hah, *Q*; foole! Hah? *F*   190 though bitter]
((though bitter)*); and bitter *Oxf¹ (Craven)*   192.1] *Rowe*; *Enter the Prince, Hero, Leonato, Iohn and
B*orachio, and Conrade. Q*; *Enter the Prince. F*   193–295+ SP DON PEDRO] *Capell (D. Pe.)*; *Pedro
Q*   193 signor] *(*signior*)*

BENEDICK   Troth, my lord, I have played the part of Lady   195
Fame. I found him here as melancholy as a lodge in
a warren. I told him, and I think I told him true, that
your grace had got the good will of this young lady, and
I offered him my company to a willow tree, either to
make him a garland, as being forsaken, or to bind him   200
up a rod, as being worthy to be whipped.

DON PEDRO   To be whipped? What's his fault?

BENEDICK   The flat transgression of a schoolboy, who,
being overjoyed with finding a bird's nest, shows it his
companion, and he steals it.   205

DON PEDRO   Wilt thou make a trust a transgression? The
transgression is in the stealer.

BENEDICK   Yet it had not been amiss the rod had been
made, and the garland too; for the garland he might
have worn himself, and the rod he might have bestowed   210
on you, who, as I take it, have stolen his bird's nest.

DON PEDRO   I will but teach them to sing, and restore
them to the owner.

BENEDICK   If their singing answer your saying, by my
faith you say honestly.   215

---

lady at 198 can suggest that Hero is
present; Q's 'this' could, though, be a
misreading of copy 'his'.

195–6 **Lady Fame** a spreader of news;
Virgil's Fama (*Aeneid*, 4.181–90) has
many eyes, ears and tongues (much like
Shakespeare's Rumour personified in *2H4*
Prologue), and in this sense communicates
information more generally rather than
exclusively connoting notoriety or
celebrity.

196–7 **lodge . . . warren** isolated hunting
lodge in a game park

198 **good will** agreement

200 **garland** i.e. of willow

203 **flat** outright

transgression . . . schoolboy i.e. error of
youth and naivety

205 **he** i.e. the companion; the purloining of a
nest belonging to another is in fact the
habit of the cuckoo, from which the word
'cuckold' derives.

206 **Wilt . . . transgression** i.e. are you
interpreting a trust as a transgression? Don
Pedro questions the logic of Benedick's
metaphor.

212 **them** perhaps a reference to both Leonato
and Hero, both of whom must be consulted
in the transaction; the 'song' is an
agreement to wed.

214 **answer** corroborate

215 **say honestly** speak in good faith

197 think I told] thinke, told *F*   198 good will] *(goodwil); will F*   201 up] *om. F*

DON PEDRO   The Lady Beatrice hath a quarrel to you.
The gentleman that danced with her told her she is
much wronged by you.

BENEDICK   O, she misused me past the endurance of a
block! An oak but with one green leaf on it would have   220
answered her; my very visor began to assume life and
scold with her! She told me, not thinking I had been
myself, that I was the prince's jester, that I was duller
than a great thaw, huddling jest upon jest with such
impossible conveyance upon me that I stood like a man   225
at a mark, with a whole army shooting at me. She
speaks poniards, and every word stabs. If her breath
were as terrible as her terminations there were no living
near her, she would infect to the North Star. I would
not marry her though she were endowed with all that   230
Adam had left him before he transgressed. She would

216 **to** with
218 **wronged by you** injured by your slanders
219 **misused** abused
220 **block** insensible object; cf. *JC* 1.1.36: 'You blocks, you stones, you worse than senseless things!'
   with . . . leaf immature; with the faintest sign of life
222 **scold** argue, but the verb implies Beatrice's shrewish identity
223–4 **duller . . . thaw** more boring than the spring rainy season (when roads were impassable and visiting impossible)
224 **huddling** piling up
225 **impossible conveyance** incredible dexterity; outrageous expression
226 **mark** target; a man standing near a target could, albeit perilously, inform the archers of how close their arrows were to their object – as in e.g. John Webster, *The White*

Devil (1612), 3.2.24–5: 'I am at the mark, sir: I'll give aim to you / And tell you how near you shoot.'
227 **poniards** daggers; cf. Philip Massinger, *The Duke of Milan* (1623), 2.1.377–8: 'euerie word's a Poynard, / And reaches to my Heart' (Massinger, 1.244).
228 **terminations** descriptive terms (Shakespeare's sole use and the *OED*'s sole citation for this use, solicited perhaps by the tempting alliteration and rhythm)
229 **she . . . Star** i.e. she would pollute the entire universe
230 **marry her** Benedick has obviously thought of Beatrice as a marriage partner, just as she has of him at 10–15.
231 **Adam . . . transgressed** Before disobeying God's instruction to eschew the fruit of the tree of knowledge of good and evil, Adam lived in paradise, whose benefits

223 jester, that] Iester, and that *F*   228 her] *om. F*

have made Hercules have turned spit, yea, and have
cleft his club to make the fire too. Come, talk not of her,
you shall find her the infernal Ate in good apparel. I
would to God some scholar would conjure her, for   235
certainly while she is here a man may live as quiet in
hell as in a sanctuary, and people sin upon purpose
because they would go thither — so indeed all disquiet,
horror and perturbation follows her.

Enter CLAUDIO *and* BEATRICE.

included freedom from death, sin and labour, and, theoretically, dominion over the rest of creation, including his wife (Genesis, 2.16–17, 3.1–23). Benedick perhaps wants his audience to recall also that Adam's wife Eve provoked the fall of man ('The woman thou gavest to be with mee, she gave mee of the tree, and I did eat', Genesis, 3.12).

231–3 **She . . . too** i.e. she would have out-henpecked Omphale of classical legend; see 29–30n.

232 **have turned** For duplication of the perfect tense, see Abbott, 360.
turned spit Turning the roasting spit over the fire was considered the most menial of Elizabethan kitchen tasks. Hercules' club was a massive (and phallic) one, and splitting it into firewood would have been an arduous as well as emasculating task for him to undertake. The misogyny of Benedick's caricatures increases as he elaborates them.

233 **cleft** split

234 **Ate . . . apparel** the classical goddess of discord (pronounced 'ah-tay'), and eldest daughter of Zeus, beautiful in appearance but usually clad in rags, and instigator of the Trojan war; cf. *JC* 3.1.271–3: 'Ate . . . come hot from hell, / Shall . . . / Cry havoc'; and *KJ* 2.1.63: 'An Ate, stirring him to blood and strife'. *The Lamentable*

Tragedy of Locrine (1595) presents Ate as a chorus, entering 'with thunder and lightning, all in black, with a burning torch in one hand and a bloody sword in the other', and warning that 'a woman was the only cause / That civil discord was then stirred up' (*Locrine*, Epilogue, 200–1). The image of Beatrice here joins other female figures of dissent with misleadingly pleasant appearance, such as Duessa and Ate in Spenser's *Faerie Queene*: 'in face / And outward shewe faire semblance they did beare; / [though] vnder maske of beautie and good grace, / Vile treason and fowle falshood hidden were, / That mote to none but to the warie wise appeare' (*FQ*, 4.1.17.5–9); cf. Claudio's speech to Hero at 4.1.56–9: 'You seem to me as Dian in her orb . . . / But you are more intemperate in your blood / Than Venus'.

235 **conjure her** Scholars were thought adept at both summoning spirits and exorcising them back again to the place whence they came.

236 **here** i.e. on earth

237 **sanctuary** religious refuge

238 **thither** i.e. to hell

239.1 The timing of this entrance can affect the tenor of Benedick's speech; he may, for instance, shift at once into a different tone of voice.

239.1 BEATRICE] *Beatrice, Leonato, Hero.* F

DON PEDRO   Look, here she comes.   240

BENEDICK   Will your grace command me any service to
the world's end? I will go on the slightest errand now to
the Antipodes that you can devise to send me on. I will
fetch you a toothpicker now from the furthest inch of
Asia; bring you the length of Prester John's foot; fetch   245
you a hair off the Great Cham's beard; do you any
embassage to the Pygmies, rather than hold three words'
conference with this harpy. You have no employment
for me?

DON PEDRO   None, but to desire your good company.   250

243 **Antipodes** region and people on the other
side of the earth (and thus the soles of
whose feet 'are as it were planted against'
our own, *OED* 1); Benedick's desire to
undertake far-fetched and exotic journeys
of derring-do in order to avoid a woman
associated, through Ate, with sorcery
recalls the type of the male adventurer
Odysseus fleeing Circe for home, or
Aeneas fleeing Dido for duty. Both are
cited by Ovid in his *Remedies of Love* as
examples of how to swear off love (sig.
C1ᵛ).

244 **toothpicker** i.e. like the objectives he
lists, a trivial pursuit for such an arduous
errand (but presumably worth it if it
allows him to avoid Beatrice). Toothpicks
were considered fashion accessories; in
AW they are outmoded (1.1.158–9); in *KJ*
(1.1.190) they are considered the
affectation of travellers.

245 **Prester John's foot** Prester John was a
figure of medieval legend, a Christian
ruler sometimes identified with the king /
emperor-priest of Abyssinia (a fabulously
rich kingdom in the East). Presumably
securing the measurement of his foot, like
procuring a beard-hair of the Great Cham,

would be a difficult enterprise. All the
exotic locales Benedick speaks of are
mentioned in the travel writings of Sir
John Mandeville and Marco Polo.

246 **Great Cham** the title of the Mongol
emperors (Khan of Tartary), e.g. Khublai
or Genghis (who defeated Prester John in
battle). Another powerful figure of oriental
rule.

247 **Pygmies** The battle of the Pygmies (a race
of tiny people) and the Cranes was an
ancient Greek folk tale. The Pygmies are
mentioned in passing by Homer (*Iliad*,
3.5–7); later Pliny the Elder, in his *Natural
History*, set the story in India. The
encounters of a traveller with dwarfish
peoples was a stock feature of medieval
and classical legend.

248 **harpy** a term for a cruel and vicious
woman, from the Greek verb 'to seize',
and in classical legend a monster with the
head and body of a beautiful woman and
the wings and claws of an eagle; cf.
haggard at 3.1.36. Like Ate (234) and her
sisters, a duplicitous figure that combines
an alluring female appearance with
danger. It is a comment which nevertheless
notes Beatrice's beauty.

246 off] of *Steevens–Reed*

BENEDICK   O God, sir, here's a dish I love not; I cannot
endure my Lady Tongue!   *Exit.*

DON PEDRO   Come, lady, come; you have lost the heart of
Signor Benedick.

BEATRICE   Indeed, my lord, he lent it me awhile, and I   255
gave him use for it, a double heart for his single one.
Marry, once before he won it of me with false dice;
therefore your grace may well say I have lost it.

DON PEDRO   You have put him down, lady, you have put
him down.   260

BEATRICE   So I would not he should do me, my lord, lest I
should prove the mother of fools. I have brought Count
Claudio, whom you sent me to seek.

DON PEDRO   Why, how now, Count? Wherefore are you
sad?   265

CLAUDIO   Not sad, my lord.

DON PEDRO   How then? Sick?

252 **Lady Tongue** like the 'good continuer'
Lady Disdain (1.1.136, 112), a figure of
female shrewishness and garrulousness;
cf. *Lady Fame*, 2.1.195–6.

255–6 **I . . . it** I paid him interest on the use of
his heart (i.e. Beatrice returned her own
heart – *a double heart* – in addition to, or
in exchange for, his). Along with 1.1.138–
9, a suggestion of a past romantic
disappointment (which would make
Benedick and Beatrice's history analogous
to Claudio and Hero's in consisting of
an initial setback followed by a
reaffirmation).

257 **it** i.e. his – or perhaps her own – heart
false dice dice that have been weighted so
as to permit cheating in a game of chance.
Beatrice implies that at some point in the

past Benedick broke faith with her despite
her own generous terms of 100 per cent
interest (usury was, however, itself a
suspect practice).

259–60 **put him down** defeated or demeaned
him. Beatrice's response sexualizes the
phrase, and, as John Traugott observes,
'Beatrice is forever thinking of (or being
made to think of) the ultimate female
position in the congress of the sexes – put
down, overmastered, lying in woolen,
dancing the love dance down into the
grave' (Traugott, 173).

262 **fools** errant humans; additionally, any
children of Benedick's might resemble
their foolish father, the Prince's jester.

265 **sad** solemn, serious; an implied SD for
the actor playing Claudio

252 my Lady Tongue] this Lady tongue *F*   256 his] a *F*

CLAUDIO   Neither, my lord.

BEATRICE   The count is neither sad, nor sick, nor merry,
nor well – but civil count, civil as an orange, and   270
something of that jealous complexion.

DON PEDRO   I'faith, lady, I think your blazon to be true;
though I'll be sworn if he be so his conceit is false. Here,
Claudio, I have wooed in thy name, and fair Hero is won.
I have broke with her father, and his good will obtained.   275
Name the day of marriage, and God give thee joy!

LEONATO   Count, take of me my daughter, and with her
my fortunes. His grace hath made the match, and all
grace say amen to it.

BEATRICE   Speak, Count, 'tis your cue.   280

CLAUDIO   Silence is the perfectest herald of joy; I were
but little happy if I could say how much. Lady, as you

[Handwritten marginalia: She gets / No Clue / like a / cue of / meant / are K / cunt even / work / to / Swoon / her]

---

270 **civil** grave, with a pun on Seville, the Spanish town renowned for oranges of a bittersweet flavour (i.e. like Claudio, neither sweet nor sour); the words could be and often were spelled the same in Elizabethan orthography. Cam¹ cites Nashe, *Strange News, Of the Intercepting Certain Letters* (1592): 'For the order of my life, it is as civil as a civil orange' (Nashe, 1.329). In the contrast between their bitter rind and sweet fruit, oranges were also a figure of deception; see 4.1.30n.

271 **jealous complexion** Yellow was considered the symbol of jealousy and suspicion, perhaps because of the melancholy attendant upon jaundice (the word comes from the Old English *geolo*, related to the word for gall). Cf. Robert Greene's *Quip for an Upstart Courtier* (1592): 'Amongst the rest was a yellow daffodil, a flowre fit for gelous Dottrels, who through the bewty of their honest wives grow suspicious' (Greene, *Courtier*,

213); and see *WT* 2.3.105–7. Seville oranges also have a greenish tint, which makes them an apt emblem of the green-eyed monster.

272 **blazon** a poetic technique (derived from the term for the heraldic representation of armorial bearings) for describing the (usually female) person of the beloved in discrete parts; cf. *TN* 1.5.286–7: 'Thy tongue, thy face, thy limbs, actions, and spirit / Do give thee five-fold blazon'.

273 **conceit** idea (i.e. that Hero has been wooed by the Prince for himself)
   Here This could imply a SD for Don Pedro to hand Hero to Claudio.

275 **broke** broached the matter

278–9 **all grace** God (i.e. the source of all grace)

279 **say amen** bless; confirm

280 Beatrice's prompt implies a pregnant pause following Leonato's speech.

281 **herald** announcer, one who blazons

282 **how much** i.e. how happy I am; Claudio's reticence would have

271 that] a *F*   275 obtained.] obtained. *Don Pedro signals; enter Leonato with Hero Oxf¹ (Jenkins)*

are mine, I am yours. I give away myself for you, and
dote upon the exchange.

BEATRICE   Speak, cousin, or, if you cannot, stop his   285
mouth with a kiss and let not him speak neither.

DON PEDRO   In faith, lady, you have a merry heart.

BEATRICE   Yea, my lord, I thank it, poor fool, it keeps on
the windy side of care. My cousin tells him in his ear
that he is in her heart.   290

CLAUDIO   And so she doth, cousin.

BEATRICE   Good Lord, for alliance! Thus goes everyone
to the world but I, and I am sunburnt. I may sit in a
corner and cry 'Hey-ho for a husband'.

DON PEDRO   Lady Beatrice, I will get you one.   295

BEATRICE   I would rather have one of your father's
getting. Hath your grace ne'er a brother like you? Your

been uncharacteristic of a typical
Renaissance lover, who was thought to be
rendered garrulous by the strength of his
feelings (see 1.1.287n.).

289 **windy side** upwind (a location which
would allow care to be blown away from
one, or from which one could, by blocking
the wind, prevent it from accelerating
care's momentum)
tells . . . ear an indication for Hero's stage
action

292 **alliance** marriage, or the association of
families thereby produced (a response to
Claudio's calling her his cousin)

293 **the world** i.e. the married state of the
majority, worldly and carnal compared
with the innocence of celibacy. Cf. *AW*
1.3.18; and Genesis, 19.31, where one of
Lot's daughters says to her sister, 'Our
father is old, and there is not man in the
earth to come unto us after the manner of
all the world.'
sunburnt (1) unhoused by marriage,
and hence exposed to the elements;

(2) unattractively browned by the sun; cf.
5.4.38, 'I'll hold my mind were she an
Ethiope', and *TC* 1.3.282–3, 'The Grecian
dames are sunburnt, and not worth / The
splinter of a lance.' The comment could
also reflect that Beatrice's colouring (like
her *too brown* cousin's, 1.1.164) departs
from the conventional Renaissance norm
of fair beauty.

293–4 **in a corner** the resting place of
wallflowers and spinsters

294 **Hey-ho . . . husband** the proverbial sigh
(Dent, H833) of the woman on the shelf,
and the title of a ballad (subtitled 'or, a
willing Maids wants made known'). Cf.
Burton's *Anatomy of Melancholy*, 3.231:
'Hai-ho for a husband, cries she, a bad
husband, nay the worst that ever was, is
better than none' (Burton, 3.231).

297 **getting** begetting; cf. *get* at 295.
ne'er . . . you Don Pedro does indeed have
a half-brother (Don John), though one
presumably not so like him as to inhibit
Beatrice's rejoinder.

290 her] my *F*   294 'Hey-ho . . . husband'] *Staunton;* heigh ho . . . husband *Q;* 'heigh-ho' . . . husband
Theobald

235

father got excellent husbands, if a maid could come by them.

DON PEDRO   Will you have me, lady?   300

BEATRICE   No, my lord, unless I might have another for working days. Your grace is too costly to wear every day. But I beseech your grace pardon me, I was born to speak all mirth and no matter.

DON PEDRO   Your silence most offends me, and to be 305 merry best becomes you, for out o'question, you were born in a merry hour.

BEATRICE   No, sure, my lord, my mother cried; but then there was a star danced, and under that was I born. [*to Hero and Claudio*] Cousins, God give you joy!   310

LEONATO   Niece, will you look to those things I told you of?

BEATRICE   I cry you mercy, uncle. [*to Don Pedro*] By your grace's pardon.   *Exit.*

298–9 **come by them** acquire one (implies the rarity of Don Pedro's kind)

302 **costly** well born; expensive

304 **no matter** nothing of substance or sense; cf. 1.1.260–1: 'I have almost matter enough in me for such an embassage.'

305 **Your . . . me** i.e. I don't want you to inhibit your speech

307 **merry hour** i.e. both astrologically and auspiciously

308 **my mother cried** a corrective characteristic of Beatrice's emotional realism – as well as her scriptural sense; see Genesis, 3.16: 'Unto the woman he said, I will greatly multiply thy sorrow and thy conception, in sorrow thou shalt bring forth children, and thy desire shall be to thy husband, and he shall rule over thee.'

309 **a star danced** as the sun was reputed to dance on Easter morning; a shooting star

under . . . born i.e. born at the time when a benign astrological sign was predominant, and hence possessing a character influenced by that planet. Cf. 1.3.10–11: 'being as thou sayst thou art, born under Saturn'; 5.2.39–40: 'No, I was not born under a rhyming planet.'

311–12 Leonato could be saving Beatrice – or the Prince – from further embarrassment by inventing for her an excuse to leave.

313–14 Beatrice apologizes to her uncle and excuses herself from the Prince's company; the second phrase could also serve as apology for any offence her humour may have caused.

300, 305, 315SP] *Capell (D. Pe.); Rowe (Pedro); Prince Q*   300 me, lady?] *Rowe;* me? lady. *Q*   306 o']
(a); of *F*   309–10 SD] *Oxf¹*   313 SD] *Oxf¹*

DON PEDRO   By my troth, a pleasant-spirited lady.   315

LEONATO   There's little of the melancholy element in her, my lord. She is never sad but when she sleeps, and not ever sad then; for I have heard my daughter say she hath often dreamt of unhappiness and waked herself with laughing.   320

DON PEDRO   She cannot endure to hear tell of a husband.

LEONATO   O, by no means. She mocks all her wooers out of suit.

DON PEDRO   She were an excellent wife for Benedick.

LEONATO   O Lord, my lord, if they were but a week 325 married, they would talk themselves mad.

DON PEDRO   County Claudio, when mean you to go to church?

CLAUDIO   Tomorrow, my lord. Time goes on crutches till Love have all his rites.   330

LEONATO   Not till Monday, my dear son, which is hence a just sennight – and a time too brief, too, to have all things answer my mind.

DON PEDRO   Come, you shake the head at so long a

---

316 **melancholy element** one of the four humours, believed to be engendered by black bile (the other three provoked by blood, phlegm and cholar), and, like earth, dry and cold. Leonato's diagnosis contradicts Beatrice's own description of her *cold blood* at 1.1.124; here, she is temperamentally the opposite of the saturnine Don John.

317, 318 **sad** serious

318 **ever** always

318–20 **she ... laughing** i.e. even in her sleep, if she is visited by sad dreams, she recovers her good humour; cf. 2.1.18 and

n., another image of Beatrice as possessing a mixed emotional constitution.

323 **suit** courtship

329 **on crutches** i.e. slowly and painfully

330 **Love** i.e. Cupid, a god requiring observances
all his rites religious solemnities; sexual consummation, or marital 'rights'. The senses are indistinguishable in performance.

332 **a just sennight** exactly a week

333 **answer my mind** arranged to my liking

334 **shake the head** an indication for Claudio's gesture

315 pleasant-spirited] *(pleasant spirited), Theobald*   321 SP] *Capell (D. Pe); Pedro Q*   324+ SP] *Capell (D. Pe); Prince Q*   327 County] *(Countie); Counte F*   332 sennight] *(seuennight)*   333 my] *om. F*

breathing, but I warrant thee, Claudio, the time shall 335
not go dully by us. I will, in the interim, undertake one
of Hercules' labours, which is to bring Signor Benedick
and the Lady Beatrice into a mountain of affection
th'one with th'other. I would fain have it a match, and
I doubt not but to fashion it, if you three will but 340
minister such assistance as I shall give you direction.

LEONATO   My lord, I am for you, though it cost me ten
nights' watchings.

CLAUDIO   And I, my lord.

DON PEDRO   And you too, gentle Hero?   345

HERO   I will do any modest office, my lord, to help my
cousin to a good husband.

DON PEDRO   And Benedick is not the unhopefullest
husband that I know. Thus far can I praise him: he is
of a noble strain, of approved valour and confirmed 350
honesty. I will teach you how to humour your cousin

---

335 **breathing** interval, pause
warrant promise
335–6 **time . . . us** Don Pedro's proposal
savours of the kind of courtly pastime
found in the worlds of Baldasarre
Castiglione's *Il libro del cortegiano* (*The
Courtier*) (1528) or Lyly, *Anatomy*.
337 **Hercules' labours** In classical legend
Hercules was sentenced by Apollo to
serve the Argive king Eurystheus in
penance for having slain his own family;
the latter imposed 12 nearly impossible
tasks of strength and skill upon him, such
as cleaning the capacious Augean stables,
capturing the Cretan bull, obtaining the
apples of the Hesperides, etc.
338 **mountain** large quantity
339 **fain** gladly
340 **fashion** engineer. For some heartless
critics, this language of artifice is proof that
the ultimate union of Beatrice and Benedick
is more indebted to social convention and
machination than voluntary feeling; e.g.
Stephen Greenblatt in the Norton

Shakespeare: 'they are tricked into marriage
against their hearts . . . [they] constantly
tantalize us with the possibility of an
identity . . . deliberately fashioned to resist
the constant pressure of society. But that
pressure finally prevails. Marriage is a
social conspiracy' (Greenblatt, 1386);
compare, however, the play's contrast
between malicious and beneficent ('honest',
3.1.84) slanders, the latter sometimes a
paradox but in this play argued to be true.
341 **minister** administer, provide, afford
343 **nights' watchings** wakeful nights; the
term (like *candle-wasters*, 5.1.18) implies
that the task will require much study as
well as observation.
346 **modest office** seemly role
348 **unhopefullest** most unpromising
350 **strain** birth or lineage (*JC* 5.1.57);
temperament (*KL* 5.3.41)
approved proven
351 **honesty** honour
humour put her in such a humour; indulge
so as to persuade; manipulate

that she shall fall in love with Benedick; [*to Claudio and
Leonato*] and I, with your two helps, will so practise
on Benedick that, in despite of his quick wit and his
queasy stomach, he shall fall in love with Beatrice. If we   355
can do this, Cupid is no longer an archer; his glory shall
be ours, for we are the only love-gods. Go in with me
and I will tell you my drift.   *Exeunt.*

[2.2]   *Enter* [DON] JOHN *and* BORACHIO.

DON JOHN   It is so; the Count Claudio shall marry the
            daughter of Leonato.
BORACHIO   Yea, my lord, but I can cross it.
DON JOHN   Any bar, any cross, any impediment will be
            medicinable to me. I am sick in displeasure to him, and   5
            whatsoever comes athwart his affection ranges evenly
            with mine. How canst thou cross this marriage?

353–4 **practise on** scheme upon
354 **quick wit** i.e. sharp intelligence, and his
     intellectual defence against marriage;
     Draper (262) observes that 'quick wit,
     though sometimes attributed to the
     sanguine type and to certain sorts of
     melancholy, was thought on the authority
     of Aristotle to be a common effect of
     choler . . . [albeit] such under the influence
     of the sun, [which] . . . made men strong,
     valiant, honest, and loyal' (unlike choleric
     persons under the influence of Mars, who
     tended to be brawlers).
355 **queasy stomach** fastidious pride; delicate
     appetite (for love)
356 **Cupid . . . archer** The cherubic god of
     love wounded his victims with arrows;
     Don Pedro suggests they will trump his
     efforts.

358 **drift** plan, intention
2.2 The location is a space in Leonato's house
     or its environs.
1–2 Don John's remark could indicate that his
     entrance overlaps with the exit of the
     previous scene, and thus is a comment
     upon what can be observed of Hero and
     Claudio's behaviour.
3   **cross** prevent, hinder
4   **bar** impediment, obstacle
     cross affliction, trouble
5   **medicinable** salutary, healing **to** with
6   **comes athwart** crosses the path of,
     impedes or hinders (as of a ship's course)
     affection desire, inclination
     ranges evenly lines up with (*OED* range
     v.[1] II 5b); the metaphor derives from
     printing practice (*ranges evenly* is a
     tautology).

352–3 SD] *Kittredge*   358 SD] *Rowe; exit Q*   **2.2**] *Capell*   0.1] DON] *Rowe*   1+ SP DON JOHN] *Capell
(D. Jo.); Iohn Q*

BORACHIO   Not honestly, my lord, but so covertly that no
   dishonesty shall appear in me.

DON JOHN   Show me briefly how.   10

BORACHIO   I think I told your lordship, a year since, how
   much I am in the favour of Margaret, the waiting-
   gentlewoman to Hero.

DON JOHN   I remember.

BORACHIO   I can, at any unseasonable instant of the night,   15
   appoint her to look out at her lady's chamber window.

DON JOHN   What life is in that to be the death of this
   marriage?

BORACHIO   The poison of that lies in you to temper. Go
   you to the prince your brother; spare not to tell him that   20
   he hath wronged his honour in marrying the renowned
   Claudio – whose estimation do you mightily hold up
   – to a contaminated stale, such a one as Hero.

DON JOHN   What proof shall I make of that?

BORACHIO   Proof enough to misuse the prince, to vex   25
   Claudio, to undo Hero and kill Leonato. Look you for
   any other issue?

DON JOHN   Only to despite them I will endeavour
   anything.

---

15 **unseasonable instant** late hour
16 **appoint** instruct
   chamber bedroom
19 **temper** concoct, mix
22 **estimation** reputation and / or worth
   hold up maintain, affirm
23 **contaminated stale** depraved prostitute;
   stale was the term for a decoy, including
   the prostitute used by thieves to lure
   victims (*OED n.*³ 4).
24 How will I demonstrate that?
25 **misuse** abuse, deceive
   vex injure, distress (stronger than the

modern sense of irritate)
26 **undo** ruin in reputation
   kill Leonato As if to underscore the
   degree to which the assault on Hero's
   honour is an attack on male identity,
   Borachio considers the effects of the
   slander to be more lethal to the aged
   Leonato than to his daughter or the others
   abused.
27 **issue** result
28 **despite** maliciously or contemptuously
   injure; Shakespeare's only use of the word
   as a verb

12–13 waiting-gentlewoman] *(*waiting gentlewoman*), Rowe*

BORACHIO   Go, then. Find me a meet hour to draw Don   30
Pedro and the Count Claudio alone. Tell them that you
know that Hero loves me. Intend a kind of zeal both to
the prince and Claudio – as in love of your brother's
honour, who hath made this match, and his friend's
reputation, who is thus like to be cozened with the   35
semblance of a maid – that you have discovered thus.
They will scarcely believe this without trial; offer them
instances, which shall bear no less likelihood than to
see me at her chamber window, hear me call Margaret
'Hero', hear Margaret term me 'Claudio'. And bring   40
them to see this the very night before the intended
wedding (for in the meantime I will so fashion the
matter that Hero shall be absent), and there shall
appear such seeming truth of Hero's disloyalty that

30   **meet hour** convenient time
32   **Intend** pretend
     zeal fervent loyalty
35   **cozened** cheated
36   **semblance** mere appearance
     maid virgin
     discovered revealed
     thus i.e. that Hero consorts with Borachio
37   **trial** proof
38   **bear . . . likelihood** seem no less
     convincing
40   **Claudio** Some editors read 'Borachio' for
     Claudio, on the grounds that for Claudio to
     overhear a supposed Hero call to Claudio
     might suggest that she were herself
     deceived; but presumably it would be
     easier to convince the socially ambitious
     Margaret ('Why, shall I always keep below
     stairs?', 5.2.9–10) to dress as her mistress
     and play-act with Borachio the love affair
     of Hero and Claudio, in a kind of sex
     game of social class, and it would also

doubly injure Claudio to watch Hero mock
him by calling her lover by his name.
Shakespeare's sources have the man
actually entering the bedroom window, as
opposed to merely speaking at it, and it is
worth noting here that Shakespeare renders
this scene in report only, although some
productions choose to stage it, a choice
which can either (if convincingly staged)
mitigate Claudio's rejection of Hero or
(if not plausibly incriminating) make his
distrust of her all the more repellent;
Shakespeare however leaves the audience
to judge his decision to reject her on the
basis of our imagination of the scene, given
aural evidence alone. Like many of
the characters, we too are dependent on
report.
42   **fashion** contrive, arrange; cf. 2.1.339–40:
     'I would fain have it a match, and I doubt
     not but to fashion it.'
44   **disloyalty** unfaithfulness

30 Don] on *F*   33 – as] (as *Q*   in] in a *F*   34–6 match, . . . maid –] *Capell;* match) . . . maid, *Q*   39
Margaret] *(Marg.)*   40 'Hero'] *this edn;* Hero *Q* 'Claudio'] *this edn;* Claudio *Q;* Borachio *Theobald*   42
meantime] *(mean time)*   44 truth] truths *F*

jealousy shall be called assurance, and all the   45
preparation overthrown.

DON JOHN   Grow this to what adverse issue it can, I will
put it in practice. Be cunning in the working this and
thy fee is a thousand ducats.

BORACHIO   Be you constant in the accusation and my   50
cunning shall not shame me.

DON JOHN   I will presently go learn their day of marriage.

Exeunt.

[2.3]   *Enter* BENEDICK *alone.*

BENEDICK   Boy!

[Enter Boy.*]*

BOY   Signor.

BENEDICK   In my chamber window lies a book. Bring it
hither to me in the orchard.

BOY   I am here already, sir.   5

---

45 **jealousy** suspicion
  assurance certainty
46 **preparation** i.e. for the wedding
47 **Grow this** let this grow
  what issue whatever outcome
48 **working this** i.e. working of this (Abbott, 93)
49 **ducats** A ducat was a gold or silver coin worth about 9s 4d (i.e. about 47p, or a modern equivalent of around £20).
51 **cunning** guile, underhanded cleverness
52 **presently** at once, directly
2.3 The location is Leonato's orchard. The staging needs to provide for Benedick's concealment from the gullers (though he must be visible to the audience); its elaborateness will depend on the nature

of the production (on the Elizabethan stage, presumably the actor playing Benedick concealed himself downstage behind the pillars). Modern production choices have included shrubbery, trees, lattice, garden furniture, etc., as well as arbours, both imaginary and actual. Property arbours did exist in Elizabethan staging practice (one is featured on the title page of the 1615 edition of Kyd's *Spanish Tragedy*; see p. 118).

5 **already** i.e. immediately; cf. *AW* 2.2.65: 'I am there before my legs.' There is no SD for the boy's rentery (and Cam¹ suggests that he exists merely to let Benedick identify the location in his address to him), although many productions have

---

50 you] thou *F*   52 SD] *Rowe; exit Q*   **2.3**] *Capell*   0.1] *Enter* Benedick *and a boy. / Rowe* 1.1] *Collier*   2+ Signor] *(Signior)*

BENEDICK   I know that, but I would have thee hence and
here again.   *Exit [Boy]*.
I do much wonder that one man, seeing how much
another man is a fool when he dedicates his behaviours
to love, will, after he hath laughed at such shallow   10
follies in others, become the argument of his own
scorn by falling in love. And such a man is Claudio. I
have known when there was no music with him but the
drum and the fife, and now had he rather hear the tabor
and the pipe. I have known when he would have walked   15
ten mile afoot to see a good armour, and now will he lie
ten nights awake carving the fashion of a new doublet.
He was wont to speak plain and to the purpose, like
an honest man and a soldier, and now is he turned

successfully had him reappear and attempt
to deliver the book to the concealed
Benedick while the latter frantically
attempts to maintain his concealment.
7   SD Q marks this at 5, perhaps so as to avoid
inserting a SD in Benedick's long speech,
but if this direction is followed Benedick
can address himself to the retreating boy, or
to no one in particular (as if he were
puzzling over the phrase *here already*).
9–10 **dedicates . . . love** fashions his actions in
the habits of a lover. The notion suggests a
set of conventional gestures and attitudes
appropriate to a lover; see 3.2.38n.
11 **argument** subject
12 **And . . . Claudio** Draper (264) comments
that Benedick's reading himself 'a lengthy
lecture against marriage' is 'quite a
needless task for a truly confirmed
bachelor!'
14 **drum . . . fife** i.e. instruments usually
reserved for military music
14–15 **tabor . . . pipe** The tabor was a
small drum, used principally as an

accompaniment to the whistle, or pipe, i.e.
instruments for dances and love songs
(and often played by fools). Cf. *R3* 1.1.5–8,
24: 'Now are . . . / chang'd . . . / Our
dreadful marches to delightful measures
. . . in this weak piping time of peace . . .';
and Lyly, *Campaspe*, 2.2.35–9: 'Is the
warlike sou[n]d of drumme and trumpet
turned to the soft noyse of lire and lute?
The neighing of barbed steeds . . .
conuerted to dilicate tunes and amorous
glaunces?' (*Works*, 2.330). Claudio's
entrance at 34 with musicians bears out
Benedick's criticism.
16 **armour** i.e. suit of armour
17 **carving** designing
    doublet upper part of a man's dress, a
close-fitting jacket with detachable sleeves
18–19 **like . . . soldier** Shakespeare also
associates a soldier's speech with a blunt
and unornamented style in *H5* 5.2.148–9:
'I speak to thee plain soldier.'
19–20 **turned ortography** become the
very spirit of an over-polished or

7 SD] *Johnson; exit. opp. 5 Q; after* that *6 Collier*

ortography; his words are a very fantastical banquet, 20
just so many strange dishes. May I be so converted and
see with these eyes? I cannot tell; I think not. I will not
be sworn but love may transform me to an oyster, but
I'll take my oath on it, till he have made an oyster of me
he shall never make me such a fool. One woman is fair, 25
yet I am well. Another is wise, yet I am well. Another
virtuous, yet I am well. But till all graces be in one
woman, one woman shall not come in my grace. Rich

fastidious style; cf. *LLL* 5.1.19, 'such
rackers of orthography', who 'draweth out
the thread of his verbosity finer than the
staple of his argument' (16–17). The word
turned, like *converted* (21), suggests that
Claudio has undergone a metamorphosis of
Ovidian proportions. Editors since Rowe
have emended to 'orthography' (or
sometimes 'orthographer') but Q's spelling
could equally be a colloquialism.
20 **fantastical banquet** Benedick's choice of
metaphor suggests the irony of this silver-
tongued man disdaining verbal prowess.
22–3 **I will . . . may** I cannot promise that love
might not
23–4 **transform . . . oyster** (1) render me a
mollusc, one of the more ignominious
animals in the divine hierarchy, and tight-
lipped in the manner of a melancholy
lover; (2) split me wide open: Dent, O116,
cites as proverbial 'Undone as you would
do an oyster'. Cf. Lyly, *Anatomy*, 97,
where an oyster represents a man made
vulnerable to a perfidious female appetite:
'Think this with thyself, that the sweet
songs of Calypso were subtle snares to
entice Ulysses, that the crab which catcheth
the oyster when the sun shineth . . . that
women when they be most pleasant
pretend most treachery.' The image recalls
the anecdote of Albertus Magnus (1208–
80) in his *De Animalibus*: 'Ambrose relates

that a crab would willingly reach within
the shell of a mollusc to eat its inhabitant,
but out of fear of having its claw trapped
and crushed in the bivalve's shell, it dares
not enter. Consequently, it watches until
the mollusc is relaxed by the warm rays
of the sun, and opens its shell. Then, using
its scissor-like claw, the crab inserts a
stone between the halves of the shell,
preventing them from closing, and finally
eats the mollusc at leisure' (Albertus,
24.23).
28 **in my grace** into my favour
28–33 **Rich . . . God** Despite his professed
disdain for marriage, Benedick apparently
finds it difficult to lay the fascinating subject
to rest. His criteria here recall Beatrice's at
2.1.13–15. They also reflect those of
conduct-book recommendations for the
choice of a spouse (see pp. 39–41) as well as
the terms of the formal controversy about
women; see Tasso, *Of Marriage and
Wiving*: 'Demosthenes, writing vnto the
Tyrant *Corynthus* . . . what qualities one
should seeke to finde in a woman that he
ment to marry withal, returned him this
answere: "First, shee must be rich, that
thou maist have wherewithall to live in
shewe and carrie a port; next, she must be
nobly borne, that thou maist be honoured
through her bloud; then she must be
yong, that she may content thee; then

24 an] *(and)*, F

she shall be, that's certain; wise, or I'll none; virtuous,
or I'll never cheapen her; fair, or I'll never look on her;   30
mild, or come not near me; noble, or not I for an angel.
Of good discourse, an excellent musician, and her hair
shall be of what colour it please God. Hah! The prince
and Monsieur Love. I will hide me in the arbour.
[*Withdraws.*]

Enter DON PEDRO, LEONATO, CLAUDIO
[*and* BALTHASAR], *with Music.*

DON PEDRO
Come, shall we hear this music?   35
CLAUDIO
Yea, my good lord. How still the evening is,

faire, that thou need not to hunt after other
game; and lastly, honest and vertuous,
that thou maiest not take the paines to
provide a spie to watch her" ' (sig. B2ᵛ).
No mention is made in the play of
Beatrice's fortune (unlike Hero's), and
she has been played both as a grand lady
of independent means and as a poor
relation.
29 **I'll none** i.e. I'll have nothing to do with
her, have none of her
30 **cheapen** bid or bargain for
31 **noble** well-born; a coin worth one-third of
a sovereign (7s 6d or about 37p)
   angel celestial being; a coin worth half of a
sovereign, i.e. more than a noble (so called
because it pictured the archangel Michael
vanquishing a dragon)
32 **Of good discourse** well spoken; despite
the early modern horror of talkative
women, the ideal woman was nonetheless
supposed to be conversationally adept
when called upon (see 1.1.163–5n.).
33 **of . . . God** i.e. an issue of little matter,
that could be left to chance, although there
is perhaps some sense that the colour
should be natural; the Elizabethan 'Homily
on Excess of Apparel' inveighed 'who can
paint her face, and curl her hair, and change
it into an unnatural colour, but there doth
work reproof to her Maker, who made her,
as though she could make herself more
comely than God hath appointed the
measure of her beauty' (*Homilies*, 315).
Women also wore false hair (cf. 3.4.12–13:
'I like the new tire within excellently, if the
hair were a thought browner').
34 **Monsieur Love** Mr Love, i.e. Claudio; the
French implies affectation.
   hide me The actor must conceal himself so
that his responses are visible to the audience.
34.2 *and* BALTHASAR See List of Roles 5n.

31 I] *om. F*   34 SD] *Theobald*   34.1 DON PEDRO] *Rowe; prince Q*   34.2 *and* BALTHASAR] *Rowe; after 45 Q (Enter Balthaser with musicke)*   with Music] *and Iacke Wilson F*   35+ SP] *Capell (D. Pe.); Prince Q*

   As hushed on purpose to grace harmony!
DON PEDRO [*aside to Claudio and Leonato*]
   See you where Benedick hath hid himself?
CLAUDIO [*aside*]
   O, very well, my lord. The music ended,
   We'll fit the kid-fox with a pennyworth.   40
DON PEDRO
   Come, Balthasar, we'll hear that song again.
BALTHASAR
   O good my lord, tax not so bad a voice
   To slander music any more than once.
DON PEDRO
   It is the witness still of excellency
   To put a strange face on his own perfection.   45
   I pray thee sing, and let me woo no more.
BALTHASAR
   Because you talk of wooing I will sing,
   Since many a wooer doth commence his suit

---

37 **grace harmony** favour music
39 **The music ended** once the music is over
40 **fit** get even with
kid-fox young fox, or cub; the epithet conveys both Benedick's own sense of his cunning, and his naive vulnerability to the charade about to be played upon him. Editors unpersuaded of Benedick's actual youth (and requiring it for the metaphor) have emended this to 'hid fox', based on the evidence of Don Pedro's use of *hid* at 38, Hamlet's line 'hide Fox, and all after' (4.2.29 in the Folio text), and the Elizabethan game of 'Fox i'th' hole', in which children hopped on one leg and pursued one of their fellows (the fox),

who emerged from hiding and ran for home.
pennyworth a bargain, often a bad one, though here Claudio's meaning is perhaps 'we'll give him what – or more than – he bargained for'. Cf. Lyly, *Anatomy*, 195: 'thou shalt haue repentaunce . . . at suche an vnreasonable rate, that thou wilt curse thy hard penyworth'.
41 **again** This corroborates Benedick's report that Claudio has recently been given over to love songs.
42 **tax** burden, make demands
43–4 A casting-off error in F reprints these two lines at the top of fol. 108.
44–5 The mark of skill is ever to disparage or misrepresent itself.

38, 39 SD] *Capell* 40 kid-fox] hid fox *Warburton;* cade fox *Hanmer* 44 excellency] excellency, / to slander Musicke any more then once. / *Prince.* It is the witnesse still of excellencie, *F*

To her he thinks not worthy, yet he woos,
Yet will he swear he loves.
DON PEDRO   Nay, pray thee, come,   50
Or if thou wilt hold longer argument,
Do it in notes.
BALTHASAR   Note this before my notes:
There's not a note of mine that's worth the noting.
DON PEDRO
Why, these are very crotchets that he speaks.
Note notes forsooth, and nothing!   [*Balthasar plays.*]
BENEDICK   Now, divine air! Now is his soul ravished!   56
Is it not strange that sheep's guts should hale souls out
of men's bodies? Well, a horn for my money, when all's
done.

49 **To . . . worthy** i.e. Don Pedro flatters Balthasar's music much as a lover flatters a lady he doesn't truly believe worthy of his love, but woos nonetheless, out of custom or duplicity; this exchange and the song that follows are marked by an unusual (for this play) recognition of the role of male amatory untrustworthiness in female perfidy.

52 **notes** i.e. musical ones

54 **crotchets** musical notes; nonsense. Like a true euphuist, Don Pedro joins Balthasar in his lame punning even as he scolds him for it.

55 **nothing** In Elizabethan pronunciation, the *o* in 'nothing' was long, and the *th* could be sounded as *t*, so that 'noting' and 'nothing' sounded the same. See Kökeritz, 132; *WT* 4.4.614–15: 'no hearing, no feeling, but my sir's song, and admiring the nothing of it'. Possible puns here (as with the title of this play) include noticing; knowing; commenting; musical notes;

nought; female or male genitalia; and virginity: cf. Philip Massinger, *Maid of Honour* (1621), 2.2.9, where the oath 'by my virginity' is described as 'a perlous oath / In a waiting-woman of fifteene, and is indeed a kinde of nothing' (Massinger, 1.139). The brothers Tasso (sig. C3ᵛ) elaborate: 'a woman that hath no being, but onely what is given to her, (as it were of Almes) from the ribbe of Man, shall without doubt fall under this infamous consideration of such a Non ens being nothing, or a thing without substance'.

56 **ravished** i.e. carried away with rapture, though literally raped or robbed, bereft of itself

57 **sheep's guts** i.e. the prosaic material that furnished the strings of a musical instrument
hale drag, haul

58 **horn** a hunting horn, which like the fife and the drum was a masculine instrument (with the usual emasculating innuendo)

55 nothing] noting *Theobald*   SD] *Capell subst.; Malone (Musick.)*

BALTHASAR *(Sings.)*

    Sigh no more, ladies, sigh no more,   60
      Men were deceivers ever;
    One foot in sea, and one on shore,
      To one thing constant never.
    Then sigh not so, but let them go,
      And be you blithe and bonny,   65
    Converting all your sounds of woe
      Into 'Hey, nonny, nonny'.

    Sing no more ditties, sing no more,
      Of dumps so dull and heavy;
    The fraud of men was ever so,   70
      Since summer first was leavy.
    Then sigh not so, but let them go,
      And be you blithe and bonny,
    Converting all your sounds of woe
      Into 'Hey, nonny, nonny'.   75

DON PEDRO   By my troth, a good song.

60–75 The song's theme of male inconstancy would be more portentous for the play's audience at this point than for the audience within the play (we are aware of Don John's intentions), although it is perhaps worth noting that Don Pedro and Balthasar consider the song's subject unremarkable, or innocent, or fashionable enough for a love song. W.H. Auden observes that 'the song is actually about the irresponsibility of men and the folly of women taking them seriously, and recommends as an antidote good humour and common sense. If one imagines these sentiments being the expression of a character, the only character they suit is Beatrice' (Auden,

115). Shakespeare's other betrayed-maiden songs include Ophelia's (*Ham* 4.5.23–66) and Desdemona's (*Oth* 4.3.39–46).
65 **blithe and bonny** merry and comely
67 **nonny, nonny** i.e. careless nothings; 'a meaningless refrain, formerly often used to cover indelicate allusions' (*OED* nonny-nonny)
69 **dumps** sad songs; drooping dances; melancholic moods
    dull melancholic
    heavy ponderous; tedious
71 **leavy** full of leaves, i.e. the beginning of the season of lovemaking
76 **troth** truth, faith (a form of asseveration)

---

60 SP] *Capell* SD] *Capell subst. (The Song.); as heading before 60 Q* 67 'Hey, nonny, nonny'] *this edn;* hey nony nony *Q* 68 ²more] *F2;* moe *Q* 70 was] *were F* 71 leavy] *leafy / Pope* 72–5] *Brooke;* Then sigh not so, &c. *Q*

BALTHASAR And an ill singer, my lord.

DON PEDRO Ha? No, no, faith; thou sing'st well enough
for a shift.

BENEDICK [*aside*] An he had been a dog that should have   80
howled thus, they would have hanged him. And I pray
God his bad voice bode no mischief. I had as lief have
heard the night-raven, come what plague could have
come after it.

DON PEDRO Yea, marry, – dost thou hear, Balthasar? I   85
pray thee get us some excellent music, for tomorrow
night we would have it at the Lady Hero's chamber
window.

BALTHASAR The best I can, my lord.

DON PEDRO Do so. Farewell.   *Exit Balthasar.*
Come hither, Leonato. What was it you told me of   91
today? That your niece Beatrice was in love with Signor
Benedick?

CLAUDIO [*aside*] O ay, stalk on, stalk on, the fowl sits.
[*Raises his voice.*] I did never think that lady would have   95
loved any man.

LEONATO No, nor I neither. But most wonderful that she
should so dote on Signor Benedick, whom she hath in
all outward behaviours seemed ever to abhor.

---

79 **a shift** i.e. in a pinch, as a stop-gap

82 **lief** readily

83 **night-raven** a proverbial harbinger of
doom. Cf. Dent, R33: 'The croaking raven
bodes disaster'; *FQ*, 2.12.36.5: 'The hoars
night-rauen, trump of dolefull drere'; and
Lyly, *Sappho and Phao*, 3.359–60: 'the
owle hath not shrikte at the window, or the
night Rauen croked, both being fatall'
(*Works*, 2.397).

85 **Yea, marry** addressed to either Claudio or
Leonato (whoever has made the

suggestion about providing a serenade at
Hero's chamber window); the phrase
indicates the conversation in progress
between the conspirators while Benedick
speaks to the audience.

86 **get . . . music** i.e. get us some (more)
excellent music, although asking Balthasar
to procure (other) excellent music perhaps
could corroborate Benedick's estimate of
Balthasar's talents

94 **stalk . . . sits** proceed carefully, our prey is
waiting to be caught

---

80 SD] *Johnson* An] *(And)*   82 lief] *F;* liue *Q*   90 SD] *after 89 Q; Exeunt Balthasar and Music /
Capell*   94 SD] *after* sits *Johnson subst.* ay] *(I)*   95 SD] *Oxf¹*

BENEDICK   Is't possible? Sits the wind in that corner?   100

LEONATO   By my troth, my lord, I cannot tell what to think of it. But that she loves him with an enraged affection, it is past the infinite of thought.

DON PEDRO   Maybe she doth but counterfeit.

CLAUDIO   Faith, like enough.   105

LEONATO   O God! Counterfeit? There was never counterfeit of passion came so near the life of passion as she discovers it.

DON PEDRO   Why, what effects of passion shows she?

CLAUDIO [*aside*]   Bait the hook well, this fish will bite!   110

LEONATO   What effects, my lord? She will sit you – you heard my daughter tell you how.

CLAUDIO   She did indeed.

DON PEDRO   How, how, I pray you? You amaze me! I would have thought her spirit had been invincible   115
against all assaults of affection.

LEONATO   I would have sworn it had, my lord; especially against Benedick.

100 **Sits ... corner** proverbial (Dent, W419: 'Is the wind in that door?'), e.g. 'Is that the way the wind blows?' The wind was thought to blow from one of the four quarters of the earth (i.e. north, south, east or west).

102 **enraged** i.e. passionate

102–3 ***it. But ... it** Q's light punctuation (see t.n.) allows for two different meanings: (1) 'I cannot avoid thinking that she loves him to distraction'; (2) 'The degree to which she loves him distractedly passes the utmost reach of thought.'

103 **past ... thought** unthinkable but true

108 **discovers** displays, reveals

109 **effects** signs; love-melancholy was understood to be accompanied by a host of distinctive behaviours, or 'signs

diagnosticke' (Ferrand, 106), such as Beatrice is reported to exhibit at 140–2. Cf. 3.2.37–8: 'If he be not in love with some woman there is no believing old signs.'

111 **sit you – you** Q's punctuation (see t.n.) can be read as a use of the Latin ethical dative, which emphasizes the hearer's interest in the answer (Furness); in performance, however, the sense likely to be conveyed is that of Leonato drawing a blank as to how to answer the Prince's question, stuttering, and then attempting to appeal to Claudio (or to the Prince) for reply: 'Sit – you, you'. The use of the future tense (*will sit*) indicates a repeated action in the past (as at 132).

102–3 it . . . affection,] *Oxf¹ (Pope); it, . . . affection, Q; it, . . . affection; Steevens²*   110, 122 SD]
Theobald   111 sit you – you] *(sit you, you)*

BENEDICK   I should think this a gull, but that the
    white-bearded fellow speaks it. Knavery cannot, sure,   120
    hide himself in such reverence.

CLAUDIO [*aside*]   He hath ta'en th'infection; hold it up!

DON PEDRO   Hath she made her affection known to
    Benedick?

LEONATO   No, and swears she never will. That's her   125
    torment.

CLAUDIO   'Tis true indeed, so your daughter says. 'Shall
    I,' says she, 'that have so oft encountered him with
    scorn, write to him that I love him?'

LEONATO   This says she now, when she is beginning to   130
    write to him; for she'll be up twenty times a night, and
    there will she sit in her smock till she have writ a sheet
    of paper. My daughter tells us all.

CLAUDIO   Now you talk of a sheet of paper, I remember a
    pretty jest your daughter told us of.   135

LEONATO   O, when she had writ it, and was reading it
    over, she found 'Benedick' and 'Beatrice' between the
    sheet?

CLAUDIO   That.

119 **gull** hoax
120 **white-bearded fellow** i.e. Leonato
    Knavery trickery
121 **himself** itself
    reverence esteemed old age
122 **ta'en th'infection** i.e. swallowed the bait;
    the metaphor connotes the status of love as
    an illness. Claudio's comment indicates
    some action on Benedick's part that would
    demonstrate his having become persuaded
    or further intrigued by what he overhears.
    hold it up keep the jest going
132 **smock** chemise

have writ has written; in Leonato's jest, as
in her own behaviour (revealed in 5.4),
Beatrice demonstrates her love by writing
to Benedick.
135 **pretty jest** droll incident
136 **she** i.e. Beatrice
    it . . . it i.e. the piece of paper
137–8 **between the sheet** literally, between
the (folded) sheet of paper, but with
sexual innuendo, i.e. bedsheets, cf. *TGV*
1.2.123–9
139 **That** yes, that one (jest; with perhaps an
eye-roll at its familiarity)

120 white-bearded] *(white bearded), F*   127–9 'Shall . . . him?'] *Capell subst.;* shall . . . him? *Q*   135 us
of] *F;* of vs *Q*   137 'Benedick' . . . 'Beatrice'] *Cam¹;* Benedick . . . Beatrice *Q*

LEONATO   O, she tore the letter into a thousand halfpence,   140
railed at herself that she should be so immodest to
write to one that she knew would flout her. 'I measure
him', says she, 'by my own spirit; for I should flout him,
if he writ to me – yea, though I loved him I should.'

CLAUDIO   Then down upon her knees she falls, weeps,   145
sobs, beats her heart, tears her hair, prays, curses, 'O
sweet Benedick! God give me patience!'

LEONATO   She doth indeed; my daughter says so. And the
ecstasy hath so much overborne her that my daughter
is sometime afeard she will do a desperate outrage to   150
herself. It is very true.

DON PEDRO   It were good that Benedick knew of it by
some other, if she will not discover it.

CLAUDIO   To what end? He would make but a sport of it
and torment the poor lady worse.   155

DON PEDRO   An he should, it were an alms to hang him.
She's an excellent sweet lady, and, out of all suspicion,
she is virtuous.

CLAUDIO   And she is exceeding wise.

DON PEDRO   In everything but in loving Benedick.   160

LEONATO   O my lord, wisdom and blood combating in so
tender a body, we have ten proofs to one that blood hath

---

140 **halfpence** i.e. small pieces (pronounced 'hàypense')
141 **railed at** berated
142, 143 **flout** disdain, scorn
149 **ecstasy** transport, frenzy
153 **other** i.e. other persons
   discover reveal
156 **An** if
   alms act of charity
157 **out . . . suspicion** beyond all doubt

158–9 **virtuous . . . wise** The uncanny way in which these particular attributes echo Benedick's own criteria at 28ff. could suggest a staging of this scene in which the hoaxers had overheard the latter end of Benedick's description of his ideal spouse (or that they had heard him on the same subject at another time; or that such criteria were conventional considerations, qualities that any man would desire in a wife).
161, 162 **blood** passion

142–4 'I . . . should.'] *Capell subst.;* I . . . should. *Q*   144 loved] *Oxf¹ (Wells);* loue *Q*   146–7 'O . . . patience!'] *Capell subst.;* O . . . patience. *Q*   154 make but] but make *F*   156 An] *(And)*

the victory. I am sorry for her, as I have just cause, being her uncle and her guardian.

DON PEDRO   I would she had bestowed this dotage on me.   165
I would have doffed all other respects and made her
half myself. I pray you tell Benedick of it and hear what
'a will say.

LEONATO   Were it good, think you?

CLAUDIO   Hero thinks surely she will die, for she says she   170
will die if he love her not, and she will die ere she
make her love known, and she will die if he woo her,
rather than she will bate one breath of her accustomed
crossness.

DON PEDRO   She doth well. If she should make tender of   175
her love 'tis very possible he'll scorn it, for the man, as
you know all, hath a contemptible spirit.

CLAUDIO   He is a very proper man.

DON PEDRO   He hath indeed a good outward happiness

CLAUDIO   Before God, and in my mind very wise.   180

DON PEDRO   He doth indeed show some sparks that are
like wit.

CLAUDIO   And I take him to be valiant.

DON PEDRO   As Hector, I assure you. And in the
managing of quarrels you may say he is wise, for either   185

---

165 **bestowed this dotage** conferred this love
166 **doffed** set aside; cf. 5.1.78 and n. **respects**
consideration (such as difference in rank);
Don Pedro has a habit of imagining himself
the lover of his subordinates' women.
167 **half myself** i.e. my other half
173 **bate** forgo
174 **crossness** intemperance, cussedness,
obstructiveness
175 **tender** offer
177 **contemptible** contemptuous, scornful,
but also worthy of contempt (hence

Claudio's defence)
178 **proper** handsome; admirable (although
Don Pedro's reformulation weakens this
sense)
179 **outward happiness** external appearance
181 **sparks** traces (signs of fire)
182 **wit** intelligence
184 **Hector** valiant Trojan leader in Homer's
Iliad, slain by Achilles, who subsequently
dragged Hector's corpse three times
around Troy's walls (22.465ff.)
185 **wise** prudent

166 doffed] *Pope (*doft*); daft *Q*   168 'a] he *F*   180 Before] 'Fore *F*   183 SP] *Leon. F*

he avoids them with great discretion, or undertakes
them with a most Christian-like fear.

LEONATO   If he do fear God, 'a must necessarily keep
peace; if he break the peace, he ought to enter into a
quarrel with fear and trembling.   190

DON PEDRO   And so will he do, for the man doth fear God,
howsoever it seems not in him by some large jests he
will make. Well, I am sorry for your niece. Shall we go
seek Benedick and tell him of her love?

CLAUDIO   Never tell him, my lord. Let her wear it out   195
with good counsel.

LEONATO   Nay, that's impossible; she may wear her heart
out first.

DON PEDRO   Well, we will hear further of it by your
daughter. Let it cool the while. I love Benedick well,   200
and I could wish he would modestly examine himself to
see how much he is unworthy so good a lady.

LEONATO   My lord, will you walk? Dinner is ready.

CLAUDIO [*to Don Pedro and Leonato*]   If he do not dote on
her upon this, I will never trust my expectation.   205

DON PEDRO [*to Leonato and Claudio*]   Let there be the
same net spread for her, and that must your daughter
and her gentlewomen carry. The sport will be when
they hold one an opinion of another's dotage, and no
such matter. That's the scene that I would see, which   210

---

187 **Christian-like** i.e. with his mind duly on
his mortal end (with a suggestion of
cowardice)
192 **by** to judge by
large broad, indelicate
196 **counsel** advice
200 **it** i.e. love

202 **unworthy** undeserving of
203 **walk** i.e. within doors
205 **expectation** ability to predict
208 **carry** manage
209–10 **they . . . matter** each holds the same
opinion of the other's being in love, and
none of it is true

187 most] *om. F*   194 seek] see *F*   202 unworthy] vnworthy to haue *F*   204, 206 SD] *Theobald*
208 gentlewomen] gentlewoman *F*   209 one . . . another's] an opinion of one another's *Pope;* one
opinion of the other's *Oxf¹ (Craven)*

will be merely a dumb-show. Let us send her to call
him in to dinner.   [*Exeunt all but Benedick.*]
BENEDICK [*Emerges.*] This can be no trick. The
conference was sadly borne; they have the truth of this
from Hero. They seem to pity the lady. It seems her   215
affections have their full bent. Love me? Why, it must
be requited. I hear how I am censured: they say I will
bear myself proudly if I perceive the love come from
her. They say too that she will rather die than give any
sign of affection. I did never think to marry. I must not   220
seem proud; happy are they that hear their detractions
and can put them to mending. They say the lady is fair
– 'tis a truth, I can bear them witness. And virtuous –
'tis so, I cannot reprove it. And wise, but for loving
me. By my troth, it is no addition to her wit – nor no   225
great argument of her folly, for I will be horribly in
love with her. I may chance have some odd quirks and
remnants of wit broken on me because I have railed so
long against marriage. But doth not the appetite alter?
A man loves the meat in his youth that he cannot   230

---

211 **dumb-show** a mimed dramatic practice used to preview the events of a plot (as in *Ham* 3.2.137 SD), and by the time of *MA*'s composition, a device of somewhat archaic reputation (Gurr, 174); i.e. both notoriously witty parties will be at an uncharacteristic loss for words, which is indeed what happens at 4.1.255ff.
214 **sadly borne** seriously conducted
216 **bent** scope (as in a drawn bow)
Love ... it Derek Jacobi, in the 1984 RSC production, directed by Terry Hands, delivered these words as 'Love me? Why? It'.
217 **censured** judged

218–21 **proudly . . . proud** disdainfully . . . disdainful
221 **detractions** faults criticized
224 **reprove** disprove
226 **argument** proof, evidence
227 **chance have** happen to have by chance, perhaps
quirks quibbles, quips
228 **remnants** dregs, rags; see 1.1.266–7 for a similar comparison of wit and clothing: 'The body of your discourse is sometime guarded with fragments'. **broken on** levelled against; see 5.1.137n.
railed ranted
230 **meat** with a pun on 'mate', as at 1.1.44, 115

212 SD *Exeunt*] *(Exeunt.)* F   *all but Benedick*] *Capell subst.*   213 *Emerges*] *Capell subst.; advances from the Arbour / Theobald*   216 their] the F   225 wit –] *(wit,)*

endure in his age. Shall quips and sentences and these
paper bullets of the brain awe a man from the career of
his humour? No, the world must be peopled. When I
said I would die a bachelor, I did not think I should
live till I were married   235

Enter BEATRICE.

Here comes Beatrice. By this day, she's a fair lady! I do
spy some marks of love in her.

BEATRICE   Against my will I am sent to bid you come in
to dinner.

BENEDICK   Fair Beatrice, I thank you for your pains.   240

BEATRICE   I took no more pains for those thanks than you
take pains to thank me. If it had been painful I would
not have come.

BENEDICK   You take pleasure, then, in the message?

BEATRICE   Yea, just so much as you may take upon a   245
knife's point and choke a daw withal. You have no
stomach, signor? Fare you well.   *Exit.*

---

231 **sentences** maxims, Latin *sententiae*
232 **paper bullets** literary clichés; flimsy
weapons
awe dissuade, intimidate
232–3 **career ... humour** (race)course or path of
his desire (*OED* career *sb.* 1b); cf. 5.1.134–
5: 'I shall meet your wit in the career an you
charge it against me.'
233 **peopled** populated; one of the standard
'causes for which matrimony was
ordained', as noted in the *Book of Common
Prayer*: 'the procreation of children to be
brought up in the fear and nurture of the
Lord, and praise of God' (*BCP*, 290)
240 Benedick's first lover-like address to
Beatrice is a verse line, perhaps an

involuntary instance; Beatrice pointedly
does not respond in kind.
246 **choke a daw** silence a jackdaw (a small
crow easily taught to imitate human
speech, and a proverbially stupid bird), i.e.
as much pleasure as you would get from
blocking the throat of a small and gullible
bird (very little, presumably). A daw was a
common term for a foolish person. The
image is of feeding morsels to a tame bird
from the point of a knife.
withal with; the strong form derives from
the awkwardness of the preposition at the
end of the sentence.
246–7 **You ... stomach** i.e. aren't you hungry

236 SD] *after 237 Q*   246 choke] not choke *Oxf¹ (Collier* MS*)*   247 signor] *(*signior*)*

BENEDICK Ha! 'Against my will I am sent to bid you come
in to dinner' – there's a double meaning in that. 'I took
no more pains for those thanks than you took pains to 250
thank me' – that's as much as to say, 'Any pains that I
take for you is as easy as thanks.' If I do not take pity of
her I am a villain; if I do not love her I am a Jew. I will
go get her picture.   *Exit.*

[**3.1**]   *Enter* HERO *and two gentlewomen,*
MARGARET *and* URSULA.

HERO
Good Margaret, run thee to the parlour;
There shalt thou find my cousin Beatrice

248–52 **Against . . . thanks** 'Whereas
we have previously seen that Benedick
does not want to marry, and have been
amused by the specious way in which
he used logic to avoid that issue, now
we see that he does want to marry, and that
the same tools serve his turn . . . he turns
inside out the conventions of repartee
which Shakespeare has so thoroughly
established. For instead of taking an
unflattering second meaning and returning
it with addition, he takes an insolent
surface meaning and then bends all his
wits to discover a hidden compliment'
(Vickers, 185).
253 **a villain** of base character, a scoundrel
(from the French *vilein*, serf or peasant)
Jew i.e. ungenerous person (from the
Elizabethan caricature of Jews as
rapacious usurers, void of Christian
charity); person of no faith (from a

Christian perspective). Many modern
productions change this word to another
(e.g. villain, fool), or delete it altogether.
254 **her picture** Aristocratic Elizabethan
lovers were wont to commission miniature
portraits of their beloveds – one of the
behaviours dedicated to love (see 109n.).
3.1 The location is the orchard; as in the
previous scene, some place must exist for
Beatrice to conceal herself, and this scene
can pose a difficulty for actresses playing
Beatrice, who are faced with the problem of
how not to repeat Benedick's choices.
Sometimes her hiding place has provided an
explanation for the cold Beatrice has
contracted as of 3.4 (for instance wet
laundry, a pond, or under plants that are
watered by Hero and Ursula). It is not clear
how much time has passed between this and
the previous scene, in which Benedick was
called in to dinner.

248–51 'Against . . . dinner' . . . 'I . . . me'] *Theobald subst.;* against . . . dinner . . . I . . . me
Q 251–2 'Any . . . thanks.'] *Alexander subst.;* any . . . thanks: *Q* **3.1**] *Actus Tertius F;* scene
i *Rowe* 0.1 gentlewomen] Gentlemen *F* 0.2 URSULA] *(Vrsley)*

257

Proposing with the prince and Claudio;
Whisper her ear and tell her I and Ursley
Walk in the orchard, and our whole discourse   5
Is all of her. Say that thou overheard'st us,
And bid her steal into the pleached bower
Where honeysuckles ripened by the sun
Forbid the sun to enter, like favourites
Made proud by princes that advance their pride   10
Against that power that bred it; there will she hide her
To listen our propose. This is thy office,
Bear thee well in it, and leave us alone.

MARGARET   I'll make her come, I warrant you, presently.

                                                    [*Exit.*]

HERO

Now, Ursula, when Beatrice doth come,   15
As we do trace this alley up and down
Our talk must only be of Benedick.
When I do name him, let it be thy part
To praise him more than ever man did merit;

---

3   **Proposing** conversing; along with *propose*
    at 12, Shakespeare's only use of the term in
    this sense
4   **Ursley** a familiar pronunciation of
    Ursula
7   **pleached bower** pleachèd: see 1.2.8. A
    bower is an arbour or alley formed of
    intertwined branches, in this case with
    honeysuckle vine growing over it.
9–11 **like . . . it** like privileged courtiers who
    seek to challenge the authority of the ruler
    who favours them; these lines are often cut
    in production. Harry Berger Jr observes that
    'this is displaced analysis of the whole
    situation . . . Beatrice is the rebellious
    favorite advancing her virgin pride against
    the masculine forces that ripen it – the
    solar energy of parents, princes, admirers'

(Berger, 306).
11 **her** herself
12 **our** perhaps spoken with an emphasis to
    distinguish it from the proposing of the
    men in the parlour
    propose conversation; F's 'purpose' is
    viable (if unmetrical), and this is the only
    location in Shakespeare where *propose*
    means conversation, but the repetition
    from 3 argues for Q's form.
    office duty, charge
13 **Bear . . . it** perform it skilfully
14 **presently** immediately; Q's punctuation
    (see t.n.) does not indicate whether the
    word refers to Margaret's action or to
    Beatrice's.
16 **trace** tread, follow the direction of
    alley bordered garden path

---

4 Ursley] *Vrsula F*   12 propose] purpose *F*   14 you, presently] you presently *Q*   14 SD] *F2*

My talk to thee must be how Benedick 20
Is sick in love with Beatrice. Of this matter
Is little Cupid's crafty arrow made,
That only wounds by hearsay.

Enter BEATRICE[, *who hides*].

Now begin,
For look where Beatrice like a lapwing runs
Close by the ground to hear our conference. 25
URSULA [*to Hero*]
The pleasant'st angling is to see the fish
Cut with her golden oars the silver stream
And greedily devour the treacherous bait;
So angle we for Beatrice, who even now
Is couched in the woodbine coverture. 30
Fear you not my part of the dialogue.
HERO [*to Ursula*]
Then go we near her, that her ear lose nothing

---

23 **only wounds** wounds only
24 **lapwing** a ground-nesting bird (plover)
noted for its cunning in drawing intruders
away from its nest by various diversionary
tactics, 'who fearing her young ones to be
destroyed by passengers, flieth with a false
cry far from their nests, making those that
look for them seek where they are not'
(Lyly, *Euphues*, 4); the term perhaps
suggests the erratic nature of Beatrice's
motion across the stage. The bird was also
a figure of a specifically female deceit, as
in e.g. *The Court of Good Counsel* (1607):
'those women whose minds are not deckt
of virtue, are those which labour aboue all
others in decking up their bodies, thinking
belike to haue as good luck as the lapwing,
who though but a vile bird, and liueth most

in durty lakes and desert places, yet at the
marriage of the eagle, she was honourable
aboue all other birds, because of the
crowne on her head, and of her dyed
feathers' (W. B., sig. D3ᵛ).
26 **angling** fishing; much as Benedick's
gullers describe him as prey in the previous
scene, Beatrice is imagined here as a fish
about to be caught.
27 **oars** i.e. fins
28 **treacherous** because it hides a hook
30 **couched** couchèd: hidden; ensconced
closely
woodbine coverture honeysuckle
covering, canopy
31 i.e. don't worry about my ability to play
my part

---

23 SD *Enter* BEATRICE] *Oxf¹; after 25 Q; after 23 F who hides*] *Theobald subst. (running towards the
arbour)* 26 SD] *Foakes* 30 woodbine] *(wood-bine), Theobald* 32 SD] *Foakes*

Of the false sweet bait that we lay for it.
[*They approach Beatrice's hiding place.*]
– No, truly, Ursula, she is too disdainful.
I know her spirits are as coy and wild   35
As haggards of the rock.

URSULA   But are you sure
That Benedick loves Beatrice so entirely?

HERO

So says the prince and my new-trothed lord.

URSULA

And did they bid you tell her of it, madam?

HERO

They did entreat me to acquaint her of it;   40
But I persuaded them, if they loved Benedick,
To wish him wrestle with affection
And never to let Beatrice know of it.

URSULA

Why did you so? Doth not the gentleman
Deserve at full as fortunate a bed   45
As ever Beatrice shall couch upon?

---

35 **coy** evasive

36 **haggards** untamed mature female hawks (as opposed to those raised from nestlings by human hands, in order to hunt), and hence a figure for unruly women of deceptive wiles and feigned reluctance. Cf. *TS* 4.2.39: 'this proud disdainful haggard'; Lyly, *Anatomy*, 219: 'I know not whether it is peculiar to that sex to dissemble with those who they most desire, or whether they haue learned outwardly to loth that which they most loue, yet wisely did she cast this in her head, if she should yeelde at the first assault he woulde thinke hir a lighte huswife, if she should reiect him

scornfully a very haggard.' Edmund Bert's *Treatise of Hawks and Hunting* (1619) notes that 'your haggard is very loving and kinde to her keeper, after he hath brought her by his sweet and kind familiarity to understand him' (Bert, cited in Furness). Beatrice employs similar imagery in her soliloquy at the end of the scene (112).

38 **new-trothed** trothèd; newly pledged or betrothed

42 **affection** his passion

45–6 ***at . . . upon** fully as blessed a marriage bed as Beatrice will inhabit (*OED* full *a., sb.*³ and *adv.* B 1); Q's 'as full' may be a compositor's error for 'at full'.

33 SD] *Steevens subst. (they advance to the bower); approaching Beatrice's hiding place Oxf* 38 new-trothed] *(new trothed), Theobald* 42 wrestle] *(wrastle)* 45 at full] *this edn; as full Q*

HERO

O god of love! I know he doth deserve
As much as may be yielded to a man.
But Nature never framed a woman's heart
Of prouder stuff than that of Beatrice.   50
Disdain and Scorn ride sparkling in her eyes,
Misprising what they look on, and her wit
Values itself so highly that to her
All matter else seems weak. She cannot love,
Nor take no shape nor project of affection,   55
She is so self-endeared.

URSULA   Sure, I think so.
And therefore certainly it were not good
She knew his love, lest she'll make sport at it.

HERO

Why, you speak truth. I never yet saw man –
How wise, how noble, young, how rarely featured –   60

---

48 **yielded** allowed, credited
51 **sparkling** flashing; the metaphor animates
Disdain and Scorn (as at 1.1.114, 'Is it
possible Disdain should die?').
52 **Misprising** misconstruing, misvaluing,
with the connotation of seeing it as worse
than it is in fact
they her eyes; Disdain and Scorn
54 **All matter else** anyone else's conversation
55 **take . . . affection** understand the form or
nature of love
56 **self-endeared** enamoured of herself
59–68 Such exaggerations and conversions of
virtues into defects as Beatrice reputedly
performs were described by Lyly as a
particularly female form of euphuism: 'Dost
thou not know that women deeme none
valyaunt, vnlesse he be too venturesome?
That they accompte one a dastarde, if he
be not desperate, a pinch penny and if he

be not prodigall, if silent a sotte, if ful of
wordes a foole'; 'If he be cleanly, then
terme they him proude, if meane in apparel,
a slouen, if bolde, blunte, if shamefaste, a
coward' (Lyly, *Anatomy*, 249, 254). Such
conversions were recommended to men
by Ovid in his *Remedies of Love Translated
and Intituled to the Youth of England*
(1600) as a means of avoiding or exorcising
love: 'If she be fat, that she is swollen say: /
If browne, then tawny like the Affrike Moor
/ If slender, leane, meger, and worne away /
If courtly, wanton, worst of worst before / If
modest, strange, as fitteth woman-head, /
Say she is rusticke, clownishe, and ill-bred'
(Ovid, *Remedies*, sig. D1ᵛ, and paraphrased
in Lyly, *Anatomy*, 102). Cf. Petruchio's
reversal of the convention in *TS* 2.1.171–
81, 237–56.
60 **rarely** exceptionally, handsomely

---

56 self-endeared] (selfe indeared), Rowe   58 she'll] she *F*

But she would spell him backward. If fair-faced,
She would swear the gentleman should be her sister;
If black, why Nature, drawing of an antic,
Made a foul blot; if tall, a lance ill-headed;
If low, an agate very vilely cut;   65
If speaking, why, a vane blown with all winds;
If silent, why, a block moved with none.
So turns she every man the wrong side out,
And never gives to truth and virtue that
Which simpleness and merit purchaseth.   70

URSULA
Sure, sure, such carping is not commendable.

HERO
No, not to be so odd and from all fashions
As Beatrice is cannot be commendable.
But who dare tell her so? If I should speak,
She would mock me into air. O, she would laugh me   75

---

61 **spell him backward** misrepresent his virtues as vices; witches were imagined to conjure devils by praying in reverse.
   fair-faced of light complexion (a stereotypical female virtue); fresh faced
63 **black** of dark colouring
63–4 **Nature . . . blot** Nature, caricaturing a grotesque, or clown, blotted her composition (or created an ugly image); cf. 5.1.96, *Go anticly*.
64 **lance ill-headed** spear with a dull point
65 If short, an ill-fashioned dwarf; an agate was a gemstone often carved with diminutive figures. Cf. *2H4* 1.2.16–17, for Falstaff's description of his page: 'I was never manned with an agate till now'; and *RJ* 1.4.55–6: 'In shape no bigger than an agate stone / On the forefinger of an alderman'.

66 **vane . . . winds** implies verbose but also inconstant or indiscriminate speech; a vane is a weathervane.
67 **block** See 2.1.220n.
   moved movèd
70 **simpleness** straightforward integrity; cf. *MND* 5.1.82–3: 'never anything can be amiss / When simpleness and duty tender it'.
   purchaseth earn, deserve; for the singular verb after two subject nouns see Abbott, 336.
71, 73 **commendable** pronounced with an accent on the first and third syllables
72 **from all fashions** contrary to, eccentrically divergent from, customary compliment and female decorum
75 **mock . . . air** i.e. ridicule me into nothingness
75–6 **laugh . . . myself** i.e. reduce me to silence

---

61 fair-faced] *(faire faced)*, *F4*   63 antic] *F (anticke); antique Q*   64 ill-headed] *(ill headed)*, *F2*   65 agate] *(agot)* vilely] *(vildly)*

262

Out of myself, press me to death with wit!
Therefore let Benedick, like covered fire,
Consume away in sighs, waste inwardly.
It were a better death than die with mocks,
Which is as bad as die with tickling.   80

URSULA
Yet tell her of it; hear what she will say.

HERO
No, rather I will go to Benedick
And counsel him to fight against his passion.
And truly, I'll devise some honest slanders
To stain my cousin with: one doth not know   85
How much an ill word may empoison liking.

URSULA
O, do not do your cousin such a wrong!
She cannot be so much without true judgement,
Having so swift and excellent a wit

---

76 **press ... death** a figure based on the torture of the '*peine forte et dure*' ('strong and severe punishment'), in which heavy weights were loaded upon the criminals who refused to plead. Most figurative uses referred to the silence of the victim; cf. *R2* 3.4.71–2: 'O, I am pressed to death / Through want of speaking!'; *Son* 140.1–2: 'Be wise as thou art cruel, do not press / My tongue-tied patience with too much disdain'.

77 **covered fire** either fire that will burn all the more fiercely for being damped down (proverbial: 'Fire that's closest kept burns most of all', Dent, F265), or fire that will sputter out for want of oxygen. Either case implies that Benedick must keep his passion concealed.

78 **Consume away** A sigh was thought to cost the heart a drop of blood.
sighs i.e. draughts of air (and the wordless hallmark of the lover). Cf. 1.1.190.

80 **tickling** three syllables

84 **honest slanders** Hero proposes to defame her cousin, albeit 'honestly', by concentrating on foibles rather than sins, much in the same way that Don John plans to 'stain' her own reputation; honest slanders were unlikely to attack chastity (or 'honesty').

86 **empoison** Cf. 2.2.19: 'The poison of that lies in you to temper.'

89 **so . . . wit** a female virtue, according to Nicholas Breton in *The Praise of Virtuous Ladies* (1606): 'Nowadays, men are so fantastical (I dare not say foolish) that if a woman be not so wise as to make a man a fool, she is no wise woman. No, forsooth, but he is a very wise man to match with such a woman. Women have wit naturally; wisdom must be had by grace; grace was given to our Lady; then who wiser than a woman?' (Breton, *Praise*, 61). Lyly's Fidus concurs: 'of all creatures

79 than] *(then); to F*

As she is prized to have, as to refuse 90
So rare a gentleman as Signor Benedick.

HERO

He is the only man of Italy –
Always excepted my dear Claudio.

URSULA

I pray you, be not angry with me, madam,
Speaking my fancy. Signor Benedick, 95
For shape, for bearing, argument and valour,
Goes foremost in report through Italy.

HERO

Indeed, he hath an excellent good name.

URSULA

His excellence did earn it ere he had it.
When are you married, madam? 100

HERO

Why, every day, tomorrow! Come, go in,
I'll show thee some attires, and have thy counsel
Which is the best to furnish me tomorrow.

URSULA [*to Hero*]

She's limed, I warrant you! We have caught her,
madam!

---

the woman's wit is the most excellent, therefore have the poets feigned the muses to be women, they nymphs, goddesses, ensaumples of whose rare wisdomes and sharp capacities would nothing but make me commit idolatry of my daughter' (Lyly, *Euphues*, 263).

90 **prized** esteemed; like Benedick's gullers, Hero and Ursula solicit the intellectual vanity of their prey to the cause of loving.
91 **rare** exceptional
92 **only** unrivalled
95 **fancy** conviction

96 **bearing** deportment
argument reason, discourse
97 **Goes . . . through** i.e. has the best reputation in
99 i.e. he came by it through merit
101 **every day, tomorrow** as of tomorrow, forever
102 **attires** clothing
104 **limed** caught (from birdlime, an adhesive substance fashioned from the bark of holly trees, used to capture small birds). Ursula's observation suggests some revealing stage action by Beatrice.

---

91 as Signor Benedick] as Benedick *Pope* 91, 95 Signor] *(signior)* 96 bearing,] *F4;* bearing *Q*
101 day, tomorrow!] *Rowe (*Day, to morrow;*);* euerie day tomorrow, *Q* 104 SD] *Capell* limed] tane *F*
104] *Pope; Q lines* you, / madame. /

HERO [*to Ursula*]

If it prove so, then loving goes by haps;   105
Some Cupid kills with arrows, some with traps.

[*Exeunt all but Beatrice.*]

BEATRICE

What fire is in mine ears? Can this be true?
Stand I condemned for pride and scorn so much?
Contempt, farewell; and maiden pride, adieu;
No glory lives behind the back of such.   110
And Benedick, love on, I will requite thee,
Taming my wild heart to thy loving hand.
If thou dost love, my kindness shall incite thee
To bind our loves up in a holy band.
For others say thou dost deserve, and I   115
Believe it better than reportingly.   *Exit.*

[**3.2**]   *Enter* DON PEDRO, CLAUDIO,
BENEDICK *and* LEONATO.

DON PEDRO   I do but stay till your marriage be
consummate, and then go I toward Aragon.

---

105 **haps** chance, accident; Cupid's blindfolded marksmanship always involves some element of chance.
107 Beatrice speaks verse here (an abbreviated sonnet) for the first time in the play (a rare event for her, though we will see her capable of composing it in 5.4).
fire . . . ears i.e. Beatrice's ears are burning, both because she hears herself being spoken of, and because what she hears hits home.
110 **lives . . . of** attends, follows
such persons possessed of such qualities
112 Beatrice's language picks up on the imagery of wild birds used by her gullers,

although she herself will be the one doing the taming, rather than submitting to another's rule. It was thought that a hawk could be tamed only by love; see 36n.
114 **a holy band** i.e. marriage
116 **better than reportingly** i.e. intrinsically, on grounds other than hearsay (an unusual conviction in a play where so much is construed as a result of report). Many modern productions break for intermission at this point.
3.2 The location is Leonato's house or environs.
2   **consummate** celebrated ritually (but also in a sexual sense). See also *predestinate*, 1.1.128 and n.

105 SD] *Capell (aside)*   106 SD] *Rowe (Exeunt); Exeunt* Hero, *and* Ursula. Beatrice *advances / Theobald; Exit. F; not in Q*   111 on] *Qc, F; one Qu*   3.2] *scene ii Pope*   0.1 DON PEDRO] *Rowe; Prince Q*   1+ SP] *Rowe (Pedro.); Capell (D. Pe.); Prince Q*

CLAUDIO   I'll bring you thither, my lord, if you'll
vouchsafe me.

DON PEDRO   Nay, that would be as great a soil in the new   5
gloss of your marriage as to show a child his new coat
and forbid him to wear it. I will only be bold with
Benedick for his company, for from the crown of his
head to the sole of his foot, he is all mirth. He hath
twice or thrice cut Cupid's bowstring, and the little   10
hangman dare not shoot at him. He hath a heart as
sound as a bell, and his tongue is the clapper: for what
his heart thinks, his tongue speaks.

BENEDICK   _Gallants, I am not as I have been._

LEONATO   So say I; methinks you are sadder.   15

CLAUDIO   I hope he be in love.

DON PEDRO   Hang him, truant! There's no true drop of
blood in him to be truly touched with love. If he be sad,
he wants money.

BENEDICK   I have the toothache.   20

DON PEDRO   Draw it.

BENEDICK   Hang it!

---

3   **bring you thither** escort, accompany you thither (i.e. to Aragon, his home)
4   **vouchsafe** allow
5   **soil in** stain on
7   **be bold with** ask
8–9 **from . . . foot** proverbial (Dent, C864)
9   **all mirth** This comment is given an ironic edge applied to a Benedick freshly shaven and complaining of a toothache to conceal the fact.
11   **hangman** i.e. rascal, rogue; cf. *TGV* 4.4.53–4: 'stolen from me by the hangman's boys'.
11–12 **as . . . bell** proverbial (Dent, B272)

12–13 **for . . . speaks** proverbial (Dent, H334); Don Pedro perhaps varies the proverb 'as the fool thinks, so the bell chinks'.
15   **sadder** more serious, or, as at 49, melancholic – a mark of a lover
17   **Hang him, truant** hang him, the fickle one; Q's punctuation (see t.n.) also suggests the possibility of 'hang him for a truant', i.e. as a truant to love or to his own vow to disdain love.
18   **blood** passion
19   **he wants** it is because he lacks
20   **toothache** See 24–5n.
21   **Draw** extract

---

17 Hang him, truant!] *Theobald (*hang him, truant,*); Hang him truant, *Q*

CLAUDIO   You must hang it first and draw it afterwards.

DON PEDRO   What? Sigh for the toothache?

LEONATO   Where is but a humour or a worm.   25

BENEDICK   Well, everyone can master a grief but he that
has it.

CLAUDIO   Yet, say I, he is in love.

DON PEDRO   There is no appearance of fancy in him,
unless it be a fancy that he hath to strange disguises: as   30

---

23 Hanging and drawing (disembowelling) was the punishment for traitors. Cf. Middleton, *The Widow* (1652), 4.1.105–6: '*Martino:* I pray, what's good, sir, for a wicked tooth? / *Ricardo:* Hang'd, drawn, and quartering' (Middleton, 5.193). Teeth were also hung in shop windows to indicate that dentistry was performed within.

24–5 **toothache . . . humour . . . worm** Toothaches and love were associated ailments. Cf. Francis Beaumont and John Fletcher, *The False One* (1620), 2.3.109–10: 'You had best be troubled with the tooth-ach too, / For Lovers ever are'; and Massinger, *The Parliament of Love* (1624), 1B.30–2: 'I am troubled / With the tooth ach, or with love, I know not whether: / There is a worme in both' (Massinger, 2.113). Toothache in Elizabethan medical thought was caused by humours descending from the head / or by worms penetrating the tooth; cf. Bateman, 'Of the teeth', in *Upon Bartholomew*: 'The cause of such aking is humours that come downe from the heade . . . Also sometime teeth be pearced with holes & sometime by worms they be changed into yellow colour, greene, or black' (Bateman, 5.20). If Benedick is truly suffering (as opposed to hiding his newly shorn face in a towel), then his toothache joins Beatrice's cold as a

physical sign of emotional vulnerability. He is either claiming not to be sad because of love, or ostentatiously claiming he bears the marks of true love.

26–7 proverbial: 'All commend patience but none can endure to suffer' (Dent, A124), and 'The healthful man can give counsel to the sick' (M182); cf 5.1.35–6: 'For there was never yet philosopher / That could endure the toothache patiently'.

29–30 **fancy . . . fancy** love . . . whim; the wordplay is repeated at 34–6.

30 **strange disguises** *strange* = foreign, outlandish. Presumably Benedick's transformation into a lover has been indicated sartorially, by an attempt at excessively fashionable dress; if so, he appears as the commonplace caricature of English gallants, who borrowed with indiscriminate enthusiasm from other countries' styles. Cf. *MV* 1.2.72–3, where Portia guesses that her English suitor 'bought his doublet in Italy, his round hose in France, his bonnet in Germany'; and Dekker's *Seven Deadly Sins*: 'For, an English-mans suite is like a traitors bodie that hath beene hanged, drawne, and quartered, and is set vp in seuerall places: the coller of his Dublet and the belly in Fraunce: the wing and narrow sleeue in Italy . . . thus wee that mocke euerie Nation, for keeping one fashion, yet steale patches

---

26 can] *Pope;* cannot *Q*

to be a Dutchman today, a Frenchman tomorrow – or
in the shape of two countries at once, as a German from
the waist downward, all slops, and a Spaniard from the
hip upward, no doublet. Unless he have a fancy to this
foolery – as it appears he hath – he is no fool for   35
fancy, as you would have it appear he is.

CLAUDIO   If he be not in love with some woman there is
no believing old signs. 'A brushes his hat o'mornings:
what should that bode?

DON PEDRO   Hath any man seen him at the barber's?   40

CLAUDIO   No, but the barber's man hath been seen with
him, and the old ornament of his cheek hath already
stuffed tennis balls.

LEONATO   Indeed, he looks younger than he did by the
loss of a beard.   45

from euerie one of them, to peece out our
pride, are now laughing stockes to them,
because their cut so scuruily becomes vs'
(Dekker, *Sins*, 60).

31–4 **or ... doublet** This passage was omitted
from F, perhaps because the play had been
cut for performance at Court during the
wedding festivities of the Princess
Elizabeth and the Elector Palatine in 1613;
or perhaps because, as a Scot, King James
was sensitive to English caricatures of
foreigners.

33 **slops** large loose breeches

34 **no doublet** i.e. all cloak, the hip-length
Spanish cape, according to Malone,
concealing a doublet (see 2.3.17n.). A
person dressed to this description would be
veritably overflowing in fabric.

34–6 **Unless ... is** i.e. unless it be the case that
he is given to this kind of dress, as it
appears he is from his attire, then he is no
lover, as you would construe it

38 **old signs** conventional marks; cf. the
'marks' of love denoted in *AYL* 3.2.364–72:
'A lean cheek . . . a blue eye and sunken . . .
an unquestionable spirit . . . a beard
neglected . . . your hose should be
ungartered, your bonnet unbanded, your
sleeve unbuttoned, your shoe untied, and
everything about you demonstrating a
careless desolation.'
    brushes his hat i.e. in order to clean it
(presumably, a mark of fastidiousness that
the soldierly Benedick would have forgone)

39 **bode** indicate

43 **stuffed tennis balls** an actual practice. Cf.
Dekker, *The Shoemaker's Holiday* (1600),
5.5.23–4: 'yet I'll shaue [my beard off] and
stuffe tennis balls with it to please my bully
king' (*Works*, 1.84). Ard² surmises that
perhaps Benedick is aware of Beatrice's
preference at 2.1.26–7; Benedick's action
anticipates Borachio's vision of the shaven
Hercules at 3.3.131–2.

31–4 or . . . doublet] *om. F*   36 it] it to *F*   38 o'] *(a)*

DON PEDRO   Nay, 'a rubs himself with civet. Can you
smell him out by that?

CLAUDIO   That's as much as to say the sweet youth's in love.

DON PEDRO   The greatest note of it is his melancholy.

CLAUDIO   And when was he wont to wash his face?   50

DON PEDRO   Yea, or to paint himself? For the which I
hear what they say of him.

CLAUDIO   Nay, but his jesting spirit, which is now crept
into a lute-string and now governed by stops.

---

46 **civet** a foppish perfume obtained from the
scent glands of the civet cat; cf. *AYL*
3.2.60–1: 'The courtier's hands are
perfumed with civet.'

47 **smell him out** smell his perfume; detect
his secret; proverbial (Dent, S558)

50 **wash his face** perhaps with perfume (though
not with civet): 'In Shakespeare's time our
race had not abandoned itself to that reckless
use of water, either for ablution or potation,
which has more recently become one of its
characteristic traits' (White, cited in
Furness). Oxf¹ comments more generously:
'Benedick deserves the benefit of the doubt;
he probably washes his face, though
possibly more often pale-Beatrice.'

51 **paint himself** use cosmetics
the which i.e. his use of cosmetics;
according to Burton, the most damning of
the love-stricken man's traits: they 'go
beyond women, they wear harlot's colours,
and do not walk but jet and dance, he-
women, she-men, more like players,
Butterflies, Baboons, Apes, Antickes, than
Men . . . in a short space their whole
patrimonies are consumed' (Burton, 3.101).

51–2 **For . . . him** i.e. and I know what
rumours *that* is generating

53 **but** but what of

53–4 **now . . . now** at times . . . at other times

54 **lute-string** The plaintive lute was a
conventional instrument of the love-lorn;
cf. *1H4* 1.2.70–2: 'as melancholy as . . . an
old lion, or a lover's lute'.
stops the frets, or points on a lute's neck
where the fingers press in order to regulate
sounds; or the holes on a pipe (also a
favourite of lovers): i.e. Benedick's jesting
spirit 'at times conceals itself in a lute string,
and at other times permits itself to be played
upon (in, by implication, a melancholy
fashion) like the finger-holes of a recorder'
(Wells, *Re-editing*, 45). Claudio puns on the
notion of the pauses that have crept into
Benedick's heretofore free-wheeling wit.
(The notion that love robs one of one's wit
when it doesn't render one garrulous is
expressed both by Don Pedro, at 2.3.208–11
– 'The sport will be when they hold one an
opinion of another's dotage . . . That's the
scene that I would see, which will be merely
a dumb-show' – and by Margaret, at 3.4.63,
in her reply to Beatrice's 'how long have
you professed apprehension?': 'Ever since
you left it.') Of course, Don Pedro and
Claudio are hardly letting Benedick get a
word in edgeways, even if he were in a
mood to cross wits with them.

---

49 SP] *F (Prin.); Bene. Q*   51+ SP DON PEDRO] *Rowe (Pedro.); Capell (D. Pe.); Prince Q*   53 now crept]
new-crept *Cam¹ (Boas)*   54 now] new *Dyce*

DON PEDRO   Indeed, that tells a heavy tale for him.   55
Conclude, conclude: he is in love.

CLAUDIO   Nay, but I know who loves him.

DON PEDRO   That would I know too; I warrant one that
knows him not.

CLAUDIO   Yes, and his ill conditions, and in despite of all   60
dies for him.

DON PEDRO   She shall be buried with her face upwards.

BENEDICK   Yet is this no charm for the toothache. [*to
Leonato*] Old signor, walk aside with me. I have studied
eight or nine wise words to speak to you which these   65
hobby-horses must not hear. [*Exeunt Benedick and Leonato.*]

DON PEDRO   For my life, to break with him about
Beatrice!

CLAUDIO   'Tis even so. Hero and Margaret have by this
played their parts with Beatrice, and then the two bears   70
will not bite one another when they meet.

---

55 **heavy** incriminating, conclusive
58–9 **I warrant . . . not** i.e. I swear it's someone who doesn't know what a curmudgeonly woman-scorner he is.
60 **Yes . . . conditions** i.e. You're wrong. She does know his bad qualities and is still in love with him.
61 **dies** pines away
62 Don Pedro pursues Claudio's *double entendre* by implying that she who loves Benedick will only be buried while 'dying' under his body in the sex act. Cf. *WT* 4.4.131–2: 'Not like a corpse; or if – not to be buried, / But quick, and in mine arms'. The innuendo of the passage posed a problem for eighteenth- and nineteenth-century editors, who were unwilling or unable to grant its sexual content, and hence, after Theobald,

often emended *face* to 'heels', citing proverbial instances of the latter.
63 **charm** cure
65–6 **wise . . . hear** Benedick addresses Leonato on the same subject in our hearing at 5.4.21, which suggests either that he loses his nerve here, or, more likely (since in performance the repetition generally passes unnoticed), that Shakespeare must isolate Don Pedro and Claudio in order to further Don John's plot.
66 **hobby-horses** buffoons, from the practice of the morris dance and the stage, where a performer would don a wickerwork horse-costume and imitate the antic movements of a high-spirited horse
69 **'Tis even so** i.e. you're right
Margaret Actually, Ursula was the more instrumental agent: either a slip

---

56 conclude] *om. F*   62 face] heels *Theobald*   63 toothache.] *Rowe;* tooth-ake, *Q*   64 signor]
(signior)   66 SD] *Theobald*

Enter [DON] JOHN *the bastard.*

DON JOHN   My lord and brother, God save you!
DON PEDRO   Good e'en, brother.
DON JOHN   If your leisure served, I would speak with you.
DON PEDRO   In private?   75
DON JOHN   If it please you; yet Count Claudio may hear,
    for what I would speak of concerns him.
DON PEDRO   What's the matter?
DON JOHN   [*to Claudio*] Means your lordship to be
    married tomorrow?   80
DON PEDRO   You know he does.
DON JOHN   I know not that when he knows what I know.
CLAUDIO   If there be any impediment, I pray you discover
    it.
DON JOHN   You may think I love you not. Let that appear   85
    hereafter, and aim better at me by that I now will
    manifest. For my brother – I think he holds you well and
    in dearness of heart – hath holp to effect your ensuing
    marriage; surely suit ill spent and labour ill bestowed.
DON PEDRO   Why, what's the matter?   90
DON JOHN   I came hither to tell you; and, circumstances

by Shakespeare, or evidence of an original
intention subsequently changed in order to
balance the two waiting gentlewomen's
roles; or an error by a Claudio ignorant of
the details (and assuming that the more
mischievous Margaret would be the active
party to the deception).
73 **Good e'en** [God give you] good evening
    (i.e. any time after noon)
76 **yet . . . hear** perhaps an indication that

Claudio moves to excuse himself
83 **discover** disclose, reveal
85 **that** i.e. whether I love you or no
86 **aim better at** judge better of
87 **For** as for
    holds you well has a high opinion of you
88 **dearness of heart** friendship
    holp helped
89 **suit** pursuit
91 **circumstances** explanations, details

71.1 DON] *Rowe*   72, 74, 76 SP] *Rowe (John); Bastard Q*   73 e'en] *Oxf;* den *Q*   77 of concerns] *Qu;* of,
concernes *Qc*   79, 82, 85, 91 SP] *Rowe (John); Bast. Q*   79 SD] *Rowe*   87–8 brother . . . heart –] brother
(I thinke, . . . heart) *Qc;* brother, I think, . . . heart *Rowe;* brother, I thinke, . . . heart, *Qu*   88 holp] *Qc*
(holpe); hope *Qu*

shortened – for she has been too long a-talking of – the
lady is disloyal.

CLAUDIO Who, Hero?

DON JOHN Even she: Leonato's Hero, your Hero, every   95
man's Hero.

CLAUDIO Disloyal?

DON JOHN The word is too good to paint out her
wickedness; I could say she were worse. Think you of a
worse title, and I will fit her to it. Wonder not till 100
further warrant. Go but with me, tonight you shall see
her chamber window entered, even the night before her
wedding day. If you love her then, tomorrow wed her.
But it would better fit your honour to change your mind.

CLAUDIO May this be so?   105

DON PEDRO I will not think it.

DON JOHN If you dare not trust that you see, confess not
that you know. If you will follow me I will show you
enough, and when you have seen more and heard more,
proceed accordingly.   110

92 **too . . . of** Don John insinuates that for a woman to be a subject of general conversation was in itself a dubious portent of female reputation. He echoes an opinion also shared by Rich in his *Excellency of Good Women*: 'Thucydides will needs approve that women to be most honest, that is least knowne, and I think indeed that the most honest woman is least spoken of, for they doe please the least in member, and vertue was never graced by the multitude' (sig. C2ʳ).

93, 97 **disloyal** unfaithful

98 **paint out** depict fully; Don John's verb suggests the link between female untrustworthiness and the use of cosmetics.

101 **warrant** proof
   Go but only go

102 **chamber window entered** This contrasts with Borachio's plan of 2.2 and the accusation of 4.1.91, that Hero did merely 'Talk with a ruffian at her chamber window'. In the sources Claudio's counterpart does indeed witness her chamber window entered (e.g. Bandello: 'he who simulated the lover climbed up and entered the house as if he had a mistress within. When the unhappy Sir Timbreo saw it, being convinced . . . he felt himself swooning', Bullough, 117).

104 **honour** reputation

107–8 **If . . . know** a difficult line, to the effect of 'if you won't believe your eyes, then you must refuse the knowledge they present'
   that . . . that what . . . what

92 – for . . . talking of –] *Qc* ((for . . . . talking of)*; for . . . talking, *Qu* has] hath *F* a-talking] *(a talking)* 95 SP] *Rowe (John.); Bastar. Q* 98, 107 SP] *Rowe (John.); Bast. Q* 101 me, tonight] *Qu;* me tonight *Qc* 103 her then,] *Hanmer;* her, then *Q*

CLAUDIO　If I see anything tonight why I should not
marry her, tomorrow in the congregation where I
should wed, there will I shame her.

DON PEDRO　And as I wooed for thee to obtain her, I will
join with thee to disgrace her.　　　　　　　　　　115

DON JOHN　I will disparage her no farther till you are my
witnesses. Bear it coldly but till midnight, and let the
issue show itself.

DON PEDRO　O day untowardly turned!

CLAUDIO　O mischief strangely thwarting!　　　　　　120

DON JOHN　O plague right well prevented! So will you say
when you have seen the sequel.　　　　　　　[*Exeunt.*]

[**3.3**] *Enter* DOGBERRY[, *the constable*], *and his compartner*
[VERGES,] *with the* Watch[, *among them*
George SEACOAL *and Hugh Oatcake*].

111 **why** i.e. that would provide a reason
why

112 **in the congregation** Unlike his precedents
in the prose and poetic sources, who
communicate their rejection of Hero by
messenger to the bride's father, Claudio
immediately plots a very public repudiation
of Hero. In Ariosto, he withdraws from
the court without a murmur (*Orlando*,
96.56), is believed a suicide, and it is
his grief-stricken brother Lurcanio who
'undertakes before them all, / To give
them perfect notice and instruction, /
Who was the cause of Ariodante's fall'
(97.63.3–5).

117 **coldly** calmly; without betraying you
know it

118 **issue** outcome

119 **untowardly turned** unhappily altered

120 **mischief** evil plight (*OED sb.* 1a), i.e.
Hero's infidelity

strangely thwarting unaccountably
obstructive (*OED* strangely *adv.* 5)

121–2 **So . . . sequel** 'The exit of Don John
with this string of sibilants cannot be
accidental' (Craik, 304).

122 This point in the action has often been the
location of an interpolated scene of
Borachio's assignation with Margaret
(Cox, *Shakespeare*, 156). See p. 91 for
discussion of the ramifications of such a
production choice.

3.3 The location is a street, with a church
bench in it and a *penthouse* (100), or
overhanging shed or porch roof; see 100n.

0.1 *constable* the chief civil officer of a parish,
nominally holding office for a year. The
post was unpaid and was meant to rotate
amongst citizens, although some holders
(like *MM*'s Elbow) were persuaded to
occupy it for a price, so as to spare others
their turn. Proverbially witless ('You might

112 her, tomorrow in] *Alexander;* her tomorrow, in *Rowe;* her to morrow in *Q;* her; to morrow, in
Capell congregation] *Qu;* congregation, *Qc* 116, 121 SP] *Rowe (John); Bastard Q* 117 midnight]
night *F* 122 SD] *F2; Exit. F* **3.3**] *Capell (*SCENE III*)* 0.1 *the constable*] *this edn* 0.2 VERGES]
Rowe 0.2–3 among . . . Oatcake] *this edn*

DOGBERRY   Are you good men and true?

VERGES   Yea, or else it were pity but they should suffer
salvation, body and soul.

DOGBERRY   Nay, that were a punishment too good for
them, if they should have any allegiance in them, being   5
chosen for the prince's watch.

VERGES   Well, give them their charge, neighbour
Dogberry.

DOGBERRY   First, who think you the most desertless man
to be constable?   10

1 WATCHMAN   Hugh Oatcake, sir, or George Seacoal, for
they can write and read.

be a constable for your wit', Dent,
C616).
compartner fellow office-bearer; the
only use of this word in Shakespeare's
works
0.2 *the* **Watch** a neighbourhood citizen patrol;
their number could include at least four
men (Oatcake, Seacoal, the speaker who
distinguishes them, and perhaps one other
from whom they are distinguished). As
Seacoal is the only speaker whose speeches
can be identified, he is alone in being
specified in the SPs.
3   **salvation** i.e. damnation. A feature of
Dogberry's unique attempt at an elevated
diction is frequent malapropisms which
sound somewhat like the correct words
for the circumstances he intends; whereas
the characters of higher rank delight
in deliberate word-play and semantic
conversions, Dogberry, 'in his obsessive
quest for polysyllables as symbols of
status' (Davis, 10), inadvertently says the
opposite of what he means. John Barton's
1976 RSC production of the play rendered
this verbal slippage by casting the members

of the Watch as a band of colonized Sikhs
under the British Raj, i.e. locals for whom
English was not their first language. The
British (and rural) names of the local
constabulary mark them as different in
fictional register from the higher-ranking
and etymologically Latinate Messinese.
5   **allegiance** Dogberry's error for disloyalty
6   **prince's watch** Elizabethan society had no
regular police force (or standing army).
7   **charge** assignment; instructions
9   **desertless** malapropism for 'deserving'
10 **constable** deputy leader of the Watch in the
absence of Dogberry
11 SP Q distinguishes between SPs for
individual watchmen only at the beginning
and the ending of the scene: Watch 1 appears
at 11, 157 and 162; Watch 2 (George
Seacoal) at 17, 27, 159 and 165. The
remainder are assigned to the undifferentiated
'*Watch*'. Various assignments of all the
lines are possible; many editions assign
the lion's share of the undifferentiated
lines (e.g. the questions to Dogberry) to
Watch 2, on the grounds that this
character, once designated leader, further

11 SP] *(Watch* 1*)*; SECOND WATCHMAN *Oxf*; A WATCHMAN *Oxf[1]*   Oatcake] *(Ote-cake)*, *F4*   11, 13 Seacoal]
(Sea-cole), *F4*

DOGBERRY   Come hither, neighbour Seacoal; [*Seacoal
   steps forward.*] God hath blest you with a good name. To
   be a well-favoured man is the gift of fortune, but to   15
   write and read comes by nature.
SEACOAL   Both which, master constable –
DOGBERRY   You have. I knew it would be your answer.
   Well, for your favour, sir, why, give God thanks, and
   make no boast of it; and for your writing and reading,   20
   let that appear when there is no need of such vanity.
   You are thought here to be the most senseless and fit
   man for the constable of the watch, therefore bear

questions Dogberry about his duties, and then, assuming the mantle of authority, orders his men about. Line 121 ('I know that Deformed') generally goes to Watch 1 because 162 ('And one Deformed is one of them') does in Q, and both seem to indicate a personage of some pretensions to criminology (which could be in keeping with Watch 1's being the first to reply to Dogberry at 11, and his initiative at 157); it is not necessary, however, that they be the same person, and there may be greater flexibility for a production if they are left as in Q (so that 162 could be an attempt to assert an authority usurped at 121). Similarly, the assignment of the other speeches exclusively to Watch 2 weights the dialogue heavily in favour of that actor at the expense of awkward silence for whatever other actors are present. Productions more often distribute 37–123 amongst the other actors in the Watch, returning (as here) to Watch 2 / Seacoal for the directives at 86–7, 93 and 103. With the exception of these three directives, this edition leaves the undifferentiated assignments as in Q, on the assumption that the indeterminacy (a result of printing practice as well as playing) permits the reader to imagine Dogberry besieged by multiple voices, and frees a director to assign roles according to the resources and talents of the company.

Oatcake The oaten cake was a Scottish food; like Seacoal's name, it identifies its bearer as hailing from northern parts considered provincial by London standards.

14   **a good name** Seacoal was high-grade coal shipped from Newcastle (a city of north-east England), as opposed to the charcoal sold in London by colliers.

15   **well-favoured** handsome
   fortune Lady Luck; cf. Lyly, *Euphues*, 15: 'To bee rich is the gift of Fortune, to be wise the grace of God.' Dogberry, however, attributes hereditary features to chance and literacy to heredity.

17   Seacoal's prompt suggests that a mysterious pause may occur after Dogberry's sentence.

19   **favour** appearance

22   **senseless** malapropism for 'sensible'

13–14 SD] *Bevington*   14 name. To] *Qc (*name: to*); name, to *Qu*   15 well-favoured] *(welfauoured)*, F   17 SP] *Bevington²; Watch 2 Q;* FIRST WATCHMAN *Oxf;* A WATCHMAN *Oxf¹*   constable] *Rowe*; Constable. *Q;* Constable *F*

you the lantern. [*Hands Seacoal the lantern.*] This is
your charge: you shall comprehend all vagrom men.   25
You are to bid any man stand, in the prince's name.

SEACOAL   How if 'a will not stand?

DOGBERRY   Why then, take no note of him, but let him
go, and presently call the rest of the watch together, and
thank God you are rid of a knave.   30

VERGES   If he will not stand when he is bidden, he is none
of the prince's subjects.

DOGBERRY   True, and they are to meddle with none but
the prince's subjects. You shall also make no noise in
the streets, for for the watch to babble and to talk is most   35
tolerable, and not to be endured.

WATCHMAN   We will rather sleep than talk; we know what
belongs to a watch.

DOGBERRY   Why, you speak like an ancient and most quiet
watchman. For I cannot see how sleeping should   40
offend. Only have a care that your bills be not stolen.

---

24 **lantern** On the Renaissance stage the
lantern would have indicated that it was
night time.
25 **comprehend** malapropism for 'apprehend'
vagrom malapropism for 'vagrant'
26, 27, 31   **stand** halt
28 **note** notice
29 **presently** immediately
31–2 **none . . . subjects** i.e. not subject to the
Prince's jurisdiction
36 **tolerable** malapropism for 'intolerable'.
Cf. *TS* 5.2.94: 'Intolerable, not to be
endur'd!'; Smith notes that 'This famous
phrase at once took root in the language'
(Smith). See also Thomas Heywood's *Fair
Maid of the Exchange* (1607), 4.3.157–8:
' 'tis most tolerable, and not to be indured'

(Heywood, *Maid*, 140). It may have been
suggested by an expression in John
Northbrooke's *Treatise against . . . Plays*
(1577): 'Plays and Players are not tolerable
nor to be endured' (Northbrooke, 76).
37 **sleep** The comic indolence of watchmen
was noted in Thomas Dekker's *Gull's
Hornbook* (1609): 'If you smell a watch,
and that you may easily do, for commonly
they eat onions to keep them in sleeping,
which they account a medicine against
cold' (Dekker, *Hornbook*, 63).
38 **belongs to** becomes, is appropriate for
39 **ancient** experienced
41 **bills** halberds, long wooden weapons with
a pointed axe head on top
stolen i.e. whilst you are napping

---

24 SD] *this edn (RP)*   27 SP] Bevington²; *Watch* 2 Q; FIRST WATCHMAN *Oxf*; A WATCHMAN *Oxf¹*   35 for
for] for, for Q   and to] and F   37, 44, 48, 53 SP] *(Watch); Watch* 2 / Rowe; SEACOAL *Folg²*

Well, you are to call at all the alehouses, and bid those
that are drunk get them to bed.

WATCHMAN   How if they will not?

DOGBERRY   Why then, let them alone till they are sober. If   45
they make you not then the better answer, you may say
they are not the men you took them for.

WATCHMAN   Well, sir.

DOGBERRY   If you meet a thief, you may suspect him, by
virtue of your office, to be no true man. And for such   50
kind of men, the less you meddle or make with them,
why, the more is for your honesty.

WATCHMAN   If we know him to be a thief, shall we not lay
hands on him?

DOGBERRY   Truly, by your office you may; but I think they   55
that touch pitch will be defiled. The most peaceable
way for you, if you do take a thief, is to let him show
himself what he is, and steal out of your company.

VERGES   You have been always called a merciful man,
partner.   60

DOGBERRY   Truly, I would not hang a dog by my will,
much more a man who hath any honesty in him.

VERGES   If you hear a child cry in the night you must call
to the nurse and bid her still it.

---

46 **better** more tractable
47 **for** to be
50 **true** honest
51 **meddle or make** have to do; proverbial
(Dent, M852)
52 **more is** better it is
56 **touch . . . defiled** proverbial: 'He that
toucheth pitch shall be defiled' (Dent,
P358, from Ecclesiastes, 13.1)
57–8 **show . . . is** reveal his true nature
61 **hang a dog** Animals were sometimes
subject to legal penalties; cf. 2.3.80–1: 'An

he had been a dog that should have howled
thus, they would have hanged him.'
62 **more** i.e. less
64 **still** quiet (ironic given that the Watch
themselves are calling out); the expectation
for quiet night-time hours is emphasized
in *The Statutes of the Street* (1595): '22. No
man shall blow any horn in the night,
within this citie, or whistle after the hour
of nyne of the clock in the night, under
paine of imprisonment . . . 30. No man
shall, after the houre of nyne at night,

42 those] them *F*

WATCHMAN   How if the nurse be asleep and will not hear   65
us?

DOGBERRY   Why then, depart in peace, and let the child
wake her with crying; for the ewe that will not hear her
lamb when it baas will never answer a calf when he
bleats.   70

VERGES   'Tis very true.

DOGBERRY   This is the end of the charge. You, constable,
are to present the prince's own person. If you meet the
prince in the night you may stay him.

VERGES   Nay, by'r Lady, that I think 'a cannot.   75

DOGBERRY   Five shillings to one on't with any man that
knows the statutes. He may stay him – marry, not
without the prince be willing, for indeed the watch
ought to offend no man, and it is an offence to stay a
man against his will.   80

VERGES   By'r Lady, I think it be so.

DOGBERRY   Ha, ah ha! Well, masters, good night; an there

keepe any rule, whereby any suche suddaine outcry be made in the still of the night, as making any affray, or beating his wyfe or seruaunt, or singing, or reuyling in his house, to the disturbaunce of his neighbours.'

69 **calf** can mean fool (i.e. the Watchman) (*OED* calf¹ 1c); Dogberry's formulation lends this sentiment the force of a proverb.

73 **present** i.e. represent, take on the authority of

74, 77 **stay** arrest, stop for questioning

75, 81 **by'r Lady** by our Lady

77 **statutes** Acts of Parliament (though the law in question governing apprehension of the Prince belongs to the common law). F's 'Statues' is most likely an error in keeping with Dogberry's own; F2 restores Q's spelling.

79 **offend no man** A watch's efficacy was no doubt compromised by the difficulty, or snobbery, in a hierarchical society of members of a lower status apprehending those of a higher social station (who were themselves exempt from serving as watchmen); on these grounds, Dekker's *Hornbook* recommends that those abroad after curfew who meet a watch call out the name of a nobleman, e.g. ' "Sir Giles." It skills not though there be none dubbed in your bunch; the watch will wink at you, only for the love they bear to arms and knighthood' (63).

82 **Ha, ah ha!** most likely a triumphant exultation over Verges' error (e.g. Ha, I told you so!); Smith suggests that the first 'Ha' be interrogative.

65 SP] *(Watch); Watch 2 / Rowe*   77 statutes] Statues *F*   82 an] *(and)*

be any matter of weight chances, call up me. Keep your
fellows' counsels, and your own, and good night. [*to*
Verges] Come, neighbour. [*Dogberry and Verges begin to*   85
exit.]

SEACOAL   Well, masters, we hear our charge. Let us go sit
here upon the church bench till two, and then all to bed.

DOGBERRY [*Returns.*]   One word more, honest neighbours. I pray you watch about Signor Leonato's
door, for the wedding being there tomorrow, there is a   90
great coil tonight. Adieu. Be vigitant, I beseech you.

Exeunt [*Dogberry and Verges*].

Enter BORACHIO *and* CONRADE.

BORACHIO   What, Conrade!

SEACOAL [*aside*]   Peace, stir not.

BORACHIO   Conrade, I say!

CONRADE   Here, man, I am at thy elbow.   95

BORACHIO   Mass, and my elbow itched; I thought there
would a scab follow!

---

83   **any . . . weight** anything important

83–4 **Keep . . . own** The oath of a grand-jury
man was 'The King's counsel, your
fellows' and your own you shall observe
and keep secret' (Cam); cf Dent, C682:
'The counsel thou wouldst have another
keep, first keep thyself.'

91   **coil** hubbub, to-do
vigitant malapropism for 'vigilant'. In
many productions the Watch retire upstage,
or down, or otherwise dispose themselves
inconspicuously, often to sleep (although
on the Renaissance stage it was a
convention that separate parties could be
invisible and inaudible to each other).

92   **What** hey there

96   **Mass** i.e. by the Mass (for a late sixteenth-
century Protestant Englishman, an outdated
oath; Borachio is of course Italian or
Spanish)
my elbow itched An itchy elbow was an
omen presaging unsavoury company: 'My
elbow itched, I must change my bedfellow'
(Tilley, E98).

97   **scab** lesion; parasitic rascal. Cf. *Cor*
1.1.163–5: 'What's the matter, you
dissentious rogues, / That, rubbing the poor
itch of your opinion, / Make yourself scabs?'

84–5 SD] *Oxf¹*   85 SD] *Folg²*   86 SP] *Bevington²; Watch 2 / Rowe; Watch Q*   88 SD] *this edn (*RP*)*
89 Signor] *(*signior*)*   91 SD *Dogberry and Verges*] *Pope; Exeunt Q*   93 SP] *Capell; Watch Q:* FIRST
WATCHMAN *Oxf*   SD] *Rowe*

CONRADE   I will owe thee an answer for that. And now, forward with thy tale.

BORACHIO   Stand thee close, then, under this penthouse, 100 for it drizzles rain, and I will, like a true drunkard, utter all to thee.

SEACOAL [*aside*]   Some treason, masters. Yet stand close.

BORACHIO   Therefore, know I have earned of Don John a thousand ducats. 105

CONRADE   Is it possible that any villainy should be so dear?

BORACHIO   Thou shouldst rather ask if it were possible any villainy should be so rich. For when rich villains have need of poor ones, poor ones may make what price 110 they will.

CONRADE   I wonder at it.

BORACHIO   That shows thou art unconfirmed. Thou knowest that the fashion of a doublet, or a hat, or a cloak, is nothing to a man. 115

CONRADE   Yes, it is apparel.

---

100 **close** near; hidden
   penthouse overhanging canopy; on the unlocalized Renaissance stage, the word could establish a location for the audience, or perhaps indicate that Borachio and Conrade situated themselves under the tiring-house canopy.

101 **true drunkard** Cf. the Latin proverb '*in vino veritas*' ('in wine there is truth'), and Borachio's own name (see List of Roles 7n.). Borachio and Conrade are often played as if drunk in this scene.

103 **Yet** for now
   close together; nearer; hidden; implicitly another SD

107 **dear** expensive, precious

113 **unconfirmed** ignorant

113–37 **Thou . . . fashion** Borachio's digression on fashion (usually cut in performance) seems, as Conrade suggests, rather far afield from his story, unless we take it as a meditation on the fickleness of *all the hot-bloods* (127–8) when it comes to choice of either clothing or women; or perhaps as a reflection on the misleading connections between clothing and identity (crucial to Margaret's impersonation of Hero); or, indeed, on the discrepancy between the conduct and the rank of apparent gentlemen Don John, Claudio and Don Pedro.

114 **doublet** See 2.3.17n.

115 **nothing to a man** tells us nothing about a man; does not matter to a man (another play on the word, which Conrade's reply compounds); cf. *TS* 3.1.117

---

103 SP] *Bevington²; 2 Watch / Capell; Watch Q*   SD] *Johnson*   104 Don] *F;* Dun *Q*

BORACHIO I mean the fashion.

CONRADE Yes, the fashion is the fashion.

BORACHIO Tush, I may as well say the fool's the fool. But
seest thou not what a deformed thief this fashion is?   120

WATCHMAN [*aside*] I know that Deformed. 'A has been
a vile thief this seven year; 'a goes up and down like a
gentleman; I remember his name.

BORACHIO Didst thou not hear somebody?

CONRADE No, 'twas the vane on the house.   125

BORACHIO Seest thou not, I say, what a deformed thief
this fashion is, how giddily 'a turns about all the
hot-bloods between fourteen and five-and-thirty,
sometimes fashioning them like Pharaoh's soldiers in
the reechy painting, sometime like god Bel's priests in   130

---

120 **deformed** deforming

122 **seven year** a number denoting an indefinite
term (Furness)

goes . . . down walks about

122 3 **like a gentleman** In a culture of
(largely flouted) sumptuary laws (which
decreed that a person's clothing must
indicate his or her social station and
gender) it is possible to impersonate
another status by wearing its designated
apparel (much as actors do). The 'Homily
on Excess of Apparel' exhorts that 'every
man behold and consider his own vocation,
inasmuch as God hath appointed every
man his degree and office, within the limits
whereof it behoveth him to keep himself.
Therefore all may not look to wear like
apparel, but everyone according to his
degree . . .' (*Homilies*, 310).

124 Borachio's question indicates either that
the Watchman's speech is audible, or, in
productions that cut the passages on
fashion, that the Watch betray their

presence in some other way (often by
dropping a weapon or the lantern).

125 **vane** weathervane

the house may refer both to the fictional
setting and to the roof of the playhouse

129 **Pharaoh's soldiers** soldiers of Pharaoh,
king of Egypt, who were drowned along
with their leader in the Red Sea while
pursuing the escaping Israelites (Exodus,
14.23–8)

130 **reechy** smoke-begrimed, discoloured;
Borachio refers here and in the following
lines to visual representations of biblical
and classical subjects (which would have
portrayed ancient persons in the fashion
contemporary to the painter's own
moment, e.g. a becodpieced Hercules).

god Bel's priests the priests of Baal, or the
Sumerian god of winds and agriculture. The
reference is to the apocryphal story 'Bel and
the Dragon', once attached to the Book of
Daniel; the story tells how Daniel overthrew
the priests of Bel by convincing their

---

120 deformed] *Qc;* deformed *Qu*   121 SP] *(Watch); First Watch / Capell; 2 Watch / Bevington;* SEACOAL
Bevington² SD] *Capell* Deformed] *Rowe;* deformed *Q*   122 year] yeares *F* year;] *Qc (*yeere,*);* yeere
Qu   123 I] *Qc; not in Qu*   128 five-and-thirty] *(fiue and thirtie), Cam*   130 reechy] *(*rechie)

the old church window, sometime like the shaven
Hercules in the smirched worm-eaten tapestry, where
his codpiece seems as massy as his club.

CONRADE   All this I see, and I see that the fashion wears
out more apparel than the man. But art not thou thyself   135
giddy with the fashion, too, that thou hast shifted out of
thy tale into telling me of the fashion?

king (Cyrus of Persia) that Bel was not a
deity but a mere image. God Bel's priests,
as idolators, were no doubt richly clothed
(Tudor–Stuart Protestantism posited a
strong connection between idolatry and
sartorial excess, the whore of Babylon, or
the Roman Church, being a chief exemplar
of the trend).

131 **old church window** The idolatrous
stained-glass window was a hallmark of
Catholic practice.

131–2 **shaven Hercules** likely to be a
confusion with the shorn Samson (Judges,
16), but perhaps a reference to Hercules in
the house of Omphale (see 2.1.231–3 and
2.1.29–30n.), except that Hercules in the
latter circumstance is not usually shaven
though he is dressed as a woman (much
being made of the contrast between his
beard and his clothing): 'So in Hercules,
painted with his great beard and furious
countenance, in a woman's attire, spinning
at Omphale's commandment, it breedeth
both delight and laughter' (Sidney,
Defence, 68). Or, as Cam² suggests,
Hercules at the crossroads, a popular
representation of the youthful (and
beardless) Hercules poised between the
paths of virtue and vice. The drunken
Borachio may be garbling his allusions, but
the thrust of his comparison seems to point
to the image of an overly preened (clean-
shaven, such as Benedick is in 3.2) and
ornately dressed figure of a man, by

contrast with his bedraggled tapestry.

132 **smirched** besmirched, grimy

133 **codpiece** laced-up attachment to a man's
breeches, covering his genitals. In
Elizabethan fashion (to 1580) codpieces
were often outsized and ornately
bejewelled in order to draw attention to,
and suggest, the proportions and capacities
of their contents. Cf. Montaigne, 'On some
verses of Virgil': 'what was the meaning of
that ridiculous part of the breeches worn by
our fathers, which is still seen on our
Swiss? What is the point of the show we
make even now of the shape of our pieces
under our galligaskins, and what is worse,
often by falsehood and imposture beyond
their natural size?' (Montaigne, 653). Like
the *reechy painting* and the *worm-eaten
tapestry*, the codpiece was outdated by
1600.

    club i.e. prodigious object (Hercules being
known for his strength, and the
corresponding heft of his club). Borachio
here draws a distinction between actual
strength (the club) and the mere (and often
fallacious) representation of it. Borachio's
observations contribute to the play's
thematic fascination with what constitutes
'a man' (see pp. 61–2).

134–5 **wears … man** consumes more clothing
than is strictly needed by its wearer

136 **giddy with** entranced by
    shifted out pun on changing one's shift, or
shirt

134 and I] and *F*

BORACHIO   Not so neither. But know that I have tonight
   wooed Margaret, the Lady Hero's gentlewoman, by the
   name of Hero; she leans me out at her mistress'   140
   chamber window, bids me a thousand times goodnight
   – I tell this tale vilely. I should first tell thee how the
   prince, Claudio and my master, planted and placed and
   possessed by my master Don John, saw afar off in the
   orchard this amiable encounter.   145
CONRADE   And thought they Margaret was Hero?
BORACHIO   Two of them did, the prince and Claudio,
   but the devil my master knew she was Margaret. And
   partly by his oaths, which first possessed them, partly
   by the dark night, which did deceive them, but chiefly   150
   by my villainy, which did confirm any slander that Don
   John had made, away went Claudio enraged, swore he
   would meet her as he was appointed next morning at
   the temple, and there, before the whole congregation,
   shame her with what he saw o'ernight, and send her   155
   home again without a husband.
1 WATCHMAN [*Starts out upon them.*]   We charge you in
   the prince's name, stand!

140 **leans me out** leans out towards me; cf.
   1.3.55 and n.
141 **thousand times goodnight** Borachio and
   Margaret apparently played a conventional
   lovers' leave-taking scene in the tradition
   of *RJ* (2.2).
144 **possessed** primed, or deluded, by the
   (false) story of what they were about to
   see; with possibly a 'sense of demoniac
   possession, inasmuch as Borachio refers in
   his next sentence and at 148 to "the devil,
   my master" ' (Furness). Borachio's syntax
   is somewhat garbled (with drink or the
   pleasures of alliteration?); *planted and*

   placed can refer to all three witnesses,
   though *possessed* only to the Prince and
   Claudio.
   afar off from far off (presumably a distance
   at which the deception of Margaret's
   borrowed garments would be plausible)
149 **possessed** prejudiced
150 **dark** Unlike Shakespeare's sources, which
   note the brightness of the scene ('the night
   was not very dark but very still', Bullough,
   116), Claudio's error is mitigated by the
   tenebrousness of the evening.
154 **temple** i.e. the church
158 **stand** i.e. stand forth, don't move; this

143 prince, Claudio] *Rowe;* prince Claudio *Q*   146 SP] *Qc (Conr.); Con Qu*   they] thy *F*   157, 162 SP]
(Watch 1); 2 Watch Ard²; SEACOAL *Cam²*   157 SD] *Capell*

283

SEACOAL   Call up the right master constable! We have
here recovered the most dangerous piece of lechery   160
that ever was known in the commonwealth!

1 WATCHMAN   And one Deformed is one of them. I know
him, 'a wears a lock.

CONRADE   Masters, masters –

SEACOAL   You'll be made bring Deformed forth, I   165
warrant you.

CONRADE   Masters –

SEACOAL   Never speak, we charge you! Let us obey you
to go with us.

BORACHIO [*to Conrade*]   We are like to prove a goodly   170
commodity, being taken up of these men's bills.

command follows Dogberry's prescribed formula at 26 ('You are to bid any man stand, in the prince's name'), but may derive added humour from the fact that Conrade and Borachio are in fact already standing ('Stand thee close, then, under this penthouse', 100).

159 **right** an honorific intensifier, as in 'right honourable', 'right worshipful'

160 **recovered** malapropism for 'discovered'. Dogberry's malapropisms are seemingly contagious (as at 168). Folg² provides an exit for the Second Watchman at 161 and a re-entrance for him along with Dogberry and Verges at 165 (the uncorrected Q in fact prints the SP at 164 and 167 as *Con.*). See t.n.
lechery malapropism for 'treachery'

163 **lock** a lock of hair grown longer than its fellows, and often ornamented with tokens

of the beloved. William Prynne wrote an entire treatise against the affectation (*The Unloveliness of Love-Locks*, 1628); Sidney's Astrophel, on the other hand, argues in sonnet 54 of *Astrophel and Stella* for the originality of his love despite his lack of tokens: 'Because I breathe not loue to euery one, / Nor doe not vse set colours for to wear, / Nor nourish special locks of vowèd hair. . . .'.

164 **Masters** i.e. officers (*OED sb.*[1] III 19a)

168 **obey** malapropism for 'order', 'command'

170–1 **goodly commodity** valuable article; goods obtained on credit from an usurer, typically at exorbitant interest

171 **taken up of** under arrest, at the point of; received on credit for
bills halberds; bonds given as security for goods

159, 165 SP] *Folg²; Watch 2 Q; First Watch Ard²;* A WATCHMAN *Oxf*   159 constable!] constable! *Second Watchman exits Folg² (Cam²)*   163 lock.] lock. *Enter Dogberry, Verges, and Second Watchman Folg²*   164, 167 SP] *(Conr) Qc; Con. Qu;* DOGBERRY *Folg² (Cam²)*   164 masters –] *Theobald;* masters. *Q*   167–8 CONRADE . . . Never] *Theobald subst;* Conr Masters, neuer *Qc;* Con. Masters, neuer *Qu;* DOGBERRY Masters, never *Folg² (Cam²)*   168 SP] *Bevington²; First Watch / Theobald; Sec. Watch / Bevington;* A WATCHMAN *Oxf*   170 SD] *Oxf*

CONRADE   A commodity in question, I warrant you.
Come, we'll obey you.   *Exeunt.*

[**3.4**]   *Enter* HERO, MARGARET *and* URSULA.

HERO   Good Ursula, wake my cousin Beatrice and desire
her to rise.

URSULA   I will, lady.

HERO   And bid her come hither.

URSULA   Well.   [*Exit.*]

MARGARET   Troth, I think your other rebato were better.   6

HERO   No, pray thee, good Meg, I'll wear this.

MARGARET   By my troth, 's not so good, and I warrant
your cousin will say so.

HERO   My cousin's a fool, and thou art another. I'll wear   10
none but this.

MARGARET   I like the new tire within excellently, if the
hair were a thought browner. And your gown's a most
rare fashion, i'faith. I saw the Duchess of Milan's gown
that they praise so.   15

HERO   O, that exceeds, they say.

---

172 **in question** (1) sought after; (2) subject to
legal trial or interrogation (cf. *2H4* 1.2.60:
'He that was in question for the robbery');
(3) doubtful

3.4 The location is the interior of Leonato's
house, sometimes Hero's chambers
(although Ursula's scene-changing
command to *withdraw* at the arrival of the
menfolk (87) suggests that Hero's
preparations take place in a public space).

5   **Well** yes

6   **Troth** in truth (a mild oath)
rebato a stiff collar or ruff; also used to
describe the wire architectural support of

the lace or linen

7, 10, 16 SP F's '*Bero.*' might suggest
setting from an unknown uncorrected state
of Q.

12   **tire** complete head dress, including false
hair and ornaments, viewed by some with
the same contempt reserved for male
affectations such as the love-lock
within i.e. in another room

13   **a thought browner** a bit, slightly more,
brunette (i.e. more closely allied to Hero's
own colouring)

14   **rare** exceptional

16   **exceeds** i.e. excels, outdoes (all praise)

---

172 SP] *Qc (Conr); Con Qu*   **3.4**] *Capell (SCENE IV)*   0.1 HERO,] *Rowe; Hero, and Q*   1 Good] *Qc;*
God *Qu*   5 SD] *Hanmer*   8, 17 troth, 's] *Capell;* troth's *Q*   7, 10, 16 SP] *Bero. F*

MARGARET   By my troth, 's but a night-gown in respect of
    yours – cloth o'gold, and cuts, and laced with silver, set
    with pearls, down sleeves, side sleeves and skirts round
    underborne with a bluish tinsel. But for a fine, quaint,   20
    graceful and excellent fashion, yours is worth ten on't.
HERO   God give me joy to wear it, for my heart is
    exceeding heavy.
MARGARET   'Twill be heavier soon by the weight of a
    man.   25
HERO   Fie upon thee! Art not ashamed?
MARGARET   Of what, lady? Of speaking honourably? Is
    not marriage honourable in a beggar? Is not your lord
    honourable without marriage? I think you would have
    me say, saving your reverence, 'a husband'. An bad   30
    thinking do not wrest true speaking, I'll offend nobody.
    Is there any harm in 'the heavier for a husband'? None,

17   **'s** it is
     night-gown dressing gown
     in respect of compared with
18   **cuts** slashed openings on the edge or in the
     body of the overdress which would have
     revealed the rich lining inlaid beneath
     laced trimmed; embroidered
18–19 **set with pearls** Pearls were often sewn
     into the fabric of ornate garments.
19   **down sleeves** tight-fitting sleeves to the
     wrist
     side sleeves ornamental sleeves draped
     away from the shoulders down the back
19–20 **round underborne** trimmed all the
     way around underneath; or held out by an
     ornamental petticoat
20   **tinsel** a fine silk tissue laced with silver or
     gold
     quaint elegant
21   **on't** of it

24   **heavier** Margaret's sexual innuendo
     compares with Don Pedro's at 3.2.62 that
     the woman who loves Benedick will be
     'buried with her face upwards'.
26   **Fie** expresses serious offence
     Art not i.e. art thou not
28   **honourable . . . beggar** proverbial (Dent,
     M683). Protestantism encouraged the
     appropriateness of marriage for all people
     (including priests); the *Book of Common
     Prayer* proclaims that 'Matrimony . . . is an
     honourable estate . . . commended of Saint
     Paul to be honourable among all men'
     (*BCP*, 290).
30   **saving your reverence** a formula for
     excusing the mention of an indelicate subject
     a husband i.e. instead of the indeterminate
     man (25)
     An if
31   **wrest** twist the meaning of

17 in] *F;* it *Q*   18 o'] *(a)*   30 saving . . . 'a husband'] *Pope;* 'saving . . . a husband' *Cam;* sauing . . . a
husband *Q*   An] *(&)*   32 'the . . . husband'] *Pope;* the . . . husband *Q*

I think, an it be the right husband and the right wife;
otherwise 'tis light and not heavy.

Enter BEATRICE.

Ask my lady Beatrice else; here she comes.   35
HERO   Good morrow, coz.
BEATRICE   Good morrow, sweet Hero.
HERO   Why, how now? Do you speak in the sick tune?
BEATRICE   I am out of all other tune, methinks.
MARGARET   Clap's into 'Light o'love', that goes without   40
    a burden. Do you sing it, and I'll dance it.
BEATRICE   Ye light o'love with your heels? Then if your
    husband have stables enough, you'll see he shall lack
    no barns.

---

34 **light** i.c. if the husband and wife in
question are not married to one another
35 **else** i.e. if it is otherwise
36 **morrow** morning
38 **how now** i.e. what's the matter
sick tune Beatrice speaks as if she has a
head cold (cf. 58–60). 'Sick, sick' was the
name and refrain of a late sixteenth-century
tune entitled 'Captain Car', cited in
Nashe's *Summer's Last Will* (1600), 852–3:
'Sicke, Sicke, and very sicke / & sicke and
for the time' (Nashe, 3.260, also see 4.432).
Ross Duffin also cites another song, 'My
Heart is Leaned on the Land' (*c.* 1558), a
more plaintive love ballad, with a 'sick'
refrain: 'I so sick; make my bed, I will die
now' (Duffin, 369). A.P. Rossiter observes
that 'It is a notable point in Shakespeare's
contrivance that he gives both wits their
off-day, as soon as love has disturbed their
freedom' (Rossiter, 48). Many productions
account for the ailment by the choice of
Beatrice's hiding place in 3.1 (see 3.ln.).
40 **Clap's into** let us clap
Light o'love as in *TGV* 1.2.83, a popular

dance tune, probably written by Leonard
Gibson *c.* 1570, and apparently a 'light' (i.e.
wanton) one, as at 83–5: 'JULIA Best sing it
to the tune of "Light o'love". / LUCETTA It is
too heavy for so light a tune. / JULIA Heavy?
Belike it hath some burden then?' Margaret
tells Beatrice (and Hero) to cheer up.
41 **burden** refrain; bass harmonic under-song
sung by male voices; heavy weight (like
that of a man's body); child in the womb
42 **Ye . . . heels** are you, or will you be, light-
heeled, i.e. unchaste (the modern 'round-
heeled' or 'short-heeled', i.e. easily tipped
backwards). Cf. Henry Porter, *Two Angry
Women of Abingdon* (1599): 'Light aloue,
short heels, mistress Goursey' (Porter, 1.
740); and 5.4.116–17: 'that we may lighten
our own hearts and our wives' heels'.
Beatrice's question perhaps suggests some
capering stage action on Margaret's part.
light o'love wanton
43 **stables** with punning reference to its sexual
sense of 'erections'
44 **barns** with pun on bairns, the northern
(and rustic) word for children

---

33 an] *(and)*   40 'Light o'love'] *Pope;* Light a loue *Q*   42 o'love] *(aloue)*   heels?] *Capell (*heels!*);*
heels, *Q*   43 see] looke *F*

MARGARET   O illegitimate construction! I scorn that with   45
my heels.

BEATRICE   'Tis almost five o'clock, cousin; 'tis time you
were ready. By my troth, I am exceeding ill. Hey-ho!

MARGARET   For a hawk, a horse, or a husband?

BEATRICE   For the letter that begins them all: H.   50

MARGARET   Well, an you be not turned Turk, there's no
more sailing by the star.

BEATRICE   What means the fool, trow?

MARGARET   Nothing, I, but God send everyone their
heart's desire.   55

HERO   These gloves the count sent me, they are an
excellent perfume.

BEATRICE   I am stuffed, cousin, I cannot smell.

MARGARET   A maid and stuffed! There's goodly catching
of cold.   60

---

45 **illegitimate construction** false interpretation, with pun on bastard birth

45–6 **scorn . . . heels** (1) reject that with scorn, as one would grind with one's heel (*OED* heel *sb.*[1] I 3b); (2) outrun (3c), cf. *MV* 2.2.8–9: 'scorn running with thy heels'; (3) kick, as does a horse

48 **Hey-ho** a yearning sigh of regret, with, as Margaret's punning response suggests, various objects; cf. 2.1.293–4: 'I may sit in a corner and cry "Hey-ho for a husband" '.

50 **H** Both the letter and the word 'ache' were pronounced in the same way, as 'aitch'; hence quibbles such as Beatrice's on her cold, or John Heywood's *A Dialogue . . . of All the Proverbs in the English Tongue* (1546): 'H is worst among the letters in the crosse row, / For if thou find him other in thine elbow, / In thine arm, or leg, in any degree, / In thy head, or teeth, in thy toe or knee, / Into what place so euer H, may like him, / Where euer thou finde ache, thou shalt not like him.'

51 **turned Turk** i.e. converted to Islam,

changed your faith (i.e. to being in love, instead of a scorner of men). To 'turn Turk', from a Christian perspective, means to become an infidel; the phrase was proverbial (Dent, T609).

51–2 **there's . . . star** we cannot any longer navigate by the North Star, i.e. there's nothing left that we can rely on

53 **trow** I wonder

57 **perfume** Perfumed gloves were a luxury item; cf. the wares of Autolycus, *WT* 4.4.222: 'Gloves as sweet as damask roses'. Hero is perhaps trying to divert Margaret from baiting Beatrice and thus drawing her suspicion to the hoax.

58–9 **I am stuffed . . . stuffed** i.e. my nose is stuffed-up; Margaret's rejoinder turns the word to indicate the condition of pregnancy or its sexual preamble (cf. *stuffed man*, 1.1.55).

59 **maid** i.e. virgin

59–60 **goodly . . . cold** i.e. that's some cold you've caught

48 Hey-ho] *(*hey ho*), Cam*   51 an] *(*and*)*

BEATRICE   O God help me, God help me, how long have
you professed apprehension?

MARGARET   Ever since you left it. Doth not my wit
become me rarely?

BEATRICE   It is not seen enough; you should wear it in   65
your cap. By my troth, I am sick.

MARGARET   Get you some of this distilled *carduus
benedictus*, and lay it to your heart; it is the only thing
for a qualm.

HERO   There thou prick'st her with a thistle.   70

BEATRICE   *Benedictus*? Why *benedictus*? You have some
moral in this *benedictus*.

MARGARET   Moral? No, by my troth, I have no moral
meaning, I meant plain holy-thistle. You may think
perchance that I think you are in love? Nay, by'r Lady, I   75
am not such a fool to think what I list, nor I list not to
think what I can, nor indeed I cannot think, if I would
think my heart out of thinking, that you are in love, or
that you will be in love, or that you can be in love. Yet
Benedick was such another, and now is he become a   80

62 **professed apprehension** claimed to be a wit
63 **left it** gave it up
64 **rarely** infrequently, excellently
65–6 **in your cap** 'i.e., as a fool does his coxcomb' (Cam[1])
67–8 *carduus benedictus* the thistle plant, often termed 'holy' or 'blessed' (i.e. *benedictus*) for its expansive healing properties; cf. the herbal of Thomas Cogan, *Haven of Health* (1574): 'Carduus benedictus or blessed thistle, so worthily named for the vertues that it hath, . . . may worthily be called Benedictus or Omnimorbia, that is, a salue for euery sore' (cited in Furness). The plant was particularly well thought of as a remedy for 'perillous diseases of the heart' (*Gardener's Labyrinth*, 1594), 'good to be

laid upon the biting of mad dogs, serpents, spiders, or any venomous beast whatsoever' (Gerard's *Herbal*, 1597). Clearly also a pun on Benedick's name.
68 **lay . . . heart** apply it medicinally; embrace it passionately
69 **qualm** a feeling of faintness, especially about the heart (but also produced by orgasm)
70 i.e. now you've struck home (but presumably also with bawdy meaning of 'prick')
72 **moral** hidden meaning; i.e. an immoral (bawdy) one, as Margaret underlines in her response.
76 **list . . . list** wish . . . wish
80–1 **become a man** i.e. a man like any other, vulnerable to affection

74 holy-thistle] *(holy thissel), Rowe*

man. He swore he would never marry, and yet now in
despite of his heart he eats his meat without grudging.
And how you may be converted I know not, but
methinks you look with your eyes as other women do.

BEATRICE   What pace is this that thy tongue keeps?   85
MARGARET   Not a false gallop.

Enter URSULA.

URSULA   Madam, withdraw! The prince, the count,
Signor Benedick, Don John and all the gallants of the
town are come to fetch you to church.
HERO   Help to dress me, good coz, good Meg, good   90
Ursula.   [*Exeunt.*]

[**3.5**]   *Enter* LEONATO, [DOGBERRY,] *the constable,*
and [VERGES,] *the headborough.*

LEONATO   What would you with me, honest neighbour?
DOGBERRY   Marry, sir, I would have some confidence
with you, that discerns you nearly.

81–2 **in . . . heart** in spite of his former
determination (not to love)
82   **eats his meat** i.e. acknowledges his normal
human appetites
86   **false gallop** (1) a forced burst of speed, cf.
Nashe's *Terrors of the Night* (1594): 'I
haue rid a false gallop these three or foure
pages, now I care not if I breathe mee, and
walke soberly and demurely half a dozen
turnes, like a graue Citizen going about to
take the ayre' (Nashe, 1.368); (2) a canter,
a controlled gait as opposed to a full-out
gallop. Touchstone's rhymes in *AYL* 3.2
are 'the very false gallop of verses' (110),
i.e. an artificially controlled gait;

Margaret's point is that she speaks the
truth.
3.5 The location is before Leonato's house.
0.2 *headborough* parish officer, local
constable
2   **confidence** malapropism for 'conference'
('talk'). Cf. *RJ* 2.3.126–7: 'I desire some
confidence with you'; or *MW* 1.4.147–9: 'I
will tell your worship more . . . the next
time we have confidence.' Both uses are by
persons of low social caste (the nurse;
Mistress Quickly), though the term,
meaning confidential speech, is technically
apt in the circumstance.
3   **discerns** i.e. malapropism for 'concerns'

88 Signor] *(signior)*   91 SD] *Rowe*   **3.5**] *SCENE V Capell*   0.1 DOGBERRY] *Rowe (Dogb.)*   0.2
VERGES] *Rowe (Verg.)*   2, 6 SP] *Rowe; Const. Dog. Q*

LEONATO   Brief, I pray you, for you see it is a busy time
        with me.   5
DOGBERRY   Marry, this it is, sir.
VERGES   Yes, in truth it is, sir.
LEONATO   What is it, my good friends?
DOGBERRY   Goodman Verges, sir, speaks a little off the
        matter. An old man, sir, and his wits are not so blunt as,   10
        God help, I would desire they were; but, in faith, honest
        as the skin between his brows.
VERGES   Yes, I thank God, I am as honest as any man
        living, that is an old man and no honester than I.
DOGBERRY   Comparisons are odorous; *palabras*, neighbour   15
        Verges.
LEONATO   Neighbours, you are tedious.
DOGBERRY   It pleases your worship to say so, but we are
        the poor duke's officers. But truly, for mine own part, if

9   **Goodman** title for a man below the rank of
    gentleman; Dogberry is attentive to caste.
10   **blunt** malapropism for 'sharp'
11–12   **honest . . . brows** proverbial (Dent,
    S506), explained by another proverb,
    'Everyone's fault is written in his
    forehead', presumably because furrowed
    by care or conscience (Foakes); also the
    site of branding for some felonies. Brows
    are an especially charged site in this play
    full of jokes about the cuckold's horns;
    Thomas Buoni explains in *Problems of
    Beauty and All Human Affections* (1606):
    'why is the seat of Shamefastnesse in the
    forehead . . . because it is most visible and
    apparent to the eye of man' (Buoni, sig.
    O5ᵛ).
15   **odorous** malapropism for 'odious';
    proverbial (Dent, C576); cf. *Sir Giles
    Goosecap* (1606), 4.2.45: '*Goosecappe:*

Be Caparisons odious, sir Cut; what, like
flowers? / *Rudsbie:* O asse they be odorous'
(*Goosecappe*, 65).
    palabras i.e. silence, from the popular
    Spanish tag '*pocas palabras*' (few words);
    cf. *Spanish Tragedy*, 3.14.118: '*Pocas
    Palabras*, milde as the lambe'.
17   Constables were notoriously tedious
    (perhaps because they think they are witty:
    see 3.3.0.1n.). Cf. Jonson, *Cynthia's Revels*
    (1601), 2.3.82–6: 'He is his own promoter
    in every place. The wife of the ordinarie
    giues him his diet, to maintain her table in
    discourse, which (indeede) is a meere
    tyrannie ouer her other guests, for hee will
    vsurpe all the talke; ten constables are not
    so tedious' (Jonson, 4.73).
19   **poor duke's** i.e. duke's poor; see *MM*
    2.1.46 for a similar transposition on the
    part of Elbow.

7 SP] *Rowe; Headb. Q*   9 SP] *Rowe; Con. Do. Q*   off] *Steevens–Reed² (Capell); of Q*   13, 27 SP]
Rowe; Head. Q   15+ SP] *Rowe; Const. Dog. Q*

I were as tedious as a king I could find in my heart to   20
    bestow it all of your worship.

LEONATO   All thy tediousness on me, ah?

DOGBERRY   Yea, an 'twere a thousand pound more than
    'tis, for I hear as good exclamation on your worship as
    of any man in the city, and though I be but a poor man,   25
    I am glad to hear it.

VERGES   And so am I.

LEONATO   I would fain know what you have to say.

VERGES   Marry, sir, our watch tonight, excepting your
    worship's presence, ha' ta'en a couple of as arrant   30
    knaves as any in Messina.

DOGBERRY   A good old man, sir, he will be talking. As they
    say, 'When the age is in, the wit is out.' God help us, it
    is a world to see! Well said, i'faith, neighbour Verges.
    Well, God's a good man. An two men ride of a horse,   35
    one must ride behind. An honest soul, i'faith, sir,
    by my troth, he is, as ever broke bread. But, God is
    to be worshipped, all men are not alike. Alas, good
    neighbour!

---

20 **tedious** Dogberry thinks tedious means wealthy.

21–2 **of . . . on** See Abbott, 175, for *on* and *of* interchange.

24 **exclamation** i.e. acclamation (*exclamation* means loud complaint; cf. *R3* 4.4.154: 'Thus will I drown your exclamations')

28 **fain** gladly

29 **tonight** last night
excepting malapropism for 'respecting', i.e. if I may be permitted to speak in your presence; despite his own verbal difficulties, Verges at least manages to begin to state the problem.

30 **arrant** unmitigated, extreme

33 **When . . . out** as Dogberry is unabashed to admit, a proverb (although in its original form, 'When the ale is in, the wit is out', Dent, W878)

34 **a . . . see** a sight worth seeing; proverbial (Dent, W878)

35 **Well . . . man** proverbial (Dent, G195), meaning that God's dispositions are providential
An if

35–6 **two . . . behind** proverbial (Dent, T638)

37 **as . . . bread** i.e. as any in the world; proverbial (Dent, M68)

22 on me, ah?] me! ah! *Rowe;* me! ah! *Capell*   23 an 'twere] *(*and't twere*)*   pound] times *F*   30 ha'] haue *F*   32 talking. As] *Capell (*talking; as*);* talking as *Q*   33 'When . . . out.'] *Cam¹;* when . . . out, *Q*   34 see!] *Qc (*see:*);* see, *Qu*   35 An] *(*and*)*   37 he is, as] *Qc;* he is as *Qu*

LEONATO   Indeed, neighbour, he comes too short of you.   40
DOGBERRY   Gifts that God gives.
LEONATO   I must leave you.
DOGBERRY   One word, sir. Our watch, sir, have indeed
    comprehended two aspicious persons, and we would
    have them this morning examined before your worship.   45
LEONATO   Take their examination yourself, and bring it
    me. I am now in great haste, as it may appear unto you.
DOGBERRY   It shall be suffigance.
LEONATO   Drink some wine ere you go. Fare you well!

[*Enter* Messenger.]

MESSENGER   My lord, they stay for you to give your   50
    daughter to her husband.
LEONATO   I'll wait upon them; I am ready.

[*Exit with Messenger.*]

DOGBERRY   Go, good partner, go get you to Francis
    Seacoal. Bid him bring his pen and inkhorn to the jail;
    we are now to examination these men.   55
VERGES   And we must do it wisely.
DOGBERRY   We will spare for no wit, I warrant you. Here's

40 **comes too short** i.e. in speech; Dogberry interprets it as 'doesn't measure up to'. The joke is usually brought out by having Verges played by a smaller actor than Dogberry.
44 **comprehended** malapropism for 'apprehended'
    aspicious malapropism for 'suspicious'
48 **suffigance** malapropism for 'sufficient'
50 **stay** are waiting

53–4 **Francis Seacoal** either another member of the literate Seacoal family, the sexton of 4.2, or the member of the Watch whose Christian name was previously given as George
55 **examination** malapropism for 'examine'
57–8 **Here's that** we have here that which; some actors point to their heads (i.e. brains) with this line, though it could also refer to the assembled Watch.

41 SP] *Rowe; Const. Do Q*   47 it] *om. F*   48 SP] *Rowe; Constable Q*   49 well!] *Rowe;* well. *Q*   49.1] *Rowe*   52 SD] *Rowe (Ex. Leonato.); opp. 49 Q ((exit))*   55 examination these] examine those *F*

293

that shall drive some of them to a noncome. Only get
the learned writer to set down our excommunication,   59
and meet me at the jail.   [*Exeunt.*]

[**4.1**]   *Enter* DON PEDRO, [DON JOHN *the*] *bastard,*
         LEONATO, FRIAR [Francis], CLAUDIO, BENEDICK,
              HERO *and* BEATRICE [, *with others*].

LEONATO   Come, Friar Francis, be brief: only to the plain
    form of marriage, and you shall recount their particular
    duties afterwards.
FRIAR   You come hither, my lord, to marry this lady?
CLAUDIO   No.   5
LEONATO   To be married to her, Friar; you come to marry
    her.
FRIAR   Lady, you come hither to be married to this count?
HERO   I do.

---

58   **noncome** error for *non plus* (bewilderment)
    or *non compos mentis* (of unsound mind)
59   **excommunication**   malapropism   for
    'examination'
4.1 The location is a church.
0.1–3 There is no entrance for Margaret or
    Ursula here, although some productions
    have them in attendance, and hence present
    a need for some silent reaction from
    Margaret during the allegations of Hero's
    nocturnal activities.
1–2 **plain form** simple liturgical form, i.e. skip
    over   the   preliminaries.   Leonato's
    interference here is in keeping with his
    similar impulse in 5.4; see 5.4.53 SDn.
2–3 **particular duties** specific obligations
    elaborated in the *Book of Common Prayer*,
    prescribed to be read by the Minister in the
    event of there being no sermon, 'as

touching the duty of husbands toward their
wives, and wives toward their husbands';
these include, for men, loving and
honouring their spouse, and, for women,
submission and reverence, 'so that if any
[husbands] obey not the Word, they may be
won without the Word, by the conversation
of the wives, while they behold your chaste
conversation coupled with fear, whose
apparel let it not be outward, with broided
hair and trimming about with gold, either
in putting on of gorgeous apparel, but let
the hid man which is in the heart, be
without all corruption so that the spirit
be mild and quiet, which is a precious
thing in the sight of God . . . as
Sarah obeyed Abraham calling him lord;
whose daughters ye are made' (*BCP*, 297,
298–9).

60 SD] *F*   **4.1**] *Actus Quartus. F;* scene i *Rowe*   0.1 DON PEDRO, [DON JOHN *the*] *Rowe; Prince, Q*   0.2
Francis] *Dyce*   0.3 *with others.*] *Dyce subst.; and Attendants. / White² 4* SP] *Rowe; Fran. Q*   lady?]
Rowe³; lady. *Q*   6 her, Friar;] *Rowe³;* her, Frier, *Rowe;* her: Frier, *Q*

FRIAR   If either of you know any inward impediment why   10
     you should not be conjoined, I charge you on your souls
     to utter it.

CLAUDIO   Know you any, Hero?

HERO   None, my lord.

FRIAR   Know you any, Count?   15

LEONATO   I dare make his answer: none.

CLAUDIO   O, what men dare do! What men may do! What
     men daily do, not knowing what they do!

BENEDICK   How now? Interjections? Why then, some be
     of laughing, as ha, ha, he.   20

CLAUDIO

     Stand thee by, Friar. [*to Leonato*] Father, by your leave:
     Will you with free and unconstrained soul
     Give me this maid, your daughter?

LEONATO

     As freely, son, as God did give her me.

CLAUDIO

     And what have I to give you back whose worth   25
     May counterpoise this rich and precious gift?

---

10 **inward impediment** secret obstacle; the
   term *impediment* is from the Anglican
   service, which the Friar begins to follow: 'I
   require and charge you both, as ye will
   answer at the dreadful day of judgement
   . . . that if either of you know any
   impediment . . . ye do now confess it.'

18 **not . . . do** omitted in F perhaps because the
   compositor overlooked the fourth phrase
   ending in *do*

19–20 **Interjections . . . he** Benedick's
   comment on Claudio's rhetorical display
   cites William Lyly's *Short Introduction of
   Latin Grammar* (1538): 'An interiection . . .
   betokeneth a sudden passion of the minde

. . . Some are of . . . laughing, as Ha ha he'
(sig. C8ᵛ). Cf. Lyly's *Endymion* (1591),
3.3.5: 'An interiection, whereof some are of
mourning: as eho, vah' (*Works*, 3.42).
be of are to do with

21 **Stand thee by** stand aside
   by your leave with your permission.
   Claudio asks if he may put a question to
   Leonato, ironically calling him *Father*
   even as he rejects any connection with
   him; he shifts into verse for his
   denunciation.

22 **unconstrained soul** unconstrainèd: clear
   conscience

26 **counterpoise** balance

18 not . . . do!] *om. F*   20 ha, ha] *F;* ah, ha *Q*   21 SD] *Oxf¹*

295

DON PEDRO
  Nothing, unless you render her again.
CLAUDIO
  Sweet Prince, you learn me noble thankfulness.
  There, Leonato, take her back again.
  Give not this rotten orange to your friend;   30
  She's but the sign and semblance of her honour.
  Behold how like a maid she blushes here!
  O, what authority and show of truth
  Can cunning sin cover itself withal!
  Comes not that blood as modest evidence   35

27 **render** return
28 **learn me** teach me; transitive use was not at the time considered ungrammatical.
30 **rotten orange** Oranges were associated with prostitutes (perhaps because pocked skin was an effect of venereal disease); they are also a symbol of deception, as one cannot tell from their covering what taste lies within. Cf. Beatrice's comparison of Claudio to a 'civil' orange, that bittersweet fruit, at 2.1.270; or Philip De Mornay, *Work Concerning the Trueness of Christian Religion* (1617): 'The rinde of the Orrendge is hot, and the meate within it is colde' (De Mornay, 10.141). The phrase was considered unsavoury enough to be bowdlerized from most productions from Garrick (1748) to the first decade of the twentieth century, replaced by 'blemished Brilliant' (Cox, *Shakespeare*, 177).
32, 37 **maid** virgin
32 **blushes** Claudio's and the Friar's contrasting readings of Hero's blush (158ff.) reflect its identity as a complex sign in Elizabethan moral physiognomy: index of shame and innocence alike, proof that the blusher was cognizant of (and hence potentially complicit in) the nature of what provoked the blush, though still

virtuous enough to be embarrassed by it. In Dent we find 'Blushing is virtue's colour' (B480), and Erasmus writes in *De Civilitate Morum Puerilium* that a blush should denote 'a natural and wholesome modesty . . . Although even that modesty should be so moderated that it is not construed as insolence, and does not connote . . . shame' (Erasmus, 23.275). Cf. Cesare Ripa's *Iconologia* (1593), fig. 265, which glosses the Roman emblem of Chastity as 'a woman veiled, pointing with the forefinger of her right hand to her face, to signifie that she had no reason to blush'; Rich's *Excellency of Good Women*: 'the blush of a woman's face, is an approbation of chaste and honourable minde, and a manifeste signe, that shee doth not approve any intemperate actions' (sig. D3ʳ); and Lyly's *Euphues*: 'virtuous women are for to bee chosen by the face, not when they blushe for the shame of some sinne committed but for feare she should comitte any' (101). Cf. *Edward III* 2.1.1–21.
33 **authority** power to inspire belief (*OED* 6)
   show impersonation, false representation
34 **withal** with
35 **blood** i.e. blush
   modest evidence evidence of modesty

27 SP] *Rowe (Pedro.); Princn Q*

To witness simple virtue? Would you not swear,
All you that see her, that she were a maid,
By these exterior shows? But she is none;
She knows the heat of a luxurious bed.
Her blush is guiltiness, not modesty.   40

LEONATO
What do you mean, my lord?

CLAUDIO
Not to be married, not to knit my soul
To an approved wanton.

LEONATO
Dear my lord, if you, in your own proof,
Have vanquished the resistance of her youth   45
And made defeat of her virginity –

CLAUDIO
I know what you would say: if I have known her,
You will say she did embrace me as a husband
And so extenuate the forehand sin.
No, Leonato,   50
I never tempted her with word too large,
But as a brother to his sister showed
Bashful sincerity and comely love.

HERO
And seemed I ever otherwise to you?

---

36 **witness** bear witness to
38 **exterior shows** superficial signs
39 **luxurious** lecherous, lascivious
41 **What . . . mean** What are you saying?
     How can that be true? (But Claudio
     understands *mean* as 'intend to do'.)
43 **approved wanton** ~~approvèd:~~ proven slut
44 **in . . . proof** trial; experience
47 **known** i.e. sexually; 'And Adam knew
     Heva his wife, who conceiving bare Cain,
     saying, 'I have gotten a man of the Lord'
     (Genesis, 4.1).

49 **extenuate . . . sin** i.e. their imminent
     marriage would excuse the sin of pre-
     marital fornication (or anticipating
     marriage); as in the case of *MM*'s Claudio,
     Elizabethan marriage custom was divided
     on the question of whether pre-marital
     sex was wrong if both parties were
     contracted to marry.
51 **large** broad, lewd (as at 2.3.192, *large
     jests*)
53 **comely** proper, decorous

42–3] *Ard² (Dyce); Q lines* married, / wanton. /   46 virginity –] *Rowe; virginitie Q*   49–51] *Pope; Q lines*
Leonato, / large, /

CLAUDIO

Out on thee, seeming! I will write against it: 55
You seem to me as Dian in her orb,
As chaste as is the bud ere it be blown;
But you are more intemperate in your blood
Than Venus, or those pampered animals
That rage in savage sensuality.   60

HERO

Is my lord well that he doth speak so wide?

LEONATO [*to Don Pedro*]

Sweet Prince, why speak not you?

DON PEDRO   What should I speak?

55 'To hell with your pretence (to chastity); I will bear witness against / denounce it (your hypocrisy).' The ability of women to dissemble virtue, and thus the difficulty of discriminating between good women and those who were only pretending to be so, is a common theme of Renaissance literature, as in Spenser's *Faerie Queene*, or Alexander Niccholes's guide to bachelors, *How to Tell a Good Wife from a Bad* (1615): 'This undertaking is a matter of some difficulty, for good wives are many times so like unto bad, that they are hardly discerned betwixt; they could not otherwise deceive so many as they do' (Niccholes, sig. B4ᵛ). Alan Craven conjectures that 'thee' for 'thy' is a common error of Compositor A, in which case the line could read 'Out on thy seeming' (the comma is Collier's) (Craven, 48).

56 **Dian . . . orb** The Roman goddess of chastity was associated with the hunt and the changeable moon, wherein she was thought to reside (hence her ornament of crescent horns). The flower of *Agnus Castus*, or 'Dian's buds', was thought to

preserve chastity; cf. *MND* 4.1.72–3: 'Dian's bud o'er Cupid's flower / Hath such force and blessed power'.

57 **blown** fully opened

58 **intemperate** ungoverned
blood passion, lust

59 **Venus** the goddess of love (and mother of Cupid), notorious adulteress to her husband Vulcan, with Mars: 'According therefore to the opinion of the Poets, Venus was taken to be the goddess of wantonness and amorous delights as that she inspired into the minds of men, libidinous desires, and lustful appetites' (Cartari, sig. CC2ʳ).
those pampered animals perhaps pet monkeys, notoriously randy; see *Oth* 3.3.406–7: 'Were they as prime as goats, as hot as monkeys, / As salt as wolves in pride'. Well-fed horses are also a candidate; see *KL* 4.5.120–2, 'The fitchew, nor the soiled horse, goes to't with a more riotous appetite. Down from the waist they are centaurs, though women all above,' where *soiled* = indulgently fed on fresh-cut grass, and hence high in spirits.

61 **wide** wide of the mark; derangedly

55 thee, seeming!] *Collier (Knight);* thee seeming, *Q;* thee! Seeming! *(Seymour);* thy seeming! *Pope;* the seeming! *Knight*   62 SD] *this edn*   62+ SP2] *Rowe (Pedro.); Prince Q*

I stand dishonoured that have gone about
To link my dear friend to a common stale. → *prostitute*

LEONATO

Are these things spoken, or do I but dream? 65

DON JOHN

Sir, they are spoken, and these things are true.

BENEDICK

This looks not like a nuptial.

HERO

True? O God!

CLAUDIO

Leonato, stand I here?
Is this the prince? Is this the prince's brother? 70
Is this face Hero's? Are our eyes our own?

LEONATO

All this is so, but what of this, my lord?

CLAUDIO

Let me but move one question to your daughter,
And by that fatherly and kindly power
That you have in her bid her answer truly. 75

LEONATO

I charge thee do so, as thou art my child.

HERO

O, God defend me, how am I beset! → *aroused*
What kind of catechizing call you this?

64 **stale** (1) prostitute of the lowest class (cf.
2.2.23: 'a contaminated stale, such a one as
Hero'); (2) decoy
69–71 Claudio's questions go to the heart of
the play's concern with the ability to make
judgements based on visual evidence;
ironically, Don John is only the Prince's
half-brother, and Claudio has just finished
claiming that Hero's face is not an adequate
index of her identity.

73 **move** put
74 **kindly** natural (of kin)
75 **in** over
76 **as ... child** i.e. by the truth of my paternity
(a warrant whose credibility has already
been established at 1.1.100)
77 **beset** surrounded, besieged, i.e. by accusations
78 **catechizing** examination; the Elizabethan
catechism of faith is a series of questions,
beginning with 'What is your name?'

66 SP] *Rowe (John.); Bastard Q* 68 True?] 'True?' *Cam;* True, *Q* 76 so] *om. F*

299

CLAUDIO

To make you answer truly to your name.

HERO

Is it not Hero? Who can blot that name   80
With any just reproach?

CLAUDIO   Marry, that can Hero;
Hero itself can blot out Hero's virtue.
What man was he talked with you yesternight
Out at your window betwixt twelve and one?
Now, if you are a maid, answer to this.   85

HERO

I talked with no man at that hour, my lord.

DON PEDRO

Why, then are you no maiden. Leonato,
I am sorry you must hear. Upon mine honour,
Myself, my brother and this grieved count
Did see her, hear her, at that hour last night,   90

---

79 **your name** Hero's name was that of a Greek literary heroine, a priestess of Venus who nonetheless inspired the devoted love of Leander and his arduous swim across the river Hellespont on her behalf; she loyally drowned herself after his own watery demise. Her reputation thus conjoined elements of both fidelity and carnality, and Claudio and Hero's exchange turns on this crux. Claudio's intention to make Hero *answer truly* to her name perhaps recalls his memory of Borachio's calling her name (3.3.139–40). Barbara Lewalski notes that in Chapman's translation of Musaeus' *Hero and Leander* (1616) 'Hero becomes also an emblem of dissimulation in regard to chastity, in that she continues as a priestess despite her love for Leander, and is hence denounced by Venus: "Since Hero had dissembled, and disgrast / Her rites so much,

and every breast infect, / With her deceits; she made her Architect / Of all dissimulation, and since then, / Never was any trust in maides or men"' (Lewalski, 'Namesake', 178). Claudio could mean either that the unchaste Hero shames the constancy of the legendary Hero, or that the famously unchaste Hero blots any virtues this Hero might have.

80 **blot** smudge, delete, so stain, as in writing with pen and ink, a medium of slander; cf. 139–41: 'O, she is fallen / Into a pit of ink that the wide sea / Hath drops too few to wash her clean again'.

81 **just reproach** fair criticism

82 **Hero itself** the very name (by becoming henceforth a name for scandalous rather than loyal behaviour)

83 **yesternight** last night

89 **grieved** grievèd: injured; grief-stricken

86 SP] *Qc; Bero Qu*   87 are you] you are *F*

Talk with a ruffian at her chamber window,
Who hath indeed, most like a liberal villain,
Confessed the vile encounters they have had
A thousand times in secret.

DON JOHN

Fie, fie, they are not to be named, my lord,   95
Not to be spoke of!
There is not chastity enough in language
Without offence to utter them. Thus, pretty lady,
I am sorry for thy much misgovernment.

CLAUDIO

O Hero! What a Hero hadst thou been   100
If half thy outward graces had been placed
About thy thoughts and counsels of thy heart!
But fare thee well, most foul, most fair. Farewell
Thou pure impiety and impious purity.
For thee I'll lock up all the gates of love,   105

92 **liberal** free in speech or behaviour; licentious
93–4 As Beatrice's scorn will illustrate ('Talk with a man out at a window! A proper saying!', 307–8), Don John needed to bolster the evidence of the window scene with Borachio's further corroboration of its meaning.
94 In productions in which Margaret is included in this scene (contrary to the original SDs) she often begins to react to this speech, sometimes even moving to interrupt; and Don John's interjection at 95ff. serves to silence her. It is of course crucial to the development of the plot that verification of Don John's plot be delayed.
97–8 **There . . . them** i.e. there is no language decorous enough to relate them without being indelicate
99 **thy** Don John's adoption of this form could either be contemptuous or express mock pity.

much misgovernment great misconduct.
101 **outward graces** physical qualities. The relation of inner and outer properties is a chief concern of conduct books; see *Court of Good Counsel:* 'I deny not but by the lookes of a woman, a man may gather somewhat of her disposition: but seeing God hath commanded vs not to judge altogether by the face of the woman, we must yet vse a more certain and commodious way' (W. B., sig. B1ᵛ).
102 **thy thoughts** Craven (48) conjectures (as did Rowe) that Compositor A committed his trademark error of substituting 'thy' for 'the' here.
counsels promptings
103 **foul, most fair** Dent, F29, gives as proverbial 'Fair without but foul within'.
105 **gates of love** the senses, especially the eyes, which will be closed to love

95 SP] *Capell; Iohn Q*   95–6] *Q; Hanmer lines are* / of! / 96 spoke] spoken *F*   102 thy thoughts] the thoughts *(Craven)*

301

~~suspicion~~

And on my eyelids shall conjecture hang
To turn all beauty into thoughts of harm,
And never shall it more be gracious.

LEONATO

Hath no man's dagger here a point for me?
[*Hero falls.*]

BEATRICE

Why, how now, cousin! Wherefore sink you down?   110

DON JOHN

Come, let us go; these things come thus to light
Smother her spirits up.

[*Exeunt Don Pedro, Claudio and Don John.*]

BENEDICK

How doth the lady?

BEATRICE   Dead, I think. Help, uncle!
Hero! Why Hero! Uncle, Signor Benedick, Friar!

LEONATO

O Fate, take not away thy heavy hand!   115
Death is the fairest cover for her shame
That may be wished for.

BEATRICE   How now, cousin Hero?
[*Hero stirs.*]

FRIAR   Have comfort, lady.

LEONATO

Dost thou look up?

FRIAR   Yea, wherefore should she not?

---

106 **conjecture** suspicion
109 SD Hero's swoon (indicated by Beatrice's reaction at 110) follows upon her father's turning against her.
112 **spirits** vital powers
113 **Help, uncle!** This appeal can indicate Leonato's stage distance from Hero.
114 **Signor Benedick** '[Benedick] makes an

important decision when he does not leave the church with Claudio, Don Pedro, and the Bastard, as might be expected' (*Riv*, 329).
119 **look up** The ability to look (i.e. show one's face) towards the heavens was a sign of innocence; cf. *Ham* 3.3.50–1: 'Then I'll look up. / My fault is past'.

109 SD] Hanmer (*Hero swoons*)   111 SP] *Capell; Bastard Q*   112 SD] *Rowe (Exe. D. Pedro, D. John and Claudio)*   114+ Signor] *(signior)*   117 SD] *this edn (Collier MS (reviving))*

LEONATO

Wherefore? Why, doth not every earthly thing   120
Cry shame upon her? Could she here deny
The story that is printed in her blood?
Do not live, Hero; do not ope thine eyes!
For did I think thou wouldst not quickly die,
Thought I thy spirits were stronger than thy shames,   125
Myself would on the rearward of reproaches
Strike at thy life. Grieved I, I had but one?
Chid I for that at frugal Nature's frame?
O, one too much by thee! Why had I one?
Why ever wast thou lovely in my eyes?   130
Why had I not with charitable hand
Took up a beggar's issue at my gates,
Who smirched thus, and mired with infamy,
I might have said: 'No part of it is mine;
This shame derives itself from unknown loins.'   135

120–43 Cox reports that many productions from the eighteenth to the early twentieth centuries cut this speech so as to 'dignify and idealise Leonato in this scene . . . softening his resentment and self-pity and making him a more sympathetic figure than in the full text' (Cox, *Shakespeare*, 181). Unlike his prototype in the Bandello source, who 'never having found his daughter anything but honest, thought that the knight had been seized with disdain at their poverty and present lack of worldly success' (Bullough, 118–19), Leonato has no such economic explanation to fall back upon.

122 **printed . . . blood** (1) shown by her blood: 'The story which her blushes discover to be true' (Johnson); as at 55, 80 and 140, the metaphor is bibliographical; (2) the innate weakness of women

123 **ope** open

125 **spirits** vital forces, as at 112

126 **on the rearward** (1) as a rearguard action following her disgrace (a military metaphor); (2) after reproaching. The sense is that if Hero's shames do not kill her, Leonato will.

127 **Strike** This can serve as a cue for Leonato's action.
but one i.e. only one child

128 **Chid . . . that** did I complain about that; did I reproach because of that **frugal** i.e. for allowing him only one child
Nature's frame i.e. the goddess's scheme of things

129 **by** in

132 **issue** offspring

133 **smirched** smirchèd: being so soiled
mired soiled, defiled; a mire = a muddy bog

---

120 Why, doth] *Theobald;* why doth *Q*   126 rearward] *(rereward);* reward *F;* hazard *Collier MS*   133 smirched] smeered *F*   134–5 'No . . . loins.'] *Capell subst.;* no . . . loynes, *Q*

But mine, and mine I loved, and mine I praised,
And mine that I was proud on – mine so much
That I myself was to myself not mine
Valuing of her. Why she – O, she is fallen
Into a pit of ink that the wide sea   140
Hath drops too few to wash her clean again,
And salt too little which may season give
To her foul-tainted flesh.

BENEDICK   Sir, sir, be patient.
For my part, I am so attired in wonder
I know not what to say.   ⟶ Slandered   145
BEATRICE
O, on my soul, my cousin is belied!
BENEDICK
Lady, were you her bedfellow last night?
BEATRICE
No, truly, not – although until last night
I have this twelvemonth been her bedfellow.

---

138 **to ... mine** i.e. that I was worth nothing in my own eyes, compared with the value I placed upon her
142 **season give** preserve from decay; render palatable
143 ***foul-tainted** befouled; Dyce (see t.n.) hyphenated Q's 'foule tainted' on the grounds that 'foule' was the intensifier of 'tainted' rather than the other way round.
143–5 **Sir ... say** Q prints these lines as prose, and the irregularity of their rhythm (and the idea of Benedick's prosaic interjection interrupting the flow of Leonato's aria) argue for the same. However, a similar prosifying at 155–8 suggests that Q's compositor seems to have found himself with more text than expected to fit on this page (the foot of sig. G1ʳ), perhaps as a result of faulty casting off of copy (although

Newcomer suggested compositorial eye-skip between the 'I have' of 156 and that of 158). Sig G1ᵛ, being part of the inner forme, was already printed off. Hence the compositor made the fit by rendering these two passages as prose (compressing seven lines of verse into five lines), and extending his page by two lines; he may indeed have been forced to omit some of the MS text, rendering the passage difficult to explain. F's compositor followed Q's lining.
144 **attired in wonder** filled with amazement; cf. *Mac* 1.7.35–6: 'Was the hope drunk, / Wherein you dress'd yourself?'
146 **belied** slandered
149 **this twelvemonth** Beatrice is concerned here to respond to the charge that Borachio confessed to multiple *vile encounters* (93). The point is lost on Leonato.

143 foul-tainted] *Dyce (Walker);* foule tainted *Q;* soul-tainted *(Collier)*   143–5 Sir . . . say] *Pope; prose Q*   148 truly, not –] *Rowe (*truly, not;*)*; truly, not *Q;* truly: not *F*

LEONATO

> Confirmed, confirmed! O, that is stronger made   150
> Which was before barred up with ribs of iron.
> Would the two princes lie, and Claudio lie
> Who loved her so, that speaking of her foulness
> Washed it with tears? Hence from her, let her die.

FRIAR

> Hear me a little: 155
> For I have only been silent so long,
> And given way unto this course of fortune,
> By noting of the lady. I have marked
> A thousand blushing apparitions
> To start into her face, a thousand innocent shames   160
> In angel whiteness beat away those blushes;
> And in her eye there hath appeared a fire
> To burn the errors that these princes hold
> Against her maiden truth. Call me a fool,
> Trust not my reading nor my observations,   165

---

150 **that** i.e. the accusation
151 **before** already
   barred up reinforced
154 **Washed it** See Abbott, 399, for the omitted nominative. The lines provide a retrospective SD for the actor playing Claudio.
155–8 These lines are set as prose in Q at the foot of the page (sig. G1ʳ); see 143–5n. The half line at 155 gives a pause in which the other actors can quiet themselves (Leonatos have an opportunity to engage in violent stage action with *Hence from her* at 154, and thus the Friar's words are an order as well as a request).
156–8 **For . . . lady** i.e. for my silence and passivity up to this point are due only to my having observed Hero's behaviour
157 **given . . . fortune** allowed matters to proceed thus far
159–161 **apparitions . . . blushes** The Friar's

noting of Hero's physiognomy interprets her blushes as potentially incriminating signs, but he also adduces the alternating paleness of her skin as a countervailing mark of innocence. See 32n.
160 **start** rush
   innocent shames i.e. as opposed to blushes occasioned by sin; see 32n.
162–3 **fire . . . errors** The metaphor is from the burning of heretics or their books; cf. 1.1.217–18: 'the opinion that fire cannot melt out of me'. The observation suggests that Hero's response includes an element of indignation as well as devastation.
164 **maiden truth** i.e. innocence, truth of her maidenhood
165–7 **Trust . . . book** i.e. I have good intuition and lots of experience, both of which confirm my book learning / interpretation of Hero's appearance

---

152 two] *om. F*   155–8] *Pope; prose Q*   156 been silent] silent been *White²*   158 lady.] *Pope; lady, Q*   161 beat] beare *F*

Which with experimental seal doth warrant
The tenor of my book; trust not my age,
My reverence, calling nor divinity,
If this sweet lady lie not guiltless here
Under some biting error.

LEONATO   Friar, it cannot be.   170
Thou seest that all the grace that she hath left
Is that she will not add to her damnation
A sin of perjury. She not denies it.
Why seek'st thou then to cover with excuse
That which appears in proper nakedness?   175

FRIAR
Lady, what man is he you are accused of?

HERO
They know that do accuse me. I know none.
If I know more of any man alive
Than that which maiden modesty doth warrant,
Let all my sins lack mercy! – O my father,   180
Prove you that any man with me conversed

---

166 **experimental seal** the validation of experience
167 **tenor . . . book** teachings of my education
168 i.e. my solemnity, my position, nor theology
170 **biting** stinging, bitter
171 **grace** virtue, but also (with *damnation* and *sin* a theological term) invoking a notion of salvation; Leonato responds in theological terms to the Friar's warrant of his own *divinity*.
173 **not denies** does not deny; see Abbott, 305, on this construction.
175 **proper nakedness** truthful exposure
176 The Friar's question is designed to trick Hero into revealing the truth, should it be incriminating. 'He was all the while at the accusation, and heard no names mentioned

. . . had Hero been guilty, it was very probable that, in that hurry and confusion of spirits, into which the terrible insult of her lover had thrown her, she could barely have observed that the man's name was not mentioned, and so, on this question, have betrayed herself by naming the person she was conscious of having an affair with' (Warburton).
177 **I know none** Hero echoes Claudio's use of the verb at 47.
179 **that . . . warrant** i.e. the acquaintance which is appropriate to maiden innocence
180 **my father** This appeal could be directed to either the Friar or Leonato, but by 184 Hero is talking to Leonato alone.
181 **Prove** if you can prove

---

167 tenor] *(tenure)*   180 mercy!] *F (mercy.); mercy, Q*

At hours unmeet, or that I yesternight
Maintained the change of words with any creature,
Refuse me, hate me, torture me to death!

FRIAR

There is some strange misprision in the princes.   185

BENEDICK

Two of them have the very bent of honour.
And if their wisdoms be misled in this,
The practice of it lives in John the bastard,
Whose spirits toil in frame of villainies.

LEONATO

I know not. If they speak but truth of her,   190
These hands shall tear her; if they wrong her honour,
The proudest of them shall well hear of it.
Time hath not yet so dried this blood of mine,
Nor age so eat up my invention,
Nor fortune made such havoc of my means,   195
Nor my bad life reft me so much of friends
But they shall find awaked in such a kind

---

182 **unmeet** inappropriate
183 **change** exchange
184 **Refuse** disown
185 **misprision** error, misunderstanding
   the princes technically, only Don Pedro and Don John, though Benedick's response includes Claudio in royalty
186 **have . . . of** are wholly inclined to, given to; the metaphor is from archery, of a bow drawn to its full extent.
188 **practice** deceitful contrivance
   John the bastard This is the first explicit mention to the audience of Don John's illegitimacy (noted in SDs and SPs), though signs of melancholy and envy could have suggested it (in the Renaissance, signified by black clothing).
189 i.e. who devotes himself to contriving villainous plots

191–2 **if . . . it** As does the defender of the slandered princess in Shakespeare's Ariostan source, Leonato (whose softening occurs only after Benedick's entertainment of the possibility of a mistake) now turns to the postures of chivalry, 'that will in armes defend his daughter dear, / And prove her innocent in open fight' (*Orlando*, 5.68.3–4).
194 **eat** past tense, pronounced 'et'
   invention mental powers, 'policy of mind', as at 198; four syllables
195 **means** resources, perhaps financial
196 **reft** i.e. bereft, deprived
   friends includes kindred, such as his brother Antonio (who is not, however, given an entrance in this scene in Q)
197 **they** i.e. the princes
   kind manner

190 not.] *F* (not:)*;* not, *Q*

Both strength of limb and policy of mind,
Ability in means and choice of friends
To quit me of them throughly.

FRIAR   Pause awhile,   200
And let my counsel sway you in this case.
Your daughter here the princes left for dead.
Let her awhile be secretly kept in,
And publish it that she is dead indeed.
Maintain a mourning ostentation,   205
And on your family's old monument
Hang mournful epitaphs, and do all rites
That appertain unto a burial.

LEONATO
What shall become of this? What will this do?

FRIAR
Marry, this well carried shall on her behalf   210

---

198 **policy of mind** See 194n.
199 **choice of friends** i.e. to act as his seconds
     in a duel
200 **quit . . . throughly** thoroughly revenge
     myself upon them
     Pause awhile The Friar's words (as at
     155) can provide a SD for Leonato's
     behaviour.
202 ***princes** Q's 'princesse' makes a certain
     grammatical, but not social, sense.
205 **mourning ostentation** formal, public
     show of mourning; the Friar's plan to
     deceive Claudio into a recognition of true
     feeling resembles Don Pedro's plan to gull
     Beatrice and Benedick into love.
206 **monument** tomb
207 **mournful epitaphs** The writing and
     affixing of epitaphs to the hearse or tomb
     was a mourning practice. Cf. Jonson's
     Epitaph of the Countess of Pembroke:
     'Underneath this sable hearse / Lies the
     subject of all verse . . .' (Jonson, 8.433);

and the opening SD of Middleton's *A
Chaste Maid in Cheapside* (1613), 5.4:
'*enter . . . the coffin of the virgin . . . with a
garland of flowers, with epitaphs pinned
upon it*' (Middleton, 5.109). Leonato will
instruct Claudio to so hang an epitaph
upon Hero's sepulchre.
209 **become of** result from
210–22 Jonathan Bate notes a resemblance to
     the Greek myth of Alcestis, who
     volunteers to die in place of her husband
     Admetus; Hercules discovers her sacrifice
     and returns her to her husband, who, guilt-
     stricken, recognizes her true worth: 'if
     Hero is an Alcestis, Claudio is an Admetus
     who repents of and learns from earlier
     unfair conduct . . . the mock death must
     make Claudio see Hero's virtues, must
     make him into a nobler lover' (Bate,
     'Dying', 83).
210 **well carried** i.e. well carried off, well
     managed

202 princes . . . dead] *Theobald;* princesse (left for dead) *Q*

Change slander to remorse; that is some good.
But not for that dream I on this strange course,
But on this travail look for greater birth:
She, dying, as it must be so maintained,
Upon the instant that she was accused,   215
Shall be lamented, pitied and excused
Of every hearer. For it so falls out
That what we have we prize not to the worth
Whiles we enjoy it, but being lacked and lost,
Why, then we rack the value, then we find   220
The virtue that possession would not show us
Whiles it was ours. So will it fare with Claudio:
When he shall hear she died upon his words,
Th'idea of her life shall sweetly creep
Into his study of imagination,   225
And every lovely organ of her life
Shall come apparelled in more precious habit,
More moving, delicate and full of life,
Into the eye and prospect of his soul
Than when she lived indeed. Then shall he mourn   230

213 **on this travail** as a result of this effort, with a play both on travail / travel (not distinguished in early modern orthography), generated by *course* (212), and *travail*, as labourpains; cf. *birth* (213).
217 **Of** by
218 **to the worth** for what it is worth; a proverbial idea, cf. Dent, W924: 'The worth of a thing is best known by the want.'
220 **rack** stretch to the utmost (from the torture device)
223 **upon** at the sound of, as a result of
225 **study of imagination** imaginative reflection; memory

226 **organ . . . life** living feature (with some sense of actual body parts, but the more abstract sense as well)
227 **in . . . habit** more richly adorned; the Friar seems to suggest that news of Hero's death will make Claudio remember her as even more glorious than she had been in his actual experience of her. In the Bandello source, the intention is merely to make the Claudio figure confess his true motive in slandering her, i.e. his second thoughts about her social station (Bullough, 118).

221 show] *(shew)*   224 idea] *(Idæa)*   228 moving, delicate] *F2:*   moouing delicate *Q:* moving-delicate *Capell*

If ever love had interest in his liver
~~And wish he had not so accused her;~~
No, though he thought his accusation true.
Let this be so, and doubt not but success
Will fashion the event in better shape   235
Than I can lay it down in likelihood.
But if all aim but this be levelled false,
The supposition of the lady's death
Will quench the wonder of her infamy.
And if it sort not well, you may conceal her,   240
As best befits her wounded reputation,
In some reclusive and religious life,
Out of all eyes, tongues, minds and injuries.

BENEDICK

Signor Leonato, let the friar advise you,
And though you know my inwardness and love   245
Is very much unto the prince and Claudio,
Yet, by mine honour, I will deal in this
As secretly and justly as your soul

---

231 **interest in** claim upon
   liver Elizabethans often imagined the liver
   as much a seat of love as the heart (the
   brains and the genitals were also
   contenders), though the liver has perhaps
   more comical connotations than the latter.
   Cf. *TN* 2.4.98–9: 'their love may be call'd
   appetite, / No motion of the liver, but the
   palate'; *MW* 2.1.105: 'FORD Love my
   wife? / PISTOL With liver burning hot';
   LLL 4.3.73–4: 'This is the liver vein,
   which makes flesh a deity, / A green goose
   a goddess.' The liver was thought to play a
   key role in producing signs of love such as
   pallor, weight loss, hollow eyes and
   sleeplessness: 'because of the distraction
   of spirits the liver doth not performe his
   part, nor turns the aliment into blood as it
   ought, and for that cause the members are
   weake for want of sustenance' (Burton,
   3.139).

232 **accused** accusèd
234–6 Follow this plan and doubt not that its
   accomplishment will produce a better
   outcome than I can predict.
237–9 i.e. but at the very least, if the plan
   doesn't wholly succeed, her supposed
   death will silence discussion about her
   shame
237 **all aim but** every outcome except
   be levelled false fail to come to fruition
239 **wonder of** wondering at, speculation
   about
240 **sort** turn out
242 **reclusive . . . life** i.e. in a convent
243 **Out of** out of the reach of, beyond
245 **inwardness** intimacy; Shakespeare's only
   such use. Cf. *MM* 3.2.127: 'Sir, I was an
   inward of his.'
246 **Is** Abbott, 336, illustrates singular verbs
   after two or more singular nouns as
   subjects.

Should with your body.

LEONATO   Being that I flow in grief,
The smallest twine may lead me.   250

FRIAR
'Tis well consented. Presently away,
For to strange sores strangely they strain the cure.
Come, lady, die to live. This wedding day
Perhaps is but prolonged. Have patience and endure.
                    Exeunt [all but Beatrice and Benedick].

BENEDICK   Lady Beatrice, have you wept all this while?   255
BEATRICE   Yea, and I will weep awhile longer.
BENEDICK   I will not desire that.
BEATRICE   You have no reason; I do it freely.
BENEDICK   Surely I do believe your fair cousin is
     wronged.   260
BEATRICE   Ah, how much might the man deserve of me
     that would right her!
BENEDICK   Is there any way to show such friendship?
BEATRICE   A very even way, but no such friend.
BENEDICK   May a man do it?   265
BEATRICE   It is a man's office, but not yours.

---

249 **flow in** am overcome by, am swept away by (as by a current, perhaps of tears)
251–4 The Friar closes the verse with a quatrain, with the last line an alexandrine.
251 **Presently** immediately
252 **to . . . cure** Shakespeare's alliterative rendition of the proverbial phrase 'a desperate disease must have a desperate remedy' (Dent, D357)
254 **prolonged** postponed
258 **freely** of my own accord
262 **right** i.e. avenge (following from *wronged*, 260)
264 **even** straightforward, direct
266 **office** duty

but not yours i.e. because Hero should properly be revenged by a male member of her own family, or because Benedick is friends with Claudio and the Prince – or because Beatrice does not feel she has the right, given their history, to ask Benedick to do this. Cox reports that some nineteenth-century actresses delivered this phrase sarcastically, up until the performance of Ellen Terry, who delivered it as 'the afterthought of a woman . . . unwilling to expose her love to the dangers of a duel, even at the risk of his manhood being compromised' (Cox, *Shakespeare*, 189). Benedick's acceptance of her charge is tantamount

254 SD] *Rowe (Exeunt manent Benedick and Beatrice.); exit.* Q

311

BENEDICK   I do love nothing in the world so well as you.
    Is not that strange?
BEATRICE   As strange as the thing I know not. It were as
    possible for me to say I loved nothing so well as you.   270
    But believe me not – and yet I lie not. I confess nothing,
    nor I deny nothing. I am sorry for my cousin.
BENEDICK   By my sword, Beatrice, thou lovest me.
BEATRICE   Do not swear and eat it.
BENEDICK   I will swear by it that you love me, and I will   275
    make him eat it that says I love not you.
BEATRICE   Will you not eat your word?
BENEDICK   With no sauce that can be devised to it. I
    protest I love thee.
BEATRICE   Why then, God forgive me.   280

to acceptance of kinship ('Good Lord, for alliance!', 2.1.292). Rich notes in *The Excellency of Good Women* that 'I have seldom seene an honest woman . . . to haue many freendes to vndertake for her, that will quarrel for her, that will fight for her, or that will be at any great costes and charge by any means to support her, vnless it be a father, a brother a kinsman or some such like. But Thucydides will needes approve that woman to be most honest, that is least knowne, and I think indeed that the most honest woman is least spoken of, for they doe please the least in number and vertue was never graced by the multitude' (sig. Cl^v–2^r).

269 **As . . . not** i.e. as strange as anything unknown could imaginably be. Both speakers continue to quibble (significantly, on *nothing* and knowing) in their first admissions of love, as if to leave an escape clause in their declarations. 'They manage by a deft indirectness to put nothing into a syntax where the other person can choose

either its negative or its positive meaning' (Jorgensen, 30).

273 **By my sword** a mild oath, derived from the function of a sword as a guarantor of a gentleman's honour and status (as well as its cross-shape formed by the handguard, useful for swearing upon). Beatrice's reply (don't eat – or renege on – your oath / word) may pun on the more serious oath, 'God's word', which contracts to 'sword, as in *H5* 2.1.98–101: 'BARDOLPH By this sword, he that makes the first thrust, I'll kill him. By this sword, I will. / PISTOL Sword is an oath, and oaths must have their course.' Cf. Dent, W825: 'To eat one's words'.

278 **to** for

279, 283 **protest** solemnly affirm

280 **God forgive me** either for 'infringing the convention that the woman takes no initiative in love' (Ard^2), or, given her reference to a *happy hour* (282), for thinking of love in the midst of her cousin's tragedy

274 swear] *Q; sweare by it F*

BENEDICK   What offence, sweet Beatrice?

BEATRICE   You have stayed me in a happy hour; I was
about to protest I loved you.

BENEDICK   And do it, with all thy heart.

BEATRICE   I love you with so much of my heart that none   285
is left to protest.

BENEDICK   Come, bid me do anything for thee.

BEATRICE   Kill Claudio.

BENEDICK   Ha, not for the wide world.

BEATRICE   You kill me to deny it. Farewell. [*Moves as if to   290
leave.*]

BENEDICK   Tarry, sweet Beatrice. [*Stays her.*]

BEATRICE   I am gone, though I am here. There is no love
in you; nay, I pray you, let me go.

BENEDICK   Beatrice –

BEATRICE   In faith, I will go.   295

BENEDICK   We'll be friends first.

BEATRICE   You dare easier be friends with me than fight
with mine enemy.

BENEDICK   Is Claudio thine enemy?

BEATRICE   Is 'a not approved in the height a villain, that   300
hath slandered, scorned, dishonoured my kinswoman?
O, that I were a man! What, bear her in hand until they

---

282 **stayed me** stopped me (perhaps
   physically, as at 291, or by interrupting
   her with his query at 281); caught me,
   found me
   happy hour lucky moment
286 **protest** quibble on the meaning at 279,
   283
288 **Kill Claudio** This line, its delivery and its
   reception, by both Benedick and the
   audience (laughter? shocked silence?) is
   one of the indices of a production's tenor.
   See Cox, 'Stage'.

290 **deny it** refuse my request
292 ¹**I ... here** I have left in spirit, even though
   you are forcibly retaining me.
300 **approved ... height** proved to the utmost
   extreme
302 **a man!** i.e. able to avenge Hero in a duel
   bear ... hand lead her on, delude her;
   cf. Jonson, *Volpone*, 1.1.88–90: 'still
   bearing them in hand, / Letting the cherry
   knock against their lips, / And draw it, by
   their mouths, and back againe' (Jonson,
   5.27).

290 it] *om. F*   SD] *this edn*   291 SD] *Oxf¹ (Barring her way)*   294 Beatrice –] *Theobald;* Beatrice. *Q*

313

come to take hands, and then with public accusation, uncovered slander, unmitigated rancour? O God, that I were a man! I would eat his heart in the marketplace. 305

BENEDICK   Hear me, Beatrice –

BEATRICE   Talk with a man out at a window! A proper saying!

BENEDICK   Nay, but Beatrice –

BEATRICE   Sweet Hero! She is wronged, she is slandered, 310 she is undone.

BENEDICK   Beat –

BEATRICE   Princes and counties! Surely a princely testimony, a goodly count! Count Comfit, a sweet gallant surely. O that I were a man for his sake! Or 315 that I had any friend would be a man for my sake! But manhood is melted into curtsies, valour into

303 **take hands** i.e. be wedded
304 **uncovered** barefaced; suddenly revealed
307–8 **A proper saying** a likely story; given that Beatrice knows herself to have *this twelvemonth* been Hero's bedfellow (149), and thus clear of the charge of having had 'vile encounters . . . A thousand times in secret' with Borachio (93–4) (during night-time hours, anyhow).
311 **undone** ruined (in her reputation and her future marital prospects)
313 **counties** mocking term for multiple countships
314 **a goodly count** a fine excuse for a nobleman; a fine story (account); a likely accusation (cf. *testimony*). Beatrice's rage seems only to hone her quibbling power.
Count Comfit Count Sweetmeat, 'i.e. a specious nobleman made out of sugar' (Steevens), with the sense of insubstantial concoction – *conte confect*, French for invented tale (White, cited in Furness); Beatrice apparently found Claudio's loverly demeanour as cloying as Benedick once did. Cf. Sir Thomas Overbury's Theophrastian character of an Amorist: 'his fashion exceeds the worth of his weight. He is never without verses, and muske comfects, and sighs to the hazard of his buttons' (Overbury, 10–11).
317 **curtsies** Q's 'cursies' can be read either as 'curtsies' (a subservient and / or scraping bow, as at 2.1.46–7: 'it is my cousin's duty to make curtsy'); or 'courtesies': fancy manners (which might include curtseying).

304 rancour?] rancour – *Rowe*   306, 309 Beatrice –] *Collier;* Beatrice. *Q*   307 window!] *Malone;* window? *Hanmer;* window – *Rowe;* window, *Q*   312 Beat –] *Theobald;* Beat? *Q*   314 count! Count] *Q (*Counte, Counte*);* Count, *F*   317 curtsies] *(*cursies*);* curtesies *F3*

compliment, and men are only turned into tongue, and trim ones, too. He is now as valiant as Hercules that only tells a lie and swears it. I cannot be a man 320 with wishing, therefore I will die a woman with grieving.

BENEDICK   Tarry, good Beatrice. By this hand, I love thee.

BEATRICE   Use it for my love some other way than swearing by it.

BENEDICK   Think you in your soul the Count Claudio 325 hath wronged Hero?

BEATRICE   Yea, as sure as I have a thought or a soul.

BENEDICK   Enough, I am engaged. I will challenge him. I will kiss your hand, and so I leave you. By this hand, Claudio shall render me a dear account. As you hear of 330 me, so think of me. Go comfort your cousin. I must say she is dead, and so farewell.   *[Exeunt by different doors.]*

---

318 **compliment** insubstantial flattery (such as Benedick's offer to 'do anything for thee', 287)

  are . . . tongue have become words only

319 **trim** fine, glib

321 **with** by

322 **By this hand** either hers, which he has taken, or his own, which he holds up as proof of his sincerity

327 a solemn oath, and a relatively novel possibility for a woman in this period, when the female possession of souls was still, for some, a matter of at least mock debate. See, for instance, John Donne, *Certain Problems* (1623): 'Why hath the Common Opinion afforded Women Soules? Wee deny soules to others equall to them in all but in speech . . . Haue they so many aduantages and meanes to hurt vs that we dare not

displease them, but giue them what they will . . . doe we somewhat (in this dignifying of them) flatter Princes and great personages that are so much gouerned by them? Or do wee in that easinesse and prodigality wherein we daily lose our owne soules to wee care not whom, so labour to perswade ourselues, that sith a woman hath a soule, a soule is no great matter?' (sig. G2ᵛ–3ʳ). Women do have souls in the King James Bible, e.g. Genesis, 35.18.

328 **engaged** committed, i.e. contracted to fight on her behalf. This crucial switch of allegiance from the word of his male companions to a woman's belief is a defining moment for Benedick.

330 **dear account** costly payment (with perhaps some pun, similar to Beatrice's at 314, on *count*)

---

329 I] *om. F*   331 cousin] *(coosin)*   332 SD] *F2 (Exeunt.)*   by different doors] *this edn*

[4.2] *Enter the constables*[, DOGBERRY *and* VERGES],
and the [Sexton *as*] *town clerk, in gowns,* [*with the*
Watch,] BORACHIO [*and* CONRADE].

DOGBERRY   Is our whole dissembly appeared?
VERGES   O, a stool and a cushion for the sexton.
SEXTON [*Sits.*]   Which be the malefactors?
DOGBERRY   Marry, that am I, and my partner.
VERGES   Nay, that's certain; we have the exhibition to   5
examine.
SEXTON   But which are the offenders that are to be
examined? [*to Dogberry*] Let them come before, master
constable.

4.2 The location is a prison.
0.2 **the* **Sexton** This term was inserted by
Capell (following the SP at 3ff.). A sexton
was a minor church official in charge of
church property; here, presumably, being
the *learned writer* named at 3.5.59, he also
moonlights as the town clerk.
in gowns Black gowns were the official
robes of Elizabethan constables.
1+ SP *The original SPs throughout this
scene, which denote actors' (or intended
actors') names, betray the marks of the
play's composition, and perhaps that the
copy-text that served as the basis for Q was
a promptbook used in the theatre (and hence
puzzled over by a compositor). Dogberry's
part is rendered variously as '*Kemp*' (or
'*Keeper*', '*Ke.*', '*Kem.*') or '*Andrew*', for
the actor Will Kemp, who often took the
parts of the clown (or the 'Merry Andrew')
in the company of the Lord Chamberlain's
Men (until 1599; see pp. 26, 134). Verges,
similarly, is assigned to '*Cowley*' or
'*Couley*', for the actor Richard Cowley, or

'*Const.*' (at 53). The speeches of the Watch
are assigned to '*Watch 1*', '*Watch 2*' and
'*Watch*', which may or may not correspond
to the assignments of 3.3 (e.g. some editions
assign Watch 1 here to Seacoal, given his
promotion in the earlier scene to head of the
Watch).
1 **dissembly** malapropism for 'assembly'
2 From this line it appears that Verges is in
charge of arranging the examination room
(this directive may serve to finesse the
scene change, if the moving of stage
furniture is involved).
4 **that am I** It is not entirely clear what
misunderstanding of *malefactor* leads
Dogberry and Verges to come forward
here, although it probably relies on the
meaning of 'factor' as steward (Cam[2]).
5 **exhibition** i.e. commission (given to them
by Leonato in 3.5)
8 ***before**, i.e. to the fore; the punctuation
(or enunciation) of this line to include
a pause after *before* (and so to render
it an instruction to Dogberry

4.2] *Capell (SCENE II)*   0.1 DOGBERRY *and* VERGES] *Rowe subst.*   0.2–3 *and . . .* BORACHIO] *Capell subst.; Borachio, and the Towne clearke in gownes. Q; Borachio, Conrade, the Town Clerke and Sexton in gownes / Rowe*   0.3 *and* CONRADE] *Rowe*   1 SP] *Capell; Keeper Q; To. Cl. / Rowe*   2, 5 SP] *Capell; Cowley Q; Dog. / Rowe*   3 SD] *Oxf*   4 SP] *Capell; Andrew Q; Verg. / Rowe*   8 before, master] *this edn;* before maister *Q*   SD] *this edn*

DOGBERRY   Yea, marry, let them come before me. [*Watch*   10
    lead Borachio and Conrade forward, then step back.]
    [*to Borachio*] What is your name, friend?

BORACHIO   Borachio.

DOGBERRY [*to the Sexton*]   Pray write down 'Borachio'. [*to
    Conrade*] Yours, sirrah?

CONRADE   I am a gentleman, sir, and my name is   15
    Conrade.

DOGBERRY   Write down 'master gentleman Conrade'.
    Masters, do you serve God?

CONRADE, BORACHIO   Yea, sir, we hope.

DOGBERRY   Write down, that they hope they serve God;   20
    and write God first, for God defend but God should
    go before such villains. Masters, it is proved already
    that you are little better than false knaves, and it will
    go near to be thought so shortly. How answer you for
    yourselves?   25

CONRADE   Marry, sir, we say we are none.

DOGBERRY   A marvellous witty fellow, I assure you. But I
    will go a bout with him. [*to Borachio*] Come you hither,

---

to let the malefactors come forward) makes his interpretation at 10 yet another instance of construing the Sexton's commands as a comment on his own self-importance.

14 **sirrah** fellow (a term of contempt, which Conrade's insistence on his status seeks to rebuff)

19–22 **Yea . . . villains** omitted in F, presumably to comply with the 1606

statute against profanity and the taking of God's name in vain in plays

21 **defend** forbid (cf. 2.1.83)

22 **Masters** a term of deference, hence perhaps comically inappropriate

28 **a bout** a round (as in sparring, or dancing – cf. 2.1.76); heard as '(go) about' = deal with, outmanoeuvre

him i.e. Borachio (unless *a bout* = 'about', in which case *him* = Conrade)

10 SP] *Capell; Kemp Q; To. Cl. / Rowe*   10–11 *Watch . . . forward*] *Folg² (Conrade and Borachio are brought forward)*   11 *then step back*] *this edn*   12 SD] *this edn*   13 SP] *Capell; Ke. Q; Kem. F; To. Cl. / Rowe*   SD] *Oxf* 'Borachio'] *Capell subst;* Borachio *Q*   13–14 SD] *Oxf*   17 SP] *Capell; Ke. Q; Kee. F; To. Cl. / Rowe* 'master gentleman Conrade'] *Capell subst.;* master gentleman Conrade *Q*   19–22 CONRADE . . . villains.] *om. F*   19 SP] *Q (Both); Con , Bor / Capell*   20 SP] *Capell; Kem. Q; To. Cl. / Theobald*   27 SP] *Capell; Kemp Q; To. Cl. / Rowe*   28 a bout] about *Q*   SD] *Bevington*

sirrah. A word in your ear. Sir, I say to you, it is thought
you are false knaves.   30

BORACHIO   Sir, I say to you, we are none.

DOGBERRY   Well, stand aside. 'Fore God, they are both
in a tale. [*to the Sexton*] Have you writ down, that they
are none?

SEXTON   Master constable, you go not the way to   35
examine. You must call forth the watch that are their
accusers.

DOGBERRY   Yea, marry, that's the eftest way. Let the
watch come forth. [*Watch come forward.*] Masters, I
charge you in the prince's name, accuse these men.   40

1 WATCHMAN   [*Indicates Borachio.*]   This man said, sir,
that Don John the prince's brother was a villain.

DOGBERRY   Write down 'Prince John a villain'. Why, this
is flat perjury, to call a prince's brother villain!

BORACHIO   Master constable –   45

DOGBERRY   Pray thee, fellow, peace! I do not like thy look,
I promise thee.

SEXTON   What heard you him say else?

2 WATCHMAN   Marry, that he had received a thousand
ducats of Don John for accusing the Lady Hero   50
wrongfully.

DOGBERRY   Flat burglary as ever was committed!

VERGES   Yea, by mass, that it is.

SEXTON   What else, fellow?

---

29 **in your ear** Dogberry hopes to extort a
confession by interrogating the male factors
separately, despite the fact that Borachio has
just heard the exchange with Conrade.

33 **in a tale** in collusion

35 **go . . . way** i.e. do not go about the proper
way

38 **eftest** a nonsense word; he seems to mean
'most expedient', or some combination of
'deftest' and 'easiest'.

29 ear. Sir] *Cam subst.*; eare sir, *Q*   32, 38, 43, 46, 52, 58 SP] *Capell; Kemp Q; To. Cl. / Rowe*   33 SD] *this edn*   38 eftest] easiest *Rowe;* deftest *(Theobald)*   39 SD] *this edn*   41 SP] *(Watch 1)*   SD] *this edn*   43 'Prince . . . villain'.] *Capell subst.*; prince . . . villaine: *Q*   45 constable –] *Capell (*Constable, –*);* Constable. *Q*   49 SP] *(Watch 2);* SEACOAL *Folg²*   52 SP] *Capell; Const. Q; Dog. / Rowe*   53 by mass] by th'masse *F*

1 WATCHMAN   And that Count Claudio did mean, upon   55
    his words, to disgrace Hero before the whole assembly,
    and not marry her.

DOGBERRY   O villain! Thou wilt be condemned into
    everlasting redemption for this.

SEXTON   What else?   60

WATCH   This is all.

SEXTON   And this is more, masters, than you can deny.
    Prince John is this morning secretly stolen away;
    Hero was in this manner accused, in this very manner
    refused and, upon the grief of this, suddenly died.   65
    Master constable, let these men be bound and brought
    to Leonato's. I will go before and show him their
    examination.   [*Exit.*]

DOGBERRY   Come, let them be opinioned.

VERGES   Let them be in the hands – [*Watch move to bind   70
    them.*]

CONRADE   Off, coxcomb!

DOGBERRY   God's my life, where's the sexton? Let him
    write down the prince's officer coxcomb! Come, bind

55–6 **upon his words** on the strength of his
    words
59 **redemption** malapropism for 'perdition'
    or 'damnation'
65 **refused** disowned (both by Claudio and by
    her father)
69 **opinioned** malapropism for 'pinioned'
70–1 *Q gives both these lines, as one sentence
    (see t.n.), to '*Couley*' (Verges); F gives them
    to '*Sex.*', and Theobald to '*Conrade*' (on the
    grounds that neither Verges nor the Sexton

would refer to a watchman as a coxcomb).
Malone redistributed the text as here
(following Warburton, who gave 'Let them
be in hand' to the Sexton, and 'Off, Coxcomb'
to Conrade). Cam[1] suggests that the
compositor perhaps found 'Cou.' and 'Con.'
on successive lines and took the speakers to
be the same. Equally Borachio might speak
71 (although the gentleman Conrade seems
more disposed to stand on ceremony).
72 **God's my life** God save my life

55 SP] SEACOAL *Folg*[2]   67 Leonato's] *Leonato F*   68 SD] *Theobald*   69 SP] *Rowe; Constable Q* 70 SP
VERGES] *Capell; Couley Q; Sex. F; Conrade / Theobald*   SD] *this edn; Watchmen seize Conrade and
Borachio Oxf[1]; he offers to bind Conrade Cam[1] (Brae)*   70–1 in 1 . . . coxcomb!] *Malone; Warburton (*in
hand. *Exit. / Conr.* Off Coxcomb!*); in the hands of Coxcombe. Q; in bands. Con.* Off, coxcomb! *Capell;* be
bound; in the – / Con. Hands off! coxcomb! *(Lloyd (Kinnear)); in the hands of – Con.* Coxcomb! *Staunton;*
– in the hands. *Conrade.* Off, coxcomb! *Cam[1] (Brae)*   72, 76 SP] *Rowe; Kemp Q*

them. [*to Conrade, who resists*] Thou naughty varlet!

CONRADE   Away! You are an ass, you are an ass!   75

DOGBERRY   Dost thou not suspect my place? Dost thou
not suspect my years? O, that he were here to write me
down an ass! But masters, remember that I am an ass;
though it be not written down, yet forget not that I am
an ass. No, thou villain, thou art full of piety, as shall be   80
proved upon thee by good witness. I am a wise fellow,
and which is more, an officer, and which is more, a
householder, and which is more, as pretty a piece of
flesh as any is in Messina, and one that knows the law
– go to! – and a rich fellow enough – go to! – and a   85
fellow that hath had losses, and one that hath two
gowns, and everything handsome about him. – Bring
him away. – O, that I had been writ down an ass!

Exeunt.

[**5.1**]   *Enter* LEONATO *and his brother* [ANTONIO].

ANTONIO

If you go on thus you will kill yourself,
And 'tis not wisdom thus to second grief

---

74 **naughty varlet** worthless knave, rascal
76, 77 **suspect** malapropism for 'respect'
77 **years** age, but perhaps an unwitting pun, if *years* is heard as 'ears'. Craik (309) cites *Misogonus* (1570), 1.2.63–4: 'nothinge greues me but my yeares be so longe / my master will take me for balames asse'.
80 **piety** malapropism for 'impiety'
83 **householder** person qualified to vote by the ownership of property
83–4 **as … flesh** i.e. impressive, in appearance but also in social reputation; there is a stage tradition of playing Dogberry as corpulent; there could also be an (unwitting?) sexual

innuendo, on *flesh* as penis, cf. *RJ* 1.1.29: 'Me they shall feel while I am able to stand; and 'tis known I am a pretty piece of flesh.'
85 **go to!** an intensifying exclamation; a command to move forward
86 **hath had losses** i.e. has been wealthy enough to afford to lose money, and still have *two gowns*
5.1 The location is before Leonato's house. The action takes place on the evening of the wedding day.
2 **second** reinforce; act as a second to (as in a duel)

---

74 them. Thou] *F3* (them; thou*)*; them, thou *Q;* them thou *F*   SD] *Oxf¹*   75 SP] *Rowe; Couley Q*   84 is] *om. F*   88 SD] *Pope; exit. Q*   **5.1**] *Actus Quintus. F;* scene i *Rowe*   0.1 ANTONIO] *Rowe*   1+ SP ANTONIO] *Rowe; Brother Q;* LEONATO'S BROTHER *Folg²*

Against yourself.

LEONATO   I pray thee cease thy counsel,
Which falls into mine ears as profitless
As water in a sieve. Give not me counsel,   5
Nor let no comforter delight mine ear
But such a one whose wrongs do suit with mine.
Bring me a father that so loved his child,
Whose joy of her is overwhelmed like mine,
And bid him speak of patience.   10
Measure his woe the length and breadth of mine,
And let it answer every strain for strain,
As thus for thus, and such a grief for such,
In every lineament, branch, shape and form.
If such a one will smile, and stroke his beard   15
And sorrow; wag, cry 'hem', when he should groan,

---

7 **suit** compare
9 **overwhelmed** drowned (in tears)
11 **Measure** measure against
12 **strain for strain** The word *strain* has three possible meanings here: (1) burst, pang; (2) stretch, stress; (3) perhaps with musical connotation, one phrase answering another
14 **lineament** contour
15–16 **stroke . . . 'hem'** To stroke the beard and cry 'hem' (or 'ahem') in order to clear the throat were regarded as overtures to dull or platitudinous speech; cf. *TC* 1.3.165–6: 'Now play me Nestor; hem, and stroke thy beard, / As he being dressed to some oration.'
16 **sorrow** grieve; this passage was first deemed a crux by Capell, who changed it to 'Bid sorrow, wag; cry hem!' (i.e. 'drive grief away by croaking platitudes', Ard²), an emendation which initiated a history of similar efforts, though his version is

generally adopted. The wording of Q was followed only by Johnson, whose punctuation rendered it as 'And, Sorrow wag! cry; hem, when'. Another possibility (RP) is that 'sorry wag' = miserable joker; as 'sorry' was often spelt 'sor[r]ie' the mistaken setting of 'sorrow' in its place would not be impossible. This edition retains Q's wording on the grounds of its intelligibility, emotional descriptiveness, and rhythm (i.e. in the two three-part syntactic units generated by the enjambment of 15–16, and the caesura of 16, Leonato refines and condenses his sentiment through repetition).
wag play the wag, or mischievous prankster, i.e. pretend to be light-hearted
cry 'hem' i.e. clear away or disguise with a cough; cf. *AYL* 1.3.16–18: 'ROSALIND . . . these burrs are in my heart. / CELIA Hem them away.'

---

6 comforter] comfort *F* 7 do] doth *F* 16 And . . . 'hem',] *Cam²;* And sorrow, wagge, crie hem, *Q;* And hallow, wag, cry hem *F3;* And Hollow, wag, cry hem, *F4;* And Sorrow wage; cry, hem! *Theobald;* And sorrow waive, cry hem, *Hanmer;* And sorrowing, cry 'hem' *Halliwell (Heath);* And, Sorrow wag! cry; hem, *Johnson;* In sorrow wag! cry hem *Steevens–Reed;* In sorrow wag; cry hem, *Malone;* Cry – sorrow, wag! and hem, *Steevens–Reed² (Johnson);* And sorrow, wag! cry hem, *Collier;* Bid sorrow, wag; cry hem! *Capell;* And sorrow raze *(Craven)*   'hem'] *Cam;* hem *Q*

Patch grief with proverbs, make misfortune drunk
With candle-wasters, bring him yet to me,
And I of him will gather patience.
But there is no such man. For, brother, men   20
Can counsel and speak comfort to that grief
Which they themselves not feel. But tasting it,
Their counsel turns to passion which before
Would give preceptial medicine to rage,
Fetter strong madness in a silken thread,   25
Charm ache with air and agony with words.
No, no, 'tis all men's office to speak patience
To those that wring under the load of sorrow,
But no man's virtue nor sufficiency
To be so moral when he shall endure   30
The like himself. Therefore give me no counsel;
My griefs cry louder than advertisement.

ANTONIO

Therein do men from children nothing differ.

LEONATO

I pray thee peace; I will be flesh and blood.
For there was never yet philosopher   35

17 **Patch . . . proverbs** attempt to assuage sorrow with clichés

17–18 **make . . . candle-wasters** inundate grief with philosophical precepts, *candle-wasters* being a term used to express contempt for scholars; cf. Jonson, *Cynthia's Revels*, 3.2.2–3: 'a whoreson booke-worme, a candle-waster . . . Foh, he smells all lamp-oil with studying by candlelight' (Jonson, 4.84).

18 **yet** then; even now

19 **patience** three syllables

22 **not feel** For the omission of the auxiliary verb 'do' before 'not' see Abbott, 305, and *Tem* 5.1.38: 'Whereof the ewe not bites'.

24 **preceptial medicine** balms composed of moral precepts, the *moral medicine* disdained by Don John at 1.3.12

25 **Fetter** chain

26 **air** breath, i.e. talk, words

27 **office** duty

27–31 **No . . . himself** Cf. Dent, A124: 'All commend patience, but none can endure to suffer.'

28 **wring** suffer

29 **sufficiency** ability, capacity

30 **moral** glibly comforting with moral precepts
   shall must

32 **advertisement** precept (*OED* 2); good advice. Pronounced (as in British English) with the stress on the second syllable.

35–6 i.e. even philosophers, with all their wisdom, cannot avoid feeling pain; cf. 3.2.26–7: 'Well, everyone can master a grief but he that has it.'

That could endure the toothache patiently,
However they have writ the style of gods
And made a push at chance and sufferance.

ANTONIO

Yet bend not all the harm upon yourself;
Make those that do offend you suffer too.   40

LEONATO

There thou speak'st reason. Nay, I will do so:
My soul doth tell me Hero is belied,
And that shall Claudio know, so shall the prince
And all of them that thus dishonour her.

Enter DON PEDRO *and* CLAUDIO.

ANTONIO

Here comes the prince and Claudio hastily.   45

DON PEDRO

Good e'en, good e'en.

CLAUDIO   Good day to both of you.

LEONATO

Hear you, my lords?

DON PEDRO   We have some haste, Leonato.

LEONATO

Some haste, my lord! Well, fare you well, my lord.

---

37 **writ . . . of** claimed the title of (*OED* style
sb. 18a) by claiming a divine indifference to
misfortune (a trait of the Stoic philosophers)
38 **made . . . at** defied, scoffed
chance and sufferance accident and
predestination; the line is about philosophers
who, while they might, remarkably, have
attempted to solve the puzzles of free will
and divine prescience, are still unable to
endure a simple toothache.

39 **bend** direct, aim; the metaphor is from
archery
45 **comes** For singular verbs preceding
plural subjects see Abbott, 335. See also
5.4.7: 'I am glad that all things sorts so
well'; and 5.4.52: 'Here comes other
reckonings.'
46 **Good e'en** [God give you] good even[ing]
(i.e. any time after noon)
47 **Hear you** will you hear me

38 push] pish *Oxf* 44.1 DON PEDRO] *Rowe (Pedro); Prince Q* 46+ SP] *Pedro / Rowe; Prince Q* e'en . . .
e'en] *Oxf;* den . . . den *Q* 47 lords?] Lords! *Rowe;* lords, – *Capell*

Are you so hasty now? Well, all is one.
DON PEDRO
Nay, do not quarrel with us, good old man.   50
ANTONIO
If he could right himself with quarrelling,
Some of us would lie low.
CLAUDIO   Who wrongs him?
LEONATO
Marry, thou dost wrong me, thou dissembler, thou!
Nay, never lay thy hand upon thy sword;
I fear thee not.
CLAUDIO   Marry, beshrew my hand   55
If it should give your age such cause of fear.
In faith, my hand meant nothing to my sword.
LEONATO
Tush, tush, man, never fleer and jest at me!
I speak not like a dotard nor a fool,
As under privilege of age to brag   60
What I have done being young, or what would do
Were I not old. Know, Claudio, to thy head,
Thou hast so wronged mine innocent child and me
That I am forced to lay my reverence by,
And with grey hairs and bruise of many days   65

49 **all is one** it makes no difference
52 **lie low** i.e. in death, perhaps with a pun on 'base lying'. It is not clear whether Antonio knows that Hero's death is feigned, as the entry SD at 4.1 does not include him in the wedding party (though he is often present in productions).
53 **thou** Leonato uses the more familiar pronoun to address Claudio (reserving the respectful *you* for the Prince).
54 an indication for Claudio's stage action, and perhaps for a threatening gesture on Leonato's part

55 **beshrew** curse
57 **my ... sword** my hand intended nothing in moving toward my sword
58 **Tush** a contemptuous exclamation
    fleer sneer, mock
59 **dotard** senile person
60 **under . . . age** excused by senility, or the reverence due to an elderly person
62 **to thy head** to your face; cf. *MND* 1.1.106: 'I'll avouch it to his head'.
64 **lay ... by** set my age aside
65 **bruise** injuries, wear and tear

52–3 him? / Marry] him? Marry? *Malone*   63 mine] my *F*

Do challenge thee to trial of a man.
I say thou hast belied mine innocent ch.
Thy slander hath gone through and throu,
And she lies buried with her ancestors –
O, in a tomb where never scandal slept,
Save this of hers, framed by thy villainy.

CLAUDIO

My villainy?

LEONATO   Thine, Claudio; thine, I say.

DON PEDRO

You say not right, old man.

LEONATO   My lord, my lord,
I'll prove it on his body, if he dare,
Despite his nice fence and his active practice,   75
His May of youth and bloom of lustihood.

CLAUDIO

Away! I will not have to do with you.

LEONATO

Canst thou so doff me? Thou hast killed my child;
If thou kill'st me, boy, thou shalt kill a man.

ANTONIO

He shall kill two of us, and men indeed.   80
But that's no matter, let him kill one first.
Win me and wear me! Let him answer me.

---

66   **trial . . . man** a duel. Leonato's chivalric
gesture is modelled after that of Genevra's
defender in Shakespeare's Ariostan source
(see 4.1.191–2n.); it is often accompanied in
production by some action signifying a
challenge (the drawing of Leonato's sword,
his flinging of a glove at Claudio's feet, etc.).

71   **framed** plotted, engineered

74   **prove it** Trial by combat was considered a
method of judicial inquiry, the victory
being decided by God.

75   **nice fence** fancy fencing skill

76   **May . . . lustihood** prime of life and peak
of vigour

78   **doff me** put me off, brush me aside; cf. *Oth*
4.2.177: 'Every day thou doff'st me with
some device'. Cf. 2.3.166 and n.

82   **Win . . . me!** a challenge: i.e. if you subdue
me, then you may do with me as you wish;
proverbial (Dent, W408).
      Let . . . me i.e. let him fight me in a duel;
or perhaps a directive to Leonato

78   doff] *(daffe)*

me, follow me, boy. Come, sir boy, come, follow me,
Sir boy! I'll whip you from your foining fence!
Nay, as I am a gentleman, I will.   85

LEONATO

Brother –

ANTONIO

Content yourself. God knows, I loved my niece,
And she is dead, slandered to death by villains
That dare as well answer a man indeed
As I dare take a serpent by the tongue.   90
Boys, apes, braggarts, jacks, milksops!

LEONATO   Brother Anthony –

ANTONIO

Hold you content. What, man? I know them, yea,
And what they weigh, even to the utmost scruple.
Scambling, outfacing, fashion-monging boys,
That lie, and cog, and flout, deprave and slander,   95
Go anticly and show outward hideousness,
And speak off half a dozen dangerous words

to refrain from restraining Antonio (*Let him answer me*). Antonio's enthusiasm for the fight (so at odds with his earlier counsel of patience) risks parodying Leonato's own challenge; some productions have underscored the humour of his indignation by portraying him as literally deaf to Leonato's pleas.

84 **foining fence** thrusting sword-play, as in fencing (as opposed to striking in earnest, and putting himself at risk)

89 **answer . . . indeed** fight a real man

91 **apes** imitations of real men
jacks rascals
milksops cowards

93 **scruple** a small apothecary's weight

(20 grains)

94 **Scambling, outfacing, fashion-monging** contentious, brazen, dandified

95 **cog** cheat
flout jeer
deprave defame

96 **Go anticly** go about in grotesque manner or dress; cf. 3.3.127–33: 'how giddily 'a turns about all the hot-bloods between fourteen and five-and-thirty. . . .'.
outward hideousness appearance of ferocity. Rowe's addition of 'an' serves to smooth the metre; 'an' could have been omitted by haplography or eye-skip (an / ou).

97 **speak off** casually throw out
dangerous threatening

85 gentleman, I] *F;* gentleman I, *Q*   86 Brother –] *Theobald (*Brother, –*);* Brother. *Q*   91 Anthony –] *Theobald;* Anthony. *Q*   94 Scambling] Scrambling *Craig*   96 anticly] *(*antiquely*), Rowe*   outward] an outward *Rowe*   97 off] *Theobald;* of *Q*   dangerous] *(*dang'rous*)*

How they might hurt their enemies, if they durst –
And this is all.

LEONATO

But brother Anthony –

ANTONIO   Come, 'tis no matter.   100
Do not you meddle; let me deal in this.

DON PEDRO

Gentlemen both, we will not wake your patience.
My heart is sorry for your daughter's death,
But on my honour she was charged with nothing
But what was true and very full of proof.   105

LEONATO

My lord, my lord –

DON PEDRO   I will not hear you.

LEONATO   No?
– Come, brother, away. I will be heard.

ANTONIO

And shall, or some of us will smart for it.

Exeunt Leonato and Antonio.

Enter BENEDICK.

DON PEDRO   See, see: here comes the man we went to
seek.   110

CLAUDIO   Now, signor, what news?

BENEDICK [*to Don Pedro*]   Good day, my lord.

DON PEDRO   Welcome, signor. You are almost come to
part almost a fray.

98 **durst** dared
99 **And . . . all** i.e. they are nothing but
    words
102 **wake** disturb

112 **my lord** Benedick's address to Don Pedro
    ignores Claudio's greeting.
113–14 **You . . . fray** You are nearly in time to
    part what was almost a fight.

100 Anthony –] *Theobald;* Anthonie. *Q*   SP2] *F (Ant.); Brother Q*   106 lord –] *Pope;* Lord. *Q*   106–7
No? . . . heard] *one line Q* (No come brother, away, I wil be heard)   108 SD] *opp. 107 Q (Exeunt amb.);
after 107 F (Exeunt ambo.)*   111, 113 signor] *(signior)*   112 SD] *Oxf*

327

CLAUDIO   We had liked to have had our two noses 115
snapped off with two old men without teeth.

DON PEDRO   Leonato and his brother. What think'st
thou? Had we fought, I doubt we should have been too
young for them.

BENEDICK   In a false quarrel there is no true valour. I 120
came to seek you both.

CLAUDIO   We have been up and down to seek thee, for
we are high-proof melancholy and would fain have it
beaten away. Wilt thou use thy wit?

BENEDICK   It is in my scabbard. Shall I draw it? 125

DON PEDRO   Dost thou wear thy wit by thy side?

CLAUDIO   Never any did so, though very many have
been beside their wit. I will bid thee draw as we do the
minstrels – draw to pleasure us.

DON PEDRO   As I am an honest man, he looks pale. Art 130
thou sick, or angry?

CLAUDIO   What, courage, man! What though care killed a
cat, thou hast mettle enough in thee to kill care.

BENEDICK   Sir, I shall meet your wit in the career an you
charge it against me. I pray you choose another subject. 135

---

115 **We had liked** i.e. we were in danger of having
116 **with** by
118 **I doubt** I'm afraid
123 **high-proof** in the highest degree
fain gladly
126–8 **wit . . . wit** Don Pedro attempts a sally on the notion of being 'besides one's wits' (i.e. at the end of one's wits with frustration), which Claudio turns into the notion of being separated from one's wit (i.e. foolish). Claudio here assumes that Benedick's role is indeed that of 'the prince's jester' (2.1.223).
128–9 **as . . . minstrels** i.e. as we bid the minstrels draw their bows across the strings. Claudio deflects the menacing meaning of Benedick's *draw* at 125.
129 **pleasure** entertain
132–3 **What though . . . cat** proverbial (Dent, C84). Claudio perhaps jests about what he thinks is Benedick's lovelorn condition, although the main drift of this sequence is that he cannot believe Benedick is in earnest.
134 **in the career** galloping at full speed; the metaphor is from jousting.
135 **charge** level, aim; urge it on
another subject i.e. other than Beatrice, or love

115 liked] *(likt); like F2*   123 high-proof] *(high proofe), Theobald*   134 an] *(and)*

CLAUDIO   Nay, then, give him another staff; this last was
     broke cross.
DON PEDRO   By this light, he changes more and more. I
     think he be angry indeed.
CLAUDIO   If he be, he knows how to turn his girdle.   140
BENEDICK   Shall I speak a word in your ear?
CLAUDIO   God bless me from a challenge.
BENEDICK [*aside to Claudio*]   You are a villain. I jest not.
     I will make it good how you dare, with what you dare
     and when you dare. Do me right, or I will protest   145
     your cowardice. You have killed a sweet lady, and
     her death shall fall heavy on you. Let me hear from
     you.
CLAUDIO   Well, I will meet you, so I may have good cheer.
DON PEDRO   What, a feast, a feast?   150
CLAUDIO   I'faith, I thank him, he hath bid me to a calf's

---

136 **staff** lance-shaft
137 **broke cross** broken across, as in a failed
     attempt at the tilt in a joust, such that the
     spear is broken across the body of an
     opponent rather than by the push of the
     point (Claudio still believes they are
     having a combat of wits); cf. *AYL* 3.4.37–
     41: 'He . . . swears brave oaths, and breaks
     them bravely, quite traverse, athwart the
     heart of his lover; as a puisny tilter that
     spurs his horse but on one side breaks his
     staff.'
140 **turn his girdle** indicate his unwillingness
     to fight. The proverbial expression (Dent,
     B698) is of uncertain origin, and could
     possibly mean either to rotate a belt in
     order to bring the dagger or scabbard
     (usually worn behind) within range of the
     grasp, or, more likely, to turn a belt so that
     the buckle was behind the body to signify
     that one had decided to bear with a
     provocation rather than contest it.
143 SD *added by Cam on the strength of

Benedick's request to speak a word *in
your ear,* and Don Pedro's query at 150
(although it is clear at 192 that Don Pedro
had gathered what passed between the
two)
144 **make it good** i.e. make good my word,
     prove that Claudio is a villain by fighting
     and defeating him
     with . . . dare i.e. offering Claudio his
     choice of weapon
145 **Do me right** i.e. meet my challenge
     protest proclaim; denounce
149 **so** provided, on condition that
     good cheer entertainment (make it worth
     my while)
151–4 **calf's head . . . capon . . . woodcock**
     types of likely feasting food, but also
     insults: a calf's head is a fool (a calf being
     a type of immaturity); a capon (a castrated
     rooster) is a figure for cowardice; the
     woodcock, for stupidity, as it is a bird
     easily captured (cf. the ironic proverb 'As
     wise as a woodcock', Dent, W746).

143 SD] *Cam*   151 him,] *F;* him *Q*

head and a capon, the which if I do not carve most
curiously, say my knife's naught. Shall I not find a
woodcock too?

BENEDICK   Sir, your wit ambles well; it goes easily.   155
DON PEDRO   I'll tell thee how Beatrice praised thy wit the
other day. I said thou hadst a fine wit. 'True,' said she,
'a fine little one.' 'No,' said I, 'a great wit.' 'Right,' says
she, 'a great gross one.' 'Nay,' said I, 'a good wit.' 'Just,'
said she, 'it hurts nobody.' 'Nay,' said I, 'the gentleman   160
is wise.' 'Certain,' said she, 'a wise gentleman.' 'Nay,'
said I, 'he hath the tongues.' 'That I believe,' said she,
'for he swore a thing to me on Monday night, which
he forswore on Tuesday morning. There's a double
tongue; there's two tongues.' Thus did she an hour   165
together trans-shape thy particular virtues. Yet at last
she concluded, with a sigh, thou wast the properest
man in Italy.
CLAUDIO   For the which she wept heartily and said she
cared not.   170
DON PEDRO   Yea, that she did, but yet for all that, an if she
did not hate him deadly, she would love him dearly.

---

153 **curiously** cleverly
   naught useless, blunt
155 **ambles** moves (as in – ironic – praise for a
   horse's gait)
   goes easily doesn't exert itself; goes away
   quickly, i.e. is of no import
157 **fine** excellent; diminutive
159 **Just** just so
161 **a wise gentleman** Johnson suggests that
   'perhaps "wise gentleman" was in that age
   used ironically, and always stood for silly
   fellow'.
162 **hath the tongues** speaks various
   languages; cf. *TGV* 4.1.33–5: '2 OUTLAW
   Have you the tongues? / VALENTINE
   My youthful travel therein made me

happy, / Or else I often had been
miserable.'
164–5 **a double tongue** *double* = deceitful.
   Beatrice's alleged comment paraphrases
   her own account of her personal history
   with Benedick, delivered to the Prince at
   2.1.255–6.
166 **trans-shape** metamorphose (as Hero
   claims she does at 3.1.59–70)
167 **properest** most handsome, finest
171–2 **an . . . dearly** proverbial: 'A woman
   either loves or hates to extremes' (Dent,
   W651); cf. Lyly, *Anatomy*, 238: 'I haue
   heard that women eyther loue entirely or
   hate deadly.'
171 **an if** if

157 said she] saies she *F*   157–65 'True . . . tongues.'] *Capell subst.;* True . . . tongues *Q*   171 an] *(and)*

The old man's daughter told us all.

CLAUDIO   All, all. And moreover, God saw him when he
was hid in the garden.   175

DON PEDRO   But when shall we set the savage bull's horns
on the sensible Benedick's head?

CLAUDIO   Yea, and text underneath: 'Here dwells Benedick
the married man.'

BENEDICK   Fare you well. Boy, you know my mind. I will   180
leave you now to your gossip-like humour. You break
jests as braggarts do their blades, which, God be
thanked, hurt not. My lord, for your many courtesies,
I thank you. I must discontinue your company. Your
brother the bastard is fled from Messina; you have   185
among you killed a sweet and innocent lady. For my
Lord Lack-beard there, he and I shall meet, and till
then peace be with him.   [*Exit.*]

DON PEDRO   He is in earnest.

CLAUDIO   In most profound earnest. And, I'll warrant   190
you, for the love of Beatrice.

DON PEDRO   And hath challenged thee?

CLAUDIO   Most sincerely.

---

173 **old man's daughter** i.e. Hero

174–75 **God . . . garden** The allusion in
Claudio's hint about Benedick's eavesdropping in 2.3 is to Genesis, 3.8, when God
discovers Adam and Eve in a state of post-
lapsarian shame in the wake of eating from
the tree of the knowledge of good and evil:
they 'heard the voice of the Lord walking in
the garden in the cool of the day: and . . . hid
themselves from the presence of the Lord
God amongst the trees of the garden'.

181 **gossip-like humour** talkative women's
mood

181–2 **break jests** crack jokes

182 **as . . . blades** as cowardly boasters break
their swords in order to give the impression
they've been fighting; cf. *1H4* 2.4.296–8,
where Falstaff 'hacked [his sword] with
his dagger, and said he would swear truth
out of England but he would make you
believe it was done in fight'.

184 **discontinue your company** Benedick is
resigning from his service to the Prince.

187 **Lord Lack-beard** i.e. Claudio, a reference
to his youth and / or his lack of manliness
meet in a duel

177 on] *(one)* 178–9 'Here . . . man.'] *Capell subst.;* here . . . man. *Q* 180 well.] *this edn (RP);* wel,
Q 187 Lack-beard there,] *F;* Lacke-beard, there *Q* 188 SD] *Rowe*

DON PEDRO   What a pretty thing man is when he goes in
his doublet and hose, and leaves off his wit!   195
CLAUDIO   He is then a giant to an ape; but then is an ape
a doctor to such a man.
DON PEDRO   But soft you, let me be. Pluck up, my heart,
and be sad – did he not say my brother was fled?

Enter Constables [DOGBERRY *and* VERGES, *with the*
Watch], CONRADE *and* BORACHIO.

DOGBERRY   Come you, sir. If justice cannot tame you, she   200
shall ne'er weigh more reasons in her balance. Nay, an
you be a cursing hypocrite once, you must be looked to.
DON PEDRO   How now? Two of my brother's men bound?
Borachio one.
CLAUDIO   Hearken after their offence, my lord.   205
DON PEDRO   Officers, what offence have these men done?
DOGBERRY   Marry, sir, they have committed false report.
Moreover they have spoken untruths, secondarily they

194 **goes in** i.e. goes about only in
195 **leaves . . . wit** forgets to wear his intelligence (like a cape covering his other clothing, which a person would remove in preparation to fight)
196–7 **is then . . . man** i.e. seems heroic to a fool (*ape*), but the fool is a scholar compared with such a man. The ape could also be a literal one, cf. *Ham* 4.2.15–18: 'such officers do the King best service in the end: he keeps them, like an ape, in the corner of his jaw – first mouthed, to be last swallowed'; and *MM* 2.2.121–3: 'His glassy essence – like an angry ape / Plays such fantastic tricks before high heaven / As makes the angels weep.'
198 **soft you** wait a moment
198–9 **Pluck . . . sad** rouse yourself, my mind, and be serious
201 **reasons** In Elizabethan pronunciation this

word would have sounded the same as 'raisins', and so there is perhaps an inadvertent joke in the image of the icon of Justice – a blindfolded woman holding a set of scales – weighing reasons much as a shopkeeper weighs fruit; cf. *1H4* 2.4.232–3: 'If reasons were as plentiful as blackberries . . .'. See Cercignani, 243. Dogberry's meaning seems to be that if Justice cannot punish the scoundrel in question (whether he means Conrade or Borachio is not clear), she should hang up her scales.
201–2 **an . . . to** if you are a 'lying imposter' (Kittredge), in a word (Abbott, 57), you must be punished
205 **Hearken** enquire
208 **secondarily** Dogberry attempts to enumerate his claims in the manner of a logical proposition.

198 up,] *Steevens; vp Q*   199.1–2] *after 195 Q*   DOGBERRY . . . Watch] *Rowe subst. (Enter* Dogberry, Verges, Conrade *and* Borachio, *guarded.)*   200, 207 SP] *Rowe; Const. Q*   201 an] *(*and*)*

332

are slanders, sixth and lastly, they have belied a lady,
thirdly they have verified unjust things, and, to 210
conclude, they are lying knaves.

DON PEDRO   First I ask thee what they have done, thirdly
I ask thee what's their offence, sixth and lastly why they
are committed, and, to conclude, what you lay to their
charge?   215

CLAUDIO   Rightly reasoned and in his own division; and,
by my troth, there's one meaning well suited.

DON PEDRO   Who have you offended, masters, that you
are thus bound to your answer? This learned constable
is too cunning to be understood. What's your offence? 220

BORACHIO   Sweet Prince, let me go no farther to mine
answer. Do you hear me, and let this count kill me. I
have deceived even your very eyes. What your wisdoms
could not discover, these shallow fools have brought to
light, who in the night overheard me confessing to this 225
man how Don John your brother incensed me to
slander the lady Hero; how you were brought into
the orchard and saw me court Margaret in Hero's
garments; how you disgraced her when you should
marry her. My villainy they have upon record, which I 230
had rather seal with my death than repeat over to my
shame. The lady is dead upon mine and my master's

209 **slanders** malapropism for 'slanderers'
210 **verified** Dogberry's error for 'sworn to'
214 **committed** i.e. to custody
216 **in . . . division** according to his own rhetorical enumeration
217 **well suited** neatly set out (by various phrasings)
219 **bound . . . answer** required to respond; tied up in preparation for your trial
220 **cunning** clever, ingenious
221–2 **go . . . answer** reply without preamble; travel no further (especially in Dogberry's company?) to my punishment

226 **incensed** provoked, as in *MW* 1.3.95–6, 'I will incense Ford to deal with poison', and *KL* 2.2.499, 'what they may incense him to'
228–9 **in Hero's garments** 'This important touch is added for the first time in this, the last account of the midnight episode' (Smith); it is never explained why Margaret would do this.
231 **seal** i.e. prove, pay for; the metaphor is from sealing wax.
232 **upon** in consequence of

false accusation, and, briefly, I desire nothing but the
reward of a villain.

DON PEDRO

Runs not this speech like iron through your blood?   235

CLAUDIO

I have drunk poison whiles he uttered it.

DON PEDRO

But did my brother set thee on to this?

BORACHIO

Yea, and paid me richly for the practice of it.

DON PEDRO

He is composed and framed of treachery,
And fled he is upon this villainy.   240

CLAUDIO

Sweet Hero! Now thy image doth appear
In the rare semblance that I loved it first.

DOGBERRY   Come, bring away the plaintiffs. By this
time our sexton hath reformed Signor Leonato of the
matter. And masters, do not forget to specify, when   245
time and place shall serve, that I am an ass.

VERGES   Here, here comes master Signor Leonato, and
the sexton too.

Enter LEONATO, *his brother* [ANTONIO] *and the* Sexton.

LEONATO

Which is the villain? Let me see his eyes,
That when I note another man like him   250
I may avoid him. Which of these is he?

---

235 **like iron** i.e. as a sword; Don Pedro shifts
into verse here.
238 **practice** accomplishment
239 **framed of** shaped by (*OED v. 5*)
242 **rare   semblance**   exceptional,   or

exceptionally lovely, likeness
that in which; see Abbott, 394, and 5.2.45.
243 **plaintiffs** for 'defendants'
244 **reformed** malapropism for 'informed'

244, 247 Signor] *(Signior)*   247 SP] *Rowe; Con.2 Q*   248.1 *his* . . . Sexton] *om. F*   ANTONIO] *Rowe*

BORACHIO
    If you would know your wronger, look on me.
LEONATO
    Art thou the slave that with thy breath hast killed
    Mine innocent child?
BORACHIO   Yea, even I alone.
LEONATO
    No, not so, villain, thou beliest thyself.   255
    Here stand a pair of honourable men;
    A third is fled that had a hand in it.
    I thank you, princes, for my daughter's death;
    Record it with your high and worthy deeds.
    'Twas bravely done, if you bethink you of it.   260
CLAUDIO
    I know not how to pray your patience.
    Yet I must speak. Choose your revenge yourself.
    Impose me to what penance your invention
    Can lay upon my sin. Yet sinned I not
    But in mistaking.
DON PEDRO   By my soul, nor I.   265
    And yet to satisfy this good old man
    I would bend under any heavy weight
    That he'll enjoin me to.
LEONATO
    I cannot bid you bid my daughter live –
    That were impossible. But I pray you both,   270
    Possess the people in Messina here
    How innocent she died. [*to Claudio*] And if
        your love

---

256 **honourable men** presumably a sarcastic
reference to Don Pedro and Claudio; cf.
JC 3.2.83–4: 'For Brutus is an honourable
man, / So are they all, all honourable men.'

261 **patience** three syllables
263 **Impose** subject
    invention imagination
271 **Possess** inform

253–4 Art . . . child] *prose F*   255 thou] thou thou *F*   272 SD] *this edn*

Can labour aught in sad invention,
Hang her an epitaph upon her tomb
And sing it to her bones. Sing it tonight.   275
Tomorrow morning come you to my house,
And since you could not be my son-in-law,
Be yet my nephew. My brother hath a daughter,
Almost the copy of my child that's dead,
And she alone is heir to both of us.   280
Give her the right you should have given her cousin,
And so dies my revenge.

CLAUDIO   O noble sir!
Your over-kindness doth wring tears from me.
I do embrace your offer, and dispose
For henceforth of poor Claudio.   285

LEONATO

Tomorrow, then, I will expect your coming;
Tonight I take my leave. This naughty man
Shall face to face be brought to Margaret,
Who I believe was packed in all this wrong,
Hired to it by your brother.

BORACHIO   No, by my soul she was not,   290
Nor knew not what she did when she spoke to me,
But always hath been just and virtuous
In anything that I do know by her.

273 **labour . . . invention** bestir itself at all in serious creation; *invention* has four syllables.
274 **an epitaph** as suggested by the Friar; see 4.1.207 and n.
280 **alone . . . us** Antonio's son, mentioned at 1.2.1–2, is quite forgotten; see pp. 144–5.
281 **right** just treatment, with pun on rite (of marriage)
284 **dispose** you may dispose
285 The metre of this line is irregular. It is possible that *dispose* (284) belongs at the beginning of this line, and something has been dropped from the end of 284.
287 **leave** Don Pedro and Claudio often exit here (in which case 316–18 are brought forward to this point or cut).
naughty wicked
289 **packed** in league, an accomplice; cf. *CE* 5.1.219–20: 'That goldsmith there, were he not pack'd with her, / Could witness it'. See 2.2.40n. and 5.4.4n. for speculation about Margaret's awareness of her role in the plot.
293 **by** of

281 given] *(giu'n)*   283 over-kindness] *(ouer kindnesse), Rowe*

DOGBERRY   Moreover, sir, which indeed is not under
white and black, this plaintiff here, the offender, did   295
call me ass. I beseech you let it be remembered in his
punishment. And also the watch heard them talk of one
Deformed; they say he wears a key in his ear and a lock
hanging by it, and borrows money in God's name, the
which he hath used so long, and never paid, that   300
now men grow hard-hearted and will lend nothing for
God's sake. Pray you examine him upon that point.

LEONATO
I thank thee for thy care and honest pains.

DOGBERRY   Your worship speaks like a most thankful and
reverent youth, and I praise God for you.   305

LEONATO [*Gives him money.*]   There's for thy pains.

DOGBERRY   God save the foundation!

LEONATO   Go, I discharge thee of thy prisoner, and I
thank thee.

DOGBERRY   I leave an arrant knave with your worship,   310
which I beseech your worship to correct yourself, for
the example of others. God keep your worship! I wish
your worship well! God restore you to health! I humbly
give you leave to depart, and if a merry meeting may be
wished, God prohibit it! Come, neighbour.   315

[*Exeunt Dogberry and Verges.*]

LEONATO

Until tomorrow morning, lords, farewell.

294–5 **under . . . black** i.e. written down
298 **a key** In Dogberry's garbled apprehension,
Deformed's love-lock has acquired a key,
and the man himself the financial habits of
a borrower who invokes God's name like a
beggar.
299–300 **the which** i.e. the trick of persuading
men to lend for God's sake
300 **paid** repaid

305 **reverent** malapropism for 'reverend'
youth malapropism for 'elder'
307 the usual thanks given by recipients of
charity, especially at the entrances to
convents or monasteries
310 **arrant** (1) thorough; (2) perhaps a mistake
for 'errant'
314 **give** malapropism for 'ask'
315 **prohibit** malapropism for 'permit'

294 SP] *Rowe (Dog.); Const. Q*   301 hard-hearted] *(hard hearted), F*   305 reverent] reuerend *F*   306
SD] *Oxf*   315 SD] *F (Exeunt.) after 316*

337

ANTONIO
Farewell, my lords. We look for you tomorrow.
DON PEDRO
We will not fail.
CLAUDIO   Tonight I'll mourn with Hero.
LEONATO [*to the Watch*]
Bring you these fellows on. We'll talk with Margaret, 319
How her acquaintance grew with this lewd fellow. *Exeunt.*

[**5.2**]   *Enter* BENEDICK *and* MARGARET.

BENEDICK   Pray thee, sweet mistress Margaret, deserve
well at my hands by helping me to the speech of
Beatrice.
MARGARET   Will you then write me a sonnet in praise of
my beauty?   5
BENEDICK   In so high a style, Margaret, that no man
living shall come over it; for in most comely truth thou
deservest it.
MARGARET   To have no man come over me? Why, shall I
always keep below stairs?   10

---

320 **lewd** worthless, wicked, rascally, as in e.g.
Acts, 17.5: 'the Jews . . . took unto them
certain lewd fellows of the baser sort'
5.2 The location is the vicinity of Leonato's
house.
0.1 Capell's addition (see t.n.) interposes a
separation between Benedick and Margaret,
although their dialogue (e.g. Margaret's
knowledge of Benedick's literary efforts)
could equally suggest the possibility that
they are in mid-conversation upon entry; or
that she observes him in the act of
composition.
1–2 **deserve . . . hands** i.e. earn a reward from
me
2 **to . . . of** to speak with

6 **style** with pun on 'stile' (a step for climbing
over a fence); cf. Chaucer, *The Squire's
Tale*, 97–8: 'Al be it that I can nat sowne
his style, / Ne can nat clymen over so high
a style.'
7 **come over** surpass; climb over
comely pleasant
9 **come over me** cover me in the act of
intercourse
10 **keep below stairs** remain a servant (rather
than, according to the convention of
sonnets, become a mistress to a servant-
lover); Margaret perhaps also suggests that
she would like to improve her social rank
via marriage to someone in possession of a
house, stairs and servants.

319 SD] *Cam* 319–20] *Pope; prose Q* **5.2**] *Capell (SCENE II)* 0.1] *meeting / Capell* 9 me? Why]
Rowe; me, why *Q*

BENEDICK　Thy wit is as quick as the greyhound's mouth, it catches.

MARGARET　And yours as blunt as the fencer's foils, which hit, but hurt not.

BENEDICK　A most manly wit, Margaret, it will not hurt a　15
woman. And so, I pray thee, call Beatrice. I give thee the bucklers.

MARGARET　Give us the swords; we have bucklers of our own.

BENEDICK　If you use them, Margaret, you must put in　20
the pikes with a vice, and they are dangerous weapons for maids.

MARGARET　Well, I will call Beatrice to you, who I think hath legs.　　　　　　　　　　　　　　*Exit.*

BENEDICK　And therefore will come.　　　　　　　25
　　[*Sings.*]
　　　　　　The God of love
　　　　　　That sits above,
　　　　And knows me, and knows me,
　　　　How pitiful I deserve –

11　**greyhound's mouth** Greyhounds were used as hunting dogs.
12　**catches** seizes swiftly
13　**foils** blunted rapiers used in fencing practice
16–17　**I give . . . bucklers** I concede (to your superior wit). A buckler was a small shield with a detachable spike screwed (sexual pun intended) into the centre; 'to give the bucklers is to yield, or to lay by all thought of defence' (Johnson).
18　**swords** innuendo for penises
　　bucklers innuendo for hymens or vulvas, or thighs, protecting the vulva
21　**pikes** spikes
　　vice (1) screw (with sexual innuendo); (2) clamp used to screw an item into place;

(3) sin; (4) thighs closed in intercourse as the screw of a vice compresses its jaws
24　**hath legs** can move
25　**come** come when called; yield, be favourably moved (*OED v.* II 16)
26–9　the first stanza of a popular song by William Elderton, printed in 1562, of a melancholy lover praying for grace from his disdainful mistress. Duffin (175) writes that 'the melody survives under "The Gods of love" and other names, including "Turkeylony", which may be a corruption of the Italian "Tordiglione" . . . The mismatch of the plural subject with the singular verb of the first line in the original poem ("the gods off love yt sytts a bove") along with the orthography of

13 yours] *(your's)*　24 SD] *(Exit Margarite.)*　25 SD] *Pope*　26–9] *Capell; prose Q*

I mean in singing; but in loving, Leander the good   30
swimmer, Troilus the first employer of pandars and
a whole bookful of these quondam carpet-mongers,
whose names yet run smoothly in the even road of a
blank verse, why, they were never so truly turned over
and over as my poor self in love. Marry, I cannot show   35
it in rhyme. I have tried; I can find out no rhyme to
'lady' but 'baby' – an innocent rhyme; for 'scorn', 'horn'
– a hard rhyme; for 'school', 'fool', a babbling rhyme:
very ominous endings. No, I was not born under a
rhyming planet nor I cannot woo in festival terms.   40

"Gods" in some sources (i.e. "Godes," "Goddes"), may suggest that the song originally began, "The Goddess of love. . . .".'

30 **Leander** a famously and tragically loyal lover, who contrary to Benedick's (ironic?) estimate of his athletic prowess drowned while swimming the Hellespont. See 4.1.79n. Marlowe's poem *Hero and Leander*, was published in 1598, although echoes of the poem in *MND* suggest that Shakespeare knew it in manuscript.

31 **Troilus** another hapless hero of faithful love, loved and left by Criseyde, after he was assisted to her bed by her go-between uncle Pandarus; their story was celebrated by Chaucer in his poem *Troilus and Cresyde* and by Shakespeare himself in his play of 1601–2.

32 **quondam** erstwhile, bygone
carpet-mongers literally, carpet salesmen, but Benedick seems to mean something along the lines of 'pretend lovers' (in the senses of fictional, literary and lightweight), or the twentieth-century 'bedroom warriors'; from the term 'carpet-knight', a lover as opposed to a fighter, one awarded a knighthood for service not in battle but at court, 'on carpet consideration' (*TN* 3.4.235)

34 **verse** Benedick's examples are literary ones. The versifying effects of love are noted elsewhere in Shakespeare's works, e.g. Berowne in *LLL* 4.3.13–14: 'By heaven, I do love, and it hath taught me to rhyme, and to be melancholy'; and *Ham* 2.2.119–20: '*I am ill at these numbers. I have not art to reckon my groans.*'

37 **innocent** childish (but perhaps ominously so, as suggesting the consequences of loving ladies)
horn cuckold's horn; erect penis

38 **hard** (1) harsh, in sound, in import (because the horn was the mark of a cuckold), and in material substance, and hence (2) erect
fool (1) speaker of nonsense, or babble (*babbling* comes from the term for the speech of infants); (2) a cuckolded father of bastards

39 **ominous endings** incompetent rhymes; inauspicious ends (to be brought to by love)

40 **rhyming planet** astrological sign conducive to verse-making; cf. 1.3.10–11: 'being as thou sayst thou art, born under Saturn'; and 2.1.306–9.
festival terms (1) lighthearted, holiday language, cf. *1H4* 1.3.46–7: 'With many holiday and lady terms / He questioned me'; (2) conventionally

37–8 'lady'. . . 'fool'] *quotation marks as Pope; none in Q*   40 nor] for *F*

Enter BEATRICE.

Sweet Beatrice, wouldst thou come when I called thee?

BEATRICE   Yea, signor, and depart when you bid me.

BENEDICK   O, stay but till then.

BEATRICE   'Then' is spoken; fare you well now. And yet,
ere I go, let me go with that I came for, which is, with   45
knowing what hath passed between you and Claudio.

BENEDICK   Only foul words – and thereupon I will kiss
thee.

BEATRICE   Foul words is but foul wind, and foul wind is
but foul breath, and foul breath is noisome, therefore I   50
will depart unkissed.

BENEDICK   Thou hast frighted the word out of his right
sense, so forcible is thy wit. But I must tell thee plainly:
Claudio undergoes my challenge, and either I must
shortly hear from him, or I will subscribe him a coward.   55
And I pray thee now tell me, for which of my bad parts
didst thou first fall in love with me?

BEATRICE   For them all together, which maintained so
politic a state of evil that they will not admit any good
part to intermingle with them. But for which of my   60
good parts did you first suffer love for me?

---

sentimental love poetry   like another
soldier of professed incompetence at love
language, Henry V (*H5* 5.2.132–3): 'Marry,
if you would put me to verses, or to dance
for your sake, Kate, why, you undid me.'
Benedick nonetheless does manage to
produce a sonnet in 5.4.
44 **fare you well** This often serves as a cue for
Beatrice to move as if to exit.
45 **that** what; see 5.1.242n. on *that*.
49 **Foul . . . but foul wind** Cf. Job, 6.26: 'Do
you imagine to reprove words, that the

talke of the afflicted should be as the
winde?'; Dent, W833.
50 **noisome** offensive
52 **his** its
54 **undergoes** has received
55 **subscribe** publish, publicly proclaim over
a signature
59 **politic** well-governed; canny. Beatrice's
metaphor invokes that of the body
politic.
61 **suffer** undergo, but with (as Benedick
glosses) a sense of resistance

40.1] *F; after 41 Q*   42+ signor] *(signior)*   44 'Then'] *Malone;* Then, *Q*   45 came for] *Rowe¹;* came *Q*

341

BENEDICK   'Suffer love'! A good epithet. I do suffer love
indeed, for I love thee against my will.

BEATRICE   In spite of your heart, I think. Alas, poor heart!
If you spite it for my sake, I will spite it for yours, for I   65
will never love that which my friend hates.

BENEDICK   Thou and I are too wise to woo peaceably.

BEATRICE   It appears not in this confession: there's not
one wise man among twenty that will praise himself.

BENEDICK   An old, an old instance, Beatrice, that lived in   70
the time of good neighbours. If a man do not erect in
this age his own tomb ere he dies, he shall live no longer
in monument than the bell rings and the widow weeps.

BEATRICE   And how long is that, think you?

BENEDICK   Question: why, an hour in clamour and a   75
quarter in rheum. Therefore is it most expedient for
the wise, if Don Worm – his conscience – find no

65–6 **If . . . hates** 'If you love me in spite of
your desire, then I will spite your heart
for your sake, for I would never love
something (a heart) which my lover
spites.'

67 **too wise** i.e. because their wit prevents
them from taking statements unequivocally
or conventionally (although the statement
could also be taken as an acknowledgement
of the risks and vulnerabilities involved in
loving)

68 **in** by

69–71 **praise himself . . . neighbours** Dent,
N117, gives as proverbial 'He has ill
neighbours that is fain to praise himself.'

70 **instance** precept

72–3 **live . . . monument** be no longer
remembered or memorialized

73 **bell** i.e. the funeral bell, or the 'passing
bell', rung as a person lay dying (nine
times for a man plus one peal for every

year of his age) in order to signify to the
community and the person in question that
the end is near (Gittings, 133)

75 **Question** i.e. good question
in clamour noise of the funeral bell, here
three-quarters of an hour longer than the
weeping of the widow; in popular
literature, widows were notorious for the
rapidity of their recoveries and remarriages.
A ballad of the period entitled 'How to
Wyve Well' includes the verse 'But when
she heres thee deade / She shifteth thee to
grave / and for she cannot weepe / With
clothe she hides her face / And shakes
her head as though / She weepte for thee
apace.'

76 **rheum** tears

77 **Don . . . conscience** The image of
one's conscience as a gnawing worm
derives from Mark, 9.46: 'Their worm
dieth   not,   and   the   fire

62 'Suffer love'!] *Capell subst.;* Suffer loue! *Q*   73 monument] monuments *F*   bell rings] Bels ring *F*

impediment to the contrary, to be the trumpet of his
own virtues, as I am to myself. So much for praising
myself, who I myself will bear witness is praiseworthy.   80
And now tell me, how doth your cousin?

BEATRICE   Very ill.

BENEDICK   And how do you?

BEATRICE   Very ill too.

BENEDICK   Serve God, love me and mend. There will I   85
leave you too, for here comes one in haste.

Enter URSULA.

URSULA   Madam, you must come to your uncle. Yonder's
old coil at home. It is proved my lady Hero hath
been falsely accused, the prince and Claudio mightily
abused, and Don John is the author of all, who is fled   90
and gone. Will you come presently?

BEATRICE   Will you go hear this news, signor?

BENEDICK   I will live in thy heart, die in thy lap, and be
buried in thy eyes – and moreover, I will go with thee   94
to thy uncle's.   *Exeunt.*

is not quenched'; cf. *R3* 1.3.222: 'The
worm of conscience still begnaw thy soul.'
Don is a term of mock-respect, although, as
Mason (258) argues, 'In a play with
characters called Don Pedro and Don John
the introduction at this late stage of Don
Worm can be read strongly; Benedick has
severed both bonds of allegiance and
friendship with Don Pedro . . . his "new
sworn brother" (1.1.68) is Don Worm, his
conscience.'

85   **mend** feel better

There i.e. with that
88   **old coil** a fine uproar
90   **abused** deceived
91   **presently** immediately
93   **die** achieve orgasm
       lap front portion of a seated body from
       waist to knees; vagina (*OED sb.*[1] 2b)
93–4   **be . . . eyes** a conventional trope of love
       poetry; Benedick seems to have mastered
       some *festival terms*, despite his earlier
       disavowal, but takes care to deflate them
       with an anticlimax.

79 myself. So] *Rowe subst.;* my self so *Q*   86.1] *after 84 F*   95 SD] *F; exit. Q*

[5.3]   *Enter* CLAUDIO, DON PEDRO, *and three or four*
[Attendants, including a Lord *and* Musicians,]*
with tapers.

CLAUDIO   Is this the monument of Leonato?
LORD   It is, my lord. *[Reads the] epitaph.*

5.3 The location is a churchyard, including the tomb of Leonato's family. This scene was frequently cut in productions from Garrick to the early twentieth century, thus removing the performance of Claudio's penance; or, given the allocation of SPs (see 2 SPn.), removing the problem of his penitence not seeming sincere enough. In more recent productions it has often been witnessed by a concealed Hero, presumably to provide her with proof of Claudio's remorse.

0.1–2 According to line 30, the company is dressed in mourning costume.

0.2 *including a* **Lord** See 2 SPn.

and **Musicians** Q does not include musicians, though they are clearly of the party at line 11; many editions include Balthasar here, given his habitual association with Claudio and Don Pedro and his affiliation with music, but since he was asked to procure *excellent* music in the wake of his rendition of 'Sigh no more' in 2.3, it may be that his skills are not up to the more reverent task here. F's '*Iacke Wilson*' at 2.3.34.1–2 (see List of Roles 5n.) presumes a good singer here (if one artfully bad in 2.3).

tapers On the Renaissance stage, these would signify that it was night time. While this ceremony is not strictly speaking a funeral, night-time funerals (particularly for women) were coming into aristocratic vogue in the early seventeenth century (Gittings, 188).

1 **monument** family burial vault; 'the inclusion of a tomb in Henslowe's 1598 inventory of stage properties for the Rose

Theatre (Henslowe, 179) raises the possibility that a property monument may also have been used in Renaissance theatres where *Much Ado* was performed' (Cox, *Shakespeare*, 225). Alternatively, Claudio's very question helps to locate the scene verbally, obviating the need for such a visual cue.

2 SP *Q assigns the epitaph and 22–3 to the attendant Lord; or, as Capell decided, and most editors agree, fails to provide a SP before the epitaph for Claudio (who in Q speaks again at 11). Following Capell, productions usually assign the epitaph to Claudio, given that Leonato had explicitly instructed him to 'Hang her an epitaph upon her tomb / And sing it to her bones' (5.1.274–5). (However, Leonato's instruction notwithstanding, in Q he instructs others to sing to her bones.) The assumption is that 'we must assign the epitaph to the character whose importance merits the speech and who is an appropriate choice to speak it' (Myers, 415). This edition leaves the scene as in Q, agreeing in part with Cam² that 'it does not seem out of character for Claudio to do his grieving by proxy, as he did his wooing', but also on the grounds that it need not appear coldhearted for a delegate lord to read the epitaph on Claudio's behalf, and the collective behalf of the male community that has slandered Hero. On the contrary, given the highly formal, public and ritual nature of this act, it might be equally possible that the ' "I" of the unnamed lord functions as the liturgical "I" of a ritualized,

5.3] *Capell (SCENE III)*   0.1 DON PEDRO] *Rowe; Prince Q*   0.2 *Attendants*] *Rowe   including a* Lord] *this edn   and* Musicians] *this edn (Wells); Capell subst. (and Musick); Balthasar and musicians Cam¹*   2 SP] *Q; Cla. / Capell*   SD] *Cam² subst.; Epitaph Q*

Done to death by slanderous tongues
Was the Hero that here lies;
Death, in guerdon of her wrongs,   5
Gives her fame which never dies;
So the life that died with shame,
Lives in death with glorious fame.

[*Hangs scroll.*]

Hang thou there upon the tomb,
Praising her when I am dumb.   10

CLAUDIO

Now music sound, and sing your solemn hymn.   [*Music*]

ONE OR MORE SINGERS [*Sing.*]

Pardon, goddess of the night,
Those that slew thy virgin knight,

---

corporate, performative, gendered identity' (PG). The collective voice of the song ('Pardon . . . Those . . . assist our moan . . . Help us') supports the corporate nature of this act. Another reason for Claudio's silence could be that he's too upset to read the epitaph or sing himself. So too it can be argued that following the Q SP means that here (and only here) does Claudio initiate and control the action, becoming in effect director or stage manager of the scene, whereas heretofore he has been content to be directed by Don Pedro; this role lends him a new theatrical authority and weight.

5 *guerdon* recompense, reward
7 *with* as a consequence of
12–21 There is no contemporary setting extant for this song, in effect a pagan ritual of exorcism; Collier cites a reference in *Laugh and Lie Down* (1605) to a ballad sung to the tune of 'Heavily, heavily', and Duffin (302) proposes the conjectural setting of the tune 'Robin Goodfellow', 'which seems like a good match for the

structure of the poem as well as for the invocation of nocturnal spirits'.

12 SP Q does not specify a singer, despite the fact that Claudio calls for one in the previous line. Balthasar seems a plausible choice, since the actor playing him (see 0.2n. on *and* Musicians) has been responsible for singing and playing throughout; or, given the line 'Help *us* to sigh', it could be sung as a chorus by all present.

12 **goddess . . . night** Diana or Artemis, the huntress goddess of the moon and chastity (as at 4.1.56, 'You seem to me as Dian in her orb'). The image returns Hero to virgin status, and is an attempt to mollify the goddess whose anger resulted in Actaeon (the model of the cuckold) acquiring antlers (Ovid, *Met.*, 3.138–249).

13 **virgin knight** votary, follower. A frequent image of the chaste woman, like Diana the huntress, was one safely clad in male garb; cf. Spenser's armed Britomart in Book 3 of *The Faerie*

---

8 SD] *Capell (affixing it)*   10 dumb] *F (dombe); dead Q*   11 SP] *om. Capell*   SD] *Oxf¹*   12 SP] *this edn (Wells); Song Q*

For the which with songs of woe
Round about her tomb they go. 15
Midnight, assist our moan,
Help us to sigh and groan,
Heavily, heavily.
Graves yawn and yield your dead,
Till death be uttered, 20
Heavily, heavily.

LORD

Now unto thy bones good night;
Yearly will I do this rite.

DON PEDRO

Good morrow, masters. Put your torches out.
The wolves have preyed, and look, the gentle day, 25
Before the wheels of Phoebus, round about
Dapples the drowsy east with spots of grey.
Thanks to you all, and leave us. Fare you well.

CLAUDIO

Good morrow, masters; each his several way.

Queene, or the lady of Milton's *Comus*,
420–3: 'She that has [chastity], is clad in
complete steel, / And like a quiver'd
Nymph with Arrows keen / May trace huge
Forests and unharbor'd Heaths, / Infamous
Hills and sandy perilous wilds' (Milton,
Poems and Prose, 100).

15 **Round about** Clockwise circling was the
traditional way of averting evil.

19–21 **Graves . . . heavily** The meaning of
these lines is perplexing; there is perhaps
a hint of resurrection (depending on the
second meaning of *uttered*; see 20n.), in
which case F's '*Heauenly, heauenly*'

at 21 is attractive. However, the more
likely sense is that death's utterance, or
expression, is on a par with the sighing and
groaning of 17; the title of the ballad cited
by Collier (see 12–21n.) supports the latter.

20 **uttered** utterèd: expressed, commemorated;
driven out

25 **gentle day** i.e. dawn, in which case the
Midnight of 16 is figurative; this phrase
may suggest that the ceremony (and the
monument) are located out of doors.

26 **Phoebus** the Roman sun-god, who drives a
chariot pulled by the horses of the sun

29 **each . . . way** let each man go his own way

17–18] *F3; one line Q* 21] *Heauenly, heauenly F* 22 SP] *Q (Lo.); Claudio / Rowe* 22–3] *Pope; one line Q* 23 rite] *Pope; right Q* 24, 30 SP] *Rowe; Prince Q*

DON PEDRO

Come, let us hence and put on other weeds, 30
And then to Leonato's we will go.

CLAUDIO

And Hymen now with luckier issue speed's
Than this for whom we rendered up this woe. *Exeunt.*

[**5.4**] *Enter* LEONATO, BENEDICK, MARGARET,
URSULA, ANTONIO, FRIAR [Francis],
HERO [*and* BEATRICE].

FRIAR

Did I not tell you she was innocent?

LEONATO

So are the prince and Claudio who accused her,
Upon the error that you heard debated.
But Margaret was in some fault for this,
Although against her will, as it appears 5
In the true course of all the question.

ANTONIO

Well, I am glad that all things sorts so well.

30 **other weeds** more festive garments (a suggestion for costuming in this scene and in 5.4)
32 **Hymen** Roman god of marriage
issue outcome; result
speed's speed us, i.e. favour us. The distinction between the verb 'speeds' (i.e. comes quickly) and the contraction is generally lost in performance.
5.4 The location is Leonato's house.
0.3 Beatrice is absent from the SDs in Q, which may indicate the need for time for a change of costume from 5.2; on the other hand, Leonato refers to *gentlewomen all* at

10, in giving the women their instructions to return veiled. If Beatrice is absent until an entry at 51, a production could generate further speculation about her whereabouts and intentions towards Benedick.
3 **Upon** because of (Abbott, 191)
4 **some fault** presumably the fault of borrowing her mistress's clothing, if we are to take Borachio at his word at 5.1.291 that she 'knew not what she did when she spoke to me'
5 **against her will** unintentionally
6 **question** investigation (three syllables)
7 **sorts** turn out; see 5.1.45n.

32 speed's] *Theobald (Thirlby);* speeds *Q* **5.4**] *Capell (SCENE IV)* 0.2 ANTONIO] *Rowe; old man Q; Leonato's Brother / Folg²* Francis] *Rowe* 0.3 *and* BEATRICE] *Rowe* 5 will, as] *Capell;* will as *Q* 7, 17 SP] *Rowe; Old Q; Leonato's Brother / Folg²* 7 sorts] sort *F*

BENEDICK

    And so am I, being else by faith enforced

    To call young Claudio to a reckoning for it.

LEONATO

    Well, daughter, and you gentlewomen all,   10

    Withdraw into a chamber by yourselves,

    And when I send for you, come hither masked.

    The prince and Claudio promised by this hour

    To visit me. You know your office, brother:

    You must be father to your brother's daughter   15

    And give her to young Claudio.   *Exeunt Ladies.*

ANTONIO

    Which I will do with confirmed countenance.

BENEDICK

    Friar, I must entreat your pains, I think.

FRIAR

    To do what, signor?

BENEDICK

    To bind me, or undo me, one of them.   20

    Signor Leonato – truth it is, good signor,

    Your niece regards me with an eye of favour.

LEONATO

    That eye my daughter lent her? 'Tis most true.

---

8   **by faith** by a promise

9   **young** As at 16, there is a renewed emphasis on Claudio's youth.
     reckoning i.e. duel

17 **confirmed countenance** a straight face; due propriety

18 **entreat your pains ask** for your assistance

20 **bind . . . me** i.e. tie me up (in the knot of marriage) or finish me off (by marrying me

to a wife); cf. 3.1.114: 'bind our loves up in a holy band'.

22 **eye of favour** a favourable regard; as elsewhere, the sense is that different kinds of vision render their objects differently. Cf. 4.1.106–7: 'on my eyelids shall conjecture hang / To turn all beauty into thoughts of harm'.

23 **That . . . her** i.e. my daughter helped her to see Benedick in a favourable light

16 SD] *after 12 Cam*   19, 21 signor] *(Signior)*   23 her?] *this edn (RP); her, Q*

BENEDICK

And I do with an eye of love requite her.

LEONATO

The sight whereof I think you had from me,　　　25
From Claudio and the prince. But what's your will?

BENEDICK

Your answer, sir, is enigmatical.
But for my will, my will is your good will
May stand with ours this day to be conjoined
In the estate of honourable marriage;　　　30
In which, good Friar, I shall desire your help.

LEONATO

My heart is with your liking.

FRIAR　　　　　　　　　　　　And my help.
Here comes the prince and Claudio.

Enter DON PEDRO *and* CLAUDIO, *with Attendants*.

DON PEDRO

Good morrow to this fair assembly.

LEONATO

Good morrow, Prince, good morrow, Claudio.　　　35
We here attend you. Are you yet determined

24　**eye of love** an eye which sees with love; see also 22 and n.

28　**is your** is that your

29　**stand** join

33　This line is missing from F (sig. L1ʳ), due to a casting-off error. Other space-saving stratagems on this final page include the absence of space around entry directions; the abbreviation of names in SDs; the alteration of Q's '*two or three other*' (33.1) to '*with attendants*'; the shortening of SPs to avoid turnovers in verse lines (52, 55); the setting of verse as prose (75–6); the omission of *that* in 80 and 81 and *such* at 82 in order to avoid turnovers in verse lines; the treatment of an entry direction as if it were an exit (122.1); the use of tildes and abbreviations in tightly set lines (110–13); and the setting of '*FINIS*' in the direction line, usually reserved for the signature and / or catchword. F's cumulative saving is of 17 lines.

33.1　*Attendants* possibly including the Lord of 5.3

34　**assembly** four syllables

36　**yet** still

30　estate] *Johnson;* state *Q*　　33] *om F*　　33.1 DON PEDRO] *Rowe; Prince Q*　　with Attendants] *F; and two or three other Q*　　34 SP] *Rowe; Prince Q*

349

Today to marry with my brother's daughter?

CLAUDIO

I'll hold my mind were she an Ethiope.

LEONATO

Call her forth, brother. Here's the friar ready.   [*Exit Antonio.*]

DON PEDRO

Good morrow, Benedick. Why, what's the matter   40
That you have such a February face,
So full of frost, of storm and cloudiness?

CLAUDIO

I think he thinks upon the savage bull.
Tush, fear not, man: we'll tip thy horns with gold,
And all Europa shall rejoice at thee,   45
As once Europa did at lusty Jove
When he would play the noble beast in love.

BENEDICK

Bull Jove, sir, had an amiable low,
And some such strange bull leaped your father's cow

---

38 **Ethiope** i.e. an Ethiopian, foreign in both nation and race; therefore unattractive. The *OED* (Ethiop) lists a possible derivation from the Greek for 'to burn' + 'face' = burnt-face, 'later sunburnt'. Cf. 2.1.292–3: 'Thus goes everyone to the world but I, and I am sunburnt.'

41 **February face** wintry (forbidding) aspect; Benedick is either still angry with Claudio or unusually serious-looking.

44 **tip** gild; cf. 121–2.

45 **Europa** Europe the continent, but in the next line Europa is a Phoenician princess whose beauty inspired Jove to transform himself into an alluring bull in order to capture her and carry her across the sea to Crete (Ovid, *Met.*, 2.833–75). Claudio's jest attempts to mock the prospect of being horned (or cuckolded) by promising that

Benedick, like the golden calf, will become the glorious idol of a sacrilegious and widespread cult.

49 **leaped** mounted sexually; Benedick answers Claudio's jest by calling him, albeit politely, a bastard, and son of an unfaithful mother. The tone of these jests (as always) depends on their delivery in performance; the men could be portrayed as happily returning to their banter as if nothing untoward had happened, or using word-play to continue the aggression of 5.1. In either case, the recent events have done nothing to deflect the terms of their taunting away from jokes about marital infidelity, which fly thick and fast through to the end of this scene. These lines are often cut in productions eager to end on a more seemly note.

---

39 SD] *Theobald*   40 SP] *Rowe (Pedro); P. Q*   Benedick.] *(Bened.)*

And got a calf in that same noble feat   50
Much like to you, for you have just his bleat.

Enter ANTONIO, HERO, BEATRICE, MARGARET
[and] URSULA*[, the women masked]*.

CLAUDIO

For this I owe you. Here comes other reckonings.
Which is the lady I must seize upon?
[Antonio leads Hero forward.]

LEONATO

This same is she, and I do give you her.

CLAUDIO

Why then she's mine. *[to Hero]* Sweet, let me see your
face.   55

LEONATO

No, that you shall not till you take her hand
Before this friar and swear to marry her.

CLAUDIO

Give me your hand before this holy friar.

---

50 **calf** with play on 'fool'; see 5.1.151–4n.

51.2 Leonato's directive to the women at 10–12 ('you gentlewomen all, / Withdraw into a chamber by yourselves, / And when I send for you, come hither masked') suggests that all four women mask, as is often the case in production, although Theobald's SD (see t.n.) leaves open the possibility that only Hero and Beatrice do so (which could render Benedick's question at 72, *Which is Beatrice?*, especially droll). If all four mask, a director must decide when and if Margaret and Ursula unmask; likely moments include when Beatrice does, or at 78, when they are referred to by Beatrice.

52 **reckonings** accountings (for his debts); the plural refers to the number of veiled figures.

53 **seize** **upon** take possession of SD *This edition's SD preserves both the content of Leonato's directive to Antonio at 15–16 ('You must be father to your brother's daughter / And give her to young Claudio') and Q's SP at 54. Most editions substitute Antonio for Leonato in the latter SP (and also at 56), but retaining the original text's assignments provides for a Leonato who jumps in to direct matters despite his earlier directive, an action in keeping with his stage-managing presence at the original wedding.

---

50 And] A F   51.1 ANTONIO] *Theobald; brother* Q   51.2 *the women masked*] *this edn; the ladies masked / Theobald*   52 reckonings] *(recknings)*   53 SD] *this edn*   54 SP] *Antonio / Theobald*   55 SD] *Oxf¹*

I am your husband, if you like of me.
HERO [*Unmasks.*]
    And when I lived I was your other wife;   60
    And when you loved, you were my other husband.
CLAUDIO
    Another Hero!
HERO   Nothing certainer.
    One Hero died defiled, but I do live,
    And surely as I live, I am a maid.
DON PEDRO
    The former Hero! Hero that is dead!   65
LEONATO
    She died, my lord, but whiles her slander lived.
FRIAR
    All this amazement can I qualify,
    When after that the holy rites are ended,
    I'll tell you largely of fair Hero's death.
    Meantime, let wonder seem familiar,   70
    And to the chapel let us presently.
BENEDICK
    Soft and fair, Friar. [*to Antonio*] Which is Beatrice?

59 Claudio does here offer his unknown bride the right of refusal.
   like of For 'of' following 'like' see Abbott, 177.
63 **defiled** slandered
67 **qualify** mitigate, render more intelligible
67–9 Q's punctuation (retained here) leaves a choice as to whether 68 modifies the line before it or the succeeding one (i.e. 'after the rites I will explain all this amazement' or 'after the rites I'll tell you all about Hero's death').
69 **largely** in full
70 **let . . . familiar** treat these surprises as if they were natural matters

71 **presently** immediately
72 **Soft and fair** wait a moment, not so fast (*OED* soft *adv.* I 8a); the command suggests some herding or exiting stage action prompted by the Friar's previous lines.
   ***fair, Friar** See 72 SDn. on the significance of the added comma. *Friar* here is bisyllabic.
72 SD *The question is not necessarily directed to Antonio; the actor playing Benedick has a wide range of options, including addressing Leonato, Hero, the ladies in general, the lady he can already identify (by some other token) as Beatrice – anyone, in fact, except

60 SD] *Rowe*   65 SP] *Rowe (Pedro); Prince Q*   72 fair, Friar.] faire Frier, *Q*   SD] *this edn (RP)*

BEATRICE [*Unmasks.*]

    I answer to that name. What is your will?

BENEDICK

    Do not you love me?

BEATRICE   Why no, no more than reason.

BENEDICK

    Why then your uncle and the prince and Claudio   75

    Have been deceived – they swore you did.

BEATRICE

    Do not you love me?

BENEDICK   Troth no, no more than reason.

BEATRICE

    Why then my cousin, Margaret and Ursula

    Are much deceived, for they did swear you did.

BENEDICK

    They swore that you were almost sick for me.   80

BEATRICE

    They swore that you were well-nigh dead for me.

BENEDICK

    'Tis no such matter. Then you do not love me?

BEATRICE

    No truly, but in friendly recompense.

LEONATO

    Come, cousin, I am sure you love the gentleman.

---

the Friar, Don Pedro or Claudio. His purpose is to add his own wedding to that of Claudio, so he must first delay the general move towards the chapel, and then identify Beatrice. Q's punctuation ('Soft and faire Frier, which . . .') could suggest that Benedick addresses the question to the Friar; however, since it is Antonio, not the Friar, who has brought the masked ladies on stage, and who knows which is Hero, presumably he is best equipped to identify them.

75–6 F lines these as prose, which keeps Benedick and Beatrice prose speakers.

83 **but . . . recompense** but only reciprocally as a friend (which you have proved yourself by challenging Claudio)

73 SD] *Capell*   75–6] *prose F*   80, 81 that] *om. F*   81 well-nigh] *(welnigh). F* *(wel-nye)*   82 such] *om. F*   me?] *F;* me. *Q*

353

CLAUDIO

> And I'll be sworn upon't that he loves her,   85
> For here's a paper written in his hand,
> A halting sonnet of his own pure brain
> Fashioned to Beatrice.

HERO   And here's another,

> Writ in my cousin's hand, stolen from her pocket,
> Containing her affection unto Benedick.   90

BENEDICK   A miracle! Here's our own hands against our
hearts. Come, I will have thee, but by this light I take
thee for pity.

BEATRICE   I would not deny you, but by this good day I
yield upon great persuasion – and partly to save your   95
life, for I was told you were in a consumption.

LEONATO   Peace! [*to Beatrice*] I will stop your mouth.
[*Hands her to Benedick.*]

87   **halting** irregular in rhythm
  his ... brain his original composition
88–92 Many productions stage Benedick and
  Beatrice attempting to snatch these papers
  from Claudio's and Hero's hands; either in
  order to retrieve their own from view, or to
  secure that of the other. In the latter case,
  they often pause to read the poems.
91   **against** writing contrary to; pressed against
  (as if to swear by them)
92   **by this light** a familiar oath, i.e. by the
  morning sun (which, like the dancing star
  under which Beatrice was born, or the
  daylight by which she can see a church,
  draws a contrast with the night time in
  which much of the play's action has taken
  place)
97   SP Q's assignment of this speech to
  Leonato (rather than to Benedick, as in
  most editions after Theobald) is in keeping
  with his characteristic attempts to stage-
  manage this scene, and his role as

Beatrice's guardian; it also provides for a
more egalitarian accommodation between
the lovers than would Benedick's own
declaration of intent to silence Beatrice, an
egalitarianism which seems in keeping
with the tenor of their relationship
throughout. (*Peace* could in fact be
delivered to both of them.) As a directive
delivered by a third party to a couple, it has
the precedent of Beatrice's command to
Hero at 2.1.285–6, to 'Speak, cousin, or, if
you cannot, stop his mouth with a kisses
and let not him speak neither.' Leonato's
statement (and accompanying gesture
indicated in this edition's SD2) need not
imply that Benedick kisses Beatrice
(though most editions signal as such), but
merely that in handing Beatrice over to
Benedick (as Leonato is entitled to do,
being both her uncle and guardian) he will
silence her merely by getting her a
husband.

94 not] yet *Theobald*   97 SP] *Benedick / Theobald*   SD1] *this edn*   SD2] *this edn; kissing her / Theobald*

DON PEDRO

How dost thou, Benedick, the married man?

BENEDICK   I'll tell thee what, Prince; a college of wit-
crackers cannot flout me out of my humour. Dost thou   100
think I care for a satire or an epigram? No, if a man will
be beaten with brains, 'a shall wear nothing handsome
about him. In brief, since I do purpose to marry, I will
think nothing to any purpose that the world can say
against it; and therefore never flout at me for what I   105
have said against it. For man is a giddy thing, and this
is my conclusion. For thy part, Claudio, I did think
to have beaten thee, but in that thou art like to be my
kinsman, live unbruised and love my cousin.

CLAUDIO   I had well hoped thou wouldst have denied   110
Beatrice, that I might have cudgelled thee out of thy
single life, to make thee a double-dealer – which out
of question thou wilt be, if my cousin do not look
exceeding narrowly to thee.

BENEDICK   Come, come, we are friends. Let's have a   115
dance ere we are married, that we may lighten our own
hearts and our wives' heels.

LEONATO   We'll have dancing afterward.

BENEDICK   First, of my word! Therefore play, music!
Prince, thou art sad – get thee a wife, get thee a wife!   120

99–100 **college of wit-crackers** assembly of
jokers
102 **brains** i.e. products of the brain, such as
epigrams and satires
shall . . . handsome must give up all
pretensions to fashionable clothes
106–7 **this . . . conclusion** (1) this is how I've
ended (in marriage); (2) so I conclude
(that man is a giddy thing)
108 **in that** since
112 **double-dealer** married man (i.e. no longer

single); unfaithful husband. The image
also recalls Beatrice's claim that she gave
Benedick a double heart for his single one
at 2.1.256.
114 **narrowly** closely
117 **wives' heels** another innuendo about
female sexual licence, although here in
the legitimate sexuality of marriage;
cf. 3.4.42: 'Ye light o'love with your
heels?'
119 **of** by

98 SP] *Rowe (Pedro); Prince Q*   105 what] *om. F*   112 double-dealer] *(double dealer), Cam* 119 play,]
Pope; plaie Q

There is no staff more reverend than one tipped with
horn.

Enter Messenger.

MESSENGER
My lord, your brother John is ta'en in flight
And brought with armed men back to Messina.
BENEDICK   Think not on him till tomorrow; I'll devise 125
thee brave punishments for him. Strike up, pipers!

Dance. [Exeunt.]

FINIS

121 **staff** walking stick of an elderly person;
sceptre-like sign of rule; wife, who is
meant as a support for her husband
121–2 **tipped with horn** the obvious
cuckolding pun, exacerbated by the fact
that 'tip' is a variant of 'tup', a sheep-
breeder's term for the male animal and its
sexual act, as well as for the act of
furnishing with horns like a ram (*OED* tup
v. 3); as with the other horn jokes, this line
is often cut in productions seeking for a
more decorous finale. Cf. 44n.
124 **armed** armèd
126 **brave** worthy, excellent (*OED adj.* 3b);
the word carries a certain jaunty aspect.
126 SD *Dance* This is the only play of
Shakespeare's explicitly to end with a dance
for the general company (a clown's jig was
the more usual finale, taking place as a
discrete entertainment after the close of the
play). J.R. Mulryne observes that the

harmonies of dance served as a 'symbol of
order . . . every [actor's] movements allied
to his fellows' movements and the whole
governed by music', much akin to the
institution of marriage itself, 'society's
divinely-sanctioned means of controlling
and directing sexual relations' (Mulryne,
24). This ascribes perhaps a more decorous
purpose to dancing than is Benedick's (to
'lighten our . . . wives' heels', 116–17), and,
of course, the type of dance selected by a
production (pavane or tango?), as well as
the extent of its inclusiveness, determines
just what kind and degree of social order is
being represented. In the Elizabethan
theatre, a jig may well have followed this
dance, as Will Kemp (the actor who initially
played Dogberry) was famous for his jigs,
which were short, comic song-and-dance
sketches.

121 reverend] *F;* reuerent *Q*   126 SD *Exeunt.*] *Rowe*

APPENDIX
Casting Chart

This is a chart of a possible casting of this edition's text of the play. There are fifteen adult speaking parts, not counting the Watch (see 3.3.0.2n. for a discussion of the Watch numbers). These can be played by thirteen players, although a further economy could be achieved by having the mute Balthasar of 1.1 play the Messenger in 1.1 (instead of entering, as in the Quarto SD, with the soldiers at 90.1) and 5.4, as well as the Lord of 5.3 (a production relying on this actor's musical skills would be likely to have him present in 5.3 in any case).

The four female roles would have been played by boys in the Elizabethan theatre, one of whom could have also served as the boy who speaks briefly to Benedick at the beginning of 2.3. I have not assigned the parts of the Attendants or Watchmen, on the assumption that these minor roles could have been acted by members of the company; it is plausible that the players of the Watch could also serve as the Attendants.

In the Elizabethan theatre doubling no doubt took place, probably more aggressively when on tour than in London; the factors conditioning the practice would have included whether or not players of bigger parts also played minor parts, whether men played women's parts, and how much time was necessary to change costume. This chart represents only the roles noted in the Quarto, either in entry SDs or in SPs, and included in this edition (i.e. excluding the 'ghost' roles of Leonato's wife Innogen in 1.1 and 2.1 and the 'kinsman' in 2.1); however, a given production might well choose to include non-listed roles in a scene without compromising resources (Margaret, Ursula and Antonio, for instance, might or might not appear in 1.1 or 4.1, or Conrade and Borachio in 1.1, as part of the general throngs).

For an alternative version, see T. King, 193.

Actor	1.1	1.2	1.3	2.1	2.2	2.3	3.1	3.2	3.3
1	Benedick			Benedick		Benedick		Benedick	
2	Leonato	Leonato		Leonato		Leonato		Leonato	
3	Don Pedro			Don Pedro		Don Pedro		Don Pedro	
4	Claudio			Claudio		Claudio		Claudio	
5									Dogberry
6			Borachio	Borachio	Borachio				Borachio
7	Don John		Don John	Don John	Don John			Don John	
8			Conrade						Conrade
9	Balthasar*			Balthasar		Balthasar			
10		Antonio		Antonio					
11									
12									Verges
13	Messenger								
14	Beatrice			Beatrice		Beatrice	Beatrice		
15	Hero			Hero			Hero		
16				Margaret			Margaret		
17				Ursula			Ursula		
misc.						Boy			
misc.									
misc.		Attendants*		Attendants*					Watchmen

Actor	3.4	3.5	4.1	4.2	5.1	5.2	5.3	5.4
1			Benedick		Benedick	Benedick		Benedick
2		Leonato	Leonato		Leonato			Leonato
3			Don Pedro		Don Pedro		Don Pedro	Don Pedro
4			Claudio		Claudio		Claudio	Claudio
5		Dogberry		Dogberry	Dogberry			
6				Borachio	Borachio			
7			Don John					
8				Conrade	Conrade			
9				Sexton	Sexton*		(Balthasar)	
10					Antonio			Antonio
11			Friar					Friar
12		Verges		Verges	Verges			
13		Messenger					Lord	Messenger
14	Beatrice		Beatrice			Beatrice		Beatrice
15	Hero		Hero					Hero
16	Margaret					Margaret		Margaret*
17	Ursula					Ursula		Ursula*
misc.								
misc.				Watchmen	Watchmen*			
misc.							Attendants	Attendants*

* mute
( ) optional

359

ABBREVIATIONS AND REFERENCES

Quotations and references to works by Shakespeare other than *Much Ado About Nothing* are keyed to the most recently published Arden editions: for *1H4, 3H6, Per, R2* and *TGV*, the individual Arden 3 volumes; for all others, *The Arden Shakespeare: Complete Works*, gen. eds Richard Proudfoot, Ann Thompson and David Scott Kastan (revised edn, 2001). Biblical citations are from the Bishops' Bible (*The Holy Bible . . . authorized and appointed to be read in Churches*, 1588) unless otherwise indicated. Place of publication is London unless otherwise indicated.

ABBREVIATIONS

ABBREVIATIONS USED IN NOTES

*	precedes commentary notes involving readings altered from the text on which this edition is based
c	corrected state
n.	(in cross-references) commentary note
n.d.	no date
n.s	new series
SD	stage direction
SP	speech prefix
subst.	substantially
this edn	a reading adopted for the first time in this edition
t.n.	textual note
u	uncorrected state

WORKS BY AND PARTLY BY SHAKESPEARE

AC	*Antony and Cleopatra*
AW	*All's Well That Ends Well*
AYL	*As You Like It*
CE	*The Comedy of Errors*
Cor	*Coriolanus*

Cym	*Cymbeline*
E3	*King Edward III*
Ham	*Hamlet*
1H4	*King Henry IV, Part 1*
2H4	*King Henry IV, Part 2*
H5	*King Henry V*
1H6	*King Henry VI, Part 1*
2H6	*King Henry VI, Part 2*
3H6	*King Henry VI, Part 3*
H8	*King Henry VIII*
JC	*Julius Caesar*
KJ	*King John*
KL	*King Lear*
LC	*A Lover's Complaint*
LLL	*Love's Labour's Lost*
Luc	*The Rape of Lucrece*
MA	*Much Ado About Nothing*
Mac	*Macbeth*
MM	*Measure for Measure*
MND	*A Midsummer Night's Dream*
MV	*The Merchant of Venice*
MW	*The Merry Wives of Windsor*
Oth	*Othello*
Per	*Pericles*
PP	*The Passionate Pilgrim*
PT	*The Phoenix and Turtle*
R2	*King Richard II*
R3	*King Richard III*
RJ	*Romeo and Juliet*
Son	*Sonnets*
STM	*Sir Thomas More*
TC	*Troilus and Cressida*
Tem	*The Tempest*
TGV	*The Two Gentlemen of Verona*
Tim	*Timon of Athens*
Tit	*Titus Andronicus*
TN	*Twelfth Night*
TNK	*The Two Noble Kinsmen*
TS	*The Taming of the Shrew*
VA	*Venus and Adonis*
WT	*The Winter's Tale*

REFERENCES

EDITIONS OF SHAKESPEARE COLLATED
OR REFERRED TO

Alexander	*William Shakespeare: The Complete Works*, ed. Peter Alexander (1951)
Ard[1]	*Much Ado About Nothing*, ed. Grace Trenery, Arden Shakespeare (1924)
Ard[2]	*Much Ado About Nothing*, ed. A.R. Humphreys, Arden Shakespeare (1981)
Bell	*Bell's Edition of Shakespeare's Plays, as they are performed at the Theatres Royal in London*, 9 vols (1773–4)
Bevington	*Works*, ed. David Bevington (Glenview, Ill., 1980)
Bevington[2]	*Much Ado About Nothing*, ed. David Bevington, Bantam Shakespeare (New York, 1988)
Boas	*Much Ado About Nothing*, ed. F.S. Boas (Oxford, 1916)
Brooke	*Much Ado About Nothing*, ed. C.F. Tucker Brooke (New Haven, Conn., 1917)
Cam	*Works*, ed. William George Clark, John Glover and William Aldis Wright, 9 vols (Cambridge, 1863 6)
Cam[1]	*Much Ado About Nothing*, ed. J. Dover Wilson, New Shakespeare (Cambridge, 1923)
Cam[2]	*Much Ado About Nothing*, ed. F.H. Mares, New Cambridge Shakespeare (Cambridge, 1988)
Capell	*Comedies, Histories, and Tragedies*, ed. Edward Capell, 10 vols (1767–8)
Collier	*Works*, ed. J.P. Collier, 8 vols (1842–4)
Collier[2]	*Plays*, ed. J.P. Collier, 8 vols (1853–65)
Collier MS	MS annotations once thought to be by an 'Old Corrector' but probably by J.P. Collier, in his copy (the Perkins–Collier–Devonshire copy) of F2 in the Huntington Library, and entered by Collier in his own copy of the first of his editions, now in the Folger Shakespeare Library
Craig	*Works*, ed. W.J. Craig (Oxford, 1892)
Deighton	*Much Ado About Nothing*, ed. K. Deighton (1888)
Dyce	*Works*, ed. Alexander Dyce, 6 vols (1857)
F	*Comedies, Histories, and Tragedies*, The First Folio (1623)
F2	*Comedies, Histories, and Tragedies*, The Second Folio (1632)

F3	*Comedies, Histories, and Tragedies*, The Third Folio (1663)
F4	*Comedies, Histories, and Tragedies*, The Fourth Folio (1685)
Foakes	*Much Ado About Nothing*, ed. R.A. Foakes, New Penguin Shakespeare (1968)
Folg²	*Much Ado About Nothing*, ed. Barbara A. Mowat and Paul Werstine, New Folger Library Shakespeare (New York, 1995)
Furness	*Much Ado About Nothing*, ed. Horace Howard Furness, New Variorum Edition (1899, repr. New York, 1964)
Furnivall	F.J. Furnivall, *The Leopold Shakespeare* (1877)
Halliwell	*Works*, ed. James O. Halliwell, 16 vols (1853–65)
Hanmer	*Works*, ed. Thomas Hanmer, 6 vols (1743–4)
Hinman	*Much Ado About Nothing*, ed. Charlton Hinman, Shakespeare Quarto Facsimiles no. 15 (Oxford, 1971)
Johnson	*Plays*, ed. Samuel Johnson, 8 vols (1765)
Kittredge	*Works*, ed. George Lyman Kittredge (Boston, 1936)
Knight	*Works*, ed. Charles Knight, 8 vols (1839–42)
Malone	*Plays and Poems*, ed. Edmund Malone, 10 vols (1790)
Newcomer	*Much Ado About Nothing*, ed. A.G. Newcomer (1929)
Oxf	*Works*, ed. Stanley Wells and Gary Taylor, with John Jowett and William Montgomery (Oxford, 1986)
Oxf¹	*Much Ado About Nothing*, ed. Sheldon P. Zitner (Oxford, 1993)
Pope	*Works*, ed. Alexander Pope, 6 vols (1723–5)
Pope²	*Works*, ed. Alexander Pope, 6 vols (1728)
Q	*Much Ado About Nothing*, The Quarto (1600)
Riv	*The Riverside Shakespeare*, ed. G. Blakemore Evans (Boston, 1974)
Rowe	*Works*, ed. Nicholas Rowe, 6 vols (1709)
Rowe²	*Works*, ed. Nicholas Rowe, 2nd edn, 6 vols (1709)
Rowe³	*Works*, ed. Nicholas Rowe, 3rd edn, 8 vols (1714)
Smith	*Much Ado About Nothing*, ed. J.C. Smith (Boston, 1902)
Staunton	*Plays*, ed. Howard Staunton, 3 vols (1858–60)
Steevens	*Plays*, ed. Samuel Johnson and George Steevens, 2nd edn, 10 vols (1778)
Steevens–Reed	*Plays*, ed. Samuel Johnson, George Steevens and Isaac Reed, 3rd edn, 10 vols (1785)
Steevens–Reed²	*Plays*, with notes by Samuel Johnson and George Steevens, ed. Isaac Reed, 4th edn, 10 vols (1793)

Stevenson	*Much Ado About Nothing*, ed. David L. Stevenson, Signet Classic Shakespeare (New York, 1964)
Theobald	*Works*, ed. Lewis Theobald, 7 vols (1733)
Warburton	*Works*, ed. William Warburton, 8 vols (1747)
Waters-Bennett	*Much Ado About Nothing*, ed. Josephine Waters Bennett, in *The Complete Works*, gen. ed. A. Harbage, revised Complete Pelican Shakespeare (Baltimore, 1969)
White	*Works*, ed. R.G. White, 12 vols (Boston, 1857–66)
White[2]	*Works*, ed. R.G. White, 2nd edn, 6 vols (Boston, 1883)
Wilson, J.D.	See Cam[2]
Wright	*Works*, ed. William Aldis Wright and George Clark (1924)

OTHER WORKS CITED

Abbott	E.A. Abbott, *A Shakespearian Grammar*, 3rd edn (1870)
Acts	*Acts of the Privy Council, A.D. 1599–1600*, n.s., 30, 1905
Aeneid	Virgil, *The Aeneid*, trans. Robert Fitzgerald (New York, 1983)
Albertus	Albertus Magnus, *De Animalibus*, in *On Animals: A Medieval Summa Zoologica*, trans. and annotated by Kenneth F. Kitchell Jr and Irven Michael Resnick (Baltimore, 1999)
Allen	John A. Allen, 'Dogberry', *SQ*, 24 (1972), 90–112
Altick	Richard D. Altick, *Paintings from Books: Art and Literature in Britain 1760–1900* (Columbus, Ohio, 1985)
Altman	Joel Altman, *The Tudor Play of Mind: Rhetorical Inquiry and the Development of Elizabethan Drama* (Berkeley, Calif., 1978)
Anger	Jane Anger, *Her Protection for Women* (1589)
Arber	*A Transcript of the Registers of the Company of Stationers of London, 1554–1640 AD*, ed. Edward Arber, 5 vols (1876)
Aubrey	John Aubrey, *Brief Lives*, ed. O.L. Dick (London, 1949)
Auden	W.H. Auden, *Lectures on Shakespeare*, ed. Arthur Kirsch (Princeton, NJ, 2000)
Bacon	Francis Bacon, 'Of Envy', in *The Essays and Counsels Civil and Moral of Francis Bacon Lord Verulam*, ed. Oliphant Smeaton (1906)

Baker	David Baker, 'Surprise with all': rereading character in *Much Ado About Nothing*', in David Galef (ed.), *Second Thoughts: A Focus on Rereading* (Detroit, 1980), 228–45
Baldwin	Thomas Whitfield Baldwin, '*Loves Labor's Won*': *New Evidence from the Account Books of an Elizabethan Bookseller* (Carbondale, Ill., 1957)
Bandello	Matteo Bandello, *La Prima Parte de le Novelle* (1554), novella 22
Barber	C.L. Barber, *Shakespeare's Festive Comedy: A Study of Dramatic Form and Its Relation to Social Custom* (Princeton, NJ, 1959)
Barish	Jonas Barish, 'Pattern and purpose in the prose of *Much Ado About Nothing*', Rice University Studies, 60 (1974), 19–30
Bate, 'Dying'	Jonathan Bate, 'Dying to live in *Much Ado About Nothing*', in Yasunari Takada (ed.), *Surprised by Scenes: Essays in Honour of Professor Yasunari Takahashi* (Tokyo, 1994), 69–85
Bate & Jackson	Jonathan Bate and Russell Jackson, *Shakespeare: An Illustrated Stage History* (Oxford, 1996)
Bateman	Stephen Bateman, *Batman upon Bartholomew* (1582)
BCP	*The Book of Common Prayer* (1559), ed. John E. Booty (Washington, DC, 1976)
Beaumont & Fletcher	Francis Beaumont and John Fletcher, *Comedies and Tragedies* (1647)
Becon	T. Becon, *Principles of Christian Religion* (1552)
Belleforest	François de Belleforest, *Histoires Tragiques* (1569)
Berger	Harry Berger Jr, 'Against the sink-a-pace: sexual and family politics in *Much Ado About Nothing*', *SQ*, 33 (1982), 302–13
Berry	Ralph Berry, 'Problems of knowing', in *Shakespeare's Comedies: Explorations in Form* (Princeton, NJ, 1972), 154–74
Bert	Edmund Bert, *Treatise of Hawks and Hunting* (1619)
Blayney	Peter W.M. Blayney, 'The publication of playbooks', in John D. Cox and David Scott Kastan (eds), *A New History of Early English Drama* (New York, 1997), 383–422
Blazon	Benedetto Varchi, *The Blazon of Jealousy*, trans. R.T. (1615)
Breton, *Cornucopiae*	Nicholas Breton, *Cornucopiae, Pasquil's Night-Cap, or Anti-dote for the Headache* (1612)

Breton, *Praise*   Nicholas Breton, *Praise of Virtuous Ladies* (1606)
Brewer   *Brewer's Dictionary of Phrase and Fable*, 15th edn, revised Adrian Broom (1996)
Bright   Timothy Bright, *A Treatise of Melancholie* (1586)
Brissenden   Alan Brissenden, *Shakespeare and the Dance* (1981)
Bronfen   Elizabeth Bronfen, 'The day after battle: *Much Ado About Nothing* and the continuation of war by other means' *Poetica: Zeitschrift fur Sprach-und Literaturwissenschaft*, 43, no. 1–2 (2011), 63–80
Bruster   Douglas Bruster, 'The horn of plenty: cuckoldry and capital in the drama of the age of Shakespeare', *SEL*, 30 (1990), 197–215
Bullinger   Heinrich Bullinger, *Christian State of Matrimony* (1541)
Bullough   Geoffrey Bullough, *Narrative and Dramatic Sources of Shakespeare*, 8 vols (New York, 1957–75), vol. 2
Buoni   Thomas Buoni, *Problems of Beauty and All Human Affections* (1606)
Burton   Robert Burton, *The Anatomy of Melancholy*, ed. Thomas C. Faulkner, Nicholas K. Kiessling and Rhonda L. Blair, 8 vols (Oxford, 1989)
Campbell   Thomas Campbell, *Dramatic Works of Shakespeare* (1838)
Capell, *Notes*   Edward Capell, *Notes and Various Readings to Shakespeare*, 3 vols (1779)
Cartari   Vincenzo Cartari, *The Fountain of Ancient Fiction* (1599)
Castiglione   Baldasarre Castiglione, *Il libro del cortegiano* (*The Courtier*), trans. George Bull (Harmondsworth, England, 1967)
Cavell   Stanley Cavell, *Pursuits of Happiness: The Hollywood Comedy of Remarriage* (Cambridge, MA, 1984)
Cerasano   S.P. Cerasano, 'Half a dozen dangerous words', in *Gloriana's Face, Women, Public and Private, in the English Renaissance* (Detroit, 1992), 167–83
Cercignani   Fausto Cercignani, *Shakespeare's Works and Elizabethan Pronunciation* (Oxford, 1981)
Chambers   E.K. Chambers, *William Shakespeare: A Study of Facts and Problems*, 2 vols (1930)
Chaucer   *The Riverside Chaucer*, ed. Larry D. Benson, 3rd edn (Oxford, 1987)
Cheney   Patrick Cheney, *Shakespeare's Literary Authorship* (Cambridge, 2008)

Child	F.J. Child (ed.), *English and Scottish Ballads*, 8 vols (1860)
Clegg	Cyndia Clegg, 'Truth, lies and the law of slander in *Much Ado About Nothing*,' in Constance Jordan and Karen Cunningham (eds), *The Law in Shakespeare*, (Basingstoke, 2007), 167–88
Cogan	Thomas Cogan, *Haven of Health* (1574)
Coleridge	Hartley Coleridge, *Essays and Marginalia*, 2 vols (1851)
Collington, *Pennyworth*	Philip Collington, 'A "pennyworth" of marital advice: bachelors and ballad culture in *Much Ado About Nothing*,' in Karen Bamford (ed.), *Shakespeare's Comedies of Love: Essays in Honor of Alexander Leggatt*, (Toronto, 2008), 30–54
Collington, *Stuffed*	Philip Collington, '"Stuffed with all honourable virtues": *Much Ado About Nothing* and the Book of the Courtier,' *Studies in Philology*, 103, no.3 (2006), 281–312
Cook, C.	Carol Cook, 'The sign and semblance of her honor: reading gender difference in *Much Ado About Nothing'*, *PMLA*, 101 (1988), 186–202
Cook, D.	David Cook, 'The very temple of delight: the twin plots of *Much Ado About Nothing*', in Antony Coleman and Antony Hammond (eds), *Poetry and Drama 1570–1700: Essays in Honour of Harold F. Brooks* (1981), 32–46
Coryat	Thomas Coryat, *Coryat's Crudities* (1611)
Cotgrave	Randle Cotgrave, *A Dictionary of the French and English Tongues* (1611)
Coverdale	*Biblia, the Bible, That Is, the Holy Scripture . . . tr. out of Douce and Latyn into English* [by M. Coverdale] (1535)
Cox, *Shakespeare*	John D. Cox, *Shakespeare in Production: Much Ado About Nothing* (Cambridge, 1997)
Cox, 'Stage'	John D. Cox, 'The stage representation of the "Kill Claudio" sequence in *Much Ado About Nothing*', *SS* 32 (1979), 27–36
Craik	T.W. Craik, 'Much Ado About Nothing', *Scrutiny*, 19 (1953), 297–316
Crane, M.	Milton Crane, *Shakespeare's Prose* (Chicago, 1951)
Crane, W.	William G. Crane, *Wit and Rhetoric in the Renaissance* (Gloucester, Mass., 1937, reprinted 1964)

Craven, *Simmes*	'Simmes' Compositor A and Five Shakespeare Quartos', *Studies in Bibliography*, 26 (1973), 37–60
Craven, *Reliability*	'The Reliability of Simmes' Compositor A', *Studies in Bibliography*, 32 (1979), 186–97
Croll	Morris W. Croll, *Attic and Baroque Prose Style: The Anti-Ciceronian Movement* (Princeton, NJ, 1966)
Davies	Thomas Davies, *Memoirs of the Life of David Garrick*, 2 vols (1780), vol. 1
Davis	Walter Davis, Introduction to *Twentieth Century Interpretations of 'Much Ado About Nothing'* (Englewood Cliffs, NJ, 1969)
Dawson	Anthony Dawson, 'Much ado about signifying', *SEL*, 22 (1982), 211–21
Dekker, *Hornbook*	Thomas Dekker, *Gull's Hornbook* (1609)
Dekker, *Sins*	Thomas Dekker, *Seven Deadly Sins of London*, in *The Non-Dramatic Works of Thomas Dekker*, ed. Rev. Alexander B. Grosart, 5 vols (1884–6), vol. 2
Dekker, *Works*	Thomas Dekker, *The Dramatic Works of Thomas Dekker*, ed. Fredson Bowers, 4 vols (Cambridge, 1953–61)
De Mornay	Philip de Mornay, *Work Concerning the Trueness of Christian Religion . . .*, trans. Arthur Golding (1617)
Dent	R.W. Dent, *Shakespeare's Proverbial Language: An Index* (Berkeley, Los Angeles and London, 1981)
Dobranski	Stephen P. Dobranski, 'Children of the mind: miscarried narratives in *Much Ado About Nothing*', *SEL*, 38 (1998), 233–50
Dobson	Michael Dobson, 'Improving on the original: actresses and adaptations', in Bate & Jackson, 45–68
Donne, 'Indifferent'	John Donne, 'The Indifferent', in *Selected Poetry*, ed. John Carey (Oxford, 1996)
Donne, *Problems*	John Donne, *Certain Problems* (1623)
Doring	Tobias Doring, *Performances of Mourning in Shakespearean Theater and Early Modern Culture* (2006)
Drakakis	John Drakakis, 'Trust and transgression: the discursive practices of *Much Ado About Nothing*', in Richard Machin and Christopher Norris (eds), *Post-Structuralist Readings of English Poetry* (Cambridge, 1987)
Draper	John Draper, *Stratford to Dogberry: Studies in Shakespeare's Earlier Plays* (Pittsburgh, 1961)
Duffin	Ross W. Duffin, *Shakespeare's Songbook* (New York, 2004)

Dyce, *Notes*	Alexander Dyce, *A Few Notes on Shakespeare* (1853)
EC	*Essays in Criticism*
Erasmus	Desiderius Erasmus, *De Civilitate Morum Puerilium*, ed. J.K. Sowards, in *Works*, gen. ed. R.J. Schoek, 84 vols (Toronto, 1974–2003), vol. 23
Erne	Lukas Erne, *Shakespeare as Literary Dramatist* (Cambridge, 2003)
Evans, B.	Bertrand Evans, *Shakespeare's Comedies* (Oxford, 1960)
Evans, H.	Hugh C. Evans, 'Comic constables: fictional and historical', *SQ*, 20 (1969), 422–33
Evans, J.	John X. Evans, 'The villainy of one deformed: the complex word fashion in *Much Ado About Nothing*', in John H. Dorencamp (ed.), *Literary Studies: Essays in Memory of Francis A. Drumm* (Wetteren, Belgium, 1973), 91–114
Everett, 'Much Ado'	Barbara Everett, 'Much Ado About Nothing', *Critical Quarterly*, 3 (1961), 319–35
Everett, 'Unsociable'	Barbara Everett, '*Much Ado About Nothing*: the unsociable comedy', in Michael Cordner, Peter Holland and John Kerrigan (eds), *English Comedy* (Cambridge, 1994), 68–84
Faucit	Helena Faucit, *On Some of Shakespeare's Female Characters* (Edinburgh, 1891)
Fedele	Luigi Pasqualigo, *Il Fedele* (1576), trans. Anthony Munday as *Fedele and Fortunio, the Two Italian Gentlemen* (1585)
Fergusson	Francis Fergusson, '*The Comedy of Errors* and *Much Ado About Nothing*', *Sewanee Review*, 61 (1954), 24–37
Ferrand	Jacques Ferrand, *Erotomania* (1640)
Findlay	Alison Findlay (ed.), *Much Ado About Nothing: A Guide to the Text and the Play in Performance* (2011)
Fleck	Andrew Fleck, 'The ambivalent blush: figural and structural metonymy, modesty and *Much Ado About Nothing*,' *ANQ*, 19 no. 1(2006), 16–23
Forshall and Madden	*The Holy Bible Containing the Old and New Testaments, with Apocryphal Books, in the Earliest English Versions Made from the Latin Vulgate by John Wycliffe and his Follwers*, ed. Josiah Forshall and Frederic Madden (Oxford, 1850)
FQ	Edmund Spenser, *The Faerie Queene* (1590/1596)

Freedman	Penelope Freedman, *Power and Passion in Shakespeare's Pronouns* (Aldershot, 2007)
Friedman, 'Hush'd'	Michael Friedman, 'Hush'd on purpose to grace harmony: wives and silence in *Much Ado About Nothing*', *Theater Journal*, vol. 42, no. 3 (1990), 350–63
Friedman, 'Man'	Michael Friedman, ' "For Man is a giddy thing, and this is my conclusion": fashion and *Much Ado About Nothing*', *Text and Performance Quarterly*, vol. 13, no. 3 (1993), 267–82
Frye	Northrop Frye, *A Natural Perspective: The Development of Shakespearean Comedy and Romance* (New York, 1967)
Gardener's	*The Gardener's Labyrinth* (1594)
Gargantua	François Rabelais, *Gargantua and Pantagruel*, trans. Thomas Urquhart and Peter Le Motteux, 3 vols (1934)
Garrick	*Much Ado About Nothing . . . as it is Acted at the Theatres Royal in Drury Lane and Covent Garden* (1778)
Geneva Bible	*The Bible and Holy Scriptures Contained in the Old and New Testaments* (1560, 1599)
Gerard	John Gerard, *The Herbal, or General History of Plants* (1597)
Gibson	Anthony Gibson, *A Woman's Worth, defended against all the men in the world* (1599)
Gielgud	John Gielgud, *An Actor and His Time* (New York, 1997)
Gildon	Charles Gildon, 'Remarks', in Rowe (additional vol. 7), 304
Girard	René Girard, 'Love by hearsay: mimetic strategies in *Much Ado About Nothing*', in *A Theater of Envy* (Oxford, 1991), 80–91
Gittings	Clare Gittings, *Death, Burial and the Individual in Early Modern England* (1984)
Gollancz	Israel Gollancz, Introduction to *Much Ado About Nothing*, in *The Works of William Shakespeare*, 5 vols (New York, 1909), vol. 5
Goosecappe	*Sir Gyles Goosecappe*, in A.H. Bullen (ed.), *A Collection of Old English Plays*, 4 vols (1882–5), vol. 3
Greenblatt	Stephen Greenblatt, Introduction to *Much Ado About Nothing*, Norton Shakespeare (New York, 1997)

Greene, *Courtier*	Robert Greene, *A Quip for an Upstart Courtier*, in *The Life and Complete Works in Verse and Prose of Robert Greene*, ed. Rev. Alexander B. Grosart, 15 vols (1881–6), vol. 11
Greene, *Mirror*	Robert Greene, *Mirror of Modesty*, in John Payne Collier (ed.), *Illustrations of English Literature*, 3 vols (1866), vol. 3
Greg	W.W. Greg, *A Bibliography of English Printed Drama to the Restoration*, 2 vols (1962)
Gurr	Andrew Gurr, *The Shakespearean Stage, 1574–1642* (Cambridge, 1982)
Harbage	Alfred Harbage, *As They Liked It* (1947)
Hayne	Victoria Hayne, 'Measuring *Much Ado*: Davenant's *Law Against Lovers*', paper presented to the conference 'Much Ado About Nothing: A Play in History', University of California at Los Angeles, 1998
Hazlitt	William Hazlitt, *Characters of Shakespeare's Plays* (1817)
Hemming	Sarah Hemming, review of Doran production, *Financial Times*, 8 August 2002
Henslowe	*Henslowe's Diary*, ed. R.A. Foakes and R.T. Rickert (Cambridge, 1961)
Henze	Richard Henze, 'Deception in *Much Ado About Nothing*', *SEL*, 11 (1971), 187–201
Heywood, *Maid*	Thomas Heywood, *Fair Maid of the Exchange*, ed. Karl E. Snyder (New York, 1980)
Heywood, *Man*	Thomas Heywood, *How a Man May Choose a Good Wife from a Bad* (1602)
Heywood, *Proverbs*	John Heywood, *A Dialogue . . . of All the Proverbs in the English Tongue . . .* (1546)
Hogan	Charles Beecher Hogan, *Shakespeare in the Theatre, 1701–1800: A Record of Performances in London*, 2 vols (Oxford, 1952–7)
Holland	Peter Holland, *English Shakespeares* (Cambridge, 1997)
Homilies	*The First Book of Homilies* (1547), ed. John Griffiths (Oxford, 1859)
Howard	Jean E. Howard, 'Renaissance anti-theatricality and the politics of gender and rank in *Much Ado About Nothing*', in Jean E. Howard and Marion F. O'Connor, *Shakespeare Reproduced: The Text in History and Ideology* (1987), 163–87

Hunt	Maurice Hunt, 'The reclamation of language in *Much Ado About Nothing*', *SP*, 97 (2000), 165–91
Iliad	Homer, *The Iliad*, trans. Robert Fagles (New York, 1990)
Jameson	Mrs Jameson, *Characteristics of Women*, 2nd edn, 2 vols (1833)
Jenkins	Harold Jenkins, *Structural Problems in Shakespeare: Lectures and Essays by Harold Jenkins*, ed. Ernst Honigmann (2001)
Johnson on Shakespeare	*Samuel Johnson on Shakespeare*, ed. H.R Woudhuysen (1989)
Jonson	*Ben Jonson*, ed. C.H. Herford, P. Simpson and E. Simpson, 11 vols (Oxford, 1925–52)
Jorgensen	P.A. Jorgensen, 'Much Ado About Nothing', in *Redeeming Shakespeare's Words* (1962), 22–42
Kaplan, *Culture*	M. Lindsey Kaplan, *The Culture of Slander in Early Modern England* (Cambridge, 1997)
Kaplan, 'Slander'	M. Lindsey Kaplan, 'Sexual slander and the politics of the erotic in Garter's *Susanna*,' in Ellen Spolsky (ed.), *The Judgement of Susanna: Authority and Witness* (Atlanta, Ga., 1996), 73–85
Kathman, Actors	David Kathman, 'Actors names as textual evidence,' *Theater Notebook*, 63 no. 23 (2009), 70–9
Kathman, Grocers	David Kathman, 'Grocers, goldsmiths, and drapers: freemen and apprentices in the Elizabethan theater', *Shakespeare Quarterly*, LV (2004), 1–49
Kemble	*Much Ado About Nothing . . . revised by J.P. Kemble . . . as it is performed at the Theatres Royal* (1815)
King, T.	T.J. King, *Casting Shakespeare's Plays: London Actors and Their Roles, 1590–1642* (Cambridge, 1992)
King, W.	Walter N. King, 'Much Ado About Something', *SQ*, 15 (1954), 143–55
King James Bible	*The Holy Bible . . . with the former translations diligently compared and revised, by His Majesty's special command* (the Authorized Version) (1611)
Kökeritz	H. Kökeritz, *Shakespeare's Pronunciation* (1953)
Kreiger	Elliot Kreiger, 'Social relations and the social order in *Much Ado About Nothing*', *SS 32* (1979), 49–61
Lambarde	William Lambarde, *Duties of Constables, Borsholders, and Tithing Men* (1583)
Levin, Liturgical	Richard Levin, 'Liturgical quibbles in *As You Like It* and *Much Ado about Nothing*' *N&Q*, 56, no. 1 (2009), 52–3

Levin, *Prenuptial*   Richard Levin, 'Prenuptial bonding in Shakespeare and elsewhere,' *Shakespeare International Yearbook*, 7 (2007), 155–76

Lewalski, 'Love'   Barbara Lewalski, 'Love, appearance, reality: Much Ado About Something', *SEL*, 8 (1968), 235–51

Lewalski, 'Namesake'   Barbara Lewalski, 'Hero's name – and namesake – in *Much Ado About Nothing', English Language Notes*, 7 (1970), 175–9

Lindop   Grevel Lindop, review of Kaut-Howson production, *Times Literary Supplement*, 3 October 1997

Locrine   *The Lamentable Tragedy of Locrine* (1595), ed. Jane Lytton Gooch (New York, 1981)

Lodge   Thomas Lodge, Reply to Stephen Gosson's *School of Abuse* in *Defence of Poetry, Music and Stage Plays*, in *Complete Works of Thomas Lodge*, ed. E. Gosse, 4 vols (1883), vol. 1

Logan   Brian Logan, review of Donnellan production, *Observer*, 14 June 1998

Luther   Martin Luther, *First Lectures on the Psalms II: Psalms 76–126*, trans. Herbert Bouman, in *Luther's Works*, II, ed. Hilton C Oswald (St. Louis, MO, 1976), 40–1

Lyly, *Anatomy*   John Lyly, *Euphues: The Anatomy of Wit*, in Lyly, *Works*, vol. 1

Lyly, *Euphues*   John Lyly, *Euphues and His England*, in Lyly, *Works*, vol. 2

Lyly, *Grammar*   William Lyly, *Short Introduction of Latin Grammar* (1538)

Lyly, *Works*   John Lyly, *The Complete Works of John Lyly*, ed. R. Warwick Bond, 3 vols (Oxford, 1902)

McCollum   William G. McCollum, 'The role of wit in *Much Ado About Nothing*', *SQ* 19 (1968), 165–74

McEachern, 'Blush'   Claire McEachern, 'A whore at the first blush seemeth only a woman: John Bale's *Image of Both Churches* and the terms of religious difference in the early English Reformation', *Journal of Medieval and Renaissance Studies*, vol. 25, no. 2 (1995), 245–69

McEachern 'Cuckolds'   Claire McEachern, 'Why do cuckolds have horns?' *HLQ*, 71 no. 4 (2008), 607–31

McEachern, 'Fathering'   Claire McEachern, 'Fathering herself: a source study of Shakespeare's feminism', *SQ*, 39 (1988), 269–90

Magnusson   Lynne Magnusson, 'The pragmatics of repair in *King Lear* and *Much Ado About Nothing*', in *Shakespeare*

	and Social Dialogue: Dramatic Language and Elizabethan Letters (Cambridge, 1999), 141–62
Mahoney	Elisabeth Mahoney, review of Harvey production, *Guardian*, 4 June 2004
Marlowe, *Hero*	Christopher Marlowe, *Hero and Leander* (completed by George Chapman) (1598)
Marlowe, *Works*	*The Complete Works of Christopher Marlowe*, ed. Alexander Dyce, 3 vols (1850)
Marmion	Patrick Marmion, review of Doran production, *Mail on Sunday*, 4 August 2002
Martin	Gregory Martin, *The Holie Bible Faithfully Translated into English out of the Authentical Latin . . . By the English College of Doway . . .* 1609–10
Mason	Pamela Mason, 'Don Pedro, Don John, and Don . . . who? – noting a stranger in Much Adoodle-do', in Edward J. Esche (ed.), *Shakespeare and His Contemporaries* (Aldershot, England, 2000), 241–60
Massinger	Philip Massinger, *The Poems and Plays of Philip Massinger*, ed. Philip Edwards and Colin Gibson, 5 vols (Oxford, 1976)
Maus	Katherine Eisaman Maus, 'Horns of dilemma: jealousy, gender and spectatorship in English Renaissance drama,' *ELH*, 54 (1987), 561–83
Mellinkoff	Ruth Mellinkoff, *The Horned Moses in Medieval Thought and Art* (Berkeley, CA, 1970)
Middleton	Thomas Middleton, *The Works of Thomas Middleton*, ed. A.H. Bullen, 8 vols (New York, 1964)
Milton, *Poems and Prose*	John Milton, *Complete Poems and Major Prose*, ed. Merritt Hughes (New York, 1985)
Milton, *Religion*	John Milton, *Of True Religion*, in *The Prose Writings of John Milton*, ed. K.M. Burton (1958)
Misogonus	*Misogonus* (1570)
Montaigne	Michel de Montaigne, 'On some verses of Virgil', in *Essays*, trans. Donald M. Frame (Stanford, Calif., 1958)
Mueller	Martin Mueller, 'Shakespeare's sleeping beauties: the sources of *Much Ado About Nothing* and the play of their repetitions', *Modern Philology*, vol. 1, no. 3 (1994), 288–311
Mulryne	J.R. Mulryne (ed.), *Shakespeare: Much Ado About Nothing* (1965)
Musaeus, *Hero*	Musaeus, *Hero and Leander*, trans. George Chapman (1616)

Myers	Jeffrey Rayner Myers, 'An emended *Much Ado About Nothing* Act V Scene 3', *PBSA*, vol. 84, no. 4 (1990), 413–18
Myhill	Nova Myhill, 'Spectatorship in / of *Much Ado About Nothing*', *SEL*, vol. 39, no. 2 (1999), 291–311
Nashe	Thomas Nashe, *The Works of Thomas Nashe*, ed. R.B. McKerrow, 5 vols (Oxford, 1904–10)
Neely	Carol Neely, *Broken Nuptials in Shakespeare's Plays* (New Haven, Conn., 1985)
Neill	Kirby Neill, 'More ado about Claudio: an acquittal for a slandered groom', *SQ*, 3 (1952), 91–107
Niccholes	Alexander Niccholes, *A Discourse of Marriage and Wiving* (1615)
Northbrooke	John Northbrooke, *A Treatise against Dicing, Dancing, Plays, and Interludes, with other Idle Pastimes* (1577)
O'Connell	Michael O'Connell, *The Idolatrous Eye: Iconoclasm and Theater in Early Modern England*, (New York and Oxford, 2000), 129
Odyssey	Homer, *The Odyssey*, trans. Robert Fagles (New York, 1996)
OED	*Oxford English Dictionary*, 2nd edn, prepared by J.A. Simpson and E.S.C. Weiner (Oxford, 1989)
Orlando	Ludovico Ariosto, *Orlando Furioso*, trans. Sir John Harington as *Orlando Furioso in English Heroical Verse* (1591)
Ormerod	David Ormerod, 'Faith and fashion in *Much Ado About Nothing*', *SS 25* (1972), 93–105
Osborne	Laurie E. Osbourn, 'Dramatic play in *Much Ado About Nothing*: wedding the Italian novella and English comedy', *PQ* 69(2) 1990, 167–88
Overbury	Sir Thomas Overbury, *Characters*, ed. Donald Beecher (Ottawa, 2000)
Ovid, *Ars Amatoria*	*Thomas Heywood's Art of Love: The First Complete English Translation of Ovid's Ars Amatoria*, ed. M.L. Stapleton (Ann Arbor, Mich., 2000)
Ovid, *Fasti*	Ovid, *Fasti*, trans. and ed. with an introduction and notes by A.J. Boyle and R.D. Woodard (2000)
Ovid / Golding	Ovid, *The XV Books of Ovidius Naso Intituled Metamorphosis*, trans. Arthur Golding (1567)
Ovid, *Heroides*	*Ovid's Heroines: A Verse Translation of the Heroides*, Daryl Hine (New Haven, Conn., 1991)
Ovid, *Met.*	Ovid, *Metamorphoses*, trans. Rolfe Humphries (Bloomington, Ind., 1957)

Ovid, *Remedies*	Ovid, *Remedies of Love Translated and Intituled to the Youth of England*, trans. F. L. (1600)
Ovid, *Tristia*	Ovid, *Tristia*, trans. A.D. Melville (Oxford, 1992)
Page	Nadine Page, 'The public repudiation of Hero', *PMLA*, 50 (1935), 739–44
Painter	William Painter, *The Palace of Pleasure*, ed. Joseph Jacobs, 3 vols (Hildesheim, Germany, 1968)
Partridge	Eric Partridge, *Shakespeare's Bawdy* (1990)
PBSA	*Publications of the Bibliographical Society of America*
Peele	George Peele, *The Arraignment of Paris*, ed. R.M. Benbow, in *The Life and Works of George Peele*, gen. ed. Charles Tyler Prouty, 3 vols (New Haven, Conn., 1952–70), vol. 3
PG	Phyllis Gorfain, personal communication
PMLA	*Publications of the Modern Language Association*
Porter	Henry Porter, *The Pleasant History of the Two Angry Women of Abingdon* (1599)
PQ	*Philological Quarterly*
Prouty	Charles Prouty, *The Sources of Much Ado About Nothing* (New Haven, Conn., 1950)
Provenzano	Tom Provenzano, review of Plane production, *Theatre Journal*, vol. 52, no. 1 (2000), 118
Prynne	William Prynne, *The Unloveliness of Love-Locks* (1628)
Puttenham	George Puttenham, *The Art of English Poesy*, ed. Edward Arber (1906, reprinted Kent, Ohio, 1970)
R.C.	R[obert].C[leaver]., *A Godly Form of Household Government: For the Ordering of Private Families, According to the Direction of God's Word* (1612)
Rich	Barnaby Rich, *The Excellency of Good Women* (1613)
Ridley	M.R. Ridley, *Shakespeare's Plays: A Commentary* (1936)
Rimbault	E.F. Rimbault, 'Who was Jack Wilson?' (1846)
Ripa	Cesare Ripa, *Iconologia* (1593)
Rose	Steven Rose, 'Love and self love in *Much Ado About Nothing*', *EC*, 20 (1970), 143–50
Rossiter	A.P. Rossiter, 'Much Ado About Nothing', in *Angel with Horns* (1961), reprinted in *Shakespeare: The Comedies*, ed. Kenneth Muir (Englewood Cliffs, NJ, 1965), 47–57
RP	Richard Proudfoot, private communication
Schmidgall	Gary Schmidgall, *Shakespeare and Opera* (New York, 1990)

Scott	Mary Augusta Scott, 'The Book of the Courtyer: a possible source of Benedick and Beatrice', *PMLA*, 16 (1901), 476
SEL	*Studies in English Literature 1500–1900*
Sexton	Joyce Hengerer Sexton, 'The theme of slander in *Much Ado About Nothing* and Garter's *Susannah*', *PQ*, 54 (1975), 419–33
Sharpe	J.A. Sharpe, *Defamation and Sexual Slander in Early Modern England* (York, 1980)
Shattuck	Charles Shattuck, *The Shakespeare Promptbooks* (1965)
Shaw	*Shaw on Shakespeare*, ed. Edwin Wilson (New York, 1968)
Sidney, *Astrophel*	Sir Philip Sidney, *Astrophel and Stella* (1591)
Sidney, *Defence*	Sir Philip Sidney, *A Defence of Poetry*, ed. J.A. Van Dorsten (Oxford, 1966)
Smallwood	Robert Smallwood, 'Directors' Shakespeare', in Bate & Jackson, 176–96
Smith, 'Quarto'	John Hazel Smith, 'The composition of the Quarto of *Much Ado About Nothing*', Studies in Bibliography 16 (1963), 9–26
Snawsel	Robert Snawsel, *A Looking Glass for Married Folks* (1610)
SP	*Studies in Philology*
Spanish Tragedy	Thomas Kyd, *The Spanish Tragedy*, in *Works of Thomas Kyd*, ed. Frederick S. Boas (Oxford, 1901)
Spinrad	Phoebe Spinrad, 'Dogberry hero: Shakespeare's comic constables in their communal context', *SP*, vol. 89, no. 2 (1992), 161–78
SQ	*Shakespeare Quarterly*
SS	*Shakespeare Survey*
Statutes	'The Statutes of the Streets of this City, against Noysances', in *Laws of the Market* (1595)
Steed	Maggie Steed, 'Beatrice in *Much Ado About Nothing*', in Russell Jackson and Robert Smallwood (eds), *Players of Shakespeare: Further Essays in Shakespearean Performance* (Cambridge, 1993), 42–51
Straznicky	Marta Straznicky, 'Shakespeare and the government of comedy: *Much Ado About Nothing*', *SS 22* (1994), 141–71
Swinburne	A.C. Swinburne, *A Study of Shakespeare* (1880)
Tasso	Torquato and Ercole Tasso, *Of Marriage and Wiving: An excellent, pleasant, and philosophical controversy between the two Tassi*, trans. R.T. (1599)

Taylor, 'Introduction'	Gary Taylor, 'General introduction', in *TxC*
Taylor, M.	Michael Taylor, '*Much Ado About Nothing*: the individual in society', *EC*, 23 (1973), 146–53
Taylor, 'Proximities'	Gary Taylor, 'Theatrical proximities: the Stratford Festival 1998', *SQ*, 50 (1999), 334–54
Terry	Ellen Terry, *The Story of My Life* (1908)
Thompson & Thompson	Ann Thompson and John O. Thompson, *Shakespeare: Meaning and Metaphor* (Brighton, England, 1987)
Tilley	M.P. Tilley, *A Dictionary of the Proverbs in England in the Sixteenth and Seventeenth Centuries* (Ann Arbor, Mich., 1950)
Traugott	John Traugott, 'Creating a rational Rinaldo: a study in the mixture of the genres of comedy and romance in *Much Ado About Nothing*', *Genre*, vol. 15, no. 2–3 (1982), 157–81
Tyndale	William Tyndale, *The Fyrst Parte of the Bible Called the. V. Bookes of Moses* (1551)
TxC	Stanley Wells and Gary Taylor, with John Jowett and William Montgomery, *William Shakespeare: A Textual Companion* (Oxford, 1987)
Vickers	Brian Vickers, *The Artistry of Shakespeare's Prose* (1969)
Watson	Thomas Watson, *Ecatompathia* (1582)
W.B.	W.B., *The Court of Good Counsel, Wherein is set down the true rules, how as man should choose a good wife from a bad, and a woman a good husband* (1607)
Webbe	William Webbe, *A Discourse of English Poetry*, ed. Edward Arber (1871)
Weil	Herbert Weil, ' "Be vigitant, I beseech you": a fantasia on Dogberry and doubling in *Much Ado About Nothing*', *Ben Jonson Journal*, 6 (1999), 307–17
Wells, 'Crux'	Stanley Wells, 'A crux in *Much Ado About Nothing*', *SQ*, 31 (1985), 85–6
Wells, 'Foul-paper'	Stanley Wells, 'Editorial treatment of foul-paper texts: *Much Ado About Nothing* as test case', *Review of English Studies*, n.s. 31 (1980), 1–16
Wells, *Re-editing*	Stanley Wells, *Re-editing Shakespeare for the Modern Reader* (Oxford, 1984)
What You Will	John Marston, *What You Will*, in *The Works of John Marston*, ed. A.H. Bullen, 3 vols (1887), vol. 2
White Devil	John Webster, *The White Devil*, in *Three Plays*, ed. D.C. Gunby (New York, 1972)

Wiles	David Wiles, *Shakespeare's Clown: Actor and Text in the Elizabethan Playhouse* (Cambridge, 1987)
Williams, M.	Mary C. Williams, 'Much ado about chastity in *Much Ado About Nothing*', *Renaissance Papers* (1984), 37–45
Williams, R.	Roy Williams, *Days of Significance* (2013)
Wilson	F.P. Wilson, *Shakespeare and the New Bibliography*, revised and ed. Helen Gardner (Oxford, 1970)
Womack	Mark Womack, 'Balthasar's song in *Much Ado About Nothing*', in Russ McDonald, Nicholas D. Nace and Travis D. Williams (eds), *Shakespeare Up Close: Reading Early Modern Texts*, (Arden Shakespeare, 2012), 61–2
Woodbridge	Linda Woodbridge, *Women and the English Renaissance: Literature and the Nature of Womankind, 1540–1620* (Urbana and Chicago, 1984)
Wright, L.	Louis B. Wright, *Middle-Class Culture in Elizabethan England* (Chapel Hill, NC, 1935)
Wright, N.	Nancy E. Wright, 'The legal interpretation of defamation in Shakespeare's *Much Ado About Nothing*,' *Ben Jonson Journal*, 13 (2006), 281–312.

MODERN STAGE, FILM AND TELEVISION PRODUCTIONS CITED

Alexander	RSC, Royal Shakespeare Theatre, Stratford-upon-Avon, directed by Bill Alexander, 1990
Barton	RSC, Royal Shakespeare Theatre, Stratford-upon-Avon, directed by John Barton, 1976
Boyd	RSC, Royal Shakespeare Theatre, Stratford-upon-Avon, directed by Michael Boyd, 1996
Branagh	Renaissance Films / Samuel Goldwyn Production, directed by Kenneth Branagh, 1993
Craig	Imperial Theatre, London, directed by Edward Gordon Craig, 1903–4
Dench	Renaissance Theatre Company, touring production, directed by Judi Dench, 1988
Donnellan	Cheek by Jowl, Playhouse Theatre, London, directed by Declan Donnellan, 1998
Doran	RSC, Royal Shakespeare Theatre, Stratford-upon-Avon, directed by Gregory Doran, 2002
Hands	RSC, Royal Shakespeare Theatre, Stratford-upon-Avon, directed by Terry Hands, 1982–5

Harvey	Shakespeare's Globe, London, directed by Tamara Harvey, 2004
Irving	Lyceum Theatre, London, and North American tour, directed by Henry Irving, 1884–5
Kaut-Howson	Royal Exchange, Manchester, directed by Helena Kaut-Howson, 1997
Monette	Stratford Festival Theatre, Stratford, Ontario, directed by Richard Monette, 1988
O'Brien	Old Globe, San Diego, California, directed by Jack O'Brien, 1995
Planc	East Los Angeles Classic Theatre, directed by Tony Plane, 1999
Seer	Sinsheimer-Stanley Festival Glen, Shakespeare Santa Cruz festival, California, directed by Richard Seer, 1998
Stanley	Sinsheimer-Stanley Festival Glen, Shakespeare Santa Cruz festival, California, directed by Audrey Stanley, 1987
Tree	His Majesty's Theatre, London, directed by Herbert Beerbohm Tree, 1905
Trevis	RSC, Royal Shakespeare Theatre, Stratford-upon-Avon, directed by Di Trevis, 1988
Zeffirelli	BBC Television Production, directed by Franco Zeffirelli, 1967

http://www.theskinny.co.uk/film/features/304769-joss_whedon_much_ado_about_nothing

http://www.vulture.com/2013/06/joss-whedon-much-ado-about-nothing-interview.html

http://www.theguardian.com/culture/2011/jun/02/much-ado-david-tennant-catherine-tate

INDEX